For the Love of Food

The Complete Natural Foods Cookbook

For the Love of Food

The Complete Natural Foods Cookbook

Jeanne Marie Martin

Note to Readers: The information in this book is presented for educational purposes. It is not intended to replace the services of healing professionals for conditions that require them.

Published by:
  Alive Books
  PO Box 80055
  Burnaby BC Canada
  V5H 3X1

Cover Design: Peter Virag and Terence Yeung
Format Design and Typesetting: David Janik-Jones
Illustrations: Kathryn Lissack
Front Cover Photo: Ron Crompton
Cover Recipe: Easy Cheesecake

Inside Color Photography by Ron Crompton and Siegfried Gursche
Food Styling by Stephen Case (and Jeanne Marie Martin)
Tableware Courtesy of The Market Kitchen at Granville Island, Vancouver BC

Hardcover
First Printing: October 1996

Canadian Cataloguing in Publication Data
Martin, Jeanne Marie, 1951-
  For the love of food

ISBN 0-920470-71-8 (bound)

  1. Cookery (Natural foods) 2. Vegetarian cookery. 3. Natural foods. I. Title.
TX741.M37 1996   641.5'63   C96-910327-1

Printed and bound in Canada

Dedication

To All People
This book should really be called *For the Love of People* because it was written in an effort to help people lead healthier, happier lives.

Special thanks to these people who gave assistance and encouragement while I was writing this book: Robert Lee Betts, Esther A. Albrecht, Lois Kempton, and Patrick Keefe, DC. And, also thanks to whose who helped with the new edition: Christine Olsen, Katherine Zia, Kitty Cates, Gisela Temmel, Michele Holman, and Mac and Penny Macdonald.

And especially – thank God for the creative energy, faith, endurance, and grace given to complete this work.

Books by Jeanne Marie Martin

For the Love of Food: The Complete Natural Foods Cookbook

The All Natural Allergy Cookbook

Hearty Vegetarian Soups and Stews

Vegan Delights: Gourmet Vegetarian Specialties

201 Fat Burning Recipes (with Cathi Graham)

Return to the Joy of Health (with Dr. Zoltan Rona)

Jeanne Marie Martin's Light Cuisine: Seafood, Poultry and Egg Recipes
    for Healthy Living

Complete Candida Yeast Guidebook

Recipes for Romance: Passionate Poetry, Aphrodisiacs and Menus for Loving

Expert's Comments on For the Love of Food:

"This book is designed to be of help to those who need help. It is a compilation of information that has been discovered by the author as being effective in the preparation of healthful food items. Sometimes it is difficult to discover 'how to'. This book paves the way by telling you how to cook properly for a better quality of life. Because I believe anything that allows the body to function naturally is good, so do I believe there is much merit contained in this book."

Patrick T. Keefe, DC, Professor of Clinical Science, Dean of Continued Education, Palmer College of Chiropractic, Davenport, Iowa, USA

"Changing your nutritional habits to eat for a longer and healthier life, may require eliminating some of your favorite but unhealthy foods. **For the Love of Food** *introduces you to new tastes that will bring a smile to your face, superb flavors to your palate and healthful foods for your body. Whether you are a beginner or an experienced chef, you will find this book to be an easy-to-follow guide to healthy and delicious natural foods. Ms. Martin has a special gift for educating with creativity to expand your culinary talents. I highly recommend this book to all of my patients."*

Dr. Steven Small, "Nutritionist to the Stars"
Optimum Health Associates, Beverly Hills, California

"In the field of natural health care, the cry 'Stop the Insanity' is in itself an insane slogan. Various popular concepts like megavitamins, hypoglycemia, vegetarianism, food combining rules and candida come and go. The general public gets more confused with the appearance of each new nutrition guru and few educators know how to help people sort out myth from reality. Fortunately for readers, Jeanne Marie Martin's books provide substantial intellectual relief amidst this chaos.

Jeanne Marie is one of those rare individuals who has an ability to help her readers understand seemingly complex issues in simple terms. She also has the insight to know just what the public needs to know about health at any given time. With this new book, her timing couldn't be any better. I think most of us have read and heard enough about food dogma, chemistry and technology. We might just be ready to enjoy what we eat for a change. Jeanne Marie's talents as an author and teacher are well displayed here with wise practical advice that is sure to dispell guilt and foster a healthier and happier feeling about the things we eat. **For the Love of Food** *may well be her finest and best effort to date."*

Zoltan P. Rona, MD, MSc, author of *Return to the Joy of Health*
and *Childhood Illness & the Allergy Connection*

"An immensely readable, novel, and informative feast of facts and ideas, for everyone interested in whole foods - the selection, preparation, storage and enjoyment."

Dr. John Travis, MD, author of the *Wellness Workbook*

*"In addition to being a book of recipes, **For the Love of Food** contains a comprehensive description of a sensible approach to natural foods—including tips on menu planning, guidelines for the efficient use of time and money, and valuable cooking techniques. For those interested in more balanced eating habits, this book is a wise investment."*

Dr. William Bahan, DC, founder of the Whole Health Institute

*"It was a pleasure to encounter so sensible a book on food - one, I might add, which promises to whet anybody's appetite for healthier eating. We used to think that the only food that tasted good, was not good for our bodies. Jeanne Marie Martin has changed this attitude. Her great recipes, combined with rock-solid nutritional guidelines, make clear: healthy eating can also satisfy anybody's most discriminating palate. I for one am going to keep **For the Love of Food** in our kitchen, prominently displayed so that we may enjoy all of her wonderful, healthy, delicious recipes."*

David Steinman, author of
The Safe Shopper's Bible and *Living Healthy in a Toxic World*

"For over twenty-five years, I have been cooking with natural foods; teaching cooking and nutrition. My 'success' experience with Jeanne Marie's recipes is a common one. She is an excellent teacher and has written the book so that the most uninitiated can begin to cook with natural foods and have 'tasty success.'"

Joan S. Calkins, PhD, California

"Besides being filled with delicious recipes, this book has such complete information on nutrition, foods, utensils, meal ideas and buying tips that I have chosen it as the textbook for my natural food and nutrition classes. It's also selling faster than any cookbook in my natural food store. I've been looking for a complete book like this for years."

Karen Walker Ehmke, MS, RD, Wisconsin

**"The doctor of the future will give no medicine
but will interest patients in the care of the human frame,
in proper diet, and in the cause and prevention of disease."**

Thomas A. Edison

Table of Contents

1 The Importance of Eating Well

2 Help for the Cook

3

Recipes & Food Preparation Guidelines

Charts, Tables, Glossaries, & Guides

List of Tables

List of Illustrations

Foreword

by Michael T. Murray, ND

The famous Greek physician, Hippocrates, is credited with saying "Let your food be your medicine and let your medicine be your food." In *For the Love of Food*, Jeanne Marie Martin provides a comprehensive and practical guide to the creation of meals that not only promote health, but also taste delicious.

There is an ever growing appreciation of the role of diet in determining our level of health. Most people now accept the fact that "we are what we eat," yet have trouble making dietary changes. As people are learning more about the value of proper nutrition, they often become confused when trying to actually prepare a meal. They need a tool to help them make the transition to a health promoting diet. *For the Love of Food* is the ideal tool. It provides the guidance for the natural foods novice as well as the experienced "health nut."

It it now well established that certain dietary practices cause, as well as prevent, a wide range of diseases. In addition, more and more research is accumulating that indicates certain diets and foods offer immediate therapeutic benefit. The basic underlying theme is that humans function best when consuming a diet rich in plant foods and low in animal foods.

There are many reasons why humans need to eat a diet high in nutrient-rich plant foods. First of all, the human digestive system is better suited for predominantly vegetarian diet. Secondly, plant foods are rich not only in nutrients like vitamins and minerals, but also in compounds often referred to as "phytochemicals." These phytochemicals do not possess any true nutritional effects, but are known to produce many health promoting effects.

Most of the health conditions that are quite rampant in developed countries are referred to as "chronic degenerative diseases." Included in this category are heart disease, cancer, diabetes, and arthritis. These conditions owe their origin largely to dietary and lifestyle choices. The chief dietary link is a diet that is high in animal foods, saturated fats, and refined sugar; low in nutrient-rich plant foods. In *For the Love of Food* Jeanne Marie addresses this problem by offering recipes that focus on providing a high intake of a wide and varied amount of plant foods.

Ralph Waldo Emerson once said "The first wealth is health." Many people wait until their health is in a precarious state before they truly appreciate Emerson's words. The human body is the most remarkable thing on earth, yet many people have lost sight of just how important it is to provide the high quality nourishment our bodies require. Our bodies, the vessel of our soul, are something to be cherished. I urge you to treat your body as your most prized possession. I firmly believe that the quality of one's life is directly related to the quality of the foods routinely ingested. I strongly encourage you to love your body by incorporating into your life the recipes and recommendations contained in *For the Love of Food*.

Michael T. Murray, ND
Author of the *Encyclopedia of Natural Medicine*

Dr. Murray, graduate and faculty member of the Bastyr University, is an accomplished writer, educator, and lecturer, and the editor of *The American Journal of Natural Medicine*. He is the co-author of *A Textbook of Natural Medicine*, a physician's guide to naturopathic medicine, and the author of twelve other books including *Encyclopedia of Nutritional Supplements*, *The Healing Power of Foods* and *Natural Alternatives to Over-The-Counter and Prescription Drugs*.

 *Chapter Before the First*

Beginning with Natural Foods

The Right Way to Begin

Get off to a good start with natural foods. Your first impression of health foods or natural foods can be a lasting impression of like or dislike. Natural foods should not be eaten just because they are "good for you," but because they are delicious as well as wholesome and nutritious.

People often think of a natural food or vegetarian diet as rabbit food. Salads, salads, and more salads. Little do they know that a natural food diet has tremendous variety, more so than the average meat-eater's diet. You could make thousands of cooked gourmet delights and other healthful dishes and never have to repeat one recipe or touch a salad. Vegetarian dishes are filling, yet do not leave you with a heavy feeling in your stomach.

Still unconvinced? Read on for a new and wonderful experience in the land of natural foods.

" I am convinced from experience that to maintain oneself on this earth is not a hardship but a pastime, if we live simply and wisely."

Thoreau - Walden

What This Book Is All About

First — *For the Love of Food* is not just a recipe book. Recipe books are everywhere. In this book, there are hows and whys for each step of the way toward better eating, as well as exciting recipes.

Second — All the healthful dishes in this book are delicious. One can make terrible-tasting natural food dishes. Some people thrive on the idea that they are better for you. This is not true. There are no such unpleasant recipes in this book. Try to develop a taste for new foods and give your taste buds time to adjust. If a dish is completely unappealing, do not eat it.

Third — One need not be an expert cook in order to follow these recipes and have them turn out great. Measurements are exact when they need to be and tips on cooking techniques, spicing, and adding colorful touches are included. These recipes are pretested to ensure they work.

Fourth — These foods are interesting, practical, and fun to make as well as being appealing to the eye.

Fifth — There are tips on how to shop and save money, and many recipes call for inexpensive ingredients.

Sixth — There are ideas on how to save preparation time and how to select, store, and stock foods, as well as make use of leftovers.

Seventh — This book offers special information and recipes for vegans, vegetarians, macrobiotics, and for health concerns such as hypoglycemia, diabetes, and Candida albicans.

Eighth — This book will change your awareness and understanding of natural foods. Reading this book once will make it easier to *improve your diet*. This is the main goal of this book. *The greater part of your food intake should be healthful, pure, body-building foods!*

Part One

♥

About Food –
The Importance
of Eating Well

 *Chapter 1*

Why Change Your Eating Habits

What Are Natural, Organic, and Health Foods?

Natural foods are foods that are eaten in as natural a state as possible, with a minimum of cooking, processing, and removing as little as possible from the original product. These foods are usually not refined and have no added chemical stabilizers, preservatives, chemicals, or drugs of any kind, and no artificial colorings and flavorings.

Organic foods are foods grown in soil that has been free of chemical fertilizers for many years, in areas where there is no concentration of air or water pollution. Also there are no chemical or unnatural pesticides or herbicides used on the plants or their products from seed through cultivation and transportation to the retail stores.

Health foods are foods that are wholesome and full of vitamins and minerals. They are conducive to good health, building a strong, healthy body, and giving a feeling of well-being. Health foods are natural and sometimes organic.

Why Are Natural and Health Foods Better for You?

1. They are more nutritious. That is, they promote growth and support and sustain the body. They contain a wide variety of vitamins and minerals.

" Most of the luxuries, and many of the so-called comforts of life, are not only indispensable, but positive hindrances to the elevation of mankind."

Thoreau - Walden

2. They contain no chemicals or additives such as cyclamates, saccharin, preservatives, or artificial colors or flavors. Many of these food additives have side effects and have been proven to harm the body, sometimes causing hyperactivity in children or even promoting diseases. Natural foods do not contain harmful and unnecessary additives.

3. Most natural foods are not refined; this means that nothing important is removed from the original product. An example is shown in this grain of wheat called a wheat berry or a wheat kernel:

- **Bran** – B vitamins plus others and about $1/5$ of the protein
- **Endosperm** – A few various vitamins and most of the carbohydrates and protein found in the wheat berry
- **Germ** – vitamin E, some B vitamins and small amount of protein and some minerals (check the vitamin chart for values of B and E vitamins)

Most of the vitamins are contained in the bran, the outer husk, and the wheat germ, the inner kernel. Some vitamins and most of the starches and protein are contained in the Endosperm. Yet to make regular white bread, the bran and germ are removed and only the endosperm used, throwing away valuable vitamins. In addition, most white flours are bleached to destroy many remaining vitamins and then artificial vitamins are readded, which are often less in value and amount than the original. These are synthetic and in some instances inadequate. (See book section for vitamin books that explain this.) This is basically the procedure used with all grains, including rice and corn in their whole form or as flours and meals.

4. A grain, bean, fruit, or vegetable, like the wheat berry, has different vitamins in the skins, remaining insides and core of the food. Often one vitamin cannot be utilized by the body without the help of another vitamin. For example: vitamin D is needed to help assimilate vitamin A in the body. In processing and refining, often these "helping" vitamins are lost. When you eat whole foods, all the necessary vitamins are present to assist one another and make it easier for all the vitamins to be assimilated by the body.

5. Natural foods are processed as little as possible. The more that is done to a food to break it down or change it, the more vitamins and energy are lost. The less processing the better. *Vitamins provide energy.* The more energy destroyed in the food, the less energy is conveyed to mind and body.

6. Refined foods are broken down and very easy to digest. The body becomes lazy

if it seldom has to do any work breaking down foods for digestion. This laziness makes it harder for the body to break down and assimilate needed vitamins from other foods. Therefore, the required vitamins often pass out of the body.

7. Refined foods enter the bloodstream too quickly since they need very little time to break down. They give the body a quick and unstable surge of energy, leaving the body needing food energy shortly after eating to keep it going. Unrefined foods enter the bloodstream slowly, allowing the body to gradually assimilate vitamins and burn fuel needed to run the body for a longer period of time. Refined items like sugar, flour products (including most pastas, breads, and dry cereals), and caffeinated coffee, quickly pass through the system, so constant refills are needed to keep the energy level stable. These non-foods give momentary energy, not usable nutrients. They are empty foods and are valueless to the body except to give it temporary energy. When the body is not getting enough nutrients, it draws on the reserve vitamins needed by other parts and functions of the body, robbing one part of the body of vital nutrients to help another.

8. Some refined foods, especially flours, make a kind of paste in the digestive system that tends to "clog the pipes." This clogging can cause indigestion or constipation, and can obstruct proper elimination of food wastes or toxins from the body.

9. There is more bulk and fiber in natural foods. These foods help clean out the intestines and aid in the elimination of waste products. A clean system keeps the body running smoothly, strengthening resistance against disease. High-fiber foods can be a good preventive measure against cancer.

10. Natural foods help keep the body weight balanced. They help stabilize the metabolism. A constant drain of energy caused by eating poor foods or eating good foods improperly can lower body resistance making it susceptible to fatigue, anxiety, disease, and possibly, after severe illness, even death. The body is naturally strong but after constant abuse, a variety of problems can develop. More than half of all sicknesses suffered by people are caused by the food they eat.

Is your present diet unhealthy and invalid?
Must you change it completely?

The answer is no. Most people already include some natural and healthful foods in their diets. The main goal is to eat healthful foods more often, such as increasing your natural food intake from 15% to 55% or 75% or more. One need not change the diet completely or become a health food nut or a vegetarian. For physical and mental well being, just improve your diet.

Moderation Is the Key to Diet and Lifestyle

This book contains many ideas on how to improve the diet and increase body energy. No one is expected to follow all these ideas and rules all the time. Familiarize yourself with the main principles of good eating and follow them whenever possible. Just by reading this book the first time and becoming aware of these ideas, one can easily improve eating habits by at least 10%. As you learn to enjoy these recipes it becomes easier to make healthful foods the greater part of your diet.

Can Proper Diet Alone Create and Maintain Health?

The answer is no. One can eat 100% natural, organic foods and follow all the eating rules in this book and still be unhealthy. Food is not the answer to all problems, but it is the answer to some. Natural foods enthusiasts can be unhealthy. Besides wholesome food a person needs:

1. Physical activity: This keeps the body machine running smoothly and provides an adequate supply of energy for all parts of the body. Everyone knows that a neglected machine gets rusty, runs sluggishly, or breaks down altogether in time. Fitness experts suggest vigorous exercise and a milder stretching form of exercise like yoga or Tai Chi each day. Anywhere from 15 minutes to an hour or more of each type of exercise is suggested for each individual according to personal need. Seek experienced advice on times and types of exercise suited for you, especially if you are over 35 years old. Vigorous exercise can include running, racket sports, dancing, biking, and swimming to name a few. Some activities like dancing and swimming may qualify as both mild and vigorous exercise depending on the styles used.

2. Chiropractic and massage: Chiropractic care can help remove nerve interferences by adjusting the spine. It keeps body energy levels high. Benefits can be discussed with a local chiropractor or you can read about it in one of the many books on the subject. Massage can relax sore muscles, relieve body tension, and reduce stress levels. It can also help to tone muscles and skin.

3. Fresh air and sunlight: These are the essentials of life. Poor quality air gives the body less energy. Why does being in a closed-up room makes you sleepy? Stale air has very little "life force" or energy. The body wants to slow down and decrease its energy needs by sleeping.

Try to keep the windows open, especially while sleeping, even if they are only open a small amount. However, it is best to avoid getting a direct draft, so open distant windows preferably. Sunlight is full of vitamins and healing energy.

Vitamins enter the body through the skin, decreasing the need for food and extra energy to run the body and keep it warm. The sun helps promote healing, but, like anything else, too much of a good thing is bad for the body. Take sunlight in moderation, depending on your own body needs. Use skin protector as needed.

4. Proper rest: The average body needs six to eight hours rest a night. Do not put excessive stress on the body by not allowing it to get its needed rest by overworking or overplaying.

Missing a night's rest or getting only a few hours sleep is not good for the body. The body can handle occasional losses of sleep, but constant loss of sleep can lower the body's resistance to disease. A sure sign of inadequate rest is having to pump yourself full of coffee and other stimulants in order to function each day.

5. Positive thinking: You are what you think! If you see yourself healthy, you most likely will be healthy. If you fear sickness or dwell on it constantly, you most surely will become ill. Have a positive attitude toward life and life will have a positive attitude toward you. Mental stress and worry lower the body's energy. A stable, secure lifestyle and personality create harmonious energy. Positive thinking is probably the most important requirement for good health.

Chapter 2

How to Change Your Eating Habits

Do It Gradually!

Everything in nature grows slowly and surely. Man, animals, birds, and trees all develop gradually. Drastic changes in diet may do more harm than good. Do everything at a pace that allows the body to adjust to the changes. A person cannot change from a heavy meat-and-potatoes-and-canned-vegetable diet to one of mostly natural foods overnight. Nor can habits of smoking and drinking alcohol be discarded all at once. An acorn does not change from an acorn to a fully developed oak tree in one day. It is essential to learn about the body's basic requirements and become aware of your individual body needs and adapt your diet accordingly. In Chapter 3 – Diet Plans for a Healthier Lifestyle, there is a series of steps or diets which can improve your present diet gradually. There is no way to do Step #2 of the changeover diet comfortably and easily without having done Step #1 first. Do not feel that you must purify your system immediately by a complete and drastic diet changeover—for any reason! Even those with major health problems or diseases need to make

" Every man is the builder of a temple called his body. We are all sculptors and painters, and our material is our own flesh and blood and bones. Any nobleness begins at once to refine a man's features, any meanness or sensuality to imbrute them."

Thoreau - Walden

appropriate diet changes step by step. (Diets for major health problems are not included in this book.)

A quick change in diet can have unpleasant side effects. If you change your diet too quickly, your body may start eliminating at too rapid a pace poisons that may have been stored in the body. This detoxification can cause headaches, nausea, lowered disease resistance, body tension, and other discomforts. If your diet is changed gradually, toxins can be eliminated slowly, causing little or no physical or mental discomforts. Take your time changing your diet and you will receive the maximum benefits possible.

When changing your diet, remember that at no time should you force yourself to eat a dish that you do not like. This will only create bad feelings about your new diet. Stick to the fancy, more flavorful dishes until you can acquire a taste for simple bean and rice dishes. Try new dishes when you are really hungry, not just curious, and you will enjoy them more.

When changing someone else's diet, be even more careful. If an individual wants to change to this new diet and understands all about it, it will be easier. If the person does not know about the diet or does not like health foods, you must begin more gradually than ever. You must introduce the tastiest and most appealing dishes, preferably ones you have already tried yourself first. Be very sure not to mention that it is health food or good for you because that person could form a mental block and decide before they taste it that they do not like it! Never, especially with a child, force someone to eat what they do not want or like. As long as you are patient and resourceful, you should not have trouble getting a person to like at least some of the new and more healthful dishes you prepare. If one likes a few dishes, as time progresses his or her tastes can change to include a wider variety of "health foods."

Also remember that some people may have individual reactions such as allergies to certain foods or nutrients. It is important that we recognize our individualized instincts as well as our needs and likes.

Tips on Introducing New Foods

For Babies:

If you start babies out on good food from the beginning, they will not want anything else. Even occasional candy and sweets will not be able to tempt them away from natural foods if their everyday diet is tasty and balanced. Avoid giving babies excessive sweets, like adding sweeteners to their liquids and foods or giving them too much fruit juice. Babies (and children) should always have their juices thinned with water, about 25 – 90% percent water for easier assimilation. Giving them frequent juices may diminish their natural taste for vegetables and other nutritious foods and may lead to a loss of vitamins and nutrients. No honey for babies! See Chapter 7 – Sweets for the Sweet for more information.

For Children:

Children can easily acquire a taste for natural foods if they are started on them at a young age. If the children are unused to natural foods, and depending on how much junk food they are currently eating, it may be hard to change their eating habits. Start out by introducing them to wholesome desserts. Then change their snacks from candy to fruit, raisins, nuts, and some fresh and frozen yogurt or dairy-free treats.

Eliminate all snacks on occasion to get them really hungry for supper. Then try a new dish or two, something simple that you think they may like. Just ask them to try it; do not push. You can promise a special dessert if they try your new dish. There are lots of incentives you can employ. Make the meal a game or let them guess what is in the dish. Often letting the children help in the meal preparation will make them eager to try what they have made themselves.

Do not overdo by wanting every single bit of food they eat to be natural. Unhealthy and unhappy babies and children are sometimes created by parents who feed them only the very best natural foods. Even good things in excess can be harmful. A little junk food once in awhile will not harm most children. Millions of kids survive in spite of even larger doses of junk foods. If you forcibly withhold junk food from children, they may seek it out at a neighbor's house. If you have a flexible attitude about junk foods, they will too. More often than not, they will not want your neighbor's candy bars, because once a taste is developed for natural food, one can actually develop a dislike for the taste of refined and junk foods.

Never force children to eat anything. This creates a negative experience. It can upset the stomach and turn them against other new foods you might like them to enjoy. However, you can use the bite system and ask them to take a bite or two of every new dish before rejecting it. Since children's tastes change rapidly, you may find they love a food today that they hated last week. They will be more likely to change their minds about a food if they have not been forced to eat it.

Appearance is important to children, so serve foods that have contrasting colors and shapes. Add pretty garnishes and make tasty, mild, well blended dips and sauces for foods children find bland or "boring."

The most important thing is to set a good example. Children like to imitate, and if you react favorably to a food, there is a good chance they will too. Do not try to get them to eat natural foods that you would not eat. Do not present awful tasting foods as wonderful as they will learn to distrust your opinion. Wholesome foods can always taste wonderful if prepared properly. Give your children choices. Generally adults do not like all foods, nor do children. Let them choose a different food, one or more items per week, that they do not have to eat if they eat their other food. This gives children a chance to express their tastes and make personal choices.

For Adults:

Talk about new food ideas with adults openly and see how they respond. Read up on natural foods and ask them to do the same. If they respond favorably to the idea of trying new foods, go ahead. Make this new experience enjoyable and never expect them to like everything. If they dislike a certain food, you can always present it occasionally in hopes that they might change their minds or their tastes.

Do not press for diet changes if they dislike the idea, just drop the subject. Bit by bit you can start incorporating natural foods into the diet by, for example, adding a cup or two of whole wheat flour to baked goods. Start buying fresh corn and vegetables rather than canned. Steam or bake vegetables and potatoes instead of boiling or frying them. Put a little soy flour or protein powder in a blender drink. Instead of sugar, use honey or other natural sweeteners in desserts. Make lots of little changes in the diet but make them subtly. When they notice how much better the food tastes and how much better they feel, you can say that you are trying out some new recipes. Only after several natural foods are incorporated into the diet and they have learned to like them should you tell them what you are adding to the foods and why. They may be surprised, and usually, you will find that they have a new opinion of "health foods."

For Adults Over Sixty:

For people who have eaten a very refined diet most of their lives, it is not a good idea to change the diet completely. Certain natural foods can be added to the diet gradually, only as their bodies accept them. Mild and easily digested natural foods are the best foods to add to the diet. Soybeans or other heavy bean dishes or too many grains could be harmful and possibly overburden their systems. Blend or mash beans for better assimilation. Avoid excessive raw vegetables or scratchy

5-, 7-, or 9-grain breads. All changes depend on the individuals and how healthy and active they are. An elderly body that is accustomed to refined food may not be able to change over to more bulky and hard-to-digest foods. Begin by adding natural oatmeal, millet, and fresh cooked vegetables to the diet. Be sure to include fresh, homemade juices and soups. Whole grains should be cooked a little softer with extra water. Gradually add heavier foods and more raw foods only if the body accepts them. Acidophilus powders, capsules, or milk is a valuable aid to digestion for the elderly or anyone with digestion problems. (For some, however, the small amount of lactose that may be contained in milk can create digestive problems. Dairy-free acidophilus is also available.) Other digestive aids including yogurt, herbal teas, and some natural enzymes may also be helpful.

Chapter 3

Diet Plans for a Healthier Lifestyle

Diet changes are easier to make when they are done in stages. The problem of rapid diet changes has just been discussed; now it is important to outline gradual, step-by-step changes that can be incorporated over a period of months or years depending on individual needs and choices.

The following diet plans can be adapted and utilized for short or long periods of time. At any one step of this plan, you may decide to stay with that step indefinitely or to proceed to the next step. The diet plan steps range from adding a variety of natural foods to your present diet to excluding unhealthful or undesirable foods, from reducing meat intake or partial vegetarianism to complete vegetarianism or veganism.

Proceed with each step at your own pace and stay with the step or diet plan that best suits your present lifestyle requirements. The health benefits and enjoyment you receive by improving your diet may help you determine how many steps you want to take. Set your own goals and use these steps to make your transition from less wholesome foods to healthful ones pleasant, exciting, and satisfying.

" If a man does not keep pace with his companions, perhaps it is because he hears a different drummer. Let him keep step to the music which he hears, however measured or far away."

Thoreau - Walden

Step One Diet Plan
The First One to Six Months: Introducing Natural Foods

What to Do:
Here are tips on what to do and buy when first introducing natural foods into the diet.

1. Experiment and introduce into the diet:
    a. Whole grain products such as breads, pasta, crackers, flours, and baked goods.
    b. Whole grain main dishes using brown rice, millet, quinoa, buckwheat, pot barley, oats, and/or whole wheat.
    c. Whole grain flours used half and half with unbleached white flour, oat flour, rice flour, or another light, natural flour.
    d. Granola, oatmeal, cornmeal, hot millet, and other warm, whole grain breakfast cereals.
    e. Honey, maple syrup, fruit concentrate, fruit and raw sugars, and other refined sugar substitutes like molasses and malt.
    f. Yogurt, sprouts, raw nuts and seeds, and nut or seed butters.
    g. Tamari soy sauce, miso, tofu, and other soy products.
    h. Main dish legumes instead of meat on occasion, like lentils, chilies, soups, stews, casseroles, or spreads.
2. Eat as many fresh fruits and vegetables as possible.
3. Drink unsweetened, preferably diluted, fruit and vegetable juices instead of pop or canned drinks sometimes.
4. Enjoy herbal teas, coffee substitutes, and nut and soy milks instead of caffeinated teas, coffee, and regular cow's milk whenever possible.
5. For snacks enjoy healthful sandwiches, yogurts, nuts and seeds, natural cheeses, fruit or vegetable salads, juices, dips with vegetables, bean spreads, and wholesome natural desserts.
6. Familiarize yourself with your local health food stores, natural food co-ops, and supermarket "health foods" and compare prices.
7. Whenever possible buy good quality natural or organic foods.
8. Bring your own healthful lunch to work or school or buy one of the few healthy dishes served in your cafeteria or nearby restaurant and bring food supplements or snacks of your own from home.
9. Start learning proper methods of cooking foods to save more of their vitamins. Practise using herbs in cooking.

10. Eat breakfast and lunch each day and enjoy a smaller supper than usual. Basically, try to follow this meal schedule:

Prebreakfast: (15 to 30 minutes before) Fresh fruit or fruit juice
Breakfast:
   a. Whole grain cereal/or bread (pancakes)/or eggs/or yogurt/or nuts or seeds/or tofu
   b. Cooked fruit/ or raw or cooked vegetables/ or sweetenings
Snack: (Optional) Fresh fruit pieces/or vegetable sticks alone or with a sauce or dip/ or nuts or seeds/ or nut butters with celery/ or puffed wheat or rice cakes with toppings/ or muffins or quick breads/or granola (bars) or rice pudding/or leftover main dishes
Lunch:
   a. Vegetables, raw or cooked
   b. Protein, a legume (bean) dish/or tofu/or nut or seed dish/or dairy product dish (or for some, meat)
   c. Whole grain product, bread/or rice/or millet/or other whole grain/or starchy vegetable
Snack: (Optional) Same as above
Supper: Same as lunch but smaller portions. If one has a proper lunch and breakfast, a large supper is unnecessary. (Some people do function better on two meals a day rather than three. If this is the case, eat at least one meal by noon and enjoy two very solid meals daily plus snacks as needed.)
Night Snack: (Optional) Same as above except avoid eating fruits or fruit juices, or raw nuts or seeds at night. Avoid eating heavily at bedtime.
(See Menus page 43 for meal suggestions.)

Stocking Your Kitchen
Where to begin? For about $25.00 you can purchase the basics needed. The following items along with some of your own kitchen herbs, fruits and vegetables, cheeses, and odds and ends will get you started eating more healthful meals and snacks. Buy these at your local natural food store, co-op, neighborhood grocery store, or ethnic shop.

Basic Health Food Stock
1 pound brown lentils
1 pound green split peas

1 pound brown rice (short grain tastes best)

Basic Health Food Stock Cont'd

1 pound unbleached white flour or whole wheat pastry flour

2 pounds whole wheat flour

$^1/_2$ – 1 pound whole wheat or other whole grain noodles(pasta)

$^1/_2$ pound quinoa

$^1/_2$ pound rolled oats

$^1/_2$ pound sunflower seeds

$^1/_4$ pound white (hulled) sesame seeds

1 – 2 pounds natural honey

8 – 16 ounces natural cooking and salad oil

8 – 16 ounces tamari soy sauce

16 ounces plain yogurt

1 pound regular or firm tofu

$^1/_8$ – $^1/_4$ pound alfalfa seeds or mung beans for sprouts

4 – 8 ounces sea salt

4 ounces sea kelp powder

Herb teas - assorted tea bags or 1 ounce each of a couple of pleasure teas in bulk or loose (See Chapter 28 - Herbal Teas)

Optional Health Food Stock

$^1/_2$ – 1 pound millet

$^1/_2$ – 1 pound cornmeal

$^1/_2$ pound nut butter or sesame tahini

coffee substitutes

Additional Items to Have on Hand

Cayenne or red pepper

Basil and parsley and other herbs

Italian herbs

Apple cider vinegar

Tomato paste

Cheddar and/or mozzarella cheese (dairy or tofu cheese)

Assorted vegetables - potatoes, mushrooms, tomatoes, green peppers

Assorted fruits

Dried fruits - coconut, raisins and/or dates

Onions and garlic

Eggs and milk (or substitutes)

Best Recipes for Beginners Found in this Book

Lentils Sweet & Sour

Rice-Cheese Loaf

Lasagne Supreme

Lasagne Rice

Tempura

Vegetable Quiche

Creamed Millet & Herbs

Macaroni & Cheese

Tomato-Lentil Soup

Split Pea Soup

Pizza

Spaghetti

Shish Kebabs

Stir-Fried Vegetables

East Indian Dahl

Yogurt & Fruit

Granola Cereal

Millet & Dates Cereal

Soaked Oats & Fruit Cereal

Any salad or dressing

Any beverage

Step Two Diet Plan
After Two to Twelve Months: Expanding the Natural Food Diet
By now you should be appreciating fresh foods and natural flavors immensely! This next step is actually easier than the first if you have really been practising the first step. Just add more natural foods to your diet and drop whatever junk foods you feel you can do without.

What to Do:
1. Expand your menu and recipe ideas. Learn as many recipes in this book and in others as possible.
2. Learn to cook all kinds of whole grains.
3. Study Chapter 19 – Legumes and practise cooking different types of legumes.
4. Check the meal planning charts and menus and try a few days a week without meat. Use instead a whole grain dish and/or a legume or tofu dish for protein. Dairy and egg dishes can also be used if desired.
5. Avoid refined products like white and brown sugars, pasta, cereals, crackers and breads, and canned products as much as possible.
6. Make sure about $1/8 - 1/2$ of your daily food intake is raw food and the rest is cooked. (Depending on the season and individual health needs.)
7. Drink mainly water, herbal teas and occasionally natural beverages like unsweetened fruit and vegetable juices.
8. Enjoy sprouts, yogurt, nut butters, tofu, and other wholesome foods on a regular basis.
9. Include powdered sea kelp or dulse almost daily and enjoy some seaweed like: nori, kombu or wakame, one or two times a week.

What to Buy:
Besides the items in Step #1, add some of the following items to your basic kitchen stock.

Additional Health Food Stock
Beans: 1 – 2 pounds each

Pinto beans	White pea or Navy beans
Adzuki beans	Black turtle beans
Kidney beans	Soybeans
Chick peas (garbanzos)	

Whole Grains: 1 pound each
Wheat berries (kernels)
Millet
Quinoa
Buckwheat
Cracked wheat or bulgur
Brown Pot barley
Buckwheat or kasha

Flours and Meals: 1 pound each
Rye flour
Oat flour
Cornmeal
Soy flour
Amaranth flour
Teff flour
Millet flour
Quinoa flour

Fruits/Nuts/Seeds: ¹/₂ – 1 pound each
(Raw and organic if possible)
Raisins
Dates
Cashew pieces
Almonds
Flax seeds
Pecans or fresh walnuts

Dry Goods: 1 – 4 ounces each
Agar-agar
Arrowroot powder
Guar gum or xanthan gum

Dry Goods Cont'd: 1 – 4 ounces each
Baking powder with no alum
Natural baking yeast
Edible food yeast (preferably engevita
  or good tasting yellow variety)

Dry Goods: ¹/₂ – 1 pound each
Carob powder
Vegetable broth powder (and/or cubes)
Protein powder
Non-instant milk powder
Unsweetened, shredded coconut

Packaged Goods: ¹/₂ – 1 pound each
Tofu
Seaweed (nori, kombu, or wakame
  are the best)
Miso
Whole grain crackers

*Jarred or Bottled Items: ¹/₂ – 1 pound
  or 8 – 16 ounces each*
Sesame tahini
Almond or cashew butter
Natural peanut butter
Natural "imitation" ketchup
Salad dressings
Natural apple cider vinegar
Natural or eggless mayonnaise
Liquid lecithin
Molasses
Real maple syrup

Step Three Diet Plan

After One Year: Natural Foods as a Way of Life
After you have added quite a few new tastes to your diet, your eating habits will
be changing, and you may find that you no longer care for certain junk foods.

Now is the time to eliminate as much junk food as possible from your diet and add more healthful items. Once you acquire a taste for good foods, you will find junk foods less and less desirable. Use up or throw away your leftover junk foods. Buy and keep only natural foods in your home and leave splurging on junk foods for eating out or visiting.

If you do not feel ready for this step, perhaps you need more work on Step #2 or prefer to stick with Step #2 permanently. Do whatever feels comfortable and fits your basic lifestyle. Now, if you are ready, continue with Step #2 and add Step #3.

What to Do:
1. Add to your diet:
    a. Yogurt three to six days a week. Try to get certified raw milk and cheeses whenever possible. Avoid eating excessive dairy foods. (Try a non-dairy day at least once a week.)
    b. Desserts using honey, maple syrup, molasses, and other unrefined sweeteners only.
    c. Buy and use mainly whole grain flours and products made from them including: breakfast cereals, pasta, breads, and crackers.
    d. Legume and whole grain combinations as the main protein in one half or more of your main meals (lunch and supper) each week. Eliminate meat at these meals.
2. Eliminate or keep to a bare minimum in your diet:
    a. Caffeinated beverages including: colas, coffee, black or green, and oriental teas, cocoa, and chocolate.
    b. All refined flours and sugars and their by-products.
    c. Almost all canned foods. Avoid frozen foods when fresh are available.
    d. All brands of supermarket cooking and salad oils and their related products: mayonnaise, tuna packed in oil, and salad dressings. Virgin olive oil is acceptable.
    e. Most alcoholic beverages and cigarettes. If you must drink alcohol, avoid hard liquor and drink beer and wine. Drink alcohol sparingly and never drink on an empty stomach.
    f. Meat for three to five days a week and use legumes and/or whole grains instead.
3. Continue experimenting and using new types of foods and recipes. All the recipes in this book can now be used.
4. The food list is the same as in Steps #1 and #2.

Step Four Diet Plan

After One to One and a Half Years: The Partial Vegetarian

This diet is for those who prefer not to eat red meats including beef, veal, pork, lamb, venison, and other game, but still enjoy or want to include white meats. This diet can also be an important first step for those who are interested in vegetarianism and vegan diets.

What to Do:

1. Continue eating all the good foods that you have already included in your diet (legumes, whole grains, eggs, dairy products, fruits, vegetables, nuts and seeds, and honey). Keep eliminating all the unnecessary foods mentioned in Steps #2 and #3.
2. Eliminate red meats from your diet. This includes all meats mentioned above.
3. Fowl, including chicken, turkey, duck, goose, quail and other birds are eaten by some partial vegetarians. The last step to being a partial vegetarian is to exclude all fowl. This can be done some time after red meats have been excluded from the diet. However, eliminating fowl is not a must for partial vegetarians.
4. The following kinds of fish and seafood are still included in the diet: tuna, salmon, cod, halibut, and other fish, octopus, squid, lobster, crab, shrimp, clams, and other shellfish.
5. Enjoy legume and whole grain foods and food combinations for one to three meals a day when meat is not served. Enjoy all the recipes in this book.
6. Poultry, fish and/or seafood can be enjoyed as little as once a month or as often as four or five times per week as a safe maximum.
7. Choose free-range or organic poultry and deep ocean fish whenever possible as more wholesome white meat selections.

Step Five Diet Plan

After One or Two Years: The Lacto-Ovo Vegetarian

What to Include:

1. Lacto – dairy products are included in the diet.
2. Ovo – eggs are included in the diet.
3. Fruits, vegetables, whole grains, legumes, honey and other natural sweeteners.

What to Eliminate:

1. All meat from the diet. Besides red meat, also exclude fowl, fish, and seafood except for seaweed. Also eliminate gelatin.

What to Do:

1. Use lots of whole grain and legume dishes in your diet—three to six servings per day or more. Legumes are a nutritional must for meat-free diets.

Note: If the diet includes dairy products but not eggs, it is Lacto-Vegetarianism. (Dairy products should not be relied on as the sole source of protein.) If the diet includes eggs but not dairy products, it is Ovo-Vegetarianism. Some Ovo-Vegetarians prefer to eat only unfertilized eggs to avoid killing potential life.

Step Six Diet Plan
After One or Two Years: The Total Vegetarian

What to Do:

1. Eliminate all meats from your diet. This includes all red meats, fowl, fish, seafood, and gelatin.
2. No dairy products or eggs whatsoever are included in this diet.
3. Continue eating fruits and vegetables, legumes and whole grains, nuts and seeds, honey, and seaweed.
4. It is preferable, in order not to defeat the healthful purposes of this diet, that there be no smoking or alcohol drinking. Some may wish to include a few social drinks, but only very occasionally.
5. Follow the rules in Chapter 23 – Dairy Products, Eggs, and Substitutes on how to eliminate dairy and egg products from the diet. Avoid recipes calling for dairy or eggs. See the recipes and menus, and Recommended Reading section.

Specialty Diets
The Vegan Diet

This is a vegetarian who follows Step #6. Besides following the diet and excluding foods of animal origin, a vegan often avoids using animal products derived from leather, horn, or other animal parts. Vegan is usually pronounced VEE-gan or VAY-gan, with a hard "g" as in garden. In the past it was pronounced VEG-an, with a soft "g" as in vegetable. Some vegans include honey and sugar in their diets and some avoid these altogether. For more information, see my book entitled: *Vegan Delights*. Also, see the books listed in the Recommended Reading section.

The Macrobiotic Diet

Macrobiotics is an Oriental approach to eating and a way of life that consists of ten different diets. The basic diet is relatively easy to follow and offers practical improvements for the average person. Each "higher" diet gets simpler and more restrictive including the final diet which contains mainly brown rice.

These higher diets can be dangerous! A few deaths have been attributed to the overzealous application of these diets. Never use them without strict supervision from a qualified health specialist. Even the benefits of these "higher" diets may be questionable.

The average macrobiotic diet, the "lower" diets, are quite practical and can be beneficial if followed properly. A balance of foods should be eaten daily with this diet. The general diet consists of the following:

1. Whole grains and legumes, especially rice, millet, and buckwheat plus adzuki, kidney, pinto and soybeans, chick peas and lentils.

2. Vegetables, especially Oriental vegetables, cabbage, celery, flower vegetables, and root vegetables.

3. Fruits that are native to your home climate. For example, if you live in northern states or Canada, eat apples, peaches, cherries, berries, and some melons. If you live in Florida, California or in other warmer climates, eat citrus fruits, avocados, palm fruits, and mangoes.

4. Dried fruits, nuts and seeds, especially: almonds, cashews, walnuts, sesame seeds, raisins, and currants.

5. Also included are herb teas, milk substitutes, seaweed, tahini, tamari soy sauce, miso, tofu, oil, vinegar, wine, arrowroot, kudzu or kuzu (for thickening and medicinal use), dried chestnuts and lotus roots, ginger and some herbs. Fish, seafood, and fertilized eggs are occasionally included.

The macrobiotic diet is based on balancing receptive energy, yin, with creative energy, yang. Foods are divided into these two categories, and a healthful diet contains a balance of both.

There are many particulars involved with these diets, more than can be mentioned here. For more information read: *Zen Macrobiotic Cooking* by Michel Abehsera, *Zen Macrobiotics* by George Oshawa, or any of the many books available on the subject. (See Recommended Reading section)

The Raw Food Vegetarian Diet

This diet is definitely not for everyone! This diet is more practical if you live in a warmer climate. Extreme caution must be taken to eat the right amounts and types of foods. Also, exercise, fresh air, and sunlight are musts!

Much of the reasoning for this diet is spiritual. Many believe that man was originally a raw food vegetarian; and supposedly, as he evolves, he will return to that diet. Living rather than "dead or dying" food should support the body according to this philosophy.

Healthy, raw foods are cleaner and keep the body and digestive system working more smoothly. Cooked foods, hot foods, and spices also irritate the stomach and take away extra energy, lowering the body's resistance to disease.

For more help with this diet, read some of the raw food books suggested in the Recommended Reading section. Seek a qualified health specialist for advice before undertaking this diet. The elderly, sick or those with allergies, severe digestive problems, weakened immune systems or chronic diseases should avoid this diet unless it is recommended for them and they are guided by their physician.

What to Do:

1. All fruits and vegetables, and nuts and seeds, everything in the diet, must be eaten raw, that is, uncooked.
2. Eliminate the following:
   a. All cooked legumes and whole grains except any grains and legumes that can be eaten raw, such as corn, peas, and green beans and those that can be sprouted.
   b. Breads, pastries, or anything baked.
   c. Eggs.
   d. Definitely, absolutely—no meats, cigarettes, alcohol, pop, coffee, caffeinated tea, refined or raw sugars or junk food of any type.
   e. No oils, salad dressings (except those made with blended vegetables or juices), or cooked sauces.
   f. No salt or spices of any kind. Herbs, however, may be used plentifully.
3. Dairy products are not included in the diet, although some raw food vegetarians do include raw milk. Certified raw milk is preferable.
4. Raw honey, honeycomb, and fresh fruits are the only sweeteners that can be used. (No sorghum or maple syrup as they are heated.)
5. Eat a variety of raw, unsalted nuts and seeds, chewed very well.
6. Eat a variety of fruits and vegetables, only eat them separately. Eat as many organic and natural foods as possible, for they are essential in order to obtain the needed vitamins. Eat only vegetables that can be eaten raw, chewed well, or soaked or sprouted before eating. Eat lots of sprouts. Sprout alfalfa, sunflower and other seeds, whole grains like wheat, oats, and barley, and legumes like mung, lentil, and chick peas. As with all raw foods, chew sprouts extremely well. Sun-dried fruits are also included in the diet.

7. Include dried and fresh seaweed in the diet, especially nori. For other types of seaweed, rinse and soak them until tender before chewing well.

8. Beverages may include fresh and bottled waters, fresh juiced or squeezed juices (no bottled juices as most are heated), and herbal sun teas. Occasional raw, blended vegetable and fruit soups may be enjoyed. It is best to avoid tap water.

9. There are varied opinions on how much to eat and how often. Basically: eat when you are hungry, but not until you are stuffed.

The Fruitarian Diet

This diet is based on a spiritual concept: destroy no life for your food. Take only that which nature gives freely, with no harm to her creatures. Fruits fall on the ground when ripe or can be picked without harming a plant. Vegetables are often important to a plant, and you destroy or harm it when the vegetables are removed. For example, beets, carrots, and other root vegetables are the main parts of their plants. Broccoli, cauliflower, lettuces, spinach are removed by harming their plants; therefore, these vegetables are not included in the fruitarian diet. Also in this diet, food is not taken from an animal. Besides meat, this means not taking milk from cows, eggs from chickens, or honey from bees. This diet is all raw foods. "Life need not be killed to give life to another" is a guiding principle of this diet.

So, this diet is very limited and is suggested only for those living a "spiritual" or meditative lifestyle, preferably in a warm climate. Here again, a qualified, holistic health specialist should be consulted before engaging in this diet which can be quite harmful to people whose body types are not suited for it.

This Diet Includes:

1. All fruits, vegetables, nuts and seeds, and beans and grains that can be plucked without harming the plants. For example, cucumbers, peas, corn, green beans, summer squash, tomatoes, and peppers. Seeds and nuts that fall easily from a tree can be enjoyed.

2. Whole grains and beans that can be gathered without harming the plants and can be sprouted or soaked before being chewed well.

3. Some herbs can be eaten fresh or dried and crushed over food. Herbal sun tea may be used as a beverage.

4. Drink mainly fresh spring water. (No tap water.)

5. Eat only raw foods. (No blended or processed foods whatsoever.)

 *Chapter 4*

Meal Planning

How to Eat Your Food: The Fine Art of Serving, Eating, and Digesting Your Food

Preparation and Serving

The feelings and vibrations you put into foods are as important as the food itself. Make and serve food in love, with love. Appreciate or bless the food as it is being prepared. Most important of all, one must like the food and enjoy the preparation. One must desire to make an attractive, delicious, and healthful meal. The kitchen is the center of the home. The kitchen atmosphere can be either pleasant, warm, and friendly or empty, cold, and messy. It can be a place for family fun, togetherness, sharing, and exchanging ideas or it can be a place for criticism, arguments, and aggression. Hastily put together, poor-tasting, poor-quality food prepared in a begrudging manner helps create a bad atmosphere. It is sad that many people and even television, radio, and ads speak of the kitchen as a place to hurry and "get out of," a place of drudgery. Yet, cooking can be a hobby, something to explore and enjoy. It can be fun and challenging like any sport or game. Kitchen work can become play. If the cook enjoys preparing the food, others will enjoy eating it. Eating has always

"I learned in my two years experience that… a man may use as simple a diet as the animals and yet retain health and strength."

Thoreau - Walden

been a major social event. Families, businesses, friends, and lovers use the meal as a way of pleasant social interaction. Ask a businessperson what a luncheon with an important client can do. Ask romantics how much they enjoy a candlelight dinner or ask someone who has been home all day how much they like dining out with friends or family. Good meals can be a major factor in family unity. Meals should always be pleasant experiences shared with others as often as possible. Here are some ideas for making your meals at home more pleasant.

Preparation and Serving Ideas:
1. Enjoy preparing the food. Prepare something you like.
2. Choose something that is tasty, attractive and healthful.
3. Bless the food. Eat it with appreciation for the Maker, the cook, and your own bodies. You may want to join hands and silently appreciate or take turns giving a blessing.
4. Set a neat table. Get rid of clutter and mess before the meal. Stack dirty dishes neatly out of the way or wash them beforehand.
5. Set an attractive table. Choose a pretty table cloth, placemats, or napkins and use color accents for the table. Fresh flowers add to any table arrangement. Flowers need not be expensive, even a few wildflowers in a vase or bottle can be a pleasing addition.
6. Candlelight and dress-up dinners can be a special treat for birthdays or other occasions.

Eating and Digesting
It takes energy to digest food. In order to digest food easily, assimilate more vitamins and conserve body energy, follow these important tips. Remember that 50% or more of all illnesses are brought about by the food we eat. Illness can be caused by overeating, poor digestion, eating toxic or poor quality foods, eating improperly prepared foods, improper food combining, and eating quickly or when under stress.

Good Digestion Tips:
1. Preparing and eating meals in a positive manner is good for digestion. Foods are harder to digest when one is under stress. Do not eat when upset, angry, overtired, or tense. If you must eat, eat only fruits, beverages, or very simple, easy-to-digest foods.
2. Eat in a calm, peaceful atmosphere. Pleasant, low music can be a plus. Avoid

watching television or reading while eating as it takes concentration and energy away from digesting food. Pleasant scenery or window views can assist in relaxing you and slowing down the eating process, thus aiding digestion. Take a few slow, deep breaths to relax and slow you down before eating and between mouthfuls.

4. Eat only when you are hungry and eat only enough to feel satisfied. Never stuff yourself. It is better to let food spoil in the garbage or compost than to let it spoil in the digestive tract. Excessive food clogs the system, robs body energy, contributes to sluggishness, fatigue and illness, and, of course, adds inches to your waistline.

5. Chew your food well. For the millionth time, digestion begins in the mouth! It is essential to break down the food into tiny bits and mix enough saliva (which is full of digestive enzymes) with it before it is swallowed. Gandhi's wise words offer the best guidelines: "Drink your foods and chew your liquids."

6. Eat slowly. If you eat slower, you generally eat less and absorb more nutrients. If you are prone to eating too fast, make a sign to sit on the table in front of you that says: "eat slowly" or "chew well." Use the sign for every home meal until you can remember to "slow down" and savor your food.

7. Do not eat when restless, bored, tired or unhappy. Find busy work to do with your hands, like sewing, sorting grains or beans, doodling, playing cards or crafts.

8. Eat two to three meals a day and possibly one to three snacks. Do not nibble all day long. Chew on a carrot stick, fennel seeds, or an apple if you feel the need to exercise jaw muscles.

9. Do not eat a big meal before sleeping or lying down. Digestion sometimes takes twice as long while the body rests and calorie absorption increases. Let your stomach rest with you. If you must have something to eat before bedtime, try milk, yogurt, crackers, vegetarian paté, or another easy-to-digest snack.

10. After eating, get some mild exercise to help stimulate digestion. Try walking, slow bike riding, or washing the dishes.

11. Your meals are digested better if you have a salad first, if its a vegetarian meal. (Eat meat first if it is a non-vegetarian meal.) Also, one may have citrus fruit or juice an hour prior to the meal or yogurt with your meal as a digestive aid. Another option is to drink peppermint or chamomile tea about one hour before or after a meal to help digestion.

12. Avoid drinking liquids with meals, especially milk. Liquids dilute digestive enzymes making digestion more difficult. However, four to six ounces of water, vegetable juice or wine is sometimes acceptable and occasionally helpful, if sipped slowly, to help ease down dry foods and/or cleanse the palate.

13. Eat warm, cool, or room temperature foods whenever possible. Avoid eating too many very hot or very cold foods which require excessive body energy to cool them off or warm them up for proper assimilation.

14. Follow the food combining tips in this book as often as possible for quicker and more efficient digestion and increased body energy.

15. Eat healthful, body-building, vitamin-rich foods. Avoid junk foods whenever possible.

What to Eat

Everyday Food Needs

Why count calories, vitamins, and minerals? If you eat the right kinds of foods, in the proper combinations and the right amounts, you will not have to figure out or calculate your daily intake of B or C vitamins or the calories in a salad or a double banana split.

The following list of basic foods and proportions is easy to memorize and easy to incorporate into three meals and a snack or two a day. Forget most of the mental calculating. Learn the basics, then let the body tell you its needs and make sure you are filling them. If you feel well, you are usually eating well. If you feel unwell, and are not under stress, ill, or missing any other basic needs, check your diet and make improvements.

If you follow this chart you will get all the average daily body needs for protein, starches, iron, calcium, phosphorus, other minerals, natural oils, sweeteners, and vitamins A to Z. Also take a close look at the chart of foods to eat every week, which follows the Daily Food chart.

Dairy products and eggs are optional in some diets. If dairy products and eggs are omitted, substitute those amounts for one extra serving of green leafy vegetables and whole grains, and one extra serving of legumes, nuts or seeds.

Note: This may appear to be a large quantity of food to some, but servings are small and the number of servings varies. Most daily needs can be filled in two or three meals a day even without snacks. Two to three servings of the same types of foods may easily be had in one meal.

Daily Food Needs

Food	No. of Servings/Day	Amount Per Serving
Whole grains and starches	5-10 (At least 1 serving daily of warm cooked whole grains and only 1 serving of potatoes per day or 3 servings per week)	$1/2$ - $2/3$ cup cooked grains or 1 slice homemade bread (2 slices bought bread) or 1 medium or large potato or yam or 1 - $1\frac{1}{2}$ cups cooked starchy vegetables
Legumes, meat, or nuts and seeds	1-3 (2-3 if no dairy or eggs are eaten) (only 1 serving of meat a day or 3 servings a week and/or about 1 serving a day cooked legumes, nuts optional)	4-8 ounces or meat, poultry, or seafood or $3/4$ - 1 cup cooked legumes (only $1/2$ cups soy or fava beans) or 1-2 ounces nuts or seeds
*Dairy products and eggs or substitutes	2-4 (only 3-4 servings a week of eggs - except for those on special diets due to medical or athletic needs or for specialty diets)	8 ounces of milk or milk substitute or 4 ounces of yogurt or 2 ounces of cheese or 1 egg or 3-4 ounces tofu or 2-3 ounces of cashews, almonds, or their nut butter or 1-2 ounces sesame butter or tahini or $1/2$ cup cooked black beans, soybeans, chick peas, kidney, or pinto beans
Vegetables	3-6 (1-2 servings a day of leafy greens and 1 serving a day (3-5 weekly) of yellow or orange vegetables)	$1/2$ - 1 cup cooked vegetable or $1/2$ - 1 cup raw vegetable or salad
Fruits	1-3 (citrus fruit or juice 1 serving each day or 3-5 per week - unless allergic)	1 whole fruit or $1/2$ large fruit or $1/2$ cup berries or $1/2$ - 1 cup fruit salad or juice or cooked fruit
Water	3-4 (6-8 in hot weather)	8 ounces of water
Sweetenings	1 or less (optional - body does not need sweets - it can derive natural sugars from other foods)	4-8 ounces dessert or 1-2 teaspoons honey or other natural sweetener

* Dairy products and eggs are optional in some diets. If dairy products and eggs are omitted, substitute those amounts for vegetables, whole grains, and 1 extra serving of protein.

Eat These Foods Every Week: For everyone (except infants)
Have these foods every week. Incorporate them with other food needs on your Daily Food Needs chart. These foods and others not listed below should be eaten every week. (If you are allergic to any of these foods, avoid them. Substitutions can be made.)

Eat At Least Once, Preferably Twice a Week or More:
    Cooked carrots
    Raw carrots
    Broccoli, asparagus, artichokes(globe), or green peas (fresh)
    Cabbage, cauliflower, or Brussels sprouts
    Cucumbers, zucchini, or green peppers
    Onions, chives, garlic, or horseradish
    Kiwis, bananas, avocados, apricots, or other high potassium fruits
    Millet, quinoa, amaranth, or teff
    Raisins, other dried fruit, or molasses
    Eggs, lecithin and/or flax seeds, or flax oil
    Yogurt, acidophilus, or tofu
    Seaweed, dulse, or sea kelp

Eat Three to Four Times a Week or More:
    Spinach or other dark leafy greens
    Lettuces
    Winter squash, orange yams, or carrots
    Apples, pears, or peaches
    Oranges or other fresh citrus fruit
    Nuts and seeds, especially almonds, cashews, sesame, and sunflower
    Brown rice or other whole grains
    Legumes (beans, peas and lentils), especially black beans, chick peas,
       and pinto beans
    Whole grain cereals (cooked)
    Dairy products, tofu, or other calcium-rich foods
    Dairy products, spirulina, chlorella, or other vitamin B12 rich foods

Daily Meal Planning

Approximate Amounts of Foods for Each Day:

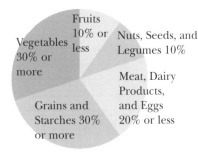

Approximate Amounts of Foods for Breakfast:

Approximate Amounts of Foods for Lunch or Supper:

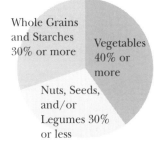

Protein Lunch or Supper

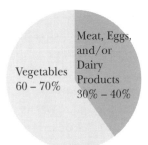

Daily Meal Schedule

On Rising: Water – 1 to 2 servings

Before Breakfast (1/4 – 1 hour before): Citrus fruit, fresh fruit and/or fresh vegetable juice – 1 serving (optional)

Breakfast: Vegetables or cooked fruit (optional) – 1 serving; dairy products or eggs – 1 serving OR whole grain or starchy vegetable – 1 serving

Mid-Morning: Water (or herb tea) – 1 serving; fruit or other snack (optional) – 1 serv.

Lunch: Vegetables – 1 to 2 servings; meat, eggs and/or dairy products – 1 serving OR legumes, nuts or seed and/or whole grains – 1 to 2 servings

Afternoon Snack (optional): Dairy products OR whole grains, legumes (nuts, seeds, or whole grain bread) – 1 serving OR fruit – 1 serving

Before Supper (at least 1/2 – 1 hour before): Water (or herb tea) – 1 serving

Supper: Vegetables – 1 to 2 servings; meat, eggs, or dairy products – 1 serving OR legumes, nuts or seeds and/or whole grains – 1 to 2 servings

After Supper (1 hour or more): Cooked fruit dessert, cake, pie, pudding, or other dessert – 1 serving (optional)

Evening Snack (optional): Dairy product and/or whole grain product – 1 serving
Note: If dairy products/eggs are omitted, substitute those amounts with one extra serving of leafy green vegetables and one extra serving of legumes, nuts or seeds.

Meal Planning Guidelines
Meals:
1. These menus need not be followed exactly. They are samples of nutritious meals, guidelines to planning meals and snacks that include all the vitamins, minerals and nutrients the average body requires. Create your own menus in similar fashion.

2. For more economical meals, serve the same dish two to four times per week or freeze leftovers for meals in later weeks. For convenience, make large batches of bean soups, chili, stews, burgers, sauces, falafel, and hummus and freeze extra to defrost later for quick meals. Most tofu and legume foods keep up to three months frozen. Tofu, legume and whole grain dishes usually keep six to eight days refrigerated if kept wrapped and perspiration, saliva and other bacteria are not allowed to spoil it. Try cooking big batches one night during the week and/or one afternoon on weekends.

3. If you are allergic to or dislike any food, substitute another similar food in that recipe, or simply choose a selection from a different menu.

4. When creating your own menus, make sure not to plan too many light or heavy foods in one day. For example, with a dry cereal breakfast, try to have a hot, heavier lunch.

5. Make sure lunches and suppers include a whole grain, legume (beans, peas, or lentils) and/or a tofu OR a protein food such as dairy, eggs (or meat).

6. About 50% of foods should be eaten raw and 50% cooked by the average person. In hot weather the proportion of raw may be increased to 75% or more, in cool weather you may want to eat fewer raw foods, perhaps as little as 25%. Cooked foods are very beneficial to many North American body types. Some nutrients are released and better assimilated in cooked or warm foods like whole grains, legumes, carrots, or winter squash. Some vegetables and other foods are more nutritious eaten raw. Include both raw and cooked foods in the diet for optimum health for the average person. Follow a diet plan that suits your body best! (Also see the Food Combining and Recipe and Food Preparation sections for more information on proper meal planning.)

Servings:

7. Enjoy two to three meals per day along with a few snacks if desired. Some people function better with two meals a day and some with three. If you wish to avoid breakfast or lunch, make sure to eat at least one of these meals by noon.

8. Do not eat any one type of food more than five to six days per week. It is better to have two servings of a certain food every other day than to have one serving everyday. Rotate foods for better digestion and health and to help prevent possible food allergies later in life.

9. Include weekly: three to ten servings of legumes, five to twelve servings of warm whole grains, and two to five servings of tofu, unless allergic or sensitive to soy products. Enjoy nuts and seeds a maximum of three to five days a week, and different vegetables everyday. (Meat, a maximum of three to seven servings.)

10. Include daily: three to six servings of vegetables (two of green vegetables), three to six servings of carbohydrates (whole grains, cereals, starchy vegetables, and pasta) and two to three servings of higher protein foods (legumes, tofu, and nuts and seeds). Fruit needs vary. Dairy or substitutes may be served two to four times.

11. A serving is: 1 piece or 1 cup fruit, $\frac{1}{2}$ – 1 cup legumes or whole grains, three to four ounces (about 100 grams) tofu, two to four tablespoons nuts, seeds, or nut/seed butters, two ounces cheese, 4 ounces yogurt or 8 ounces milk.

12. Add nutritious extras to sauces, whole grains, and legumes at the table after cooking. Sprinkle $\frac{1}{16}$ – $\frac{1}{8}$ teaspoon or less of sea kelp, dulse, or cayenne, $\frac{1}{4}$ – 1 teaspoon barley green or powdered spirulina, $\frac{1}{2}$ – 1 teaspoon ground flax seed or ground nuts or seeds, 1 – 5 teaspoons nutritious oils (like flax or pumpkin), $\frac{1}{4}$ – 1 piece nori seaweed, toasted, either whole or crumbled into food.

13. For proper food combining, always eat raw fruit 15 – 60 minutes before other foods (30 minutes is best).

14. Raw fruit may be enjoyed for snacks by itself during the day. Avoid eating raw fruit at night. Avoid eating tropical fruits too often in cold weather.

15. Cooked fruits do not contain certain enzymes found in raw fruit that mix poorly with other foods, so most cooked fruits may be eaten like other carbohydrates. Cooked fruits like apples and berries may be eaten with some meals or even after supper as a dessert.

16. Dried fruits should be eaten like fresh fruits. Eat them raw before meals and cooked with or after a meal.

17. Melons or grapes should be eaten by themselves. It is best not to eat them with other fruits. Citrus fruit may be eaten alone, or with vegetable or fruit salads to assist digestion.

18. Fruits may be interchanged in or eliminated from the menu for certain health concerns. (If you have blood sugar problems or Candida, avoid sweet fruit.) Enjoy fruit several times a week or up to two to four servings per day.

Snacks and Desserts:

19. Pick your own snacks, salad dressings and desserts to supplement these menus.

20. Snack suggestions: fresh fruit pieces, vegetable sticks alone or with sauce or dip, nuts or seeds, tahini and celery, puffed wheat or rice cakes with toppings, bread or crackers with or without nut or seed butters, muffins or quick breads, juices, cheese, yogurt, milk or milk substitutes, granola or other cereals, or left-over burgers. See also Chapter 15 – Appetizers, Snacks, and Party Foods. A few of the desserts make great snacks, such as the Rice Pudding.

21. Enjoy desserts three to eight times a week or less. There is no need for desserts in the diet, but they are enjoyable treats and anyone who is reasonably healthy and maintains a basic, balanced diet can afford to indulge in them once in a while.

22. Desserts are best served one hour after a meal, $1\frac{1}{2}$ – 2 hours after a very large meal. Raw fruits should never be served as dessert, although it is fine to eat them before a meal. For example, fresh berries or fruit salad eaten 15 minutes or more before supper is an occasional treat.

23. After a light meal, choose a heavier dessert like cake, pie or pudding. After a heavy meal, light desserts such as ice cream or a cookie or two are recommended.

Remember, no rule must be followed all the time. These are safe, wholesome guidelines for better digestion and health. A healthy individual need only follow these points most of the time. The basic rule is to follow the guidelines carefully, eat better quality foods and eat less when not feeling well. Splurge or break the rules when you feel great. Each individual's needs will vary throughout their lives. Seek authoritative nutritional counseling for special needs and problems.

Food Combining

All the recipes in this book do not follow strict food combining because healthy individuals do not need to follow strict food combining everyday. If you did, you would never have pizza, macaroni and cheese, or eggs and toast again. For optimum health, weight loss, digestion, and energy try to follow these food combining guidelines three to five days per week. Those with special health concerns should adhere strictly to these rules six to seven days per week and follow the special guidelines for healing diets in the book, *Return to the Joy of Health*. (See Recommended Reading section) Those with particular problems should consult their doctor.

Food combining is rather a complex issue as there are many conflicting points of view. I am convinced that certain combinations of food aid digestion and help to assist in the healing process. I have found it invaluable in working with allergy sufferers, cancer patients, the chronically overweight and those with other health challenges. The two most important food combining principles are:

1. Eat heavy proteins or animal products (meat, eggs, and dairy) separately from carbohydrate foods. It is alright to eat legumes and whole grains together.

2. Eat raw or dried fruit alone or before a meal so as not to hinder digestion. The enzymes in raw fruit make them the easiest foods to digest. However, upset stomach, indigestion, and fermentation of stomach contents may occur if raw fruit is eaten with other foods or after a meal. Cooked fruit or cooked dried fruit is like most other carbohydrate foods and is fine to eat after a meal, occasionally with a meal.

Other special points:

1. Do not eat citrus fruit with grains as it makes them feel heavy as lead in the system and may increase the absorption of calories.

2. Eat desserts one hour or more after a full meal of other foods to lessen their impact on the body's blood sugar level and to decrease calorie absorption. Do not eat desserts on an empty stomach.

3. Vegetarians especially should not overeat sweets. It creates an imbalance in the system and may cause cravings for alcohol and non-vegetarian foods. (It is preferable for vegetarians to avoid alcohol or indulge sparingly.)

4. Eat raw vegetables first in a meal to help stimulate and assist digestion. In a meal where meat is served, meat should be eaten first, especially red meats or poultry. Chew foods well to mix a lot of saliva with them and aid the digestive process.

5. Eat "grounding foods" if your mental energy gets scattered easily. Enjoy lots of cooked legumes, warm whole grains and warm cooked vegetables. Also eat some nut butters or tofu (or meat).

6. Yogurt and/or acid fruits are particularly good with vegetables salads as they help them to break down for better digestion and absorption of nutrients.

7. Do not mix too many foods together at one meal. Avoid 5-, 7-, and 9-grain breads as they are hard to digest. Avoid heavy foods late at night.

8. Beverages should generally be taken without other foods, preferably $\frac{1}{2}$ – 1 hour before or after a meal. Too much liquid may interfere with digestion, but four to six ounces is sometimes alright with a meal, taken in small sips as needed.

9. Always follow the suggestions that work best for and suit your individual needs. Certain body types and health problems require variations of or omission of these tips. Consult your health specialist for diet changes as needed.

Healthy Living Food Combining Chart

Key

1. A should be eaten alone.
2. B can be mixed with C but not with D.
3. C can be mixed with B or D.
4. D can be mixed with C but not with B.

ENZYME

Fresh Fruits
Apples
Apricots
Avocados
Bananas
Berries
Blackberries
Cantaloupe
Cherries (sweet)
Exotic fruits
Grapes
Honeydews
Kiwis

RAW FRUITS

Fresh Fruits, cont.
Mangoes
Melons
Other fruits
Papayas
Peaches
Pears
Plums
Raspberries
Saskatoon Berries
Strawberries
Tropical fruits
Watermelons

CLEANSING

Dried Fruits
Apricots
Coconut
Currants
Dates
Figs
Peaches
Pineapple
Raisins
Other dried fruits

ALKALINE

Whole grains
Barley
Buckwheat
Corn (dried)
Kamut
Millet
Oats
Quinoa
Rice
Rye
Spelt
Triticale
Wild rice

Cooked Fruit and Cooked Dried Fruit

CARBOHYDRATES
STARCHES

Legumes
Adzuki beans
Black beans
Chick peas
   (Garbonzos)
Haricots
Kidney beans
Lentils (red,
   brown, green)
Limas (dried)
Mung beans
Navy beans
Northern beans
Peas (dried)

Legumes, cont.
Pinto beans
Other beans
Red beans
Romano beans
Split peas
Soybeans
Tofu

**Cooked Nuts
And Seeds**
All kinds
   cooked with
   foods (not
   roasted in oil)

ENERGIZING

Starchy Vegetables
Carrots
Cauliflower
Corn (fresh)
Jerusalem
   artichokes
Parsnips
Potatoes
Pumpkins
Squash (winter)
Sweet potatoes
   (yellow)
Turnips
Yams (orange)

NEUTRAL | VEGETABLES | BUILDING

NEUTRAL	VEGETABLES	BUILDING
Artichokes (globe)	Herbs (green)	Onions
Asparagus	Eggplant (cooked only)	Parsnips
Avocado (neutral fruit)	Endive (raw)	Peas (fresh)
Beans (fresh)	Escarole (raw)	Peppers (bell or hot)
Beets and beet greens	Garlic	Radishes
Broccoli	Green onions	Rutabagas
Cabbage	Greens (others)	Shallots
Carrots	Kale	Spinach
Cauliflower	Kohlrabi	Sprouts
Celery	Leeks	Squash (summer)
Celeriac	Lettuces (raw)	Tomatoes (cooked)
Chives	Mushrooms	Turnips
Chards	Okra	Watercress
Cucumbers	Olives	Zucchini

ACID | PROTEINS | ENDURANCE

Red Meats
Beef
Lamb
Pork
Rabbit
Veal
Wild game

White Meats
Duck
Chicken
Goose
Quail
Turkey
Wild game
   birds (all)
Other poultry

Fish
Bass
Cod
Haddock
Halibut
Perch
Salmon
Shark
Sole
Snapper
Swordfish
Trout
Tuna
Turbot
Misc. fish

Shellfish
Clams
Crab
Lobster
Octopus
Oysters
Scallops
Shrimp, prawns
Squid
Others

Eggs
Duck
Hen
Goose
Quail

Dairy Products
Cheeses (all)
Milk and cream
Yogurt

Nuts (Not all True Nuts)
Almonds
Brazil nuts
Cashews
Chestnuts
Filberts
Hazelnuts
Macadamias
Pecans
Peanuts
Pistachios
Pine nuts (pignolias)
Walnuts
Other Nuts

Acid Fruits
Cherries (sour)
Currants (tart)
Cranberries
Grapefruit
Lemons
Limes
Oranges
Pineapple
Rhubarb
Tangerines
Tomatoes

Heavy Legumes
Fava beans
   (Broadbeans)
Soybeans
Tofu

Seeds
Amaranth
Chia
Flax
Pumpkin (pepitas)
Sesame
Sunflower
Teff

Miscellaneous Foods and Exceptions:

1. Certain foods are neutral and can be mixed with any food. These include avocados, butter, and natural oils.

2. Some foods can be mixed well with several different food groups and can be included in more than one category. These include avocados, carrots, cauliflower, parsnips, turnips, tofu, and soybeans.

3. Some foods can only be included in different food groups in certain forms such as raw, cooked, sweet, sour, or tart, and fresh or dried. These foods are digested differently when the form is changed by cooking or drying. These foods include beans, corn, peas, tomatoes, cherries, and currants.

4. Some foods can only be eaten in one form (raw or cooked) for optimum flavor and nutrients and digestion. These foods include rhubarb, eggplant, endive, escarole, and lettuces.

5. Desserts are not on the chart. These should be served by themselves, after a meal, preferably one to two hours after good meals. These sweet foods include carob, honey, fruit concentrate, maple syrup, molasses, and all other natural sweeteners.

6. Whole grain flours are included with the whole grain category. Items not mentioned but included are: arrowroot, tapioca, guar and xanthan gum and baking powders. It is alright to use small amounts of these in sauces for acid foods.

7. Items like coffee, black and green teas, alcohol and chocolate are not mentioned in this chart. These and all refined sugars and flours are considered toxic foods so they are not mentioned. Small amounts of these foods are perfectly safe for healthy individuals and are best consumed immediately after or one hour or so after a meal. Herb teas can be drunk frequently a half hour before or after, or in between meals but are best if not consumed during a meal.

8. Even though nuts are proteins, they are best eaten alone in their raw state and not at all when roasted in oil or commercially dry roasted. Home roasted nuts are alright to eat. (See recipe in Chapter 15 – Appetizers, Snacks, and Party Foods) A small portion of nuts, a half cup or so per recipe or two tablespoons per serving, combine well with carbohydrate foods or protein foods if cooked and mixed with other foods in these categories.

9. Certain food combinations can be used occasionally including some alkaline (starchy) foods and some acid (protein) foods with little or no unpleasant effects. Some of the exceptions are as follows:

    a. Cooked acid fruits may be eaten occasionally with starches. For example, cooked tomato sauce with pasta.

b. Starches can occasionally be eaten with fish and shellfish as both of these are lighter, easier-to-digest meats and those with good digestion could get hungry a couple hours after a seafood meal unless whole grains are eaten with them. (Some may sleep too lightly or not well after a supper of just seafood and vegetables.) For example, trout and brown basmati rice may be eaten together for some individuals.

c. Cooked cheese and eggs are also lighter and may occasionally be eaten with whole grains. For example, quiche with a whole wheat crust.

d. The raw fruit rule may sometimes be avoided but it is best to follow this rule almost always. For example, there are a wide variety of mixed foods served at weddings. It may be impolite to appear picky, so relax for special occasions or holidays like New Years. (Keep the natural digestive aids handy, just in case.)

When to Eat

Among nutritionists, there are as many differing opinions about eating habits as there are animals in the wild. Since we are all different, our needs are different too. You can learn the basics, but each individual must create from out of the basics a meal schedule to suit his or her own lifestyle. Sizes of servings and numbers of meals will vary with each individual.

If you have a desk job and sit all day, you will need fewer meals and smaller portions. If you do active work, like being on your feet all day or working outdoors, you may need more meals and larger portions.

Breakfast is supposed to be the largest meal of the day, but realistically speaking, few of us have time for or desire a heavy breakfast. Part of the reason is that we are often still full from food eaten the night before. We go to bed on a full stomach, forcing the body to work overtime. Resting slows down the body processes and lowers the energy level, so digestion takes longer.

Those who are not hungry for breakfast often end up nibbling in the morning and nibbling for lunch on non-foods like coffee, sweet rolls, candies, pop, and other junk food. After starving yourself all day, the syndrome usually continues with a few evening cocktails and then stuffing yourself at supper. It is no wonder so many people have headaches and bad tempers in the evening after forcing the body to go all day without food fuel. We would never think of driving a car around all day without first putting in the gas. After stuffing yourself at supper, it is easy to collapse in front of the television set. Another evening wasted, with seldom enough energy for hobbies, housework, exercise, or an evening out.

If you eat the needed food throughout the day, you will not be so hungry for supper. A smaller meal will usually suffice. You will have more energy in the evenings and you will go to bed without a full stomach and wake up the next day hungry when breakfast time comes.

Young and very healthy people do not always feel the effects from improper eating, but given a little time and a lot of abuse, the body will begin to show signs of poor health from bad eating habits. There is no pill or magic formula that can transform the results of wasted years of poor living habits into good health. Disease is not spontaneous, so healing may take time.

Tips on When to Eat What:

1. Rinse the mouth and drink water on rising to help cleanse the system and eliminate toxins, which are poisons stored in the body, waiting to be removed. Drink three to four cups of water a day but not with meals. Drink one hour or more before or after a meal so that the water will not dilute stomach enzymes and make digestion more difficult. Drink double this amount of water in hot weather!

2. You may have citrus fruit or juice first in the morning, one half to one hour before breakfast, to help stimulate digestion. Do not serve citrus and whole grains together in the same meal because the two make a bad combination in the stomach and may cause upset. The grains and citrus become like lead in the system and calorie absorption increases.

3. Do not eat breakfast until your body fully wakes up and your energy level is somewhat stable for the day, about at least one half hour or more after rising. Before eating, do exercise or yoga to get the body engine warmed up and energy levels normal. Then eat! If you do not have time to eat in the morning before work, pack a breakfast and eat it during your morning coffee break. By then you are hungry and digestion will be at its best. If you must have something before you go out the door, have juice, milk, yogurt, or a piece of fruit.

4. Morning snacks are not usually necessary now, but if you do choose to have one, make it juice, fruit, yogurt, whole grain, or bread, muffins, or crackers, or nuts eaten alone. Do not just have sweets and coffee, all non-foods. They have little or no vitamins whatsoever. If you must have coffee, have something of real food value with it or preferable before it.

5. Do not skip lunch and do not just eat dessert! Even dieters can have a salad, a low-fat dairy product or a low-calorie sandwich. Follow the meal schedule and note the menu suggestions. See Chapter 24 – Sandwich Ideas and Lunchbox Specials for more ideas.

6. Afternoon snacks can include vegetables or fruit or breads (or crackers) or bean dips or nuts and seeds or juices or dairy products.

7. Supper need not be a big meal, although it often can be, especially if you are eating out. In this case, skip your afternoon snack so you will have a hearty appetite. Avoid going to sleep until a couple hours or so after eating. If you have been eating well all day, you may want to have a small supper, like a vegetable salad with bread and/or a dairy product. You may want to enjoy a cooked vegetable, a protein or a legume/whole grain plus the above. Eat until satisfied but not stuffed.

8. If you have evening or bedtime snacks, a beverage like warm milk, bread, or crackers or a light, easy-to-digest food is advised. Bedtime snacks are not for everyone. Avoid fruits and sweets as sugar energy may keep you awake at night.

Menu Suggestions

Breakfasts: (Vegetarian, Dairy- and Egg-Free, Vegan)
Meal #1 – Prebreakfast – banana (or dates in cereal); Meal – millet, cooked with dates or a natural sweetener like honey.

Meal #2 – Prebreakfast – apples (or any basic fruit); Meal – oatmeal cooked with raisins or soaked oats served with cooked fruit

Meal #3 – Prebreakfast – berries (or dried fruit); Meal – whole grain bread, toast, muffin or pancakes with cooked strawberry or blueberry sauce

Meal #4 – Prebreakfast – dried fruit: dates, currants, figs, prunes, or raisins; Meal – granola or other dry, whole grain cereal served with milk substitute or heated fruit juice that has been cooled.

Meal #5 – Prebreakfast – fresh grapefruit juice; Meal – $1/_2$ baked butternut squash with cinnamon on it – delicious!

Meal #6 – Prebreakfast – melon; Meal – French toast with cooked applesauce

(Vegetarian, with dairy or eggs)

Meal #7 – Prebreakfast – one or two kiwis; Meal – sautéed vegetables with scrambled eggs

Meal #8 – Prebreakfast – pear or peach; Meal – yogurt with quiche

Lunchbox Meals: (Vegetarian, Dairy-Free, Vegan)
Meal #1 – Vegetable salad; Tofu Spread and lettuce sandwich on whole grain bread; nuts and seeds, to eat an hour afterwards

Meal #2 – Raw celery and carrot sticks; tofu cheese and/or Falafel Spread and sprout sandwich; carob or carrot cake, for a later dessert

Meal #3 – Two pieces of fruit before lunch; soy spread and lettuce or spinach sandwich on whole grain bread

Meal #4 – Raw broccoli and/or bell pepper strips; cold sweet and sour lentils with a side of cold sautéed vegetables; yogurt; whole wheat bread, crackers, or rice cakes

Meal #5 – Hot vegetable-bean soup in a thermos; Cornbread, whole grain bread or crackers; cooked fruit dessert for later

(Vegetarian, with dairy or eggs)

Meal #6 – Greek salad with feta cheese; Vegetable Quiche

Meal #7 – Cucumber yogurt, egg salad with spinach or special mixed greens stuffed in pita breads; an apple for later

Lunches and Suppers: (Vegetarian, Dairy-Free, Vegan)

Meal #1 – Vegetable salad; Sloppy Joes with a bun

Meal #2 – Super Sprouts Salad; baked potatoes; Split Pea Soup; cooked greens: kale, cabbage, or spinach, with Ginger-Nut Sauce

Meal #3 – Vegetable salad; Stuffed Green Peppers; cooked root vegetable; cake or pie for later

Meal #4 – Fruit salad or cocktail 15 minutes ahead; Soyburgers on bread or buns; steamed potatoes; natural dairy-free ice cream for later

(Vegetarian, with dairy or eggs)

Meal #5 – Spinach salad; chili; avocado or Guacamole; plain brown rice or millet; fruit juice jello for later

Meal #6 – Vegetable salad; Spinach-Potato Pie; nuts and seeds; sour cream or yogurt

Meal #7 – Beet Treat Salad; Tamale Pie and Cashew Pudding for later

Simple Suppers: (Vegetarian, Dairy-Free, Vegan)

Meal #1 – Large salad with ground nuts or tofu cheese on top; whole grain bread and veggie butter

Meal #2 – Vegetable soup; falafel sandwich

Meal #3 – Spaghetti; cooked greens: spinach, or Swiss chard

(Vegetarian, with dairy or eggs)

Meal #4 – Vegetable nut spread with crackers and yogurt

Meal #5 – Spinach-Potato Pie or Vegetable Quiche alone

* Recipes found in this book are in capitals above.

Warning Signals of Bad Eating Habits

If you do not feel well, trace back over your diet for 24 to 48 hours to see where you went wrong. Perhaps you ate too many sweets, had incomplete meals, or even skipped a meal. Did you eat too many starches or heavy foods? Your body and mind will give you warning signals when you abuse them. Look for these signals and make amends in your diet. Ignore them and you may suffer the consequences.

Here are some of the ways your body may react when and if the problem is caused by improper diet. Each body is different, so the warning signals are not always the same. This chart does not deal with major vitamin deficiencies as those symptoms are already listed in the vitamin chart in Chapter 6 – Vitamins and Minerals. This chart includes food-related problems and does not include problems caused by stress, weariness, long-term eating habits, or causes not related to diet.

If any major problems occur, contact your doctor.

Causes and Solutions for Minor Health Problems Created by Bad Eating Habits

Symptom	Cause	How to Make Amends
Dizziness, headache, shakiness	Lack of food or improper food with not enough nutrients	Stay away from junk foods for a while. If you have not eaten for a few hours, have a meal of all natural foods and avoid sweets for several days.
Shakiness, bumping into things, jumbled thoughts and depression, bruising easily	Too many sugars and refined foods in your overall diet lately or recently you had a large dose of sugar on an empty stomach	Avoid refined starches, sugars and sweets of any kind for 1-2 weeks. Increase your protein and vitamin intake with natural foods by following the meal schedules carefully.
Craving sweets or craving lots of meat or milk	Lack of nutrients or improper foods with not enough vitamins and minerals. (This is not necessarily a sign of protein deficiency.)	Make sure you are eating enough fruits and vegetables and having complete meals including protein. Watch and correct your diet for 1-2 weeks.

Symptom	Cause	How to Make Amends
Sleeplessness (insomnia)	One reason can be too many sweets in the evening. Sugar energy keeps you awake. Also, if you have not eaten enough natural foods or had incomplete meals during the day, sleeping becomes difficult. Indigestion can contribute to insomnia. See your health care practitioner for test or to acquire helpful digestive supplements.	Eat no sweets, fruit, refined starches, and or chewable vitamin C after supper or even earlier. Exercise earlier in the day. Have a balanced supper a few hours before bedtime and eat a protein or complex carbohydrate snack before bedtime. Try warm milk, toast, warm cooked yams, melted/cooked cheese on toast, warm grains, or cooked vegetables.
Heaviness, sleepiness, sluggishness, laziness	Too much food or too many starches, especially refined or heavy foods. Diet may be improperly balanced.	If a meal was just eaten, get mild exercise to wear off your heavy food. Avoid eating again until hungry. If symptoms persist, fast for a day or eat lightly for a day. Balance your meals better in the future and do not overeat.
Craving foods, especially starches and sweets, even when full of food	Improper foods with not enough nutrients. Also, lack of natural oils causes cravings for sweets and starches.	Watch your diet for a week or two. Make sure you follow the food chart. Natural oils are supplied mainly in whole grains, beans, nuts, seeds, and leafy greens.
Gas or stomach discomfort	Eating too fast, or too much. Eating improperly cooked foods or eating bad combinations of food.	Plan your meals better. Take time to eat and chew throughly or do not eat. Read over the eating rules and recheck the recipes and food combining charts related causes.
Inability to lose weight	Not enough variety of foods and therefore lacking certain vitamins. Improper food combining. Food allergies or Candida albicans.	Cut down amounts of foods, not types of foods, when dieting. The body needs natural oils even when dieting. Watch food combining. Get tested for food allergies and Candida albicans and check for other related causes.

Symptom	Cause	How to Make Amends
Inability to gain weight	If not a physical problem, diet is to blame. For some peoople overconsumption of refined foods can prevent weight gain. This and improper meal planning.	Improve the overall diet gradually to exclude all or most refined foods and consume whole foods. Eat balanced meals, lots of whole grains, legumes, vegetables, and some natural oils.
All or most of the above	Food allergy or Candida albicans yeast overgrowth.	Consult an allergist or naturopathic practitioner for testing and treatment. Avoid aggravating foods. Eat wholesome natural foods.
Inability to Quit Bad Habits (Smoking, drinking alcohol, overeating)	Overall poor diet or too many acidic foods in the diet.	Increase alkaline food intake. Surround yourself with wholesome foods to splurge on when cravings occur.

(Note: This chart does not include major illnesses or diseases indirectly related to food consumption.)

How to Improve Your Diet by Using a Meal Chart

Make a few copies of the following daily meal chart and keep a record of your meals for a week or two. Do not list the names of dishes, list the types of food in them such as rice, cheese, or bread. When your chart is completely filled in, check it over to find if each day's food contains all the foods listed on the Daily Food Needs chart. Are you eating properly? Note your deficiencies and concentrate on adding missing healthy foods to your diet and eliminating any unnecessary foods.

Make a note of changes you would like to make, and keep it in a conspicuous place, such as the refrigerator door, to remind you to make those changes. For example:

Mom: Eat more nuts and seeds, 1 serving every other day; have fruit daily, 1 –3 servings daily; cut down on sweets, only 1 serving daily; eat more legumes

Junior: Eat more vegetables, three or more servings daily; drink real diluted juices not soda pop!

Use the reminder note for two to three weeks. Then do another week or two of Daily Meal Charts to see if you have improved. If you have, and are satisfied with your diets, discard your notes and keep eating the new foods. If your diet improvement is minimal, keep your old food reminder or make a new one and follow it!

Daily Meal Chart

Daily Meal	Monday	Tuesday	Wednesday	Thursday	Friday	Saturday	Sunday
Pre-Breakfast Juice or Citrus							
Breakfast – Vegetable(s) or Cooked Fruit							
Whole Grain							
Dairy or Substitute							
Nuts/Seeds or Meat							
Beverage*							
Snack*							
Lunch – Produce							
Whole Grain							
Legume/Protein							
Beverage*							
Dairy or Substitute							
Dessert							
Snack*							
Supper – Vegetable(s)							
Whole Grain							
Legume/Protein							
Cooked Fruit*							
Beverage*							
Dairy or Substitute							
Dessert							
Snack*							

* (Optional)

Chapter 5

The Pros & Cons of Vegetarianism

Why Vegetarianism?

Should you or shouldn't you become a vegetarian? There are many reasons for vegetarianism. Many points of view. Not everyone should be a vegetarian but everyone should be aware of the reasons why meat is not needed in large quantities. Eating meat three to four times a week is more than sufficient for most people, for all protein needs along with dairy products, eggs, legumes, whole grains, nuts, and seeds to satisfy the rest of our protein needs.

Once you start eating some natural foods, you may have the desire to drop meat from your diet, partially or completely. Follow your own feelings on this and eat what feels right for you. You can be healthy whether or not you eat meat. One person may have an easier time digesting meat than another. Fresh air, exercise, eating habits, inherited tendencies, and mental attitude all have to be taken into account for good health.

Here are some facts and reasons why people become a vegetarian for both health and spiritual reasons. These are commonly accepted views, not necessarily my own. For

" *I learned this, at least, by my experiment; that if one advances confidently in the direction of his dreams, and endeavors to live the life which he has imagined, he will meet with a success unexpected in common hours.*"

Thoreau — Walden

additional information on reasons for vegetarianism see the book *Diet for a New America* by John Robbins listed in the Recommended Reading section.

Health and Practical Reasons for Vegetarianism

1. Meat is very hard to digest. It takes longer than any other food to digest, up to five or six hours or more in the stomach. This takes up a great deal of body energy.
2. Most meat is pumped full of dangerous hormones, drugs, and chemicals which can be passed on to the consumer.
3. The animals slaughtered are sometimes diseased. Some meat processors are allowed to use any diseased animals, even cancerous ones, as long as they remove the parts of the animals that are obviously diseased.
4. Eating meat may introduce harmful or irritating acids, like uric, into the body.
5. Meat makes elimination sluggish and may cause constipation, especially when combined with the wrong foods.
6. Meat creates nervous, restless energy in the body and the mind.
7. Adulterated, hormone treated, or feed lotted meat may introduce parasites and diseases into our bodies. Meat can carry cancer, tuberculosis, and other diseases.
8. Meat eating may encourage the lowering of the body's resistance to disease.
9. Meat is heavy in the system. A diet without meat generally makes one feel light, energetic, and mentally aware.
10. When animals are slaughtered they are in fear and pain. These feelings trigger the release of their bodies' stored poisons and toxins directly into their systems. This makes it easier for these poisons to be passed on to the consumer. These poisons include drugs and hormones used to increase weight gain in the animals.
11. Vegetables, legumes, and whole grains are high in protein and they have an abundant supply of all kinds of vitamins and minerals.
12. It takes approximately five to twenty pounds of vegetable protein to produce one pound of animal protein. Why waste time, energy, and money raising animal protein when vegetable protein is more economical? Countries could benefit from the grains and vegetables that would be made available for human consumption.
13. Meat is more expensive pound for pound than vegetables.

Spiritual Reasons for Vegetarianism

1. "Do not kill any developed forms of life for your food." Eat food that will cause the least pain to other creatures and living things. Plants feel pain less than animals do because they are a less conscious form of life. Also, many plants do not need to be completely destroyed to provide us with food.

2. We get firsthand energy and protein from the sun and then from plants. Why get protein thirdhand from animals when we can go up higher on the food chain to plants and get better quality protein plus vitamins. If animals get their protein from plants, why can't we?

3. Man was originally vegetarian before Noah and the Flood. It is said that as man evolves and gets closer to God and to reaching his true spiritual potential, he will return to vegetarianism.

4. Natural foods without meats are calming and conducive to a spiritual life style. "Vibrations" of vegetable foods are higher and cleaner than those of killed animals.

5. Karma! Karma is a law that what you do comes back to you. An eye for an eye, tooth for a tooth, or love for love! If you hurt life unnecessarily, kill for food when you do not need to, you will have to pay for it later on. If you are in a situation where you have to kill animals for your food or to stay alive, then that is acceptable and you will not get "bad karma." If animals are killed, it should be done reverently, only when the animals are really needed for food. If other food is available, then animals should be spared.

The Cons of Vegetarianism

1. "Junk-food vegetarians" who eat what they please with no thought of nutrition may be injuring their health.

2. Many people choose to become vegetarians but do not bother to research the protein and vitamin needs of a vegetarian. They may think they are eating well but may be protein and vitamin deficient and possibly lowering their body resistance to disease. Also, wrong food combinations may hinder digestion.

3. Some people may be more mentally and physically accustomed to meat protein and would find it too great a sacrifice or too great a strain to exclude meat.

4. It requires a good deal of time and effort to learn how to be a healthy vegetarian and to learn new cooking techniques and recipes. It may be hard to orient the taste buds in favor of natural foods and a meatless diet.

5. The following basic idea is debatable to many but is found here and there in nutrition books: Certain human bodies require certain meats to function at their optimum best. This statement, however, often refers to the eating of fish and poultry, not necessarily to red meats such as beef, pork, and lamb, which are harder to digest.

6. Vegetarians can more easily become anemic and vitamin B deficient. It is claimed that certain B vitamins, especially B12, and vitamin D are absent or insufficient in the vegetarian diet. This can be true if the vegetarian diet is not well balanced. Some

specialized vegetarian "fad" diets are examples of this. However, dairy products, eggs, millet, soybeans, brewer's yeast, special seaweeds, and herbs can provide these necessary B vitamins and other vitamins and minerals including iron and calcium.

How Not to Be a Junk-Food Vegetarian

Junk-food vegetarians are people who eat an average North American processed, refined food diet but eliminate meat. This foolish diet comes closer to suicide than almost any other self-inflicted diet. In this diet, outside of a few scattered salads and canned vegetables, there is not much to speak of in the way of food, let alone protein. Vegetarians have to eat better than anyone else.

Refined junk foods and meats are opposite extremes, meat being the hardest food to digest and refined food the easiest. They need to balance each other. You cannot eliminate one without eliminating the other! Eating one food often creates a need and a craving for the other. Most junk foods such as colas, coffee, white flour, sugar, and candies must be eliminated from the diet if one wishes to stop eating meat.

An abundance of fresh fruits and vegetables must be the foundation of your diet. Beans and whole grains come next. Refined foods should be limited in proportion to equal or preferably less than your meat intake. In other words, if you are going to have meat three times a week, make sure you do not splurge on junk foods more than three times a week.

The majority of people lose their desire for meat entirely when refined foods have been given up and more whole grains, beans, and produce are eaten. For mind and body, happiness and health, the less meat and refined foods eaten, the better!

If you are seriously interested in vegetarianism, follow the steps toward better nutrition in Chapter 3 – Diet Plans for a Healthier Lifestyle. This chapter describes in full the guidelines for being a healthy vegetarian and the preliminary steps you should take before becoming one.

The Protein Illusion

"Be sure to eat your meat! You have to get enough protein" is heard across North America and seems to be the prime concern of almost everyone. Far less is said about other nutrients. Nowhere else in the world is protein consumed in larger quantities or more readily available. We get three to four times the amount of protein that is normally needed by the body. The rest of the world is either vegetarian or consumes meat a few times a week if they can get it.

Diet Seesaw

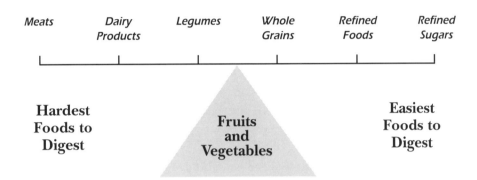

| Meats | Dairy Products | Legumes | Whole Grains | Refined Foods | Refined Sugars |

Hardest Foods to Digest

Fruits and Vegetables

Easiest Foods to Digest

When you go up and down on the diet seesaw by eating lots of meats and refined foods, your emotions and body energy go up and down too. When the foods you eat are closer to the center of the seesaw, diets and lifestyle are more balanced. (See diagram)

Besides meat, proteins are derived from the following foods: dairy products, eggs, whole grains, legumes, or some nuts or seeds.

Dairy products and/or eggs alone are not recommended as a sole source of protein. Meat and/or grains, legumes, or nuts are required for a healthy diet.

Besides the above-stated sources of protein, many vegetables and nuts are nearly complete proteins and become complete when taken in combination with other certain incomplete proteins. Some specific foods that are especially high in protein are: sprouts, avocados, leafy dark greens, almonds, cashews, sunflower seeds, and sesame seeds.

Usually only raw food vegetarians need to be concerned about getting enough protein. Many vegetarians have a higher protein level in the body than meat eaters.

Since almost everyone gets sufficient protein, the real concern is: are you getting enough vitamin A, B's, C, D, E, iron, and calcium? The majority of North American are lacking more in these essential vitamins which are derived from whole grains, legumes, fresh fruits, vegetables, and sunshine.

A general rule of thumb: Eat three to four servings of fruits and/or vegetables for every one serving of meat or a grain and/or legume combination.

Some Facts About Protein:

1. Protein is not destroyed by cooking. If it was, meat would not be considered a common source of protein.

2. Protein is derived in part from all foods, some more than others.

3. One to three servings of protein a day are completely adequate. (This does not include dairy products or eggs. More servings may be needed if these are counted.)

4. A complete protein is made up of twenty-two amino acids. All except eight can be produced by the average body. Foods or food combinations that supply all eight of these essential amino acids are called complete proteins. New food research shows that most individuals can derive adequate protein from incomplete proteins.

5. Meat is not the highest source of protein. Many legumes and grain-bean combinations have equal or more protein value.

6. Meat and dairy products and some legumes and nuts are complete proteins. Most legumes and whole grains eaten together or separately are adequate proteins.

7. Most legumes have half the calories of meat or less, and whole grains have about the same number of calories or less than meat per equal size serving.

8. A person does not use any more protein doing physical labor all day than when sitting at a desk all day! Protein is not burned up in the same way as calories. Each body is different, but the same body requires the same amount of protein daily regardless of the different amounts of work done by the individual.

9. Legumes and grains eaten together or individually as sources of protein can be exciting and tasty, even more so than meat, if prepared properly.

10. The main functions of protein in the body are to furnish energy, provide enzymes for digestion, provide antibodies and antitoxins for resistance against disease, and build and maintain the body cells.

11. Nut and seeds highest in protein include: almonds, cashews, Brazil nuts, sesame, and pumpkin seeds.

12. There is generally more protein in raw food than cooked food, but cooked protein is more digestible (more usable) for the average person.

Chapter 6

Vitamins & Minerals

The Complexity of Vitamins

The following vitamin chart is far from giving complete information on what vitamins and minerals to take and how, what amounts to take daily, or what should or should not be mixed with what. An entire book would have to be written explaining all the factors involved with vitamins. As a matter of fact, several books have been written by many knowledgeable doctors and nutritionists. Some of these books are in the Recommended Reading section.

Since some nutritionists disagree, you will have to use your own discrimination. Just remember that every body is different and has different needs. Become aware of your own needs, but do not become obsessed with taking vitamins. No one eats all the right foods and takes all the proper vitamins. The body is adaptable and will function well if all its major needs are satisfied.

There is no sure way of generalizing needs or amounts of vitamins for the average person. However, the US Federal Drug Administration (FDA) and Health Canada have issued so-called "safe" guidelines called RDA (Recommended Daily Allowances) and RDI (Recommended Daily Intake) respectively. These guidelines are for a number of vitamins and minerals, but the requirements are low and incomplete.

" If anything ail a man, so that he does not perform his functions, if he have a pain… he forthwith sets about reforming — the world."

Thoreau — Walden

The best way to ensure we are getting, as much as possible, the vitamins we need is to eat a balanced diet of vitamin-rich foods and include whatever vitamin supplements are recommended for any deficiencies we may have. Vitamin supplements should not be taken haphazardly but with knowledge of their effects and potency, and in proper combination with other vitamins. Get advice and see a doctor if deficiencies or physical problems arise.

The Big Vitamin Question

Are vitamin supplements really necessary or can we get all the vitamins we need from food? All the vitamins we need could be derived from our food alone if:

1. The foods were grown naturally, in mineral-rich soil.
2. Our foods were unrefined, unprocessed, and not chemically treated.
3. We eat daily the right variety of foods from the main food groups: protein, whole grains, produce, and dairy or dairy substitutes.
4. We have no deficiency caused by heredity, environment, stress, illness, or injury.
5. We have satisfied the body's needs for exercise, rest, sunshine, and a positive lifestyle.

Since we ourselves and our food are often lacking and incomplete, we may sometimes have to rely on extra vitamin and mineral supplements for some of our needs. But, bear these facts in mind when taking supplements:

1. Take only supplements you really need. If your body gets used to obtaining what it needs from a pill, it may get lazy and cease to produce vitamins that it usually produces on its own. Also, it may lose the ability to assimilate vitamins from food sources as that requires some breaking down of food material before usage.
2. Most vitamin needs can be obtained from natural foods.
3. Take natural rather than synthetic vitamins whenever possible. Although chemists feel there is no structural difference between natural and synthetic vitamins, there are some major differences:

    a. Synthetic vitamins are usually one or more main vitamins and sometimes some helper vitamins, whereas natural vitamins are accompanied by all kinds of other lesser vitamins and minerals that can more effectively help assimilate those main vitamins into your system. These extra lesser vitamins also help satisfy some of the body's other vitamin needs.

    b. Natural vitamins are concentrated food, not chemicals. There are no major unwanted side effects with natural vitamins. Also, there are no unnecessary chemicals present that could be stored in the body.

c. Many natural vitamins are more easily broken down by the body and assimilated whereas many synthetic vitamins take longer to break down in the body and may pass through partially undigested.

Can You Take Too Many Vitamins?

You would have to take a tremendous amount of most natural vitamins to over-dose. Usually excess vitamins just pass through the system and are eliminated. Since the need for each vitamin by each person is different, so is the maximum tolerance level. Follow the suggested dosages given by leading nutritionists and tested vitamin charts and cut down or increase the amounts slightly if you feel the need, are recommended to do so by your personal doctor or nutritionist, or if you start getting unwanted side effects. Side effects from natural vitamins are usu-ally rare and insignificant, but if any do occur, seek professional advice. Individual reactions to the binders and fillers used in vitamin preparation may occur. Avoid taking excessive amounts of fatsoluble vitamins and iron.

Vitamin Chart

Vitamin A (Carotene or Retinol which is animal derived) is fat soluble.
Functions – prevents night blindness and respiratory infections, essential for normal growth, and teeth formation.
Sources – green and yellow vegetables (especially carrots and greens), sprouts, apricots, pumpkins, fish oil, dairy products, and egg yolks.

Vitamin B1 (Thiamin) can be destroyed by too much heat and is water soluble.
Functions – essential for normal functioning of the nervous system and diges-tive tract. Essential for normal growth and proper use of starches and sugars, promotes appetite. Lack may cause constipation, diarrhea, or beriberi.
Sources – vegetables, (especially leafy greens), whole grains, legumes, wheat germ, brewer's yeast, bananas, apples, dairy products, nuts, and sprouts.

Vitamin B2 (Riboflavin) is heat stable but not light stable, and is water soluble.
Functions – helps to utilize food energy, promotes normal growth, involved with process of oxidation within body cells. Promotes healthy skin, eyes, and digestive tract. Lack can cause weakness, headaches, and digestive problems.
Sources– green leafy vegetables, citrus fruits, tomatoes, dairy products, eggs, wheat germ, brewer's yeast, legumes, whole grains, seeds, and bananas.

Vitamin B3 (Niacin) is light and heat stable and water soluble.
Functions – helps to utilize food energy. For healthy skin and digestive tract. Prevents pellagra: digestive troubles, sore tongue and skin problems.
Sources – legumes, whole grains, leafy green vegetables, dairy products, brewer's yeast, wheat germ, mushrooms, tomatoes, and peanuts.

Vitamin B6 (Pyridoxine) Destroyed by oxidation, heat, and sunlight; water soluble.
Functions – essential for protein metabolism. Helps regulate weight, prevents edema, stabilizes emotional tendencies. Helps high or low blood sugar and is good for complexion and teeth. Prevents cramps and muscle spasms.
Sources – pecans, peanuts, brewers yeast, leafy green vegetables, carrots, cabbage, avocados, and bananas.

Vitamin B12 (Cyanocobalamin) is alcohol and water soluble.
Functions – needed to form red blood cells and helps prevent anemia.
Sources – spirulina, dairy products, brewer's yeast (some varieties), wheat germ, soybeans, peanuts, seaweed, blue-green algae, and some TVP.

Vitamin C (Ascorbic Acid) is destroyed by heat and oxidation and is water soluble.
Functions – promotes healing and resistance to disease and infections. For healthy bones, teeth, and gums. Prevents scurvy. Lessens severity of colds.
Sources – citrus fruits, tomatoes, potatoes, broccoli, cauliflower, strawberries and most melons, especially cantaloupes.

Vitamin D (Calciferol) can stay stable under refrigeration and is fat soluble.
Functions – promotes calcium absorption. For normal growth and development of the body and formation of teeth and bones. Is especially needed by children and pregnant women. Lack may cause rickets and lack of energy.
Sources – sunlight, fish liver oil, sunflower seeds, coconut, almonds, and dairy products.

Vitamin E (Alpha Tocopherol) is heat stable and fat soluble.
Functions – improves the oxygen efficiency of the muscles. Said to strengthen the reproductive system and aid heart functions. Good for internal and external wounds and burns. Good for pregnant women.
Sources – leafy green vegetables, natural oils, beets, nuts, seeds, oranges, molasses, legumes, and peanuts.

Mineral Chart

Calcium

Functions – for strong bones and teeth, helps balance minerals in the body tissues, helps regulate heart beat and clot blood.

Sources – beet and turnip greens, lettuces, potatoes, dairy products, molasses, almonds, soybeans, tofu, and sesame seeds.

Iodine

Functions – for proper growth and development, regulates food use by the body, prevents goiter and enlargement of the thyroid gland.

Sources – kelp, dulse, seaweed, iodized salt, and leafy green vegetables.

Iron

Functions – helps form hemoglobin in red blood cells, transports oxygen to the blood cells, and helps prevent anemia.

Sources – leafy green vegetables, dried fruits, molasses, legumes, whole grains, almonds, and egg yolk.

Magnesium

Functions – relaxes nerves, helps digestion, and promotes new cell growth.

Sources – whole grains, eggplant, citrus fruits, egg yolk, and coconuts.

Manganese

Functions – essential for forming blood cells, helps improve memory, benefits the pancreas.

Sources – buckwheat, whole grains, sunflower seeds, legumes, bone meal, egg yolk, and brewer's yeast.

Phosphorus

Functions – for strong bones and teeth, assists waste removal and food absorption.

Sources – most vegetables, legumes, whole grains, peanuts, egg yolk, and dairy products.

Potassium

Functions – regulates the weight, good for nerves and muscles.

Sources – molasses, dried fruits, whole grains, legumes, leafy green vegetables, nuts, some fresh fruits, and bananas.

Zinc
Functions – increases blood volume, promotes healing and proper growth.
Sources – brewer's yeast, legumes, nuts and seeds, fertile eggs, and bone meal.

Other minerals that can be supplied by a balanced diet include:

Chlorine	Silicon	Sulphur
Fluorine	Sodium	Chromium
Lithium	Selenium	Copper
Molybdenum	Cobalt	

Chapter 7

Sweets for the Sweet

The Sugar Hoax

Is sugar an energy food? Perhaps it is good for temporary, empty energy, but it has no real food value or any lasting benefits whatsoever.

Since sugar is completely refined, it needs no breaking-down process in the body. Therefore it enters the bloodstream immediately and gives the body a surge of quick energy, followed soon after by a drop in energy. That is why one may eat until full of sweets one moment and be hungry the next. The sugar energy is temporary and has no real value for the body except to push the body on in short spurts.

If one obtains real raw sugar or consumes raw honey or other unrefined sweeteners, these affect the body differently. These sweeteners take time for the body to break down and to enter the bloodstream. The body gets slow, gradual fuel fed to it, with the result that one is satisfied for a longer period of time. Also, these types of sweeteners have real food value. They contain usable vitamins and minerals to support the body and its functions.

" ... and if I must have some concentrated sweet, I found by experiment that I could make a very good molasses either of pumpkins or beets, and I know that I needed only set out a few maples to obtain it more easily still, and while these were growing I could use various substitutes besides those which I have named."

Thoreau — Walden

What Is Sugar?

All refined products such as white flour and sugar are stripped of all food value. In flour a poor attempt is made to replace the lost food value with added artificial vitamins. With sugar no attempt whatsoever is made to improve it or create any food value.

In the case of sugar, the vitamins are destroyed by heat and processing. Then chemicals and additives like acid calcium phosphate, phosphoric acid, blood albumin and bone-black from animals, milk of lime, and bleach are added to break it down and "purify" it. As if it was not bad enough taking out all the food value, some harmful and unnecessary additives are added as well.

For more information about sugar, see the books listed in the Recommended Reading section.

Are Some Sugars Better than Others?

According to United States law all locally processed cane and beet sugars must be refined before they can be sold. Raw sugar is believed to be impure. Unrefined sugars are manufactured in parts of Europe and possibly in other countries but not in the United States. Many American companies that claim to sell raw sugars are using false or misleading advertising. Some sugars may only be partially refined, but they are still refined. The only difference in most sugars is how much molasses "coloring" is added, as in the case of brown sugars, or how much it is crystallized. Avoid these sugars altogether or as much as possible. This concerns all types of cane and beet sugars including the following: raw sugar, kleen-raw sugar, demerara sugar, turbinado sugar, light and dark brown sugars, granulated or powdered sugars, and in-the-raw type sugars. Some European unrefined sugars are available as imports in the USA and Canada at this time. They include Sucane®, Sweetcane®, Sucanat® or one may obtain fruit sugars like FruitSource®, Mystic Lake®, brown date sugar, and powdered malt.

Fructose or Sucrose – Which is Better?

Fructose is sugar derived from fruit. Sucrose comes from cane or beet sugar. Fructose is generally more easily digested and better for people with blood sugar problems. True, fructose is better for the body—but not if it comes in a completely refined form! Anything that looks and tastes similar to white sugar and is refined is still harmful. This included refined fructose, dextrose (corn sugar), lactose (milk sugar), date sugar, or other refined fruit sugars. A clear white or dark liquid sugar of these types is just as unhealthy whether it is sold in a health food store or supermarket. They are all the same, worthless. These liquids include fructose, corn syrup, artificial maple syrup and pancake syrup, and cooking molasses.

Dehydrated or dried brown date sugar, powdered malt, natural raw sugar, or granular sweetener are not included in this unhealthy group. These are only slightly sweet, are date or cream colored, and of coarser consistency. By the less sweet taste, one can tell these did not go through the usual sugar processes. These sugars are acceptable for use and tasty, but not always sweet enough to use alone in desserts. Use it half and half with honey or another sweetener in some recipes.

Healthful Alternatives to Sugar

There are many safe, delicious, and healthy alternatives to refined sugars. The most common of these is honey. These alternatives are recommended only if they are not refined. Preferably buy them raw and unsulphured or untreated, with no unnecessary additives.

These substitutes have vitamins and minerals. They are real foods. But, because of their sweetness, even these should be eaten sparingly. The body can make its own sugar, so none is required as food. Keep all sweets in moderation.

Substitutes:

amazake (rice culture sweetener)
barley malt powder or syrup
brown date sugar
date spread
fructose (less refined variety)
fruit butter
fruit concentrate
fruit juice
fruit juice concentrate
fruit sugar (unrefined)
honey
honeycomb
honey leaf (stevia)

maple sugar
maple syrup
molasses, blackstrap or Barbados
    (unsulphured)
natural granular fruit sweetener
    (FruitSource ®)
natural liquid fruit sweetener
    (FruitSource ®)
natural raw sugar (natural granular)
    (Sucanat ®, Sucane ®, Sweetcane ®)
rice syrup
sorghum

Recipes

Recipes using various healthful sweeteners are found throughout this and other books. Also see the substitution charts in the appendices for ways to change recipes calling for sugar into recipes using honey or other healthful sweeteners.

About Honey

It takes more than five hundred bees traveling a distance equal to once around the world or more to produce each pound of honey. Unless, of course, the bee-keeper decides to feed the bees sugar water. This cuts down the bees' work considerably and also shortens their life span. It quickens the honey-making process but lowers the quality of the honey.

Whenever possible, buy honey from a local beekeeper who can be trusted not to tamper with the bees. This is easier than it sounds. There are local beekeepers almost everywhere. Usually they sell honey in five-pound, thirty-pound, or even sixty-pound containers. Also, one can buy guaranteed pure honey at your local health food store. Most supermarket brands are not to be trusted, although some brands are pure. Look for brands that are labeled raw, unrefined, unpasteurized (unheated), or organic.

Raw, unfiltered honey is preferable and higher in vitamin and mineral content. Raw honey may be bought in liquid or solid form. Pasteurized or heated honey will always be liquid. Filtering honey also removes many other vitamins. Note: Honey quality and taste may vary widely.

Honeycomb can also be purchased and is both delicious and nutritious. The entire comb may be eaten in its own honey or by itself. Serve it with bread or toast or fruit as a snack or a dessert. It contains more vitamins than raw liquid honey but is also more expensive, so it is just for table use, not for cooking.

How to Use Honey

How to Soften Honey: Raw liquid honey can easily turn into a solid. This usually happens at cool temperatures. This hardening or recrystallizing of the honey is often a test of whether or not the honey is raw.

In order to soften raw solid honey, it must be warmed. Honey should never be heated directly. Place the honey in a pan, sink, or tub of hot water until it softens. Use water as hot as the hand can stand but no hotter. Caution: Do not put plastic containers of honey in pans of boiled water. They melt! Place a metal jar lid between the plastic container and the pan bottom and make sure the container does not touch the sides of the pan. Another way is to spoon out the hard honey and put it in a glass container before softening.

Keep honey containers covered while softening and leave them in the water just long enough to liquefy the honey. Cold temperatures can make raw honey recrystallize and harden again.

Using Every Bit: When the honey jar is empty there is usually still lots of honey sticking to the inside of the jar. Prop the jar upside down for ten to twenty minutes to get all the last drops of honey out. If there is still honey left, save the jar until the next time herb tea is made. Then swish the hot tea or water in the jar and all the honey can be completely used to sweeten the tea.

Honey Storage: Honey will keep for years on a cupboard shelf if kept in a clean covered jar and not contaminated with other food particles, dirt, perspiration, or saliva. Do not refrigerate. Keep in a warm, dry place.

Varieties of Honey

Honey varieties and flavors are determined by the types of flowers from which the bees gather nectar. The bees make honey from the nectar found in the flowers nearest to their hives. Most of the honey in North America comes from clover flowers, therefore it is called clover honey. White clover honey comes from white clover flowers. There is also red clover honey, which is just called clover honey, and alfalfa honey, wildflower honey, and others.

Here are just a few of the most popular types of honey and their qualities:

Clover – A mild-flavored honey that is quite common and plentiful. It has a pleasant taste and is useful for baking, cooking, and everyday table use. Usually the most inexpensive honey.

Alfalfa – Another mild-flavored honey. Not always available. It is usually inexpensive and great for everyday use.

Wildflower – Gathered from fields of mixed wildflowers. It has a more tangy, special flavor and is good for everyday use. Moderately priced.

Orange Blossom – From orange-tree blossoms. A delicious orange-flavored honey. It is usually expensive, so it is best kept only for table use and very special dessert recipes. Quality varies widely.

Buckwheat – It is well named the "liquor of honeys." It has a very strong, tangy flavor that is pleasant to many people and not so pleasant to others. It is dark colored. Although it is usually inexpensive, it tends to overpower all other flavors when used in cooking; so it is best kept mainly for table use and special recipes.

Fireweed – A good-tasting honey gathered from a northern American wildflower that gets its name from springing up abundantly in many areas where fires have previously occurred. The honey is moderately priced and good for all-purpose use. Quality varies. Some brands are not flavorful.

Tupelo – Special, high-quality honey, better for people with high or low blood sugar than ordinary honey. This honey can be used instead of other honey or sweeteners. It is not always available and is a bit more expensive, but is a less harmful sweet if sweets must be eaten. It is full of vitamins, but like all sweets, should be eaten in moderation.

Tips and Facts about Honey

1. Heat honey as little as possible to save vitamins and flavor.
2. To prevent sticking while measuring honey, oil the measuring cup with natural, mild-flavored oil or measure oil in the cup first before measuring the honey. It will not stick to the cup and not a drop of honey will be wasted.
3. Honey is soothing for sore throats and colds. Use it in warm milk and herb teas.
4. Babies under twenty-four months old should never be given raw honey. Young babies are unable to handle the bacteria in raw honey, which is claimed to be a contributing factor in crib deaths. Note: Infants under one year old really have no need for any sweetening. They do receive some simple milk sugars, called lactose, from milk. However, some filtered, pasteurized honey or maple syrup may be used if cooked into recipes for babies.

Tips About Sweets

1. Eat sweets in moderation. The body makes its own sugar from fruits or starches such as grains and starchy vegetables like potatoes and squash. Even too much natural sweetener is not good for the body and can cause stomach upset and lack of appetite for other important foods.
2. Sweets eaten on an empty stomach are more potent and have a stronger negative effect on the body. Sweets eaten with a meal are also harmful because they may get digested first, especially refined sweets, and the body may end up discarding other valuable nutrients in the meal. It is preferable to eat desserts and sweets one half hour to one hour after small meals and one hour or longer after large meals which also helps reduce the amount of calories that are absorbed by the body.
3. Pancakes and syrup and other sweet "foods" are often upsetting to the stomach because of their sweetness. If one must have these foods, start a meal with milk, eggs, or toast. Begin eating pancakes and syrup at the end or halfway through the meal; then stomach upset will be lessened or eliminated altogether.
4. All types of sweeteners, natural or otherwise, can be harmful to the teeth and add pounds to the body. Avoid eating sweets at night. If they must be had, brush the teeth carefully before bedtime. Refined sugars and dried fruits can be the most detrimental to teeth, especially when left on the teeth for a period of time.

Also avoid lemon juice at night which is acidic and may harm teeth enamel.

5. Craving sweets is not a sign of the body's need for sugar. It is usually a sign of either protein or vitamin deficiency. Since the majority of us overeat protein, usually a lack of vitamins is the real problem. The solution is for vitamins to be derived from real food. When craving sweets, look over your diet for the last few hours or days and make sure it was sufficient according to the meal planning charts in this book. If not, make the next meal or the food for the next few days all good foods and no sweets. Cravings should then shortly disappear unless the body has been abused for a much longer period of time.

How to Avoid Sugar and Excessive Sweets:

1. Eat fresh fruits for snacks and cooked fruits for desserts often instead of cakes or pastry.

2. Try using cooked fruit or cooked dried fruit on cereals instead of other sweeteners.

3. Drink unsweetened, natural fruit and vegetable juices and herb teas instead of soda pop and artificially sweetened or sugared fruit drinks. Dilute fruit juices or keep them to a minimum for less sweets.

4. Eat whole grain crackers, popcorn, nuts, and seeds instead of candy, cookies, and chips.

5. Eat natural whole grain cereals and breads instead of sugar-coated cereals, sweet breads, and other refined flour products.

6. Do not have desserts with every meal. Eating desserts three to four times a week is more than sufficient.

7. Use honey and molasses and other unrefined sweeteners instead of sugar in most or all dessert recipes.

8. Eat a balanced diet of all foods and sweets will be less desirable.

9. Cut down on the amounts of sweeteners used in recipes prepared at home.

10. Eat three meals a day, even if they are small meals, and snack cravings will decrease or disappear altogether.

Sugar-Related Diseases

Hypoglycemia

Hypoglycemia or low blood sugar can be caused by stress, poor diet or excessive sugar, alcohol, refined food, and/or caffeine consumption (reactive hypoglycemia), or by poor health or hereditary factors. The possible symptoms are anxiety, depression, fear, incoordination, sleeplessness, nausea, lack of sex drive, headaches, dizziness, poor memory, weakness, intense craving for alcohol, salt, or sweets, and nervousness. Hypoglycemia can result in Schizophrenia, alcoholism, diabetes, heart disease, cancer, ulcers, infections, and mental illness.

The body organ called the pancreas helps the body assimilate food sugar. When this organ is damaged or obstructed by any of the above causes, negative symptoms may develop. The pancreas pumps the body's insulin supply and provides just enough insulin to help the body assimilate food sugar. When the body is abused, the pancreas may begin to overproduce insulin and get "trigger happy." It may produce more insulin than needed. This creates extreme highs followed by lows of blood-sugar levels in the body. This in turn causes mental, physical and emotional highs and lows, leading to severe depressions, and sometimes manic emotions. Eating extra sweets, refined foods, alcohol, or caffeine during the depressed or low times increases depression and lowers energy. Avoiding sweets and alcohol prevents the pancreas from triggering too much insulin. A balanced diet keeps the pancreas quiet and the body energy levels even.

How to Find Out If You Have Hypoglycemia:
1. If you have major symptoms as mentioned above on a regular basis, you may be hypoglycemic. Try the special diet and see if it helps you.
2. You may see your doctor about taking a glucose tolerance test to determine if you have a problem. These tests are not painful but are uncomfortable and time-consuming. Warning: Many doctors do not recognize hypoglycemia as a problem and sometimes consider the symptoms to be caused by mental problems. This condition is real but may be made worse by stress and mental problems.

What to Do If You Have Hypoglycemia:
Just follow the diet outlined below. If hypoglycemia is your problem, staying on this diet will help tremendously. If the diet does not help after weeks of staying with it, seek further medical advice.

The Hypoglycemic Diet
1. Follow the diet plans outlined in this book in Chapter 3 – Diet Plans for a Healthier Lifestyle, but change the diet more quickly than suggested there, since you already have a major health problem. You may move on to Steps #2 and #3 within a month or so. Keep your diet between Steps #2 and #6 always.
2. Eliminate sweets, refined foods, alcohol, and caffeine completely, or at least keep such items at a bare minimum. Read this chapter completely and avoid

improper types of sweets. Keep flours, dry cereals, granolas, 5-, 7-, and 9-grain breads, pastas, and oatmeal to a minimum or avoid them.

3. Lower fruit intake to once or twice a day, substituting vegetables for some fruit servings. Especially avoid eating sweet fruits like pineapples, bananas, oranges, melons, mangoes, coconuts, and dates, raisins, and other dried fruits. Better to enjoy sub-acid or tart fruits like apples, pears, peaches, kiwi or berries like blueberries, raspberries, and strawberries and sometimes watermelon.

4. Eat a balanced high protein, high vitamin diet, including lots of whole grains, legumes, and vegetables. Include dairy products if desired or use soy cheese (tofu). Avoid eating excessive amounts of meat. Too much meat is stressful and hard to digest for hypoglycemics. Legumes, especially, are excellent for maintaining balanced sugar levels.

5. Have a protein snack every two to four hours to keep energy levels stable. Eat nuts and seeds or whole grains and legumes or dairy products. Vegetables may be included along with the protein foods.

6. Take one regular vitamin B complex and for those without Candida yeast problems, take one or two teaspoons or three to six tablets of nutritional yeast daily until troublesome side effects disappear. These can be taken all together or half in the morning and half in the evening. Occasional protein powder drinks are helpful for some, not all individuals. (Two to four spirulina or chlorella tablets may be taken daily instead of the yeast.)

7. Exercise – Daily vigorous exercise is also essential for good circulation and healing. Yoga is recommended in addition to physical activity.

Diabetes

Diabetes or high blood sugar has many of the same causes and symptoms as hypoglycemia except that it takes the disease one more drastic step further. In hypoglycemia the pancreas regulates the overproduction of insulin. In diabetes the pancreas cannot produce enough insulin and therefore insulin shots and pills are taken to assist the body in handling its sugar intake. With both diseases the following should be avoided: sweets, refined foods, alcohol, and caffeine. By avoiding these "food" irritants, one can avoid triggering the pancreas to over or under produce insulin that the body needs to handle these non-foods.

Follow the same diet plan for diabetes as you would for hypoglycemia along with your doctor's added recommendations.

What to Expect after Improving Your Diet

After changing your diet for the better, improvements in your mental and physical self may begin immediately. In some cases, depending on how long the body was abused, improvements may take longer. Try not to make drastic or quick dietary changes. You may feel better in days or a couple weeks. Once you feel better do not assume you can go back to your old eating habits or stop exercising. In no time at all your old symptoms may return. Stick with Steps #2 to #6 in the diet plan but allow yourself to eat more fruits as you improve. Still avoid sweet fruits and too many other sweets. My *Complete Candida Yeast Guidebook* has excellent recipes for high and low blood sugar as well.

Candida Albicans – Yeast Overgrowth

Candida albicans is one strain of hundreds of types of yeast and is found in most human bodies. It only becomes a problem when it overgrows because of a body imbalance. Then a health specialist is required to suggest a yeast killing product and acidophilus along with other possible supplements which may be needed to return the body to a natural balance.

This newly recognized disease may be prompted by excessive sugar consumption, weakened immune system, antibiotics, birth control pills, stress, vaginal yeast infections, and illness. Men, women, and children can be affected by this yeast overgrowth that can clog various parts of the body, particularly the intestines. It has many unpleasant side effects similar to those of hypoglycemia. The major symptoms include indigestion, fatigue, mental difficulties, depression, low sex drive, hyperactivity, fears, and bloating or weight gain. All sweet fruits and sweet foods and desserts must be eliminated for this health concern along with mushrooms, cheeses, food yeasts, refined foods, pastas, dry cereals, rolled oats, pickled or fermented foods, and moldy or over-ripe foods. For more information on Candida, see my book *Complete Candida Yeast Guidebook* or other books listed in the Recommended Reading section.

 *Chapter 8*

If You Want to Fast

About Fasting

Fasting is abstaining partially or completely from food, and sometimes from beverages, for one 24 hour day or longer. The purpose of fasting is to give the body a rest from digesting foods and therefore save energy that the body may use elsewhere. Perhaps the energy can be used for something more important like healing the body or giving the body a chance to remove toxins or poisons in the system. The entire eating and digesting process takes a tremendous amount of the body's energy. Often more of the energy is wasted than necessary by eating too much or too often, by eating the wrong combinations of foods, or by eating too many hard-to-digest foods.

Some laboratory tests with rats have shown that the animals that fasted on just water from birth for one day a week lived twice as long or longer than rats that ate regularly each day. Why? Their digestive systems were allowed to rest one day a week, giving the body a chance to replenish energy and heal itself. Can anyone work seven days a week and never rest or sleep? We may sleep at night but if there is food in our stomachs or digestive tract, that system is still working and wide awake! Energy saved by fasting can help make the mind clearer and more alert, and then energy can be sent

" A man is rich in proportion to the number of things he can afford to let alone."

Thoreau — Walden

to other parts of the body where it is needed. Fruit fasts rest the body system because the body has to handle only one type of food and that one food is light and easy to digest. Caution: Fasting is not a way of dieting. Do not use it as a means of losing weight. See the fasting books in the Recommended Reading section.

How to Fast

The following information is basic and brief. Read more about fasting before trying a three-day or longer fast and follow these guidelines for a more beneficial fast:
1. If you have a health problem or weakness, consult your physician before fasting. Most physicians see no purpose in fasting but will know if it may be dangerous for you. They generally will not disapprove of a partial fast. Stick with partial fasts unless you have professional assistance.
2. Abstain from all meats for at least one day before fasting and one day after.
3. Eat lightly the day before fasting. Do not stuff yourself. You will be hungrier on your fast days if you stuffed yourself the day before. Let your stomach "shrink" by eating lightly and you will crave food less or not at all while fasting.
4. Do not smoke at all or use alcohol or pharmaceutical drugs of any kind for several days before or after a fast and especially not during one! These can defeat the whole purpose of a fast. If possible avoid these for more than five days before and after a fast. Also avoid sugar and heavy starches. Natural vitamin pills may be taken before or during a fast if recommended to you by a physician or other responsible assistant. Smokers should not fast.
5. A fast should begin when you wake up in the morning, and not end until a full 24 or more hours later.
6. Beginning fasts should start with no more than a one day fast. After several successful one day fasts, one may try a three day fast. After a couple of successful three day fasts, a five day fast may be attempted. Spread these fasts out over a comfortable period of time.
7. Start gradually! Try one day a month.
8. Breaking or ending a fast improperly can ruin the entire purpose of a fast. After a short fast your first meal should be soup, yogurt and fruit, or avocado. For the next meal try salads and breads. Gradually work up to heavier foods. After a long or complete fast, begin with juices and slowly include light foods.
9. Plan your first couple fasts on days off from work until you know what you can expect to feel during a fast. Once you are accustomed to fasting, shorter fasts can be done while you continue to work. If you fast at home, keep your mind and hands busy and rest when you feel the need.

10. Drink plenty of fresh, pure water, at least two quarts a day, to help cleanse the inner body and flush out toxins and poisons. This is a must on any and every type of fast. Distilled water is best for fasting. See Chapter 27 – Beverages for more information on water. Drink water by itself, separately, not with fruits or other cleansing foods.

11. Fasting more than five days on water only is not recommended for the average person and may be dangerous.

12. Professional advice must be sought before attempting extended fasts.

Partial Fasts

These fasts can be for one, three or five days. Unsweetened herb teas may be had on any of these fasts if desired.

1. Fast on only fruits and water. Eat all you like or limit yourself to three meals of fruits a day.

2. Fast on vegetables and water only. Eat all you like or limit yourself to three meals of vegetables a day.

3. Fast on one kind of fruit only, plus water. For example, you may choose apples, bananas, berries, or grapes. Eat all you like. (Do not use fruits such as oranges, other citrus, dried fruit or coconuts.)

4. Fast on juices and water only. Use vegetable or fruit juices or a combination of both, drinking only one or the other for each meal. Do not drink a fruit juice and a vegetable juice at the same meal. Buy or borrow a juicer if possible and use freshly made juices. Drink water by itself. Drink juices slowly.

Complete Fasts

These fasts can also be for one, three, or five days. Beginners should try partial fasts first. Unsweetened herb teas may be had if desired.

1. Fast on juices and water for a day or eat lightly for a day before switching to water.

2. Fast on water only for one day or more. (Herb teas are still optional.)

If You Want to Fast a Little
Have a one day fast once every month or two.
Have a three day fast once or twice a year. (Optional)
If You Want to Fast a Lot
Have a one day fast once every two weeks.
Have a three day fast once every two months or so.
Have a five day fast once or twice a year. (Optional)

The Effects of Fasting

Depending on the length of the fast, how properly it is done, and the health of an individual, one may feel one or more temporary side effects while fasting. These side effects may sometimes be troublesome, but they indicate that the body is removing stored poisons from its system, and that is the desired effect. If you have severe problems, immediately but gradually come off the fast. Then get experienced advice before attempting to fast again. Beginning fasters usually have the hardest time, though sometimes no discomfort is felt whatsoever. Some possible temporary side effects of fasting are slight dizziness or weakness, headaches, hunger pains, light-headedness, high and low energy swings and slight nausea. Consult your health care practitioner immediately if symptoms are severe.

Part Two

♥

Help for the Cook

♥ Chapter 9

Kitchen Equipment

The Tools of the Trade

Fancy kitchen equipment has never been a prerequisite for good cooking, yet certain types of cookware and appliances are essential for wholesome, quality cooking. A good selection of pots, pans, knives, utensils and appliances can make cooking easier and more enjoyable while reducing preparation time and clean-up. Having the right utensil or piece of equipment on hand can help insure better tasting dishes if the ingredients are properly chopped, pureéd, minced, or grated according to the recipe instructions.

When selecting small metal hand tools or utensils, like spatulas (pancake turners), wire whisks, mashers, spoons, and ladles, choose restaurant supply quality utensils that are heavy-duty stainless steel from end to end. Avoid those with bolted-on-handles of plastic or other materials as these break off easily with wear or after being dropped a number of times. Also, these cheaper stainless steel items, nicknamed by myself as "stainful steel", rust quickly, within 24 hours or often less if left soaking in water. The heavy-duty, completely stainless steel utensils can be left in water for days and will not rust nor will there ever be a problem with cheap defective handles. Many of these quality stainless steel utensils are available in most kitchen shops. If specific items are hard to

" He who distinguishes the true savor of his food can never be a glutton; he who does not cannot be otherwise."

Thoreau — Walden

♥ 77

obtain, check your local restaurant supply stores as many of these will sell items to individuals though not always at the wholesale price given to businesses.

High quality pots and pans can help to produce better cooking results and more flavorful recipes as they distribute heat more effectively, cook food evenly, may retain more nutrients and eye appeal, and may reduce cooking time. Good cookware can protect food from burning too quickly and is generally easier to clean if it does. Always soak burned pots completely in water for an hour or overnight for bad burns before scrubbing. As much as 90% of the scouring time can be eliminated and use of abrasive cleansers can be reduced.

My recommendation is to have a variety of cooking pots for every kitchen: some stainless steel, enamelware, Corningware, tempered glass, one large and one small iron frying pan, and possibly one large ironware cookpot for beans and peas. It is not necessary to get expensive waterless or lifetime stainless steel cookware unless you can afford it. Medium quality stainless steel can last for decades, sometimes a lifetime if properly cared for and not scorched or mistreated. Most items can be purchased at department stores or specialty kitchen shops.

The Pros and Cons of Cookware

Stainless Steel:
- Poor heat conductor unless copper or aluminum clad
- Easy to clean and long lasting
- Price and quality varies, avoid dull finish or ribbed steel inside pots

Metal-clad stainless pots are highly recommended for most cooking. Good brands include Farberware, Revere Ware, and Lagostina.

Waterless Cookware:
- Is usually heavy-duty stainless steel or enamel
- Care and quality same as stainless steel or sturdy enamel
- Use little or no water for cooking in it
- Usually quite expensive

Highly recommended for most cooking.

Corningware and Tempered Glass:
- Poor heat conductors but hold the heat well
- Hard to clean and easy to break
- Adjust to hot or cold temperatures quickly and easily
- From average in price to expensive

- Does not give a metallic taste to food while cooking

Recommended for flavorful, natural cooking. These will crack if a cold, wet cloth touches a hot pot.

Gray Enamel:
- Only used pots are available in gray enamel
- The enamel coating is poisonous

Not recommended for any use.

New Enamel:
- Poor heat conductors and do not hold heat well
- Chips, cracks, and scratches easily if metal scouring pads or metal utensils are used. Discard pot if the inside chips down to the base metal of the pot. It may be harmful. Avoid banging pots.
- Quality varies: thick, heavy-duty pots conduct heat better and last longer.
- Some are inexpensive. Good quality, heavy-duty enamel-ware is expensive.

The inexpensive are recommended for infrequent use or as temporary cookware. If constantly in use, it needs replacing every few years due to chipping. More expensive enamel will last longer and can be used daily.

Earthenware:
- Poor heat conductor but holds heat well
- Breakable and does not adjust to quick temperature changes

Recommended for some oven baking. As with glass and other ovenware, do not touch hot pots with cold, wet cloths.

Iron:
- Poor heat conductor but holds heat well
- Rusts but cleans easily; discolors food
- Long-lasting and unbreakable
- A metal that may change flavor of food slightly, but is harmless
- Can be expensive, usually moderately priced.

Recommended for frying and cooking beans and grains. Do not use for cooking acidic foods like tomatoes. Iron must be seasoned before use. Avoid buying pre-seasoned iron cookware.

Aluminum:
- Good heat conductor but does not hold heat well
- Easy to clean and long-lasting
- May discolor food
- Can be expensive although usually inexpensive
- Metal is unstable and cooks into food. It may be harmful if used regularly and is possibly a cancer-causing agent.

Not recommended for frequent use.

Copper:
- Good heat conductor
- Very expensive and hard to clean
- May be poisonous unless lined with stainless steel or other metal

Not recommended for use unless lined. Though beautiful, it is not practical.

Tin:
- Good heat conductor
- Mars and rusts easily and is hard to clean
- Inexpensive

Recommended only for some baking

Non-stick Coated Metal:
(Various coatings over aluminum or tin or other metal, includes Teflon)
- Average heat conductor
- Hard to clean (Food clings to pan when it is cold and cooks into new food when reheated)
- Scratches easily when coating is marred, pan is unusable as base metal may be harmful; never use metal utensils or metal scouring pads
- When hot, coating may give off a harmful fluorine gas
- Chemicals and non-stick ingredients in coating may cook into food
- From average in price to expensive

Not recommended for use, but very infrequent use is alright.

Caring for Pots and Pans and Other Kitchen Utensils

Cleansing Agents:
Do not use cleansers, abrasives, or scouring powders on the insides of any pots, pans, or on any eating utensils whatsoever. Cleansers can get absorbed or

wedged into utensils and transferred to foods. These are harmful to the body and may cause constipation or possibly destroy vitamin C in the body. Use only dish soaps and gentle cleansers. Make sure these cleansers are carefully rinsed off the utensils with warm or hot water.

Cleaning Techniques:

Dishes, pots and pans, and all kitchen equipment clean easiest when washed shortly after use. If you cannot wash utensils right after use, they will still clean easily if rinsed and/or soaked in water. Burnt pans should be soaked overnight for easier cleaning.

Metal scrub pads can be used on all cookware except enamel, Corningware, earthenware, and non-stick coated pots, as the metal may scratch and damage their surfaces. A sponge, plastic, cloth, and brush scrubber may be used on these less scratch-resistant pots and pans as well as all other pots and pans, bakeware, dishes, silverware, kitchen utensils, and appliances. A little extra scrubbing may be required without the use of scouring powders and metal pads for most utensils, but the benefits to your health and your cookware are worth a little extra elbow grease.

If pots are washed well each time, they will be easier to clean. Pots with twice-baked or cooked-on foods are almost impossible to clean, and some stains are permanent.

Care of Special Kitchen Utensils

Stainless Steel:

These utensils include mashers, graters, serving spoons, strainers, squeezers, spatulas, wire whisks and beaters. Stainless steel silverware and most knives are excluded from this group.

Utensil Care: These items may be called stainless but not all are rustproof. Never leave them soaking in water for more than a half hour or so. The longer they soak the quicker they rust, especially if the item is worn. Use a plastic or mildly abrasive scrub pad and suds to clean. Do not use cleanser. Purchase more heavy-duty, restaurant quality stainless steel if you want rustproof, long lasting "real" stainless steel.

Wood:

These utensils include spoons, mallets, spatulas, cutting boards, chopping blocks, salad bowls and servers.

Utensil Care: Never soak these items in water. It is best to wash them immediately after use with warm, not hot, water and suds using a scrub brush or plastic scrubber. Rinse thoroughly and allow them to air dry completely before storing. Unlacquered salad bowls should not be washed after every use. It is best to use these only for raw salads not coated with dressings. Wipe them out between uses and dry thoroughly before storing in a cool, dry place. Cutting boards and chopping blocks should receive the same treatment.

Extra Tips about Wood:

1. Wood absorbs food and flavors and discolors, so never buy used wooden kitchen utensils of any kind.

2. If possible, keep one set of wooden spoons for sweet recipes and one set for main dishes so onion flavor is not transferred to sweets and vice versa.

3. Never leave spoons sitting in pots that are cooking.

4. Buy new wooden spoons every six to twelve months or so and throw away all old wooden spoons or wood serving utensils.

5. Never use metal scrub pads on wood because splinters of wood may be loosened and later transferred to food. Use brushes or plastic scrubbers.

Plastic:

These utensils include bowls, spatulas, storage containers, measuring cups and spoons, funnels, cookie cutters, and juice squeezers.

Utensil Care: Plastic, like wood, absorbs what it holds and discolors. Never buy used plastic utensils. Clean plastic items with a plastic scrub pad or cloth. Do not use cleansers or scouring powders of any type.

Extra Tips about Plastic:

1. Hot foods should never be used on, with, or in plastic. Plastic particles and flavors can be transferred to food this way. Let food cool before storing in a plastic container or in plastic wrap. (Exception: very hard plastic dishes or spoons.)

2. Never store food in a plastic kitchen container that has stored laundry soap or other non-food item even after it has been washed carefully.

3. Discard beat-up or discolored plastic. Re-used plastic containers from yogurt or cottage cheese should be discarded every six to twelve months, depending on use.

Iron:

These utensils include iron skillets and pots and pans.

Utensil Care: To season new iron cookware, oil the item well inside and out and place it in a 300°F oven for one hour. Then wash the pan carefully in mild suds and dry it immediately with paper towels to prevent rust. Use paper towels to avoid staining dish towels.

Extra Tips about Ironware:

1. Never leave it soaking in water or it will rust and lose its seasoned surface.

2. Wash ironware as soon as possible after each use. Use mild, diluted dishwashing suds in water. Quickly wash with a plastic scrubber and rinse in hot water. Dry immediately with paper towels and place on a hot stove element that is turned off immediately before using. Reseason when necessary.

Essential Kitchen Equipment

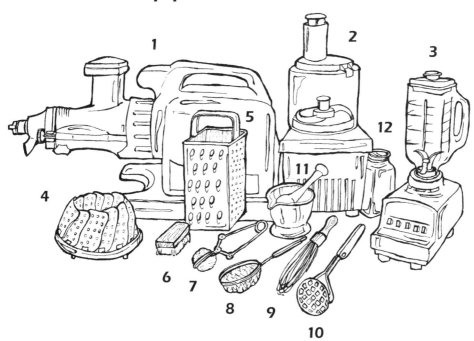

1. Juicer
2. Food Processor
3. Blender
4. Vegetable Steamer
5. Shredder/Hand Grater
6. Good Scrub Brush
7. Tea Strainer/Tea Ball
8. Wire Strainer
9. Wire Whisk
10. Hand Masher
11. Mortar and Pestle
12. Quart Jar

Tool: Good Scrub Brush

Purpose: For cleaning root vegetables and other hard vegetables and fruits. Buy a brush with strong bristles that will not break off and wedge themselves into the food. Bristles should also be flexible.

Tool: Vegetable Steamer

Purpose: For steaming vegetables. Steamers lift the food above the water so they can be cooked by steam and retain vitamins, color, and flavor. Stainless steel steamers are the best types. Bamboo may collect dirt and bacteria more easily.

*Tool: Blender ***

Purpose: For mixing, chopping, and puréeing. Good for making beverages, baby foods, dressings, sauces, puddings, and mayonnaise, etc. Also can be used for making nut flours and meals, breaking nuts into pieces, and making sesame salt.

*Tool: Food Mill ***

Purpose: For puréeing and making sauces, soups, and baby foods. (Generally not needed if you have a blender.)

*Tool: Juicer ***

Purpose: For making fresh fruit and vegetable juices and grating carrots for cakes. (Mix pulp with juice for cakes.) Some homogenizing juicers also make nut butters, ice cream, grated vegetables, baby foods, and crushed ice.

Tool: Quart and Gallon Jars

Purpose: For making yogurt and sprouts in or for storing whole grains and legumes. Canning jars are excellent. Make sure they all have lids or rings. Wire or nylon mesh (screening) and cheesecloth are also helpful for making sprouts, yogurt, or cheese.

Tool: Thermometer

Purpose: For yogurt and bread making. Choose a glass, metal, or plastic one that goes at least as low as 100°F and as high as 125°F – 150°F or more. Glass and plastic types usually need only the tip of the thermometer placed in the food for a proper temperature reading. Place metal types $3/4$ of the way or more into the food for a correct temperature reading. (Most yogurt, candy, jelly, and meat thermometers can be used.)

*Tool: Herb Grinder ***

Purpose: Whole or large, flaked herbs and seeds are fresher and have more flavor and vitamins. It is easy and practical to grind your own.

*Tool: Mortar and Pestle ***

Purpose: Can be used to grind nuts and seeds and herbs instead of a blender, herb grinder, or other appliance. Takes muscle but does the job.

Tool: Tea strainer or Tea Ball

Purpose: Bamboo or stainless steel strainers are perfect for straining bulk teas. If you do not want the mess of straining, a stainless steel (not aluminum) tea ball may be used. Just put bulk tea inside and use like a tea bag.

Tool: Hand Grinder

Purpose: Excellent for grinding beans and cooked grains for casseroles or burgers. Soft, steamed vegetables can also be pureed with it. Sometimes these come with a shredder attachment. (Note: Electric grinders will grind almost anything.)

Tool: Shredder, Hand Grater or Chopper

Purpose: Used to slice, grate, and chop vegetables and fruits for salads and cooking. A very handy tool, especially if you do not have a food processor. May sometimes be purchased with a grinder.

*Tool: Food Processor ***

Purpose: An all-purpose machine used for mixing, making dough and nut butters. Also cuts, chops, slices, purées, and grates, but tends to squash produce a bit in the process. Do not use with too much liquid.

*Tool: Grain Grinder ***

Purpose: Can be bought separately or sometimes an extra attachment can be bought for a juicer or special mixing machine. This is a perfect way to make very fresh, vitamin-rich flours, meals, cereals, and some baby foods. Stone grinders are considered the best type because they create less heat while milling and therefore destroy fewer vitamins in processing. However, some stone grinders may add gravel bits to what is being milled.

Tool: Wire Whisk (Hand Beater)

Purpose: This can be used to mix milk powder, cornmeal for cereal and thickening agents with liquids, make yogurt and whipped cream, and beat eggs. This takes muscle but does an excellent job.

*Tool: Electric Mixer ***

Purpose: Does everything the wire whisk does except it should not be used in mixing bread batter or mixing yogurt into milk. The machine does the work.

Tool: Hand Masher

Purpose: This is not the same as a potato masher. These mashers have square or oval holes in a round or oval stainless steel base. Use to mash well-cooked beans for spreads and casseroles. Also use to mash bananas, tofu, and cooked pumpkin, make egg salad, and other foods. A very essential tool.

* These are good tools, but are not essential as other kitchen utensils may be used instead.

 *Chapter 10*

How & Where to Buy Your Food

Healthy Supermarket Foods

Follow the "Shopping Tips for Natural Foods" at the end of this chapter. The following items are usually good quality and available in most supermarkets. For more detailed information and specific brand names, consult the natural food primers in the Recommended Reading section. Compare these items and their prices with foods at your local health food stores. Sometimes for the same quality and even the same brand names you can purchase the same foods for less at the supermarket. Labels saying "natural" or "health food" sometimes send prices soaring. Some foods, dry beans for instance, may cost half the price when sold at the supermarket for the same quality beans. Read the food labels to make sure no unnecessary ingredients are added.

" I went to the woods because I wished to live deliberately, to front only the essential facts of life, and see if I could not learn what it had to teach, and not, when I came to die, discover that I had not lived."

Thoreau — Walden

Healthy Supermarket Foods May Include:

Whole grain brown rice and wild rice
Whole grain crackers
Some other whole grains
Whole grain flours and sugarless
   breads and cereals
Rice cakes
Dry beans and peas and lentils
Fresh fruits and vegetables
Frozen foods with no chemical additives
Raw nuts and seeds
Some dairy products
Natural and imported cheeses
Yogurt, plain or with fruit on
   the bottom
Non-instant milk powder
Natural ice cream (no artificial ingre-
   dients, but sugar is usually added)
Butter (not margarine)

Eggs (fresh, local eggs)
Green herbs
Unsweetened fruit and
   vegetable juices
Uncaffeinated herb teas
Real maple syrup
Unsulphured molasses and honey
Peanut butter (with just salt
   and peanuts)
Apple cider vinegar
Tomato paste
Naturally fermented soy sauce
Old-fashioned rolled oats
Virgin olive oil
Tofu (make sure it has no additives)
Distilled and other pure drinking water
Mineral water

Best Buys at Your Health Food Store

For these special foods you generally must go to a health food store. Unless there is a special health food section in your supermarket, usually these foods are not carried. Buy organic whenever possible if it is high quality and reasonably priced.

Remember that buying a food in a health food store does not ensure it is good quality. Read the labels and buy with discretion. Some items may contain sugar or even chemicals. If you take the trouble to shop at a health food store, take the trouble to buy good quality. Prices vary from store to store and items may be cheaper or more expensive there than in the supermarket or other stores. On the whole, health food store products are higher quality, and the stores often contain a full line of food stuffs from soup fixings to nuts. Some carry organic produce as well.

Health Foods Store Items Usually Include:

Natural salad and cooking oils
   (not chemically processed)
Natural salad dressings
   (with no sugar or chemicals)
Whole wheat and other whole grain,
   soya, and vegetable noodles
Mayonnaise, ketchup, ice cream,
   desserts, and candies made
   only with honey
Herb teas and fresh cooking herbs
Raw milk dairy products
Rennetless cheeses
Goat milk products
Raw honey
Food yeast and protein powders
Natural vitamins and food
   supplements
Carob powder and candies
   (chocolate substitute)
Organic produce
Organic foods

Natural tofu, miso, and tempeh
Tamari soy sauce (naturally
   fermented without additives)
Seaweed (including kelp,
   wakame, nori, hijiki, dulse)
Sea salt and vegetable salts
   with no chemicals
Less common grains, whole grain
   products like kasha, cracked wheat,
   bulgur, millet, quinoa,
   amaranth, teff
Less common beans like chick peas,
soybeans, mung, adzuki, black beans
Pure, unfiltered fruit and vegetable
   juices (with no sugar or
   preservatives added)
Vegetable broth powder and cubes
Fresh peanut butter, tahini,
   and nut butters (with no
   added extras or chemicals)

Ethnic and Specialty Stores

These stores can be a gold mine of inexpensive and unusual foods. Prices on some items are cheaper here than in health food stores and supermarkets. Some high quality imported foods are also available along with specialty items that cannot be purchased elsewhere.

These shops include Chinese, Oriental, Greek, Mexican, Italian, and East Indian shops, and some delicatessens and farmers markets. Also try candy and nut shops for raw nuts, cheese stores and bakeries for special whole grain breads. Often you can buy in bulk (five pounds or more) from these shops for a cheaper price. You may want to ask about special discounts on bulk purchases. Compare prices and save as you enjoy a delicious change of taste from everyday eating.

Ethnic Stores Best Picks:

Feta and farmers cheeses
Goat cheese and milk
Other imported natural cheeses
Raw nuts and seeds
Dried legumes
Olives and pickles
Tofu, miso, tamari soy sauce,
    and other soybean products
Mineral waters
Whole grain breads and crackers

Whole grains
Yogurt
Vegetables and fruits
Vegetable noodles and tomato paste
Herbs and spices
Peanut butter, tahini, and
    other nut butters
Seafood and seaweed
Spices

Food Co-ops

Regular and natural food co-ops are primarily for those who are buying foods in bulk, but smaller quantities of one pound and less are often available depending on the type of co-op you join.

Co-ops save money on foods by buying in 20 – 50 pound or 100 pound packages or more and dividing these up among members. Usually all co-op work is divided among its members and foods are stored in someone's home or basement. Occasionally a small room or a building is rented. In larger co-ops, one person is paid to order food and handle the distribution.

Members are often expected to bring their own bags and boxes to collect food at appointed times, about once a week or once a month. Usually, not always, one or two hours or more of work per month, such as ordering, setting up, distributing, or cleaning is required of members. Sometimes a yearly membership fee is charged.

If you have a little extra time and do not care about fancy packaging, a food co-op can save you money, sometimes up to 50% on many items. Food co-ops often price foods by the one pound or five pound package and charge five, ten or fifteen percent above the actual cost the food for overhead.

Another type of co-op is the natural food store co-op, which offers a 10% – 20% discount for members who contribute work and/or membership fees. Use caution when becoming a member of a co-op. Research your local co-ops carefully and get complete information on their policies and member requirements. Most co-ops will save you money, but if your needs are small or their requirements high, you may be saving little. When calculating your savings in joining a co-op, make sure to count the time you invest in it at minimum wage (or more) per hour.

For example: For One Person

Year membership fee per person per year $25.00
    Work per month (two hours, at $5.00 per hour
    approx. minimum wage) at $10.00 per month,
    12 months equals . . . .<u>$120.00</u>
                                                              $145.00 Total

Co-op purchases per month (at reg. price) $100.00
Co-op purchases per year $1,200.00

10% off regular price:
Gross savings . . . .$120.00 year
Money and work hours spent . . . .<u>$145.00 year</u>
Loss . . . .$25.00 year

15% off regular price:
Gross savings . . . .$180.00 year
Money and work hours spent . . . .<u>$145.00 year</u>
Actual savings . . . .$35.00 year

20% off regular price:
Gross savings . . . .$240.00 year
Money and work hours spent . . . .<u>$145.00 year</u>
Actual savings . . . .$95.00 year

Food Co-op Items Available:
– Bulk goods, liquid oils, beans and grains
– Fresh, dried, canned, bottled, and packaged foods
– Fruits, vegetables, pasta, and dairy products

Other Items Available at Co-op Stores:
– Light bulbs, tissues, and cleaning supplies
– Pet food and care products (usually dry, bulk foods)

Buying in Bulk
Bulk food can be found in almost any store co-op. The five pound package is almost always cheaper by the pound than the one or two pound package. The main reason is the cost of packaging, which accounts for a good chunk of the prices of our foods. That is why natural food stores and co-ops often buy in large quantities, usually 100 pound bags or packages. They put these in bins and barrels so the customer can take his/her own bag (or a provided bag) and scoop out

the exact amount needed. This way the store can get less expensive goods and save work, time, and money by letting the customer serve himself/herself. Savings are usually passed on to the customer through lower prices.

Legumes, whole grains and whole grain products, spices, nuts and seeds, dried fruits and flours are some of the items available in bulk. Liquid items such as oils, tamari soy sauce, honey, and molasses are also available. The customer or the store may provide bottles or jars for these. These liquids come in large drums or plastic containers with dispensers.

As long as you can properly store and preserve larger quantities, you save when you buy in bulk. Compare bulk and prepackaged food prices to make sure that bulk prices are cheaper. Do not be fooled, buying in bulk may be more expensive than the same prepackaged amount. Remember, you may have to ask or bargain for bulk prices if none are offered.

Other Ways of Saving Money

1. Buy slightly defective goods at discount prices. This does not mean poor quality food. If you see slightly moldy cheese, or slightly old or overripe produce, or produce that has been bruised, ask the shopkeeper, a stock person, or produce manager (cashiers should not be asked as they have nothing to do with prices) if he/she will mark down the price. The majority of the times you ask, he/she will do it unless the store has very strict policies against this practice. Most stores do not.

2. Buy items in slightly damaged packages. Usually these are already marked down. If they are not, you may ask for a mark down. Some stores will not do this because customers have been known to damage the packages themselves in order to get a cheaper price. So do not ask for a discount too often in the same place. An easier way is to ask someone in charge when you come into the store if the store has any damaged package goods that can be sold at cheaper prices; then take your pick.

3. Buy dairy products, eggs, and/or fresh produce from farmers at their homes, roadside stands, or at farmers markets. The products are almost always high quality, fresh, and inexpensive.

4. Grow your own food. Plant a garden, or raise a few chickens for eggs, or keep goats or a cow for fresh dairy products. The freshest, best quality foods can be those you produce yourself from nutrient-rich soil and nutritious, natural animal feed without harmful additives. This is one of the few ways of obtaining natural, organic foods as soon as they are ripe and ready without a loss of vitamins due to shipping and storing time.

Shopping Tips for Natural Foods

1. Healthful foods can be bought in any kind of store. Buy foods that are not overprocessed or refined, and do not have chemical or other harmful and unnecessary additives.

2. Avoid these unnatural and harmful additives as much as possible: MSG (monosodium glutamate), BHA, BHT, alum, sulphur, saccharin, hydrogenated oils, artificial flavorings and colorings, and refined sugars such as cane or beet sugar, corn syrup and dextrose (corn sugar), fructose (usually refined fruit sugar), brown sugars, supposed raw sugars or kleen-raw sugars, turbinado, and demerara sugars. Also avoid synthetic sweeteners and other refined products, including flours.

3. Avoid instant, quick, and fast foods. Also avoid caffeinated beverages.

4. Foods labeled "Organic" are generally more expensive but much better for you. Buy them whenever possible, but know your suppliers; some are dishonest. Choose only fresh, high quality and good name brand organics.

5. Foods labeled "Natural" may or may not be better for you. This term is used loosely in an attempt to assure the buyer of goodness. Read the label for additives and buy accordingly.

6. Read all food labels. If you do not know what an additive is or what it does, do not buy the product. Buy products with few or no artificial additives.

7. Food labels list ingredients in the order of quantity: the largest ingredient first and so on. Avoid foods that have refined ingredients or unhealthful foods or additives, especially when they are listed among the first few ingredients on the labels.

8. Choose fresh produce whenever possible for better quality and nutritional value. Choose frozen foods secondly and canned foods last. (Home-canned foods would be second only to fresh garden foods.)

9. Make sure your food store is air-conditioned in summer. If it is hot inside the store, cracked, floured, or partial grains, and legumes must be refrigerated to prevent rancidity.

 *Chapter 11*

Time & Money
Saving Ideas

Time Saving Ideas

Preparing a vegetable or legume dish will take a lot more time than popping a frozen TV dinner into the oven or opening a can of soup. People returning home after a hard day at work are generally too tired to spend hours in the kitchen before dinner. Here are ways to get dinner on the table in one-half hour or less. You can cook when you have time to cook and serve it anytime you like. All the following ideas incorporate recipes from this book.

Idea #1 Make Large Batches and Freeze Extras:

Special dishes and sauces can be prepared in advance and frozen. This does not require a very large freezer. An average refrigerator-freezer will be adequate. If you have a storage space problem in winter, just place extra big batches outside in the snow or on a cold porch. They will keep until a thaw. That will give you several months of "unlimited" freezer space. In warm weather less heavy foods are needed by the body so you will not need to freeze that often.

" That man is richest whose pleasures are the cheapest."

Thoreau — Walden

Save plastic yogurt, cottage cheese, ice cream, and sour cream containers to freeze in or buy plastic containers. Label each container with a piece of masking tape and write with a pen. On the label write: Name of food, date prepared, number of servings or in the case of sauces: small, medium or large batch. For example: Pea Soup / 3-7-98 / 2 cups (or write 2 servings or 2 srv.)

The following are some examples of main dishes, sauces, and desserts that can be frozen and their uses. There are hundreds of other recipes that can be frozen. Double, triple or even quadruple recipes for large batches. Experiment with your own ideas. Sauces can be prepared and frozen, and then defrosted several hours in advance for use on fresh vegetables, grains, or beans. Entire meals and desserts can be frozen in advance and heated in minutes, but these meals contain a lot more vitamins and nutrients than any frozen TV dinner.

Approximate container sizes: small = $\frac{1}{2}$ – 1 cup; medium = 2 – 2 $\frac{1}{2}$ cups; and large = 3 – 4 cups.

A. Sauce	Use For	Container Size (2 – 4 people)
Tomato Sauce	Spaghetti	Small
	Lasagna	Large
	Pizza	Medium
	Eggplant Parmesan	Large
	Lasagna Rice	Medium or Large
Chili Sauce	Chili Beans	Medium or Large
	Tacos and Mexican Food	Small or Medium
	Plain Rice and Millet	Medium
	Cooked Vegetables	Small
Curry Sauce	Any Whole Grains	Small or Medium
	Cooked Vegetables	Small
Ketchup	Sandwiches	Extra Small
	Soyburgers	Extra Small
	Potatoes	Extra Small
	Eggs	Extra Small

B. Main Dish	Use For	Container Size (2 – 4 people)
Hummus Spread	Sandwiches Dip	Small Small
Falafel Spread	Hot Main Dish w. Veggies For Sandwiches For Dip	Medium Small Small
Soups of Every Kind	Main Dish Appetizer	Medium or Large Small or Medium
Kidney Bean Stew	Main Dish	Medium or Large
Rice-Cheese Loaf	Main Dish Side Dish	Large Small or Medium
Soyburgers	Main Dish	Wrap Separate in Wax Paper then Plastic
Sloppy Joes	Main Dish	Medium
All Bean Dishes	Main Dish Side Dish	Medium or Large Small or Medium
Spinach-Potato Pie	Main Dish Side Dish	Freeze Pie Whole or Wrap Pieces in Plastic, then in Foil
Quiche	Main Dish Side Dish	Freeze Pie Whole or Wrap Pieces in Plastic, then in Foil
Enchiladas	Main Dish	Wrap in Plastic then Foil

C. Desserts & Breads	Use For	Container Size (2 – 4 people)
Cakes of all Kinds *Pies of all Kinds, Cookies* *Yeast Breads, Quick Breads*	Desserts and Snacks	Double Wrap in Clear Wrap in Individual Pieces

Idea #2 Cook Enough for Two or More Days:

Freshly prepared grains and legumes are the most nutritious, but reheating them is acceptable when time does not permit.

A. Make a pot of a main dish grain or cereal grain. Prepare enough to last several days or a week (seven to eight days at most). Undercook the grain about five to ten minutes and store it in the refrigerator. Each day heat up a little of the grain as needed and cook it until it is hot and fully cooked. If any of the reheated grain is left over, throw it away. Do not reheat it again because most vitamins are lost after a third heating. Eat the grains plain or mixed with vegetables or herbs and spices. use the extra grain in stir-frys, steamed with vegetables, or added to soups, casseroles, veggie burgers or stews. Frozen sauces can also be defrosted for use with grains.

B. Make a pot of soup, stew, or legumes and cook it completely. (Legumes should not be undercooked.) Refrigerate the food and eat a little every day or two. Eat all the leftovers within six to eight days or freeze remaining food. Frozen sauces can also be defrosted for use with legumes.

C. Vegetable and fruit dishes are more nutritious when served fresh, but left-over dishes of this type may be served the next day if unspoiled.

Idea #3 Premixed Recipes:

1. Herb and Spice Mixes - Have ready several small jars such as baby food jars. When you have extra time, fill these with herb and spice combinations for your favorite recipes.

For example: Jars #1, #2, and #3 label - Chili Sauce Spices. (See Incredible Chili recipe.) In each jar put enough spices for one small or large batch of chili sauce. On the jar write single, double, or triple batch or for one, two, or three pounds of chili. In each jar mix all the herbs and spices needed for that recipe.

For Jar #1 Chili Sauce/one pound, put:

2 tsp sea salt	*1 tsp each, oregano, parsley, and sea kelp*
3 tsp chili powder	*$^1/_8$ – $^1/_4$ tsp red pepper*
$^1/_4$ tsp cumin seeds	*1 tsp red crushed peppers*

Fill jars #2 and #3 in the same manner or make these larger batches.

Fill other jars with herbs for spaghetti sauce, stews, soups, falafels, or any recipe calling for more than four herbs and spices. Next time you are making a recipe in a hurry, reach for one of these mixes and save time.

2. Quick Bread and Biscuit Mixes - In a plastic bag mix all dry ingredients called for in a recipe. Label each bag with the name and size of the recipe. A list of wet ingredients needed to complete the recipe can also be added to the label or on a piece of paper inside the bag. This will make it easy for your kids or spouse to help out if you are not present. These mixes can be stored in a cool, dry place for one week or more, or kept in the freezer (double-bagged) for longer periods of time and for added freshness.

3. Mix Your Own Recipes! For cereals, sandwich spreads, or salad dressings.

Quickie Meal Examples:

These meals can be prepared in one half hour or less.

Meal # 1:

Frozen Pea Soup	Heat from freezer in 15 – 25 minutes. If defrosted the night before it heats in 5 – 10 minutes.
Salad	Prepare this fresh. Approximately 10 – 15 minutes to prepare.
Whole Wheat Bread	Fresh or defrosted bread. Serve with falafel or hummus spread or veggie butter.

Meal # 2:

Soy Burgers	From the freezer. Cook in 15 – 20 minutes. Melt cheese or tofu cheese on top and use ketchup, lettuce, and bun.
Salad or Cut Vegetables	Three to ten minutes to prepare.
Optional: *Steamed Potatoes or Vegetables*	Twenty minutes to prepare and steam.

Meal # 3:

Chili	Have precooked beans in the refrigerator. Use defrosted chili sauce. Heat together on low for 20 – 30 minutes. Add a few dashes of cayenne pepper if chili is not hot enough, or a dash of honey if chili is too hot. Top with avocado, guacamole, yogurt, grated cheddar, or tofu cheese.
Salad or Cooked Vegetables	About 10 – 20 minutes to prepare.
Bread or Plain Rice or Millet	Reheat leftover rice or millet 10 – 15 minutes until hot. Pour hot chili over grains, or eat chili with a chunk of bread.
Optional	Chop 1 – 2 bell peppers and heat with chili beans and sauce as an extra vegetable.

Meal # 4:

Spaghetti with Tomato Sauce	Heat soy-wheat noodles in low-boiling water for 10 – 20 minutes until tender, not mushy. Defrost spaghetti sauce and heat it for 15 minutes, or more on low heat, until bubbling and hot. Serve spaghetti immediately when it is finished cooking.
Green Salad or Green Vegetable	Cooked spinach or broccoli is excellent with this meal, they take 10 – 15 minutes to steam.

When To Cook Big Batches

1. After dinner on week nights.
2. On weekends.
3. If time permits, make a big batch for dinner and freeze or store the leftovers.

Freezing Tips

1. Frozen foods keep from one to three months or more if wrapped properly.
2. Burgers should be wrapped in wax paper instead of foil so they will not stick and come apart. Put several wrapped burgers in a plastic bag and tie to keep them fresh and prevent freezer burn.

3. Fill freezer containers $^3/_4$ to $^4/_5$ full because the food will expand as it freezes. Overfilled containers will crack and must be rewrapped in plastic or put in a new container.

4. Do not freeze in glass containers, except special freezer glass, as they do not "give" and break easily in the freezer.

5. Wrap breads, mixes, and other bagable items in thick freezer bags or double-bag them to preserve freshness.

6. Do not pour hot foods into plastic containers because plastic particles and flavor may be transferred to food. For best results, put cool food in containers just before freezing.

7. Foods lose flavor when frozen. Add extra spices to a dish before freezing or after defrosting to perk up a dish and ensure full flavor.

8. Defrost all dairy products in the refrigerator, never at room temperature which could spoil a product or cause it to separate. Defrost other foods in the refrigerator or at room temperature. Never defrost food on a stove (hot or cold) or on top of a refrigerator or other appliance. Once foods have defrosted, refrigerate immediately.

9. Most foods that have been frozen and defrosted should not be refrozen. Exceptions include tofu, beans and peas, and some sauces.

Money Saving Ideas

1. Use leftovers in soups, stews, and casseroles. See recipes.

2. Alternate elaborate, expensive meals such as quiche or stuffed peppers with simple, inexpensive meals: chili and plain rice or millet, vegetables and rice, sweet and sour lentils, soups, soy burgers, or baked beans.

3. Cook only as much as you can eat or store.

4. Avoid using expensive items like avocados, mushrooms, and cheese whenever possible.

5. Substitute less expensive items whenever you can. For example, use in-season fruits and vegetables. Use eggplant or zucchini instead of mushrooms. Use soybeans instead of chick peas.

6. Freeze, can, and store foods from your own garden.

7. Shop comparatively. See Chapter 10 - How and Where to Buy Your Food for more money saving ideas.

♥ *Chapter 12*

Food Preparation Tips & Tricks

Kitchen Tricks

1. A quick way to break nuts into small pieces or grind them to powder for a recipe: Leave nuts in their original bag, put the bag of nuts into another plastic bag and tie it, then hit it with a mallet or hammer until the pieces are as small as you want them.

2. Before cutting dates: Oil or butter a knife or scissors and the dates will not stick together as much.

3. To measure honey easily: Before measuring honey, oil the measuring cup, or measure oil for a recipe in the cup first. The honey will slip out of the oiled cup easily.

4. To melt honey quickly and save vitamins: Put a jar of solid honey in a pan or tub of very hot water, never boiling. Caution: Plastic containers may melt if placed in water in a very hot pan! Make sure plastic containers do not touch the sides or bottom of a hot pan by using a spoon or two to prop them up in the water.

5. Use a blender to grind or chop nuts and seeds into meals. Place only about one-quarter cup of nuts in the blender at a time and grind until chopped to desired consistency. A food

" *We must learn to reawaken and keep ourselves awake, not by mechanical aids, but by an infinite expectation of the dawn which does not forsake us in our soundest sleep.*"

Thoreau — Walden

processor works even better and chops or grinds one cup or more at a time. Peanut butter can also be made by adding oil while peanuts are grinding.

6. To prevent bread dough from sticking to a baking pan, lightly oil the inside bottom and sides of the pan. Then shake flour all over the insides of the pan. Shake out excess flour. Shape the dough outside the pan and place it carefully in the pan for baking. Bread will pop right out of the pan after baking or will need only loosening with a knife.

7. Cakes can be prevented from sticking in the same way as breads or the bottom of a cake pan can be oiled and wax paper placed on the bottom. Then oil the wax paper. Pour in the cake batter and bake. After baking, loosen the cake from the sides of the pan with a knife. Turn the cake upside down on a rack and it will come out easily. Then simply peel off the wax paper from the bottom of the cake.

8. In recipes, add one to three teaspoons of gluten flour per cake or loaf of bread. This will make baked goods rise higher and taste lighter. Also use one to two teaspoons of liquid lecithin to act as a natural preservative and improve the texture of baked goods. Those with gluten allergies can use one to two teaspoons guar gum or xanthan gum instead of gluten flour to help baking powder breads and cakes to have better texture.

9. When frosting a cake, place little strips of wax paper, about 2-inches by 10-inches or 12-inches, around the base of the cake on the plate. Any frosting drippings or splatters will land on the wax paper, which can be pulled out and discarded after frosting the cake. This will keep the cake plate clean and neat.

10. The cake may look baked in the oven, but it may still be raw inside. Stick a toothpick gently into the middle of the cake. If it comes out clean, the cake is done; if not, bake for a few more minutes.

11. Do not peek in the oven while a cake is baking until it is one-half baked (half the cooking time). Then gently open the oven door. If the cake is browning too quickly, turn down the oven, or if very brown, arch a piece of tin foil over the cake for 10 – 15 minutes or so of baking time. Remove the tin foil five to ten minutes before baking is done. If the cake is cooking too slowly, turn up the oven slightly.

12. Never remove baking powder breads or cakes from the oven until they are fully cooked. Even 30 or 60 seconds out of the oven can cause these baked goods to stay doughy inside. Do toothpick tests quickly just by opening the oven door slightly.

13. Check your oven regularly with an oven thermometer to make sure it heats to the proper temperature. If the oven is too slow, turn it up higher. If the oven is hot too fast or becomes too hot, turn it lower.

14. If your oven does not heat evenly, that is, one side of the oven is hotter than the other, make sure to rotate foods while baking. For example, after a cake is half baked gently turn it around in the oven or move it from one side of the oven to the other.

15. Make sure baking pans in the oven never touch one another, or the sides of the oven as the food may burn or heat unevenly. Try to leave about an inch of space between pans, and between pans and the walls of the oven. Also, if two racks of food are filled in the oven, try not to have pans directly underneath one another. Set one rack of pans slightly to one side and the second rack slightly to the other side of the oven for more even heating.

16. Serve cakes and breads at room temperature for more flavor, especially if the baked goods have been refrigerated. Let them sit on the table for 15 – 20 minutes before serving, except for cheesecakes and chilled desserts.

17. For dough or flour stuck on a table, spread a very thin layer of water on the table and let it sit a few minutes. Then using a dough scraper or other plastic tool or scrubber, gently scrape the dough off the table. It will come off much easier than by just scrubbing when it is dry.

18. For picnics, lunches, and long trips, sandwiches and sandwich spreads can be kept fresh and unspoiled by freezing them the night before. Take them from the freezer just before departure and they can defrost along the way until lunch or suppertime. Add sandwich greens and vegetables before serving.

19. Once canned goods are opened, transfer any leftovers to plastic containers to avoid a "tinny" taste in foods and especially to prevent greater amounts of lead from being transferred to the food.

20. For onion, garlic, or fish stained hands: Rinse hands, rub a lemon over them, then wash with soap and water.

21. Two to four teaspoons of instant coffee substitute used in carob recipes gives the recipe a more chocolatey flavor.

22. For a sweet, "fresh-baked" smell in your kitchen, boil a cinnamon stick in a little water for a couple of minutes. Do not put a lid on this delightful pan.

Cooking & Eating Do's & Don'ts

Do	Because
Cook vegetables until they are tender, not crunchy or mushy. Steaming, baking, broiling, and sautéing are the best cooking methods. Avoid boiling and deep-frying.	With a bit less cooking time, more vitamins and flavor are preserved. Overcooking destroys nutrients yet undercooking does not allow foods to be broken down enough so nutrients can be properly absorbed. For example, carrots "release" more vitamin A cooked than when raw.
Eat as many raw foods as possible.	Avoid cooked foods that can be eaten raw. The more raw the foods, the more vitamins they contain. Though in some cases certain vitamins are more easily assimilated when cooked or lightly steamed.
Eat about 30% – 50% raw and the rest cooked foods. In summer, more than 50% should be raw. In winter, as little as 25% may be raw.	The combination of raw and cooked foods gives you a good variety of needed vitamins. Some vitamins are killed in heat and some are released and easier to assimilate. The variety gives the body bulk, fiber, vitamins, minerals, and energy.
Drink 3 – 4 glasses or more of water a day, on rising and between meals. Drink double this amount in hot weather.	Water cleanses the tissues and purifies the blood. Drink distilled, tested spring or filtered water.
Cook foods in their whole state or as whole as possible whenever you can.	This method saves nutrients and the flavor is better. If foods must be cut before cooking, cut them into large pieces.
Use herbs as much as possible, such as basil, parsley, thyme, sage, marjoram, bay, oregano, etc.	Herbs usually come from the leafy green parts of a low-growing plant. Herbs are natural and can be eaten in very large quantities. They may aid the body in digestion, have other helpful medicinal qualities, and add flavor, vitamins, minerals like iron and iodine, and aroma to foods.

Cooking & Eating Do's & Don'ts

Do	Because
Keep whole ground grains and flours, wheat germ, and bran in the refrigerator or a cool, dry place, or in the freezer.	Cool temperatures help preserve vitamin E as well as other vitamins and keep grains fresh, help prevent rancidity, and control bugs. Cornmeal tastes best if kept frozen.
Fast occasionally for one day or more on water or juices, or just fruits or vegetables.	Fasting cleanses the system, gives the body a rest, and helps remove toxins and poisons from the body. (See Chapter 8 – About Fasting)
Eat proper amounts of enzyme, alkaline, acid, and neutral foods each day. (See Chapter 4 – Meal Planning)	The proper combination of foods keeps the body in balance, strengthens resistance against disease, and promotes healing. It helps digestion and prevents stomach distress as well.
Try to follow the Food Combining chart when preparing meals. (See Chapter 4 – Meal Planning)	Bad food combinations cause stomach upset and poor body functioning. The greater part of your food intake should be in proper combinations.
Eat 2 – 3 servings of fruits and vegetables for every 1 serving of protein (meats or eggs) with 1 serving of grain (starch) and legume eaten each day.	This assures proper acid-alkaline balance and helps the body obtain all necessary vitamins and minerals needed every day.

Cooking & Eating Do's & Don'ts

Avoid	Because
Deep frying foods.	Greasy foods are not natural or good for the body intake. All or many vitamins may be killed in the intense heat and oil. Greasy foods can upset the stomach, liver, and gall bladder.
Hard fats, regular supermarket oils, and margarine.	Lard, animal, and commercial oils are unnatural to the body intake and have no beneficial food value. They are actually non-foods. All vitamins are usually killed in the processing. And, these oils are almost always processed and refined with dangerous chemicals. One may absorb chemical residues left over after processing. Margarine puts stress on the heart.
Mixing too many different types of food at one meal.	Mixing too many foods can cause acidity and indigestion. (See Food Combining chart)
Using baking soda or cornstarch.	They destroy vitamins in the body, especially vitamin C, hinder digestion, can can cause constipation. (Check the Substitution chart in Part 4 for healthy alternatives.)
Refined and chemically treated foods such as white sugar, white bleached flour, and white rice.	Most or all of the natural vitamins are processed out of these foods. Too much of these foods gives the body erratic energy. These are mostly non-foods and have little or no food value but lots of calories.
Baking powder with alum.	While alum helps a cake to rise higher, it adds an unnecessary additive to the body that irritates the body and may possibly be a cancer-causing agent. Alum is aluminum.
Drinking liquids with meals.	Foods should not be washed down. This makes digestion more difficult. Liquids dilute enzymes in the stomach needed for digestion of solid foods. A small drink or a few sips with a meal is all right.

Cooking & Eating Do's & Don'ts

Avoid	Because
Very hot or very cold foods.	They are unnatural to the body and shock its system. It takes extra body energy to digest these foods.
Eating fruits and vegetables together at the same meal.	This combination causes acidity and can upset the stomach. They require more body energy to digest. (There are some exceptions.)
Cutting up salads or fruits until right before eating. Eat as many fruits and vegetables whole as possible.	Once you cut a fruit or vegetable it starts to die, and nutrients escape. Cutting cells and exposing to the air hastens killing vitamins, as you can see by the brown edges of cut fruits and vegetables.
Excessive use of spices.	They may irritate the delicate stomach coatings and may lower the body energy and add toxins to the system. (Curries, chilies, black and white pepper, nutmeg, ground cinnamon, mustard, and ginger, are included.) Spices are usually from barks, roots, or strong seeds. Use sparingly.
Eating too many dairy products. Stay within or below the recommended daily allowances.	Too many dairy products are mucus forming and clog the system. They are not essential to the adult diet. Keep them at a minimum and be careful not to use them as an only source of protein as they are inadequate when overly processed. (See Chapter 5 - The Pros and Cons of Vegetarianism) Be sure to use proper dairy substitutes.
Eating tropical fruits or too many fruits in cold weather.	It is unnatural and unhealthful to eat warm climate tropical fruits in winter. This sends a message to the body that you are in hot weather and confuses the senses and body. Eat apples, pears, berries, and northern or cold climate fruits in cold weather. Also, too many fruits of any type are not "warming" foods for winter. Vegetables and other foods such as whole grains and beans help a person to retain proper body heat.

Cooking & Eating Do's & Don'ts

Never	Because
Boil foods.	It is better to steam, simmer, or cook on a low heat. The few vitamins remaining after boiling may be lost in the water. (Exceptions: Beans may be cooked at a low boil to breakdown the protein and make them more digestible. Whole squashes or whole pumpkins may be boiled.)
Cook in pots without lids.	Nutrition and flavor are lost in the open air. Foods may take as much as twice as long to cook.
Eat leftovers reheated more than once.	You will be eating food that has lost most or all of its nutritional value but not the calories. Food is best thrown away or composted after the second heating and eating.
Go to bed on a full stomach.	The stomach should be able to rest with you and not constantly be at work, which can cause indigestion and bad dreams and also lead to further stomach problems. Also, digestion time is slowed down considerably when one rests, and digestion takes much longer and takes more energy from the body.
Leave natural, unrefined oils out of the refrigerator or a cold place after opening, or mix new oil with old.	Natural oil left in a warm place or old oil mixed with new may cause rancidity, which in turn can cause poisoning, indigestion, vomiting, or gas.
Leave produce soaking to longin water to clean it.	Vitamins are lost in the water. A brief soak or rinse is all that is necessary.
Mix heavy starches and heavy legumes at the same meal, especially beans and potatoes.	When heavy acids such as soybeans and heavy alkalines such as potatoes are brought together, it can cause stomach enzymes to neutralize each other, and the foods may not be properly digested. This can cause gas and lower the body energy.

Cooking & Eating Do's & Don'ts

Never	Because
Eat raw fruits with other foods or shortly after other foods, especially meats.	Raw fruits digest very quickly and are mainly broken down in the intestines. If eaten with or shortly after other foods they will sit in the stomach and spoil and ferment before they reach the intestines. There are some exceptions. See Food Combining chart in Chapter 4 – Meal Planning.
Eat when upset, overtired, or not hungry.	Food will not be properly digested and can act like poison to the system. It takes lots of energy to digest. So save the energy if other problems are present and drink liquids or have fruit (easier to digest), yogurt, or a light food if you must have something.

♥ *Chapter 13*

How to Follow Recipes & Create Your Own

How to Choose a Recipe Book

Beginning Cooks

1. Choose a book that gives exact proportions of ingredients in its recipes.

2. Choose a book that explains the preparation procedures step by step or has pictures showing the procedures.

3. Choose a book that gives exact cooking times and temperatures.

4. The book should tell you what consistency the recipe should be and what changes to expect during preparation and cooking.

5. The best books will give suggestions for side dishes and extras to serve with main dishes.

Intermediate and Advanced Cooks

1. The book should give basic ingredients and proportions.

2. The book should give just enough information to make the recipe while the cook uses creativity to add extra touches.

3. The best books will suggest variations and possible substitutions that can be used in each recipe.

" In proportion as he (man) simplifies his life, the laws of the universe will appear less complex, and solitude will not be solitude, nor poverty, poverty, nor weakness, weakness. If you have built castles in the air, your work need not be lost; that is where they should be. Now put the foundations under them."

Thoreau — Walden

Mistakes to Watch for in Recipe Books:

1. Because cayenne red pepper is hotter in some areas of North American than in others, some natural food cookbooks call for too much or too little cayenne pepper. If books call for one teaspoon or more of cayenne (usually East Coast books), they are using very mild cayenne. If medium cayenne is used $1/16$ to $1/8$ teaspoon is the usual equivalent. Only several dashes may be required if very hot cayenne is used (usually Mid-Western books). (In this cookbook amounts are for medium or hot cayenne. Increase amounts if milder cayenne is used.)

2. Vanilla, tamari soy sauce, herbs, and a few spices in recipes are often used too sparingly. Vanilla and tamari soy sauce amounts often need to be doubled. Herbs and spices are sometimes so little in amount that the recipe is bland or, in some rare instances spices may be too much and the recipe too spicy. Usually one can judge by the list of herbs and spices in the recipe's ingredients. (Do not increase this book's amounts or amounts found in my other books.)

3. Too much salt is often used. Use a bit less where less is adequate. In rare instances a little extra salt should be added. Regular table salt is less salty than sea salt. One teaspoon sea salt equals three-quarters of a teaspoon table salt. One and one-quarter teaspoons table salt equals one teaspoon sea salt.

4. Carrot cake, banana bread, zucchini bread, and similar dessert recipes are often too doughy after baking. Use less fruit, vegetable mash, or liquid in these recipes.

5. Yeastless pie crusts and pizza doughs are sometimes too crumbly and dry. Soft butter or liquid lecithin with often help this problem. (See the recipes for pie crusts in the dessert chapter.)

How to Follow and Perfect Any Recipe

1. Read the information in this book on how to use herbs and spices before changing or making up your own recipe.

2. Use exact measurements until you are familiar with a recipe. If you are sure of your abilities, then you may approximate the amounts. Read a recipe thoroughly before beginning.

3. Do not assume that all recipes found in a book are perfect or delicious. Many books contain at least a few faulty recipes and recipes that may be bland or too spicy for your personal tastes. Make changes or add extra ingredients if you feel a recipe is inadequate.

4. Try out a recipe on yourself or your family before trying it out on friends and company. The recipe may be turn out right, but first-time attempts at any recipe can be unsatisfactory. If you are unhappy with a recipe after trying it for the first

time, write down your ideas for changes and improvements on a separate sheet of paper and place it in the cookbook near the original recipe. Next time, if the changes work out for the better, write them into your book. Almost all recipes can be changed at least a little to meet specific tastes.

5. If approximations are called for in a recipe you are not familiar with, consult another cookbook for a similar recipe that may provide more specific amounts.

6. If a new recipe does not turn out right, try it again with or without alterations. Do not expect to be a perfect cook instantly. In cooking, one is always learning and always having successes and failures.

7. If a recipe does not turn out by the second attempt and you are not sure why, get advice from experienced friends or teachers. Try to save a sample of the unsuccessful recipe for them to taste and explain your procedure and recipe step by step. If their experienced advice still leaves you unsure, have them with you the next time you use the recipe or just forget about that recipe, assume it is flawed and find another similar recipe that works better for you.

When You Forget an Ingredient in a Recipe:

1. Sometimes herbs and spices can be added by sprinkling them on top before baking a dish. Table condiments can also be used to spice up the flavor of a dish that has missing herbs and spices after it is served.

2. A missing vegetable, onions, whole grain, herbs, or other ingredient can be sautéed or cooked separately and added to a stew or other dish. Adding extras can also give flavor to reheated dishes.

3. Breads with missing salt, oil, or honey can have these ingredients kneaded into them right up to the time they are put into the pans and baked. There will be little or no loss of flavor this way. After baking, if too little yeast or any of the above-mentioned ingredients was used, the bread can be made into zwieback or bread pudding.

4. Cakes with missing sweetening or spices can be eaten like bread or broken into smaller pieces and topped with honey and cinnamon or made into bread pudding.

When You Add too Much of an Ingredient to a Recipe:

1. Usually the recipe can be extended or doubled, minus the overabundant ingredient. This prevents waste and gives a cook a second chance to patch up the recipe.

2. Soups may be extended with extra water, broth, or milk. Then adjust the other ingredients according to taste.

3. Some overspiced main dishes can be mixed with or served over plain millet or rice. Overspiced grain dishes can be mixed with plain cooked legumes or vegetables. One to four teaspoons honey or other sweetening can also help to tone down some recipes like soups or stews.

4. Mix other too-spicy dishes with bland leftovers or other non-spicy ingredients for a casserole, stew, or soup.

5. Certain strong natural oils or spices, like sage or rosemary can overpower a dish almost completely. Scoop out what you can of these extra ingredients and extend the recipe if possible. If not, discard it.

6. Tone down overspiced cakes and desserts by topping some of them with unsweetened whipped cream, tofu whipped cream, or by pouring milk or cream over them or serving them with a mild sauce.

7. Raw peeled, rinsed potatoes, or pasta noodles added to soup or stew will absorb excess herbs and spices. They can be kept in the soup or removed after they absorb excess seasonings.

Before You Make Up Your Own Recipes:

1. Make sure you have tried other recipes for a certain dish before making up your own. Do not try to create your own pumpkin pie recipe if you have never made a pumpkin pie before. Preferably you should have tried two or more different recipes for a certain dish before making your own.

2. Check a couple of recipe books for recipes you have used and see what they include for the same dish.

For example:

Carrot Cake

Recipe Book "A":

8 carrots grated fine	1 cup chopped pecans
1 cup raisins	4 beaten eggs
1/2 cup maple syrup	1/2 cup oil
2 cups flour	1 1/2 tsp baking powder (with alum)
1 tsp cinnamon	1 tsp vanilla
1 tsp salt	

Recipe Book "B":

2 cups ground carrots	1/2 cup nuts or seeds
1 cup raisins	2 beaten eggs

1 cup honey and $^1/_2$ cup milk
  or 1$^1/_2$ cups sugar and 1 cup milk

$^1/_2$ cup oil   2 cups flour
$^1/_4$ cup soy flour   2 tsp cinnamon
2 tsp vanilla   1 tsp nutmeg
2 tsp baking soda $^1/_4$ tsp sea salt

Then create your own recipe:

Your Recipe:
5 – 6 medium grated carrots
  (about 1$^1/_2$ cups)
1 cup chopped walnuts   2 tsp cinnamon
3 beaten eggs   2 tsp vanilla
1 Tbsp liquid lecithin $^1/_4$ tsp nutmeg
1$^1/_4$ cups honey $^1/_2$ tsp sea salt
$^1/_3$ cup natural oil   2 – 3 tsp no-alum baking powder
2 cups flour $^1/_2$ – 1 cup milk
  (medium whole wheat)

Why Each Ingredient Was Used in Your Recipe:

- 5 – 6 medium carrots: Fewer carrots were used so the cake would not be too moist or mushy after baking.
- 1 cup walnuts: Walnuts are a medium-priced nut with good flavor. Perfect for baked goods. (They are freshest and tastier when cracked out of the shell for recipes.)
- 3 eggs: Four eggs are really unnecessary, but three eggs are sufficient to give texture to the cake and act as a binder, especially when lecithin is added.
- 1 Tbsp liquid lecithin: Lecithin is a natural preservative that improves the texture of baked goods.
- 1 $^1/_4$ cups honey: Honey is cheaper and easier to get than pure maple syrup. Extra honey is used to give it a sweeter, more cake-like flavor and make it less like a sweet bread.
- $^1/_3$ cup oil: Only the necessary amount of oil is used. Good quality natural oil improves flavor and increases nutrients, and reduces harmful additives in recipes.

- 2 cups flour: Same as the other recipes except that medium ground whole wheat flour is specified. If medium ground flour is unavailable, use 1 cup course ground flour and 1 cup pastry flour.
- 2 tsp cinnamon and 2 tsp vanilla: Extra cinnamon and vanilla add more flavor to this recipe. One can hardly taste these ingredients in this recipe when less is used.
- $\frac{1}{4}$ tsp nutmeg; This is enough nutmeg to add extra flavor but not enough that the nutmeg tastes too strong in this recipe.
- $\frac{1}{2}$ tsp sea salt: This amount is sufficient to add flavor to the cake and help balance all the tastes in the cake. Salt complements and enhances sweetening in a recipe. Sea salt is a more healthful choice than regular table salt.
- 2 – 3 tsp no-alum (no-aluminum) baking powder: To help the cake rise and make the texture lighter.
- $\frac{1}{2}$ – 1 cup milk: For a moist but not mushy cake. Add just enough milk so the batter is stirrable, somewhat stiff and not pourable.

Changes are chosen based on previous experiences in making other recipes. Change what you want and keep what you like. Ingredients can be increased or decreased. Cooking times and temperatures can also be changed slightly if you feel that would improve your finished product. If your oven gets too hot, lower the temperature and vice versa. (See the Substitution chart for more ideas and correct amounts that can be substituted.)

Items that may sometimes be changed or interchanged are as follows:

Interchange:
    a. honey/maple syrup/fruit concentrate/rice syrup
    b. molasses/sorghum/barley malt liquid
    c. brown date sugar/natural unrefined sugar/barley malt powder
    d. yogurt/sour cream
    e. eggs/lecithin with guar gum or xanthan gum
    f. salt/vegetable salt/sea kelp/tamari soy sauce/sesame salt/potassium chloride/sea salt
    g. oil/butter/mayonnaise
    h. milk/water/juice/stock/broth
    i. baking powder/baking soda/yeast
    j. gluten flour/arrowroot powder/xanthan or guar gum
    k. cream cheese/cottage cheese/ricotta cheese/quark

Interchange:
See the individual chapters for more detailed information on interchanging the following within their own food groups:

a. vegetables
b. legumes
c. whole grains
d. dairy cheeses and soy cheeses
e. natural oils
f. herbs and spices
g. flours

Items in a recipe that can be reduced:

1. Salt can be cut down one-third to one-half the amount given in many other recipe books with little or no loss in flavor.
2. Oil or butter can be cut down one-quarter to one-half the amount given in some recipes.
3. Sweeteners can be cut down as desired in many recipes.
4. Nuts, seeds, and dried fruits can be added or subtracted as desired.
5. Items in a recipe that can *sometimes* be eliminated altogether are salt, nuts and seeds, raisins, black pepper, spices, milk and other dairy products, eggs, baking soda, and baking powder.
6. Write down your first-draft recipe. Gather your ingredients and prepare the recipe. If it is baked, you will have to wait until it is done to find out if it is a success. If it is cooked, add a little bit less herbs and spices than you think are necessary for the recipe. You may add more as it is cooking if more are needed. Write down any changes in the recipe. When the main dish is cooked or baked, judge by its flavor whether or not you are satisfied with it. Ask friends and family for opinions and use any reasonable suggestions they may offer.

If the recipe is a success, congratulate yourself for a job well done. If the recipe does not turn out as you like it, there is still more work yet to be done. Too much or too little of something was used or perhaps the recipe was over or undercooked. If the ingredients are in question, check the amounts and adjust them if necessary. Next time add more or less of the questionable ingredients. If the recipe still does not turn out, seek experienced advice.

Be patient with yourself when making up new recipes. This is an art and is not for beginner cooks, rather for intermediate or experienced cooks.

General Amounts of Herbs, Spices, & Extras to Be Used in Your Own Recipes

Legumes or Whole Grains per 1 cup dry (unsoaked and uncooked)

Sea Salt. . . . . about 1 teaspoon

Tamari Soy Sauce, Parsley. . . . . 2 – 3 teaspoons each

Sea Kelp, Thyme, Marjoram . . . . $^1/_4$ – $^1/_2$ teaspoon each

Basil, Oregano, Curry, or Chili Powder . . . . $^1/_2$ – 1 teaspoon each

Natural Oil or Butter . . . . 1 – 2 Tablespoons each

Cayenne Pepper. . . . . few dashes to $^1/_8$ teaspoon

Other herbs and spices. . . . . $^1/_4$ – $^1/_2$ teaspoon each

Soups and Stews

Same amounts as Legumes or Whole Grains per 4 cups of soup or stew.

Yeast Breads per loaf

Water or Milk. . . . . $1^1/_2$ cups

Yeast. . . . . $1^1/_2$ – 2 teaspoons

Sweetener . . . . 1 – 2 Tablespoons

Flour . . . . 1 pound or more

Sea Salt . . . . $1^1/_2$ – 2 teaspoons

Milk Powder (tapioca flour or soy milk powder). . . . . $^1/_4$ – $^1/_2$ cup if any

Eggs . . . . 1 if any

Lecithin. . . . . 1 – 2 teaspoons

Quick Breads per loaf

Water or Milk . . . . 1 – $1^1/_2$ cups

Baking Powder . . . . 1 – 3 teaspoons

Sweetener . . . . $^1/_8$ – $^1/_2$ cup

Flour. . . . . $1^1/_2$ – 2 cups

Sea Salt . . . . $^1/_2$ – 1 teaspoon

Spices . . . . $^1/_4$ – 1 teaspoon each

Eggs . . . . 1 – 2 if any

Cakes per sheet cake or two – layer round cake

Water or Milk. . . . . 1 – $1^1/_2$ cups

Baking Powder . . . . 2 – 4 teaspoons

Sweetener . . . . 1 – 2 cups

Flour . . . . $1^1/_2$ – 2 cups

Sea Salt . . . . $^1/_4$ – $^1/_2$ teaspoon

Cakes per sheet cake or two – layer round cake cont'd

Gluten Flour	1 – 2 Tablespoons
Nuts or Seeds or Raisins	$1/2$ – 1 cup or more
Lecithin	1 – 2 Tablespoons
Eggs	2 – 4 if any
Guar or Xanthan Gum (for allergy breads)	1 teaspoon
Other Sweetenings	$1/3$ – 1 cup or more
Vanilla	1 – 2 teaspoons
Cinnamon	1 – 2 teaspoons
Nutmeg, Ginger, or Allspice	$1/4$ – 1 teaspoon

Note:

In many recipes lecithin and/or eggs may be used. Also, baking powder and/or gluten flour may be used. Honey, molasses, real maple syrup, or other sweetener may also be used. Readjust the amounts of liquids and dry ingredients when necessary.

Salads and Dressings

Natural Oil (or yogurt)	2 – 4 Tablespoons
Apple Cider Vinegar or Lemon Juice	1 – 2 teaspoons or more
Parsley and Paprika	1 – 2 teaspoons crushed
Basil, Dill Weed, or Oregano	$1/4$ – $1/2$ teaspoon
Poppy, Sesame, or Sunflower Seeds	2 – 4 teaspoons
Tamari Soy Sauce	$1/4$ – 1 teaspoon if any
Other herbs and spices	$1/4$ teaspoon or less

Doubling Recipes

Salt: As recipes are doubled, salt should not be. Use about $1 1/2$ times the amount of salt called for in a single recipe when doubling a recipe. Use about two times the single amount for a triple batch recipe.

Sea Kelp: Increase amounts the same as for salt. Too much kelp can make a recipe taste "muddy."

Other Ingredients: Generally use a little less of each ingredient when doubling or tripling a recipe, especially for strong-flavored ingredients. Most mild ingredients can be doubled or tripled exactly. Knowledge of more specific techniques comes with practice.

♥ Chapter 14

Herbs, Spices, Condiments, & Natural Oils

The Art of Using Herbs and Spices

The secret of good cooking and recipe making is the proper use of herbs and spices. Proper food preparation and cooking techniques are a prerequisite.

Seasonings can enhance or detract from the flavor of foods. Herbs and spices can add flavor, color, vitamins and nutrients, texture and character to foods. A properly seasoned dish should enliven the natural flavors of the food without overpowering the subtle, natural essences of the dish. No one food, herb, or spice should predominate in a properly balanced dish. Complementing good food with a variety of seasonings that "dance together" to create wonderful sensations for your taste buds is an art, performed by any talented cook or chef. This art can be learned or acquired through practice and experimentation.

To master the use of seasonings, one must know before creating your own recipes, the individual taste and effect each herb and spice has on a dish, and which ones do or do not combine well together. Learning proper amounts of each seasoning to use is another art. Subtle herbs like

" An elderly dame, (Nature) too, dwells in my neighborhood, invisible to most persons, in whose odorous herb garden I love to stroll sometimes, gathering simples and listening to her fables...."

Thoreau — Walden

♥ 123

parsley can be used by the tablespoon while more pungent herbs like rosemary and sage must be used sparingly by the quarter teaspoon or they can easily overpower a dish and dominate all other flavors unpleasantly.

Making soups or soft desserts is an excellent way of learning how each seasoning tastes alone. Use a tried-and-true recipe from a good cookbook, prepare the soup or dessert without seasoning, slowly add one seasoning at a time, stir and taste to see how each one tastes as it is added to the recipe and how it combines with the other ingredients. Make the same recipe several times changing the order of which ingredients are added first, second and up to and including the last. Notice how a smaller or slightly larger amount of an ingredient can effect the taste.

Later try other versions of the same recipes in other books and by comparing, determine which seasonings you prefer. Note the differences and any improvement or loss of flavor from recipe to recipe. (See Chapter 13 – How to Follow Recipes & Create Your Own) These methods take a good deal of time and practice but, are among the best ways to learn about seasonings.

A balance of flavors is essential in all good tasting recipes. There are five basic flavors used in most types of cooking to which I have added a sixth— subtle. Usually a blend of two or more of these flavors is used to enhance a recipe. These flavors are like opposites or contrasting tastes. They accent, emphasize and "bring out" each others' flavors when two or more of these are used in a dish. Rarely are they all used together in one recipe.

The Six Flavors:
1. Sweet – as in: honey, maple syrup, natural and refined sugars, fruit sugar, malt, molasses, other sweeteners, some extracts like vanilla and peppermint
2. Sour – as in: lemons, limes, grapefruit, vinegar, lemon grass, yogurt, whey
3. Salty – as in: sea salt, table salt, miso, tamari soy sauce, sea kelp and seaweed, salted bouillon or cubes, salted butter
4. Spicy – as in: curry powder, chili powders, cayenne pepper, black/white/pink pepper, hot sauces
5. Pungent – as in: onions, garlic, horseradish, ginger, most herbs and spices, most flavor extracts
6. Subtle – as in: milk, herbs and spices like parsley and paprika, broth, stock, cooking wine, unsalted butter, natural oils

A cake always contains a sweet ingredient and most often a bit of salt is added. The salt actually contrasts with the sweet and makes the cake taste sweeter.

In many sauce recipes, like tomato sauce, salty and pungent items are used often with a bit of sweetening to enhance the salty and pungent flavors and accentuate them. Oriental dishes may use all six flavors. For example, a sweet and sour curried dish that includes salty, pungent and subtle items such as tamari soy sauce, onions, and broth.

Correct use of herbs and spices distinguishes a great cook from a not-so-great one. Seasoning is a fine art that must be acquired if your want to create your own recipes and not just follow the good recipes of others. A great cook can read a recipe, tell how it will taste and know what to do to improve it. A superb cook can create recipes in her head, on paper, or in a pot and make them taste wonderful on the first try.

Like all fine arts, properly using herbs and spices is not an easily acquired talent. Start by following good recipes prepared by experts, then branch out and experiment. The following information on herbs and spices and other condiments will help you get started. Skill comes with time and practice.

How to Use Herbs and Spices Properly

1. Use all seasonings carefully, a bit at a time. Too much of a wrong herb or spice can spoil a recipe. If too little is used, extra can always be added.

2. Use herbs plentifully in recipes. They are good for you and often have some medicinal qualities. Herbs include: all green, leafy parts of small plants such as basil, thyme, marjoram, parsley, oregano, and dill weed.

3. Use all spices sparingly. These are harder to digest and some are harmful to the stomach lining. These include: spices from barks of trees, most seeds, twigs, and others like: black and white pepper (cayenne is not included here as cayenne is beneficial to the body), mustard, cinnamon and sweet spices, cloves, chilies, and curries.

4. Mild flavored herbs can be used plentifully. These include: parsley, basil, thyme, marjoram, oregano, dill weed, savory, and bay leaves.

5. Strong flavored herbs should be used sparingly. These include: rosemary, sage, dill seed, tarragon, and mint leaves.

6. Seeds that are not harmful to the body include: sesame, flax, dill seed, caraway, celery, fennel, and cumin.

7. Most spices have a fairly strong flavor and should be used carefully and sparingly in recipes.

8. Many herbs and spices need to be cooked for 15 minutes or more to have their full flavors released and utilized in most recipes.

When to Add Herbs and Spices to Recipes:
Desserts and baked goods: Before cooking, baking, or chilling.
Legumes and whole grains: 20 to 30 minutes before they are finished cooking.
Soups and stews: Add after the first 20 minutes of cooking time.
Sauces and dressings: For the entire cooking time or for chilled dressings, add flavorings immediately and chill for one hour or more.
Salads: Toss with herbs after the vegetables have been tossed thoroughly with oil, or include seasonings in a dressing.

Basic Herb Cooking Chart:
Use some, not all, of the following herbs suggested for each type of food:
Beans, Lentils, and Peas: Savory, fennel, sea kelp, cayenne (red pepper), parsley, dill, oregano, basil, marjoram, thyme, sage, garlic, onions, sea salt
Whole Grains: Chives, parsley, oregano, dill weed, basil, cayenne, saffron, turmeric, paprika, marjoram, thyme, sesame seeds, sea kelp, onions, sea salt
Hot Spiced Foods: Cardamom, cumin, dill, turmeric, coriander, fennel, cayenne, curry powder, chili peppers or powder, sea kelp, marjoram, thyme, garlic, onions, sea salt
Soups and Stews: Parsley, basil, thyme, marjoram, oregano, savory, tarragon, dill, chives, cayenne, bay leaves, sea kelp, vegetable powder, mint leaves, garlic, onions, bouillon cubes, broth powder, sea salt
Salads, Salad Dressings, and Cooked Vegetables: Basil, parsley, celery seeds, chives, chervil, dill, tarragon, paprika, sea kelp, oregano, mint leaves, cumin powder, poppy seeds, sesame seeds, garlic, onions, natural oils, sea salt
Tomatoes and Tomato Sauce: Basil, parsley, rosemary, oregano, chives, bay leaves, sea kelp, marjoram, thyme, onions, garlic, sea salt
Eggs: Basil, parsley, paprika, cayenne, chives, green onion, sea salt
Breads: Caraway seeds, poppy seeds, sesame seeds, cinnamon, nutmeg, sea salt
Desserts and Cookies: Cinnamon, nutmeg, ginger, allspice, anise, poppy seeds, sesame seeds, sea salt

Table Condiments
These are herbs, spices, and extras that can be added to food after it has been served. Use one or more to add zest to cooked foods or non-spiced dishes.
Sea Salt: Can be used on any food. It is slightly saltier than regular table or earth salt. The granulated variety is best. Use sparingly as needed. It does not usually contain iodine unless specified on the label.

Sea Kelp: This powdered seaweed has a slightly salty taste and sometimes a very slight seafood flavor. It provides the body with iodine and other minerals. Sprinkle it generously or add to taste on vegetables, grains and beans.

Cayenne Pepper: This hot-tasting pepper is actually mild to the stomach and cleansing in the system. Use this sparingly instead of black or white pepper. Use $1/4$ to $1/10$ as much red pepper as you would use black pepper.

Sesame Salt: This can be used in place of table or sea salt. It contains less salt and adds more flavor to food. It can be used more generously than table or sea salt on most foods.

Vegetable Salt: Can also be used in place of table or sea salt. It usually contains vegetable powder for extra flavor and salt. Some varieties contain no actual salt. Use somewhat generously on any main dish or vegetable. Good for low-salt diets.

Salt Substitutes: Natural food stores sell various salt-free seasonings for people on special diets. These usually contain vegetable powders, yeast, herbs, and spices. These can be used like salt to flavor food. Potassium chloride can also be purchased at pharmacies and used about one quarter teaspoon or less per one teaspoon of sea salt.

Tamari Soy Sauce: A natural soy sauce that contains salt. It can be used by the teaspoon, two to three teaspoons at a time on whole grains, beans, and vegetables.

Natural Oil: Use on salads, cooked vegetables, or with legumes and whole grains. Natural oils are healthful alternatives to margarine and may be used to extend or replace butter.

Apple Cider Vinegar: Use on salads, beans, and whole grains if desired. Use a few drops at a time or measure according to taste.

Honey: This sweet extra may be used sparingly on breads, fruit salads, and some desserts. It also can be used to balance out the flavors in a sauce, soup, stew, or in recipes that use cider vinegar.

Basic Condiments Every Table Should Have:
1. A type of salt or salt substitute for flavor.
2. Sea kelp for iodine and minerals.
3. Cayenne pepper to benefit the body system and add flavor.

Recipes for Condiments

Sesame Salt (Gomashio)

Sesame seeds   **Sea salt**   **Natural Oil**

In a dry iron skillet or other heavy pan, place a thin layer ($1/8$ inch) of hulled, white sesame seeds. Cook them over a low heat, stirring occasionally until the seeds are lightly toasted. (Sesame seeds can also be toasted in the oven at 300°F and stirred often.) Do not use unhulled, brown seeds as they pop and jump out of the frying pan while cooking. Grind the sesame seeds in the blender about $1/2$ cup at a time (or use a mortar and pestle). Grind until most of the seeds are crushed fine and then mix them with sea salt, about $1/10 - 1/4$ part sea salt and $9/10 - 3/4$ parts sesame. Example: $1\frac{1}{2}$ cups ground sesame and $1/2$ cup sea salt. Optional: 1 – 2 tsp sea kelp

Vegetable Salt

Mix vegetable broth powder with sea salt about half and half or so. This can be purchased at most health food stores.

Herb Mixture (All Purpose)

$1/2$ cup parsley
1 Tbsp each basil, oregano, sea kelp, savory
2 tsp each paprika, dill weed
1 tsp each marjoram, thyme
$1/2$ – 1 tsp each cayenne, dill weed, sage (ground)
$1/4$ – 1 tsp of any of your favorite herbs or spices (3 – 4 or less)
1 – 2 Tbsp sea salt or $1/4$ – $1/2$ cup sesame or vegetable salt

Mix everything together and store in a dry place. This mixture can be used with plain legumes or grains about one to two tablespoons mixture per one cup dry legumes or grains. Stir the mixture well each time before using.

About Natural Oils

Natural oils are unrefined, unsaturated fats from vegetables, nuts, and seeds. Saturated fats are higher in cholesterol and can be found in butter, eggs, fish, poultry, and red meats. Two or more teaspoons of natural oil can be enjoyed on salads, cooked vegetables, or with legumes and whole grains. Natural oils are a healthy replacement for margarine and salad dressings. There is extensive controversy over which types of oils to use and why. It is not one of the purposes of this book to settle the dispute, but rather to shed a little light on the subject.

There are three basic processes for the manufacturing of cooking oils. The first is the solvent extraction method by which most commercial and supermarket oils are obtained. Some harmful petroleum by-products like octane, heptane and hexane are mixed with mashed seeds, beans or nuts to assist in the extraction process and obtain greater quantities of oil. Then the oil and solvents are separated because the solvents are toxic. The oil extracted this way still contains some solvent residues. For obvious reasons, these oils are not recommended.

The second method is cold-pressed. No solvents are used, and lower pressing temperatures are maintained. By this method much less oil is extracted and the product becomes more expensive. These oils are usually lightly refined to remove the stronger flavor and color which also reduces some nutrients.

The third method is expeller-pressed. Even cooler pressing temperatures are maintained during this process. While cold-pressed oils may be refined to some degree, expeller-pressed oil is merely pressed. Organic nuts and seeds are often used to make expeller-pressed oils.

Expeller-pressed oil retains the most nutrients, including valuable Omega 3 and 6 essential fatty acids, and the strongest flavor. Some oils extracted this way, like flax seed (linseed) and pumpkin oil, are best if they are used only raw in salads and with mixed raw dishes. It is important to include one or both of these oils in a vegan diet to obtain the essential Omega 3 and 6. Another way to get these oils is to grind flax seeds and sprinkle them on cereals or whole grains, and over sauces and other foods at the table. Keep refrigerated after grinding for up to one to two weeks.

Most of the other expeller-pressed oils may be used in cooking, but they must be experimented with in recipes as they have a stronger flavor and some of them can overpower the other ingredients in a dish.

I sometimes prefer to use just cold-pressed oils in general cooking, even though they are less nutritious, as I can count on a milder flavor. These types of oils are generally lighter in color. The best types of oil to cook with are the 3S': sesame, safflower and sunflower. (Not soy, which requires more processing and is less digestible.) Extra virgin olive oil is also good for some recipes and is the highest quality of olive oil. Olive oil is the only oil that can be left unrefrigerated unless it is a natural brand. It is also the only oil that need never be extracted with solvents.

In this book I specify only "natural" oil and "natural light" oil. When a recipe calls for natural oil, you may use expeller-pressed oils. They taste good only if used in the right recipes. Experiment with expeller-pressed oils, or for more uniform taste use cold-pressed oils. In all the mild-tasting recipes and desserts, I recommend "natural light" oil. To be on the safe side I generally stick with cold-pressed oils for these, but I do use some expeller-pressed almond and walnut oils in some dessert recipes.

For other specialties, toasted sesame oil is the best flavor for stir-frys. Although it is expensive, very little is used at a time, so a little bottle lasts a while. Safflower, sunflower, and olive oils are generally less expensive.

Keep all natural oils refrigerated after opening. Discard oils after the date on the label, if any, or after three to six months stored in the refrigerator after opening. Do not let perspiration, saliva, or bacteria get into the oil bottle and do not let oil sit out of the refrigerator too long, especially on a hot day. Once oil is poured out of its bottle, never pour it back into the bottle as it easily collects bacteria or dust once poured. Oil poisoning is very painful and dangerous!

For more information, see *Fats That Heal Fats That Kill* by Udo Erasmus or *The Facts About Fats* by John Finnegan.

Some recommended expeller-pressed oils are: Flora, Arrowhead Mills, and Omega. Some recommended cold-pressed oils are: Spectrum, Eden, and Lifestream.

About Margarine

Margarine has been heat processed to the point where absolutely none of the nutrients and essential fatty acids are present. It is a misconception that margarine is a heart conscious replacement for butter because the trans-fatty acids and free radicals present in margarine from the refining process are detrimental to health.

Dr. Rudolph Ballantine says in *Nutrition and Health* that the rise in heart disease directly parallels the rise in the use of margarine. He states, "It seems increasingly likely that eating margarine, instead of preventing heart attacks, actually accelerates the process which causes them." Dr. Zoltan Rona, author or *Return to the Joy of Health* states "Margarine is nothing more than plastic butter."

Natural oils can be used on bread or in recipes instead of margarine. Other alternatives include using butter sparingly or the recipes for Better Butter and Veggie Butter. (See Chapter 22 - Sauces, Spreads and Dressings) Dr. Ballantine says, "The worst butter is better than the best margarine." Margarine is an unnatural product that is unaffected by its environment. It does not become rancid or moldy, regardless of its age. Avoid all types of margarine.

Part Three

♥

Recipes and Food Preparation Guidelines

Chapter 15

Appetizers, Snacks, & Party Foods

Sweet Appetizers

 Birds Nests (Date Candies)

Pitted dates, sticky variety best
Almonds, cashews, or filberts
Walnuts or pecans
Unsweetened coconut, shredded or hulled (white) sesame seeds

Flatten a date or spread it open so the sticky side is on top. Use one medium or large date or press two small dates together for each candy. Press one almond (or other nut) and one walnut (or pecan) next to each other on the top of the date, like two eggs in a nest. If there is room, a third nut can be added. Then press the whole, flat date candy into the coconut, pressing coconut into the top and bottom of the candy. If dates are not sticky enough, dip them in water before pressing in coconut. Make dozens of these and arrange them on a plate. Refrigerate until use. Even people who dislike dates will find these candies interesting and delicious!

Dates & Cream Cheese

Use whole, firm dates and slice them almost in half lengthwise. Remove the pits if any and stuff each date with as much cream cheese as possible. Close the date up around the cream cheese partially so it looks like a sandwich with filling. Arrange them on a plate and keep them refrigerated until use.

 # Fruit-Nut Balls

Choose 2 – 3 of the following. Mix them together and grind fine.

Walnuts	*Cashews*
Pecans	*Filberts*
Sunflower seeds	*Almonds*
Other nuts	

Choose 2 – 3 of the following. Chop them very fine and mix together.

Raisins	*Currants*
Dates	*Dried apricots*
Dried peaches or pears	*Other dried fruit*

Other ingredients:
  Sesame seeds or shredded coconut
  Honey (optional)

Mix about one cup chopped dried fruit with $1/2 - 3/4$ cup ground nuts. Work them together with your hands. Add a little honey if the mixture is too dry. Shape or roll the mixture into a ball. Then roll the ball in coconut or sesame seeds making sure the entire ball is covered. If the coconut or seeds will not stick properly, roll the balls in a little honey or water before rolling them in the coconut or seeds. Refrigerate the candies before serving. Keep leftovers refrigerated. (A food processor may be used to chop and mix if desired.)

Nut Butter Balls

> $^3/_4$ *cup peanut butter, crunchy is best, or other nut butter (almond,*
> *cashew, or filbert)*
> $^1/_4$ *cup honey, maple syrup or other natural liquid sweetener*
> $^1/_4$ *cup milk powder, non-instant is best or tapioca flour*
> $^1/_4$ *cup raisins*
> *Dash or two of cinnamon*
> *Optional: almonds or cashews, whole*
> *Sesame seeds or shredded coconut*

Let the nut butter sit at room temperature for 10 – 20 minutes and then use a fork to mix it with the milk powder, honey, cinnamon, and raisins. Add a little extra milk powder if hard nut balls are wanted. Roll the mixture into little bite-size balls. As an added surprise a whole almond or cashew can be hidden in the center of each ball. Then roll the balls in coconut or sesame seeds. Keep refrigerated. Chill before serving. (Tahini or sunflower butter may also be used.)

 # *Honey-Nut Dip or Spread*

> *1 cup soy nuts, peanuts, or other nuts*
> *1 cup sunflower seeds*
> $^1/_2$ *cup orange juice*
> $^1/_4$ *cup honey*
> *2 Tbsp butter or oil*
> *Dash or two of salt*

Use a blender or food processor to blend all ingredients to desired consistency. Use it for dipping fruit pieces or spreading on crackers. Add extra juice if needed.

Appetizers

 Cheese & Nut Ball

2 cups cheddar cheese, grated or crumbled fine
2 cups cream cheese, softened
1 cup Roquefort, Blue, Brie, Feta, or Farmer's cheese, crumbled
Walnuts, pecans, or mixed nuts, ground or chopped fine
Paprika or parsley, dried

Leave the cream cheese at room temperature for an hour or more to soften it. Hand-mix the three cheeses together. Extra ingredients such as parsley, chives, or onion powder can be added to the cheeses according to personal taste. Form the cheeses into a ball and roll in paprika or parsley until it is well covered. Then roll the ball in the ground nuts, pressing the nuts into the entire ball. Then flatten one end of the ball so it will sit properly on the serving tray. Chill well before serving. Serve surrounded by crackers and use as a spread. Keeps 6 – 14 days refrigerated.

 Mild Curry Dip

1 cup plain yogurt
1 cup mayonnaise (regular or low-fat)
2 tsp curry powder
1/2 – 1 tsp turmeric
1/2 tsp each chili powder, cumin powder (cominos), ginger,
  and paprika
Sea salt or vegetable sea salt to taste
Cayenne red pepper to taste

Use a wire whisk to mix all ingredients together in a bowl. Chill thoroughly before serving. Use this tasty dip with vegetable sticks or bread chunks for parties, snacks, or lunches. Even people who dislike hot curries and spices enjoy this mild flavored, appetizing dip. Keeps one to two weeks refrigerated. Keeps longer if kept bacteria free.

 **Dilly Dip**

> *8 ounces cream cheese, softened*
> *1 cup plain yogurt*
> *4 – 6 green onion tops or handful of chives, finely chopped*
> *1/2 cup fresh parsley, finely minced (or 2 Tbsp dried)*
> *2 – 3 tsp dill weed*
> *Several dashes each sea salt and cayenne red pepper*

Leave the cream cheese at room temperature for one to two hours or more until softened, or buy soft, spreadable cream cheese. Use a fork or masher to mix all the ingredients thoroughly. Great dip for vegetables, crackers or bread. It may also be used as a sandwich spread or be stuffed into cherry tomatoes or celery sticks. Chill before serving. Keeps up to seven to eight days refrigerated.

 Tahini Yogurt Dip or Spread

> *1 1/2 cups plain yogurt*
> *1 cup sesame tahini*
> *1/3 – 1/2 cup fresh lemon juice*
> *1/4 cup finely minced parsley (or 1 Tbsp dried)*
> *1 – 2 cloves garlic, crushed*
> *1/2 – 1 tsp ground cumin*
> *1/2 tsp paprika*
> *Sea salt and cayenne red pepper to taste*

Mix all ingredients together well with a large spoon, or mix gently with a wire whisk. Chill thoroughly. Serve with veggie sticks, pita bread wedges or other whole grain bread. Makes a great party, snack, or lunch food. Keeps four to six days refrigerated.

Easy Veggie Nut Dip

2 ¹/₂ cups chopped broccoli, carrots, or asparagus,
   or 3 cups chopped spinach
¹/₂ cup sesame tahini, almond butter, cashew butter, sunflower
butter or peanut butter (or other nut butter)
2 Tbsp finely chopped parsley (or 2 tsp dried)
¹/₄ tsp or to taste of vegetable sea salt
Several dashes powdered dulse or sea kelp
Several dashes cayenne red pepper or to taste

Steam the vegetable until tender. Combine with all the other ingredients in a food processor until smooth. Serve with veggie sticks, rice cakes, crackers, or whole grain breads. Makes a tasty dip or sandwich spread for anytime. Keeps three to five days refrigerated.

 Rainbow Roll Ups

8 ounces cream cheese, softened
3 – 4 green onion tops or handful chives, finely chopped
¹/₂ red bell pepper, cut in strips and diced
¹/₂ cup finely chopped celery or ¹/₂ green pepper, cut in strips and diced
¹/₄ – ¹/₂ cup chopped black olives or green olives with pimento
1 Tbsp finely chopped parsley
¹/₄ tsp each basil, dill weed, and paprika
¹/₄ tsp vegetable sea salt or to taste
Several dashes cayenne red pepper or to taste
Optional: 1 tsp finely chopped fresh mint leaves or sorrel leaves
6 – 8 soft tortillas (some pita breads or chipatis may also be used instead)

Mix all the ingredients well and spread the mixture evenly over each tortilla (or bread) about ¹/₄ to ¹/₃-inch thick. Roll up each tortilla tightly, wrap them all and chill them in the refrigerator for two hours or more. Slice the rolls in about one-inch thick rounds and lay them flat on a plate for an attractive, colorful array of delicious snack or lunch treats. Keeps two to four days refrigerated.

♥ Cucumber-Sour Cream/Yogurt Dip

> 1 large cucumber, peeled, seeded and finely grated
> 1 cup sour cream
> 1 cup yogurt
> 2 – 3 green onion tops or small handful chives, finely chopped
> 1 – 2 Tbsp finely chopped parsley
> 1 tsp dill weed, fresh or dried
> $^1/_4$ tsp basil
> $^1/_4$ tsp tarragon and/or thyme
> Vegetable sea salt and cayenne red pepper to taste
> Optional: 1 – 2 tsp finely chopped fresh mint leaves

Mix all the ingredients together well and chill thoroughly before serving. Stuff into a large, hollowed bell pepper or two to serve as a veggie or cracker dip. Keeps three to six days refrigerated.

♥ Guacamole

> 1 ripe avocado, peeled and mashed
> 1 tsp onion, minced
> 2 – 3 tsp lemon juice (essential to keep avocado from turning brown)
> $^1/_4$ tsp chili powder
> Vegetable sea salt to taste
> Few dashes each sea kelp and tamari soy sauce
> Optional: 1 tomato, seeded and diced

Mix all the ingredients together and chill until used. Use it as a dip or spread with crackers, bread, or vegetable sticks, or as a topping or side dish with Mexican food. It also makes an appetizing sandwich spread with or without added cheese and/or sprouts. If used for a dip, bury the avocado pit in the bottom of the dip bowl. This technique will keep the dip fresh longer. Keeps one to two days refrigerated. Variations: Add chopped black olives or crumbled cheddar cheese.

Stuffed Eggs - Deviled

6 large eggs
2 – 3 Tbsp mayonnaise (regular or low-fat)
1/2 – 1 Tbsp chives or green onion tops, chopped fine
1/8 tsp each paprika and parsley
Sea salt or vegetable sea salt to taste
Few dashes cayenne red pepper
Few drops tamari soy sauce

After hard boiling the eggs, cool them in cold water and refrigerate. Peel the eggs and cut them in half lengthwise. Gently scoop out the egg yolks. Mash the yolks with remaining ingredients and refill the egg white with as much yolk mixture as possible. Sprinkle extra paprika or chives on top for added eye appeal. Chill before serving.

 # Cheesy-Cheese Dip

1/2 cup cottage cheese
1/2 cup cheddar cheese, grated
2 ounces cream cheese
2 – 4 Tbsp milk or cream
1/2 tsp each vegetable salt and onion or garlic powder
Few dashes each cayenne and paprika

Blend all the ingredients together lightly. Chill before serving. Use this dip for fruit or vegetable pieces or with crackers. Keeps two to four days refrigerated.

 # Swiss Cheese Spread

1 cup grated Swiss cheese
1/3 cup chives or green onion tops, chopped fine
1/3 cup pickles or green olives, chopped very fine

¹/₂ cup mayonnaise (regular or low-fat)
Dash or two each of vegetable salt and cayenne pepper

Be sure to drain the pickles or olives well before using them in this recipe. Add a few extra spices if desired. This spread can be used on crackers or bread. Just mix everything and serve. Keeps three to six days refrigerated.

Cucumber-Cheese Spread

16 ounces cream cheese, softened
¹/₂ cucumber, grated (save the juice)
1 – 2 Tbsp chives or 1 tsp onion powder
Few dashes each cayenne and sea kelp
1 – 2 tsp tamari soy sauce
2 – 3 tsp lemon juice
¹/₄ tsp each paprika and vegetable salt
Optional: 2 – 3 Tbsp ground nuts or tahini or nut butter

Leave the cheese at room temperature for one hour or more to soften. Mix all the ingredients together including most or all of the juice of the cucumber. Use just enough juice to make the spread smooth but not thin. Serve it as a spread or dip. Keeps three to six days refrigerated.

Home Roasted Nuts

Chopped or slivered raw nuts may be roasted in a dry pan in a preheated oven at 300°F for four to eight minutes, depending on the size of the nuts and how thinly they are layered. Stir them every couple minutes or so and turn them as needed until lightly browned and hot.

Whole nuts like almonds and hazelnuts (filberts) can be roasted in a preheated oven at 350°F for 6 – 10 minutes. Use these in recipes or as a garnish or snack. Store in a refrigerator for up to several weeks.

Soy-Cashew Nuts

> **2 cups raw cashews, whole if possible**
> **2 – 4 Tbsp tamari soy sauce**
> **Optional: several dashes cayenne**
> **Optional: 2 Tbsp butter**

Heat the butter in the frying pan if used; then add the nuts and sauté them for a couple of minutes. Add the soy sauce and a little cayenne if desired. Stir them for a few more minutes over low heat, being careful not to burn the nuts. Blanched almonds, sunflower seeds, or other nuts can be used instead, but cashews have the richest flavor. Serve the nuts like mixed nuts, either hot or cold.

Appetizer Recipes Included in Other Chapters
Marinated Vegetables – See Chapter 16 – Vegetable and Vegetable Salads
Hummus Spread – See Chapter 24 – Sandwich Ideas and Lunchbox Specials*
Soy-Spread – See See Chapter 24 – Sandwich Ideas and Lunchbox Specials*
Falafel Spread – See Chapter 20 – Main Dishes*
Tofu Cutlets – See Chapter 20 – Main Dishes (use as an appetizer or on crackers)
* Use as a spread or dip.

Celery Fills or Cracker Spreads:

Peanut butter	Hummus - Chick Pea Spread	Dilly Dip
Tahini and honey	Falafel Spread	Cheese spreads
Easy Veggie Nut Dip	Almond or cashew butter	Cucumber Dip/Spread

Cream cheese sprinkled with paprika **or** mixed with or covered with ground nuts
Nut butter and/or apple butter mixed or used separately

Cracker Toppings:

Add the following ingredients in layers:
1. Cream cheese, alfalfa sprouts, ground nuts, cucumber slices
2. Guacamole, tomato slice, ground nuts
3. Tahini, cheese (grated or sliced), honey
4. Cream cheese, jam or fruit butter, ground sunflower seeds
5. Cream cheese, tahini or nut butter, cucumber or tomato slice
6. Falafel Spread, tomato slice, grated cheese (dairy or tofu)
7. Easy Veggie Nut Dip, alfalfa sprouts, grated cheese (dairy or tofu)

Dip Sticks:

Use chips, crackers, breads, bread sticks, vegetables, or fruit pieces to dip.

♥ *Above*
Assorted breads

Below
Good foods...
Remember to eat a variety
of fruits, vegetables, whole
grains, legumes, and dairy
products or dairy substitutes
every day

♥ Left Page

Perfect for any party...

Hummus Dip (p.279) and **Myboulie** (p.229) (top) or vegetable sticks for dipping in **Dilly Dip** (p.137), **Tahini Yogurt Dip** (p.137), and a **Cheese and Nut Ball** (p.136) (bottom)

♥ This Page

Greens glorious greens in soups or salads...

Wild Green Salad (p.155) (top) or simple **Vegetable Soup Stock** (p.235) with added onions and watercress (bottom)

♥ *This Page*

For a hearty breakfast...
try **Granola** (p.179) or **Whole Wheat Pancakes** (p.180) with real maple syrup or **syrup blend** (p.182)

♥ *Right Page*

Plan your barbeque...
with **Perfect Potato Salad** (p.160), **The Best Baked Beans** (p.223), and the makings
for great **Shish Kebabs** (p.228)

♥ *Left Page*

For lunch or supper...
add **Stir-Fried Vegetables** (p.230) to brown rice (top) or try a **Hot or Cold Falafel Sandwich** (p.219) with **Cold Red Bell Pepper Soup** (p.237) (bottom)

♥ *This Page*

Spice up your menu...
with **Rice Enchiladas** (p.214) and **Mexicali Tacos** (p.215) (top) or a meal of **Spinach-Potato Pie** (p.206) with **Greek Salad #2** (p.157) and **Stuffed Tomatoes** (p.209) (bottom)

♥ *Next Page*

To satisfy your sweet tooth...
try easy-to-make **Birds Nests** (p.133) and **Fruit-Nut Balls** (p.134) with **Almond Heart Cookies** (p.328) (top) or **Tofu Cheesecake** (p.320) and **Rhubarb Sauce** cooked with dates (p.317) (bottom)

Chapter 16

Vegetables & Vegetable Salads

How to Cook Vegetables

There are five basic methods of cooking vegetables: boiling, broiling, baking, sautéing, and steaming.

1. Boiling: When cooking natural foods, very few vegetables are boiled as they lose vitamins and flavor. Some thick-skinned whole foods can be boiled whole without fear of losing their subtle qualities, such as whole winter squash: spaghetti, butternut, buttercup, acorn, and others, and pumpkins.

2. Broiling: Broiling is a limited method of cooking; some vegetables are too hard to broil effectively unless steamed first. Broiling does add superb flavor to vegetables. Easy-to-broil vegetables: bell peppers, zucchini, yellow summer squash, mushrooms, eggplant, edible pea pods, onions; also, grapefruit sections and tomatoes. Foods that can be broiled if presteamed first: broccoli, cauliflower, kohlrabi, carrots, turnips, parsnips, beets, asparagus, and artichoke hearts packed in water (drained).

3. Baking: Baking can be used to cook many vegetables. They can be flavorful when baked but may get dry and take a longer time to cook. Vegetables that can be baked whole: potatoes, orange yams, zucchini, yellow winter squash, pattypan squash, kohlrabi, small onions, bell peppers. Tomatoes may also be baked whole.

Vegetables that can be cut and baked: winter squash, carrots, beets, turnips, parsnips as well as all the vegetables that can be baked whole. Some are best if presteamed before baking. Almost all can be baked into vegetable pies, casseroles, or other dishes with multiple ingredients.

4. Sautéing: This method of cooking vegetables is quite flavorful. It does require a bit of oil. Some people avoid using oil and sauté with water or tamari soy sauce instead, but these are not true stir-frys and actually vitamins and flavor are lost when oil (or butter) is not used for stir-frying. The oil must be very hot before any vegetables are added to a stir-fry. Then the vegetables are only lightly coated in the oil and it seals in their juices and flavors. If the oil is too cool, it gets absorbed into the vegetables and destroys nutrients while saturating the vegetables. If water or tamari soy sauce are used to stir-fry, they may also permeate the vegetables, destroying valuable nutrients and flavors and the vegetables will ooze their juices while cooking, release moisture, and can become soggy. If you have digestive problems, sauté the vegetables a couple minutes longer so they are not crunchy.

5. Steaming: This is the most popular and common method of cooking vegetables for the health-minded. The flavor is in-between that of boiled and baked vegetables and the sautéed and broiled ones. Vegetables can be cooked to perfection if done properly. Buy a special steaming basket, preferably stainless steel (bamboo ones are not sanitary) and insert it in a large pot with a lid that closes completely and seals in the steam. One of the special steaming pots available at cooking shops can also be purchased. In either case the vegetables must sit above the boiling water at all times without the water touching them or they will lose flavor and nutrients.

The Importance of Steaming Vegetables:
1. Steaming preserves more nutrients. Vitamins are not boiled away or killed by high heat.
2. Steaming allows the vegetables to keep their natural flavors and bright colors.
3. Steamed vegetables retain more of their natural juices.
4. Vegetables can be cooked to perfection at a lower temperature for just the right amount of time. Overcooking is unlikely and unnecessary when vegetables are steamed.

Vegetable Steaming Guide

Approximate times given for most steamable vegetables. Cook one or more vegetables together. Put longest cooking one in pot first, add others later so each vegetable only cooks the basic allotted time.

Cooking Time	Whole Vegetable (or large pieces)	Cut Vegetable (chunks, slices, or strips)
4 – 6 minutes	snow peas, black olives, bean sprouts, lentil sprouts, green peas, garlic	bell peppers, artichoke hearts (quarters), black olives (half), water chestnuts (sliced), mushrooms, lotus root (chopped)
6 – 10 minutes	spinach, celery, green onions, zucchini	onions, garlic, bell pepper (half), yellow summer squash
8 – 14 minutes	asparagus, artichoke hearts, onions (small), chick pea sprouts, other legume sprouts	cabbage, broccoli, cauliflower, zucchini (sliced in half), Jerusalem artichokes, kohlrabi, eggplant
14 – 18	kale, collards, turnip greens, mustard greens, beet greens, swiss chard, broccoli (small stalk)	carrot, turnip, parsnip, brussels sprouts, green beans, beets, orange yams
20 – 30	brussels sprouts, green beans, kohlrabi (small), Jerusalem artichokes	winter squash (1- or 2-inch chunks), cabbage (in large wedges), white and sweet potatoes
45 minutes or more	artichokes (globe), cauliflower head, kohlrabi (large)	

The Easy Way to Grow Sprouts at Home

Varieties: Alfalfa, mung beans, lentils, wheat berries, soybeans, whole oats, and barley, and rye, unhulled millet and sesame seed, hulled sunflower seed, most peas, and beans. The following seeds, must be specially purchased in a health food store to be usable: radish, mustard, cabbage, red clover, and fenugreek.

Easiest and Most Common to Sprout:

Alfalfa: four to seven days

Mung beans: three to four days

Lentils: three to four days
Wheat berries: two and a half to three and a half days
Sunflower: three to four days

Hardest to Sprout:

Soybeans, other beans and peas, unhulled millet, mustard:
    These take approximately three to five days

Amounts of seeds per one-quart jar:
Alfalfa: three tablespoons
Mung beans and lentils: one half to one cup
Wheat berries and hulled sunflower seed and beans and peas: one cup
Other seeds as package directs.

Where and When to Sprout Seeds: A dry, cool place, like a countertop. Not in the dark, but not in direct sunlight. Ideal temperatures for growing are between 50°F – 70°F. Sprouts can be grown all year round but are especially good in winter, when most fresh vegetables are unavailable. For long, white mung sprouts for Oriental cooking, grow in a dark cupboard in an opaque container that is partly covered with a lid or fully covered with a damp cloth. For salad mung beans, grow on the countertop in a glass jar.

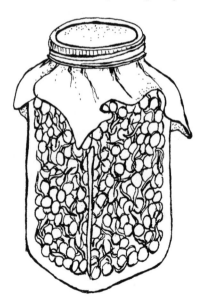

Above: Plate with paper toweling, beans and more toweling on top.

Left: Sprout jar with netting.

Materials Needed - Jars, cheesecloth, netting or clean piece of nylon stocking to cover the top of the jar, rubber bands or canning lid rings to secure cloth lid or use specially purchased sprouting jar lids, or for large amounts use pails with damp dish towels to cover them, or for hard-to-sprout varieties use damp paper toweling on a plate covered with more damp toweling, or a sprout rack made with a square frame of wood with netting or screening covering the bottom and covered with a damp cloth or plastic sheeting, or buy a sprouting rack and follow the instructions provided with it.

Perfect Sprouts

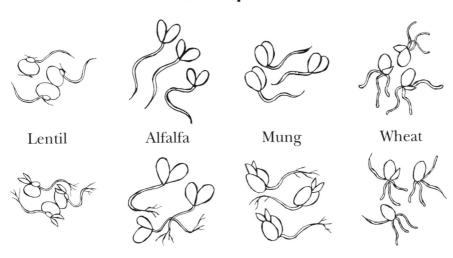

| Lentil | Alfalfa | Mung | Wheat |

Overgrown Sprouts

How to Sprout the Easy Varieties

Beginners should start sprouting in jars or with a purchased sprouting rack. For sprouting in jars, check the "Amounts of seeds per one-quart jar" list above. Place the seeds in a jar and cover it with the suggested cloth or net. Add three to four times as much water as seeds to the jar. (Example: For one-half cup of seeds, use two cups of water.) Let the seeds soak in the water overnight. In the morning drain away all the water and rinse the seeds thoroughly. Hold or place the jar upside down over the sink or dish rack for two to five minutes. Then place the jar right side up or slanted downward in a rack on the countertop. This helps remove excess water. Give the sprouts a drink two to three times a day or whenever they seem dry. Working people can rinse them in the morning, on return from work, and before bedtime. To give them a drink, fill the jar with water and let the sprouts sit in the water for a few seconds. Do not be alarmed if you forget them in the water; this is usually not harmful if it happens occasionally. Drain them thoroughly for five minutes and return them to the counter. Most of these seeds should be at least slightly green when mature. Follow the number of days given above and rinse them every day until they are ripe. On the last day of growing, let them sit on a sunny windowsill for about one hour to let them soak up vitamins, especially vitamin D and chlorophyll from the sun. On very hot days give them only indirect sun. Sprouts are most digestible and nutritious when grown the suggested number of days. Refrigerate immediately and eat them as soon as possible after they are ready. Check refrigerated sprouts every few days and rinse them if needed. Be careful not to let them freeze.

How to Sprout Harder-To-Sprout Varieties

These types are harder to sprout because they spoil easily while sprouting. Follow the basic instructions for easy-to-sprout seeds except for the following: The beans and peas should be soaked in water for 24 to 36 hours before growing them. Change the water every 12 hours. Rinse these and other hard-to-sprout varieties more often—three to five times a day or more if needed. Sprout racks or plates may be used for sprouting these. Spread these legumes and seeds one-half to one-inch thick for sprouting with these methods and keep a damp cloth or toweling over them. See Materials Needed above for more information.

How to Sprout in Large Quantities

Use buckets, pails, or large jars and fill them $1/6$ to $1/4$ full with seeds for sprouting. Soak the seeds twelve hours or so as usual. Keep a damp cloth or toweling over the container and rinse the seeds one to two times a day. This technique is not recommended for hard-to-sprout varieties.

Super Salads

Salads are fun. They look interesting and taste wonderful. Besides being a gold mine of vitamins, salads are super taste treats. Vegetables and leafy greens supply a wide range of vitamins needed for every day, including vitamins A, B1, B2, niacin, C, E, K, calcium, iron, iodine, and others.

Are your salads dull and uninteresting? Are you tired of restaurant salads full of white, wilted lettuce and a bit of pale, pink tomato and dry cucumber?

Here are some suggestions for turning a dull meal into something exciting. Besides just being a side dish or an entree, a salad can be a meal.

Warm weather is the time to increase salad intake. In the summer, everything's in season, and raw foods should make up most of the diet. Vitamins and energy are obtained from the sun, so fewer heavy foods, which produce warmth in the body in the winter, are needed in the summer. But, even in winter one needs the many vitamins found in salads. In summer, sprouts are not really needed; but in winter, with so few vitamin-rich vegetables to be found, they are a necessity. In winter, raw food intake should be about 50% or less of a person's entire food intake. In summer, raw food intake should be about 50% to 75%.

Salads are low in calories and great as meals or appetizers. Salad comes from the Roman word sal, meaning salt, which is what salad greens were originally dipped in as a kind of salad dressing.

Here are some special tips on salad storage and preparation. Follow them closely and the salad is sure to be fresh, healthful, attractive, and delicious.

About Vegetable Salads

1. Use no more than five to six different types of vegetables in each salad. Every different food takes different time and enzymes to digest. The less variety, the more body energy is saved and the quicker the digestion. Different types of lettuce count as one kind of vegetable; spinach is another vegetable and so on.

2. Choose lettuce and other greens for their heavy weight and bright color. Vegetables should be bright, crisp, and fresh. Avoid rust spots and brown edges. Even though they are not harmful, they may mean the greens are a bit old, and they make the salad less appealing.

3. The darker the greens, the more vitamins. Head lettuce or iceberg is pale, about 90% water, and very hard to digest. For a variety of flavors, and to avoid either a dull, bland lettuce salad or too strong or bitter-flavored a green salad, mix head or leaf lettuce at least half and half with spinach, a darker lettuce, or other greens.

4. Do not leave vegetables and greens soaking in water, for vitamins will be washed away. Rinse them in a colander and use a good scrub brush on hard vegetables like carrots, celery, and potatoes.

5. Store vegetables in plastic bags in the crisper section of your refrigerator or some other very cool place to preserve freshness. Do not store them wet. Wetness will make the vegetables turn brown and spoil. Keep vegetables dry. Never store produce in a brown paper bag as the paper absorbs the moisture of the produce and dries or wilts it.

6. For crisp salad greens you can wash greens an hour or less before preparing a salad. Put them in a plastic bag or container with a small bag of ice on top and refrigerate until needed. Keep salad leaves whole until it is time to prepare the salad. Before using the greens in a salad, use a salad spinner or dry them by shaking or using paper towels or a clean dish towel to absorb the excess water.

7. Tear your salad leaves rather than cutting them. It makes a more attractive salad and the leaves will not wilt or discolor as quickly.

8. Make sure to prepare salads as close to mealtime as possible. Once torn, cut, and sliced, salad starts to decay and wilt. The sooner it is eaten, the more vitamins are saved. If you have your own garden, it is best to pick your salad just before you prepare it.

9. Be careful not to drown the salad in oil or dressing. Too much dressing makes the salad wilt, so just coat it lightly by tossing. Use about one tablespoon or less of oil dressings per cup of salad or one-quarter cup per quart of salad. Use slightly more if creamy dressing is used.

10. Balance your salad. The majority of it, three-quarters or more, should be light, leafy, and easy to chew. A few root or flower vegetables, grated or chopped fine, should make up the heavier and harder-to-chew portion of the salad.

11. Whenever possible, buy or grow organic vegetables. While you may have to watch for bugs, you will also be getting food bursting with vitamins and flavor, unlike the dull taste of some store-bought produce.

12. Cut vegetables like carrots, beans, and celery on a slant. This is a French method of releasing more flavor in the food. It also makes it easier to chew and is more appealing to the eye.

13. If you have your own garden, try not to wash the vegetables at all or, if necessary, very little. Vitamins and minerals from the sun and air are lying on the leaves or skins and can easily be washed away. Unless the food is dirty or buggy, just gently brush it off, then eat or put in salads.

14. Eat a salad before your main meal (if a vegetarian meal) to help stimulate digestive enzymes. Your main meal will be digested better, and you will find you eat less of the heavier foods. Also, raw foods taste better eaten before the cooked foods.

15. Salads can be a meal or an appetizer. As a meal a salad should include some type of protein food like cheese, nuts or seeds, eggs, or yogurt. Eat two or three cups of salad with a dairy product, a whole grain bread, and/or possibly some nuts or seeds. As an appetizer, serve one-half to two cups of salad before the rest of the meal.

16. Revive wilted celery, lettuce, broccoli, or cabbage as you would flowers. Recut a thin slice off the stalks or the core bottom and place in warm water for one to four

hours until it revives. To help preserve freshness, do not remove the entire core or base of a vegetable until it is ready to be used in cooking or salads.

17. The vitamins as well as the poisons from chemical sprays and fertilizers concentrate around the seeds and in the skins of foods, so avoid eating these parts unless foods are organic or you use a natural soak to remove outer sprays from vegetables, available at some natural food stores. Even the biodegradable cleaners can remove only a small part of the sprays. For easy, natural vegetable soaks, use two to three tablespoons apple cider vinegar or two to three teaspoons baking soda in a sink full of water. Rinse carefully after soaking 15 to 20 minutes. Whenever possible, eat the skins of carrots, potatoes, and unwaxed cucumbers for the vitamins and flavor they contain.

18. Eat three vegetables that grow above the ground for every one that grows below the ground.

19. Generally, fruits and vegetables should not be had at the same meal. However, occasionally some combinations are acceptable: Apples mix well with leafy green vegetables. On occasion, raisins may be eaten with carrots.

20. Citrus fruits are always a good combination with vegetables. Citrus adds flavor and aids in digesting vegetables. Citrus juice may also be used instead of dressing. Serve a lemon wedge alongside the salad bowl. A wedge of lemon squeezed on a salad is delicious. Also, citrus juice may be added before mealtime to help preserve a salad and keep it from turning brown. Oranges are the only exception. Eat them preferably with other fruit, rather than vegetables.

21. Always include some variety of color in salads along with greens to give the salad more eye appeal and a wider variety of nutrients. Include one or more of the following: tomatoes, radishes, beets, red cabbage, radicchio, carrots, cauliflower, small yellow summer squash, red onions, mushrooms, yellow wax beans, corn, or colorful edible wildflower heads.

22. Some greens are slightly bitter but high in vitamins and should be used only a little at a time. These greens are endive, escarole, chicory, parsley, and celery leaves. Spinach and watercress are slightly strong tasting and can be used in larger quantities, depending on your own personal taste.

Vegetable Salad Possibilities

Mix and match! Here is a list of many of the different types of produce that can be included in salads. There are endless possibilities, but do not use more than five or six items per salad. Try grated raw beets, which are delicious even to those who do not like cooked beets. Be careful not to stain your clothing with its dark juice.

Also, try zucchini sliced in your salad instead of cucumbers. Soak sunflower or sesame seeds in a little water for 15 minutes before adding them to a salad so they are more digestible. Do not be afraid to experiment!

Slice thin or grate: Carrots, radishes, raw turnips or parsnips, raw potatoes (new, small potatoes are best), raw beets, cheeses

Tear: Lettuce (all kinds): romaine, bibb, head, leaf, red, Boston; spinach; cabbage (all kinds): head, Chinese, Savoy, red; endive or escarole; lemon sorrel; watercress; dandelion greens (small and young); wild greens (consult nature books); kale, exotic greens, radicchio

Slice: Tomatoes, mushrooms, green peppers, sweet red peppers, yellow, orange or purple peppers, avocados, cucumbers, zucchini (small ones only), green or wax beans, summer yellow squash (small ones only), corn (cut off the cob), hard boiled eggs, lemons (sections cubed)

Chop: Celery, broccoli, cauliflower, nuts, parsley

Dice: Green onions, leeks, garlic, chives, red or white onions, shallots

Add: Sprouts (all kinds): alfalfa, mung, sunflower, lentil; pitted olives (can slice); hulled sesame or sunflower seeds; wheat germ; fresh peas; chick peas, kidney, lima, or other beans (cooked and chilled)

Some of the More Popular Wild Greens and Flowers for Salads:

Please be sure of what you are picking and eating. Many wild plants are poisonous. Never pick these from a lawn, by the side of the road, or anywhere pesticides may have been sprayed or chemical fertilizers used.

> Lambs quarters
> Dandelion leaves (small, before the plant blooms)
> Wild violets (just the blue or purple bloom—high in vitamin C)
> Wild pea vetches (pods or blooms)
> Wild clover heads
> Mint leaves
> Wild strawberry leaves (before plant blooms—high in vitamin C)
> Plantain leaves
> Mustard leaves
> Fiddleheads (special ferns)
> Sorrels
> Watercress
> Wild rose petals
> Wild rose hips (remove inside seeds)

Vegetable Salad Recipes

(1 part equals 1 or more cups)

 Simple Tossed Salad

> **2 parts romaine lettuce, torn**
> **2 parts other lettuce or spinach, torn**
> **Tomatoes wedges**
> **Optional: green peppers or cucumbers – chopped or sliced**

Toss the salad greens and any extra vegetables and place tomato wedges on top. Serve with any dressing or a lemon wedge.

 Chef's Salad

> **3 parts crisphead or romaine lettuce**
> **1 part bibb, Boston or leaf lettuce**
> **$1/_2$ cucumber, sliced**
> **Tomatoes, wedges or slices**
> **Cheddar cheese, grated**
> **Hard-boiled eggs, chopped or sliced**

Toss everything but the tomatoes, cheese, and eggs. Place the salad in a bowl and top it with tomatoes, cheese, and egg pieces. Serve with any dressing.

 # Crisphead Carrot Salad

> *2 – 3 parts crisphead or romaine lettuce, torn*
> *1 – 2 parts leaf or red lettuce, torn*
> *1 – 2 carrots, grated fine*
> *$1/2$ cucumber, peeled and sliced*
> *1 green pepper, cut in chunks or strips*
> *Optional: 1 ear of corn, slice corn off the cob*
> *Optional: 1 – 2 green onions, chopped*

Mix the chopped and torn ingredients. Use the suggested amounts or use your own proportions. Top it all with a favorite vegetable dressing.

 # Crisphead Cabbage Combo

> *2 parts crisphead lettuce or romaine lettuce, torn*
> *1 part leaf lettuce or red lettuce, torn*
> *1 part red cabbage, chopped fine or grated*
> *4 stalks celery, chopped*
> *2 – 3 small tomatoes chopped in wedges*
> *Optional: 1 – 2 turnips or new potatoes, grated fine*

Toss the salad and use any dressing.

 # Of Radishes & Things

> *3 parts spinach, romaine or leaf lettuce, torn*
> *1 part zucchini or peeled kohlrabi, grated*
> *8 – 10 radishes, sliced into thin rounds*
> *$1/2$ – 1 cucumber, chopped*
> *Optional: $1/2$ cup lentils or alfalfa sprouts*

Mix and serve with your favorite dressing.

♥ Beet Treat Salad

> *2 – 3 parts leaf or romaine lettuce*
> *1 – 2 parts sprouts or spinach*
> *2 – 4 small beets, grated fine*
> *2 green peppers, chopped or sliced*
> *Optional: 2 – 4 small tomatoes, chopped or sliced*
> *Optional: $^1/_2$ zucchini, sliced in rounds or chopped*

Toss everything together or toss everything but the beets and add them on top of each serving of salad. Serve with any dressing. Creamy dressings are especially tasty with this salad.

♥ Wild Green Salad

> *2 – 3 parts wild greens (and edible flowers)**
> *1 – 2 parts bibb, Boston, red, or leaf lettuce*
> *1 – 2 ounces sunflower seeds, chopped nuts, or tender chick peas*
> *$^1/_2$ – 1 cup chopped green beans, peas, or corn*
> *Optional: 2 – 4 small tomatoes, chopped*
> *Optional: 1 – 2 small green onions or a handful of chives, chopped*

Serve with an oil-based salad dressing, using the same variations suggested in the sprout recipe, Sprouts to Shout About. * Use store bought exotic greens, if wild greens are unavailable.

Super Sprout Salad

> **3 parts alfalfa sprouts**
> **1 part other sprouts**
> **1 avocado, sliced or chopped**
> **2 – 4 small tomatoes chopped in small wedges**
> **4 – 6 leaves romaine lettuce or spinach, torn in small pieces**
> **$^1/_2$ cup cauliflower or broccoli flowerettes, small pieces**

Mix all ingredients and serve with yogurt and/or dressing.

 Sprouts to Shout About

> **2 – 3 parts mixed sprouts, any kinds**
> **1 – 2 parts spinach or exotic greens, torn**
> **1 – 2 small zucchini, sliced**
> **6 – 10 mushrooms, sliced thin**
> **Bread crumbs or croutons**

An oil-based salad dressing is best for this salad. Extra fresh herbs like parsley and basil can be added to the salad. Add dressing to the salad and toss until coated, then add herbs and toss again. Then chill the salad for 10-20 minutes before serving. Fresh or toasted bread crumbs can be sprinkled on top just before serving.

♥ Rice Salad

A salad or a meal in minutes. Add one cup of cold precooked rice to three or four cups of your favorite salad. Add salad dressing and enjoy. Nuts, seeds, or cheese can be added to the salad to make it a complete protein. Variation: Use millet or any other whole grain instead of rice.

Vegetable-Cheese Salad

Top your favorite salad with one to two cups yogurt or cottage cheese or $^1/_2 - 1$ cup grated cheddar or other cheese or mix one of these cheeses into the salad.

Greek Salad #1

2 parts romaine or leaf lettuce
2 parts spinach
$^1/_2 - 1$ cup pitted black olives, sliced in half
2 – 4 ounces feta cheese (soft goat or sheep milk cheese), crumbled
Optional: 2 green onions, chopped
Optional: 6 – 8 mushrooms, sliced thin

Greek Salad #2

1 green bell pepper, chopped
$^1/_2 - 1$ small cucumber, sliced and quartered
1 – 2 medium tomatoes, chopped
$^1/_2$ cup black olives, whole Greek variety or pitted
Optional: $^1/_2 - 1$ small red onion, chopped small
Optional: 2 – 4 ounces feta cheese, crumbled

Use an oil-and-vinegar-based dressing. Can be served in or with pita bread. Great served with plain yogurt or cucumber yogurt.

♥ Italian Salad

1 head Finocchio (buy this at an Italian store), chopped*
1 small bunch of spinach or romaine, torn, or
1/2 romaine lettuce, torn
1 bunch spinach or leaf lettuce, torn
(Add 1/4 tsp crushed anise seeds to 2 cups oil-based dressing
*   for this salad.)*
Plus:
2 – 4 tomatoes, wedges
1 small cucumber or zucchini, chopped
Optional: 3 – 4 stalks celery, chopped

Mix the salad and toss it with a vinegar-and-oil-based dressing. Rub the salad bowl with a piece of sliced garlic or add finely chopped garlic to the salad dressing.

Note: Finocchio is an anise-flavored, bulb-like vegetable or herb. It is best when eaten raw but the green tops can be cooked in soups and stews. Also called Fennel or Sweet-Anise. *Use lettuce if unavailable.

♥ Simple Cole Slaw

1/2 head white cabbage, grated
2 small or medium carrots, grated fine
Mayonnaise
Sea Salt to taste
1/4 – 1/2 tsp celery seed
Few dashes cayenne
Optional: 4 – 6 radishes, grated

Mix the chopped vegetables with mayonnaise and salt to taste. Add herbs plus any extra herbs if needed. Variations: Use savory or red cabbage instead of white cabbage or, top the cole slaw with a sprinkle of ground walnuts or sunflower seeds.

Tomato Salad Appetizer

1 medium or large tomato per person
Cottage cheese or mashed Tofu Cutlets à la Jim or Hummus
Cherry tomatoes or small radishes
Leaf lettuce
Creamy dressing

Place each tomato on a bed of lettuce, stem end up. Core and cut the tomato into eighths, cutting only $^3/_4$ the way down on each tomato. Scoop out a tablespoon or two of pulp from inside each tomato. Fill each tomato with cottage cheese or tofu and top each one with one radish or cherry tomato. Top it all with any favorite creamy dressing and serve.

 # Avocado-Tomato Boats

$^1/_2$ medium avocado per person, cut lengthwise
1 – 2 tomatoes, chopped
$^1/_2$ – 1 cucumber, chopped
$^1/_4$ cup chives or 1 – 2 green onions, chopped
Yogurt
Lettuce

Fill each avocado half with chopped cucumbers, tomatoes, and chives (or onion) mixed with Oil and Herb Dressing (See Chapter 22 – Sauces, Spreads, and Dressings). Top each avocado boat with yogurt (plain) and place it on a bed of lettuce. Variation: Instead of using dressing on the vegetables in the boat, marinate the vegetables before placing them in the boat. (See following recipe.)

Avocado Salad

> *8 – 10 leaves or romaine or red lettuce, torn*
> *2 avocados, chopped into big pieces*
> *2 medium tomatoes, chopped (or ¹/₂ pt. cherry tomatoes – cut in half)*
> *1 cucumber, chopped*

Toss salad gently and serve with any dressing. Creamy dressings are especially good with this salad. Serve this salad immediately as avocados can spoil easily, especially in hot weather.

 Perfect Potato Salad

> *4 cups chopped, unpeeled potatoes (steamed until tender)*
> *2 – 4 hard-boiled eggs, sliced or chopped (eggs are optional)*
> *2 – 4 green onions or handful of chives, chopped fine*
> *¹/₂ cup mayonnaise (regular or low-fat)*
> *¹/₂ tsp paprika*
> *Sea salt or vegetable sea salt to taste*
> *Several dashes of cayenne if needed*
> *Optional: ¹/₂ tsp celery seed*

Marinade:
> *¹/₂ cup oil or water or mixture*
> *3 Tbsp apple cider vinegar or 2 – 3 Tbsp lemon juice*
> *¹/₄ tsp each parsley, basil, and salt*
> *Several dashes sea kelp and cayenne*
> *Optional: 1 whole clove garlic (remove before serving)*

Marinate the potatoes in the marinade for two to four hours (or overnight) in the refrigerator, stirring every half hour or more often. Then drain off excess liquid if any and mix the potatoes with all the other ingredients. Chill thoroughly for one hour or more before serving.

♥ Marinated Vegetables

1 – 2 cups vegetables (mushrooms, cucumbers, green beans, broccoli,
*   cauliflower, tomatoes, or mixed vegetables), chopped or sliced*
1/2 cup natural oil
2 Tbsp apple cider vinegar or 1 Tbsp lemon juice
$^1/_4$ – $^1/_2$ tsp sea salt or 1 – 2 tsp tamari soy sauce
$^1/_4$ tsp each oregano, basil, and parsley
Few dashes each of sea kelp and cayenne
Optional: 1 green onion or $^1/_4$ cup chives, chopped

Beat all the ingredients together except the vegetables. Soak the chopped or
sliced vegetables and onions in the oil-and-vinegar mixture and toss it gently. Let
the vegetables soak in the mixture for one to two hours or more in the refrigerator, tossing occasionally until flavors mingle. Then drain the vegetables and let
them sit at room temperature for five to eight minutes before serving. This way
the flavors will be more distinct. Be sure to use apple cider vinegar!

♥ Easy Three-Bean Salad

1 pound (or 500ml) can cooked chick peas
1 pound (or 500ml) can cooked kidney beans
2 cups fresh green beans, chopped or fresh green limas
1 – 2 cups celery, chopped fine
4 – 5 green onions, chopped, or 1 cup chopped chives
Italian dressing (oil-based and vinegar)
Optional: 1 – 2 garlic cloves, crushed

Heat the beans and cook for five to ten minutes. Drain and chill the beans. Mix
the beans and remaining ingredients with the oil and vinegar dressing and refrigerate for four to six hours or overnight. Toss and stir every hour or so, or three
to four times before serving. Keeps four to six days refrigerated.

Marinated Three-Bean Salad Supreme

(Serves 6 – 8)

Prepare 6 – 8 hours in advance or overnight.

2 cups cooked kidney beans (about $^3/_4$ cup dry)
2 cups cooked chick peas (about $^3/_4$ cup dry)
2 cups chopped green beans or fresh green lima beans, raw
$^1/_2$ cup natural oil
6 Tbsp apple cider vinegar
$^1/_4$ – $^1/_3$ cup fresh chopped parsley (or 3 – 4 tsp dried)
1 tsp sea salt or to taste
1 tsp basil
$^1/_4$ tsp each sea kelp, oregano, and paprika
$^1/_{16}$ – $^1/_8$ tsp cayenne red pepper
1 bunch of green onions, chopped fine
4 cloves garlic, minced or pressed

Use dry, cooked or canned and rinsed beans. Dried beans will have a nicer flavor and more nutrients. Beat all the ingredients together except for the beans. Add the tender, precooked, cold beans to the marinade and mix thoroughly. Stir every 12 – 15 minutes for an hour at room temperature, unless it is a hot day, then keep in a cool place and stir three times over one half hour and then refrigerate. Stir four to eight times over a period of six to eight hours. Keeps five to seven days refrigerated. Remove marinade from fridge and cool to room temperature.

Marinated Four-Bean Salad Supreme

(Serves 6 – 8)
Prepare 6 – 8 hours in advance or overnight.

> 2 cups cooked pinto beans (about $3/4$ cup dry)
> 2 cups cooked kidney beans (about $3/4$ cup dry)
> 2 cups cooked chick peas (about $3/4$ cup dry)
> 2 cups chopped green beans or fresh green lima beans, raw
> $2/3$ cup natural oil
> 7 – 8 Tbsp apple cider vinegar
> $1/3$ – $1/2$ cup fresh chopped parsley (or 4 tsp dried)
> 1 $1/4$ tsp sea salt or to taste
> 1 $1/4$ tsp basil
> $1/2$ tsp each oregano and paprika
> $1/4$ tsp sea kelp
> $1/16$ – $1/8$ tsp cayenne red pepper
> 1 large bunch of green onions, chopped fine
> 5 cloves garlic, minced or pressed

Prepare same as the Three-Bean Salad.

Chapter 17

Fruits &
Fruit Salads

About Fruit Salads

1. For an appetizer or fruit cocktail, serve about one-half to one cup of fruit salad, using approximately one to two fruits per person. For a meal, serve two to three cups per person, about five to six fruits per person.

2. Store unripe fruit in a bowl on a counter out of direct sunlight until ripe. Then refrigerate, especially peaches, pears, apricots, and pineapples. Never keep bananas in the refrigerator. Always store them at room temperature or in a slightly cool place.

3. Unless fruits will be eaten within a day or two, do not wash them before storing. They bruise very easily and some types spoil quickly when stored wet. With berries especially, as well as other fruits, wash them before stemming to prevent bruises and also the washing away of valuable vitamins.

4. Chill fruits before peeling or cutting for a fruit salad, as the vitamins will be more easily preserved when chilled and the fruits are more easily cut.

5. Ripe fruits have more vitamins and flavor. Eat soft (not mushy) rather than crunchy fruits (except apples).

6. Leave the skins on apples, pears, peaches, and most other fruits for more vitamins and flavor especially if the fruit is organic. Discard skins from heavily sprayed fruits.

7. To preserve the color and flavor of cut fruits and to prevent fruits from turning brown and spoiling quickly, toss them very lightly and coat them with lemon juice or citrus juice, and honey if desired.

8. In order to appreciate the flavors and help stimulate digestion, serve fresh fruit salads before a meal. Served after a meal, raw fruits can contribute to indigestion and stomach upset. See Food Combining section. Serve stewed or cooked fruit with a meal or at the end of a meal or as a dessert.

9. Dried fruits have a high natural sugar content. Do not eat too many if you have a tendency to react to sugar and other sweets. If eaten before bedtime, the sugar energy may keep you awake. Eat raw dried fruits before a meal or in-between meals. Eat cooked dried fruit with a meal or as a dessert.

10. To make it easier for the body to assimilate vitamins and make digestion easier, eat whole fruits at room temperature. It takes extra body energy to digest chilled foods.

11. Raw citrus fruits and juices stimulate digestion if taken a half hour or one hour before a meal. They also help the body digest and eliminate food easily as they are full of live enzymes. If taken with starches and whole grains, they become a weight to the system. Digestion becomes more difficult and the usable calorie intake of the starches is increased. Therefore, do not have citrus fruits or juices with your meals, especially if you are serving a whole grain food. Citrus fruits including oranges, tangerines, lemons, limes, grapefruit, and tree citrons (pale yellow, thick-skinned fruits resembling a lemon, used in fruitcakes).

12. Generally fruits and vegetables should not be had at the same meal. A few vegetables are sometimes all right to eat with fruits at the same meal. Lettuce, celery, or peppers in small amounts may sometimes be eaten at the same meal with fruits. Citrus or acid fruits help to digest vegetable salads and help digest meat or dairy foods, whether raw or cooked. Avocado is a fruit but may be eaten with fruits or vegetables as it is neutral when digesting. Other exceptions are given in the Food Combining section, in Chapter 4 – Meal Planning.

Fruit Salad Possibilities

Since almost everyone is familiar with how to chop, slice, or add fruits to a salad, the listing here is by types of fruits rather than by methods of preparation. As with vegetables, be sure not to mix too many different varieties of fruits; about five to six different kinds is adequate. For detailed explanations of the more exotic fruits and how to cut them, check the Guide to Unusual Fruits. For example, be careful not to eat papaya seeds, but always eat kiwi seeds. Fruit salads are great as snacks, appetizers, or summertime meals. When cooked, they make excellent desserts or toppings for ice creams. Experiment and enjoy!

Basic Fruits: Apples, peaches, pears, apricots, nectarines, plums, kiwis, cherries, strawberries, blueberries, raspberries, blackberries, Saskatoons (service berries), grapes (best eaten alone, but they can be used in small quantities)

Acid Fruits: Grapefruits, pineapples, lemons, cranberries, gooseberries, currants, huckleberries, rhubarb (must be cooked)

Exotic or Tropical Fruits: Bananas, mangoes, papayas, tangerines, oranges, lychee nuts, persimmons, pomegranates and others

Melons: Cantaloupes, watermelons, honeydews, muskmelons, casabas, crenshaws, honey rocks, Persian melons

Dried Fruits: Raisins, dates, figs, prunes, coconut (shredded or cut small), peaches, pears, apricots

Fruit Salad Recipes

Some of these recipes do not follow food combining principles, so these salads are not for everyday. But, healthy individuals may skip food combining rules on occasion. (Soak nuts and seeds for 15 minutes in water to soften before using in recipes.)

 # *Melon Salad*

> *Cantaloupe (orange)*
> *Honeydew (green)*
> *Watermelon (red)*

Make melon balls out of equal amounts of the above three melons. For a large group of people the melon can be served in a scooped-out half of watermelon. For two to four people it can be served in a scooped-out half of a melon. Toss salad in its own juice or in lemon or orange juice and honey to keep it fresh and sweet.

 # Avocado Heaven

¹/₂ avocado per person
Strawberries or blueberries
Banana slices
Raw walnuts, pecans, or cashews, chopped
Grated coconut
Optional: yogurt, honey, or whipped cream

Cut each avocado in half and remove the pit. Fill each half with mixed fruit and chopped nuts. Top each avocado-fruit cup with plain or sweetened yogurt, honey, or whipped cream. Then sprinkle on the coconut. Place each avocado cup on a small plate in a bed of bright leaf lettuce and serve it as an appetizer. Variation: Use papayas instead of avocados.

 # Citrus Salad

4 oranges or tangerines
2 grapefruit
Optional: 1 cup chopped pineapple

Remove the seeds and section and peel each part of the oranges, tangerines and grapefruit. Toss the salad with one to two tablespoons of honey and serve.

Summer Fruit Salad

Melon, any kind(s)
1 – 2 types of berries (strawberries, blueberries, blackberries,
*   raspberries, Saskatoons)*
Plums, peaches, or pears
Pineapple chunks
Grated coconut
Optional: apples and bananas

Chop and mix all ingredients except the coconut, and drain the excess juice. Use the juice later in fruit drinks or in other recipes. Mix the coconut with the fruit salad along with lemon or orange juice and honey and serve.

Winter Fruit Salad

Apples
Bananas or Kiwis
Oranges
Raisins or chopped dates
Grated coconut
Chopped nuts
Optional: frozen or canned fruit from summer (can be strawberries,
*   blueberries, peaches, or pineapples)*

Defrost frozen fruits if any are to be used. Remove all cores, seeds, and peels and chop all ingredients into bite-size pieces. Mix them with Sweet Citrus Dressing (see Chapter 22 – Sauces, Spreads, & Dressings) and serve immediately.

♥ Exotic Pineapple-Fruit Salad

1 pineapple, whole
1 mango, peeled and pitted
1 papaya, peeled and seeded
1 avocado, peeled and pitted
1 – 2 kiwis, peeled only
1 cup blueberries or blackberries or seeded, sliced black grapes
Grated coconut

Cut the pineapple in half vertically. Leave the top stem on the fruit and scoop out the insides. Chop the pineapple and other fruit and mix all ingredients in a large bowl. Save most of the juice and leave it with the fruit salad. Mix the juice and fruit with honey to taste. Place the salad in the scooped-out pineapple halves and sprinkle it with coconut. The pineapple can be garnished with clean, fresh flowers or with fresh, whole mint leaves.

Iced Cantaloupe Surprise

(Serves 2)

1 cantaloupe
2 cups strawberries or raspberries or blueberries
2 bananas
2 peaches or 1 mango
Ice cream, sherbet, or dairy-free ice cream

Scoop out the inside of the cantaloupe. Make melon balls and mix them with the rest of the chopped fruit. Sweet Citrus Dressing may be used to keep it fresh. Place the fruit salad in the scooped-out cantaloupe and top it with one or two scoops of sherbet or ice cream. A refreshing and delicious summer treat or small meal. Nuts may be sprinkled on top.

Avocado Delight

1/2 avocado per person
Raisins
Whole almonds or cashews
Mixed chopped nuts and seeds
Yogurt, plain or honey-sweetened

Cut each avocado in half and remove the pit. Fill each half with almonds, mixed nuts and raisins. Top it with a tablespoon or two of yogurt. Place each half on a small plate on a bed of lettuce. Variation: Use cottage cheese or flavored tofu instead of yogurt. Put nuts and raisins on top of the yogurt or other filling. Mix shredded coconut with the nuts and seeds.

Green Salad

1 honeydew melon
1 – 2 cups green grapes (seed if necessary)
2 kiwis, peeled
1 avocado

Mix chopped or balled melon with grapes and cut kiwis and avocado. Toss with Sweet Citrus Dressing to keep it fresh. Serve chilled.

Orange Salad

1 cantaloupe
2 peaches
2 oranges, sectioned and peeled
1 papaya or mango

Chop and mix all ingredients. Toss with Citrus Dressing.

 **Yellow Salad**

> *1 – 2 cups pineapple*
> *2 – 4 bananas*
> *2 – 4 pears and/or 2 – 3 golden delicious apples*

Chop all fruit and mix it together with a little pineapple juice and honey. Optional: Sprinkle coconut on top.

 Red Salad

> *2 – 3 cups watermelon (seeded)*
> *2 cups strawberries, raspberries, sweet cherries, or Saskatoons*
> *2 – 3 red delicious apples*

Chop and mix ingredients. Drain off excess fruit juices. Mix salad with a Sweet Citrus Dressing and serve.

Chapter 18

Whole Grains

Whole Grains

The benefits of eating whole grains rather than partially refined grains are discussed in Chapter 1 – Why Change Your Eating Habits and the Glossary of Natural Foods. This chapter will discuss the cooking methods.

The whole grains are divided into two categories: cereal grains and main dish grains. Whole grains may be served at the same meal with legumes, nuts and seeds, or dairy products. Potatoes may be substituted sometimes for whole grains, about two to three times a week or less.

Special Tips about Grains

1. Grains are generally cooked in two cups of water or more per one cup of grain.
2. Cook grains until they are no longer crunchy but not soggy or mushy. Undercooked grains are difficult to digest.
3. See the glossary for characteristics and uses of each individual grain.
4. Very few whole grains need to be soaked before cooking. These include whole oats, rye, triticale, spelt, kamut, and wheat berries. Sometimes, only rarely, does wild rice require presoaking.
5. Raw, rolled, flaked, or crushed grains must be soaked before eating. Toasted grains may be eaten as they are or with milk, milk substitute, or fruit juice that has been heated to kill live enzymes. (See Food Combining section)
6. Before cooking, check grains for dirt balls, gravel, husks, and other foreign particles by spreading them out thinly and fingering through them.
7. Rice is usually the only grain that needs prewashing, but you may wash any grain if you feel it needs it.

8. It makes little difference if you start cooking a grain in cool or warm water. The exception is ground cereals. These get lumpy when put in hot water unless mixed carefully with a wire whisk.

9. To prevent grains from boiling over and to distribute heat evenly, water and grains together should never cover more than three-fourths of the cooking pot.

10. To make digestion easier, do not add salt to grains until the last 10 – 15 minutes of cooking.

11. Any grain in whole form (does not include rolled or broken whole grains) will never burn during its first cooking process as long as it is cooked on low heat, there is enough water, and the grain does not become overcooked to the point where it falls apart. (It usually takes $1\frac{1}{4}$ hours or more for grains to fall apart and burn.)

12. Never stir grains while cooking or they will stick or burn.

13. When reheating whole grains (second cooking), add a little extra water, about one-quarter to one-half cup per cup of grain, and simmer over a low heat so it will not burn. Do not stir.

14. One cup of dry whole grain or cereal makes about four servings.

15. The main dish grains can almost always be substituted one for the other in different recipes, except wild rice. Grains are similar but may have slight taste differences.

16. Whole grains are one of the main staples of the natural food diet. They should be eaten almost every day, even more often than potatoes. Each week you should have about three to four servings of grains for every one serving of potatoes.

Preparation of Cereal Grains
Raw Cereals
Organic Rolled Oats: These are smaller and rounder than regular, natural rolled oats and must be soaked for several hours or overnight before eating. Use $1\frac{1}{2}$ cups water per one cup of oats. These are usually found only in natural food stores and are almost always labeled "organic." After soaking the oats, drain off excess water and serve with sweetening, milk, and/or cooked fruit.

Natural Rolled Oats (Regular, Old-Fashioned, or Quick Oats): Soak one cup oats in one cup of warm water for 10 – 15 minutes. Add flavorings and/or cooked fruit and serve.

Flaked Whole Grain Cereals: Flaked oats, rye, wheat, rice, and millet may be purchased but are not always available. Prepare and serve the same as soaked organic rolled oats or toast them in the oven the same as granola and serve with milk and flavorings.

Bulgur Wheat: This cracked, parched wheat need not be cooked. Simply soak it in warm water, about $1\frac{1}{2}$ cups of water to one cup grain, and let it sit one to two hours until tender. Then drain off excess water and serve with honey, milk, and/or other flavorings or cooked fruit.

Puffed Whole Grain Cereals: These cereals include puffed oats, corn, rice, millet, wheat, and others. They are usually unsweetened. Serve them as they are with milk and sweetening as desired.

Muesli and Other Raw Whole Grain Cereals: These cereals are usually made with rolled, cracked, or flaked whole grains, ground or chopped nuts and seeds, and shredded coconut, raisins, or other dried fruits. If the cereal is organic or contains very tough, fibrous grains, prepare it the same way as organic oats. If the cereal is natural and less fibrous, prepare the same way as natural oats. Only individuals with extremely good digestion should eat raw muesli or other raw, whole grain cereals.

Granola and Other Toasted Grain Cereals: Made with toasted rolled oats, nuts and seeds, dried fruit, and sweetening. Serve with milk or simmered fruit juice or eat right out of the package. Chew well.

Cooked Cereals

Amaranth: Although amaranth grain can be cooked as a breakfast cereal, it is not that tasty. It is better to mix it with another grain or use the flour in recipes. The puffed amaranth cereal is available in some health food stores although it is not nearly as nutritious as the hot whole grain would be. Notice that it is often added to boxed cereals rather than sold by itself as a cereal. If desired, cook it in two times as much water for a rice-like texture, and $2\frac{1}{2}$ – 3 times as much water for cereal or to prepare it for bread or other recipes. Cook until tender, about 18 – 20 minutes. When cooked for shorter periods with less water, amaranth is not easily digested by most individuals.

Organic Oatmeal: Use two cups water per one cup organic rolled oats. Bring the water to a boil, then turn down heat and add oats. Stir oats constantly and cook for 10 minutes or until oats are easy to chew. Then turn off heat and cover oatmeal and let it sit 10 – 15 minutes before serving. Add flavorings or fruit as desired.

Natural Oatmeal (Regular or Old-Fashioned): Use $1\frac{1}{2}$ to two cups water per one cup natural rolled oats. Bring water to a boil then add oats. Stir for one minute over heat, then cover oatmeal, turn off heat, and let it sit for 10 – 15 minutes before serving. Add flavorings.

Cornmeal: Use about two to three cups water per one cup meal. The coarser the meal, the more water is needed and the longer the cooking time. Start water and meal cooking together in cool or lukewarm water and stir together on a medium heat. Use a wire whisk to make sure the meal and water are well mixed together to avoid lumpy cereal. After the first minute or two, the cereal must be stirred constantly for 10 minutes or more until it is no longer grainy. Add extra water if needed. It should always have a sweetener like honey added to it. Raisins, dates, or coconut and cinnamon cooked into the cereal are very delicious. Salt is optional. Store cornmeal used for cereal in a cool place or in the freezer, but never refrigerate it or it will have a damp, musty flavor.

Millet (Cereal): Use about three to four cups of water per one cup millet. More water is used for the cereal than for the main dish millet. Bring water and millet to a boil. Dates can be added now if desired. Use about one-quarter to one-half cup dates per one cup millet. Then turn down heat to a low bubble, keep pot covered, and cook about 50 to 70 minutes until the millet breaks down and is very soft and mushy. Before serving, stir the cereal to mix in the dates. Serve with milk, butter, and honey if no dates are added. Salt if desired.

Quinoa: (pronounced keen-wah) Rinse thoroughly before cooking to remove the saponin which coats it. Saponin may aggravate some allergies and irritate digestion. However, quinoa properly rinsed is a mild, beneficial, easy-to-digest food good for most allergies, sensitive stomachs and ulcers, and for babies and the elderly. Rinse the grains by rubbing them together well in a pot of fresh water and discard the water. Use a strainer when draining so as not to lose the small grains. One rinsing is enough for white quinoa, but the brown should be rubbed and rinsed three to four times with fresh water each time. (The white quinoa has had most of the saponin removed by a dry rubbing process. The brown usually has not and thus requires extra washings.) Cook like the millet above but use $2\frac{1}{2}$ – $3\frac{1}{2}$ cups water per one cup quinoa. The white cooks in 20 – 30 minutes and the brown cooks in 8 – 18 minutes.

Sweet Brown Rice: Cook and serve like millet cereal above except use two to three cups water per one cup rice and cook about 55 – 65 minutes until tender.

Teff: Bring $\frac{1}{2}$ cup teff seed and two cups of water to a boil, then turn down heat and simmer for 15 – 20 minutes or until all the water is absorbed. Like amaranth, teff is not too exciting by itself. Try cooking with raisins, currants or chopped dates, or apricots if desired. If dried fruit is not used, serve the cereal with maple syrup, honey, or another sweetener and a bit of sea salt or cinnamon. Try mixing teff with another grain.

Whole Wheat Berries, Triticale, Spelt, Kamut and Whole Oats: Cook the same as the main dish. Serve plain with salt or with butter or oil and honey, molasses, or maple syrup added.

Preparation of Main Dish Grains

Short and Long Grain Brown Rice: Put rice in a pot and fill it with water. Rub the rice together with your hands and swish it around to remove excess starches, dirt, and stray rice husks. Toss out all the water. If water was very cloudy during the first washing, repeat the process once or twice until the water is relatively clear. Then put two to three cups water per one cup rice in the pot on medium heat and bring it to a boil. Stir once, then turn down to a low bubble for 55 – 70 minutes. When rice is no longer crunchy but easy to chew, it is done. Onions, herbs, and spices (not salt) can be added during the last 15 – 20 minutes of cooking time. Keep pot fully covered while rice is cooking.

Wild Rice: This is one of the few main dish grains that will need occasional soaking in water before cooking. (Most wild rice does not need to be soaked.) If a brand is too chewy, then wash and soak one cup rice in two cups water and let it sit two hours or more. Then cook same as brown rice for about 60 minutes or more. Wild rice is often expensive and rich tasting, so it is usually mixed with brown rice. Use one part wild rice to every four to eight parts brown rice. This makes a more delicious, light-tasting, but less expensive dish. Cook the two rices separately and mix before serving, or cook wild rice for 15 – 20 minutes and then add brown rice to it and cook together for another 55 – 65 minutes. Add extra water if needed.

Natural Buckwheat and Pot Barley: Use about two cups water per one cup grain. Bring grain to a boil, then turn down heat to a low bubble. Cook onions with the grain and add herbs and salt for the last 10 minutes of cooking time. Cook grain 20 – 30 minutes or until no longer crunchy. Add extra water if needed.

Kasha (Toasted Buckwheat): Cook the same as natural buckwheat for only 15 – 25 minutes. Use slightly less water for cooking.

Millet (Main Dish): Cook the same as rice with $2\frac{1}{2}$ – 3 cups water per one cup millet. It usually does not need prewashing. Cooks in 45 – 55 minutes. Serve like rice and use interchangeably with rice in recipes calling for rice. This is the best of grains, highest in vitamins and is claimed to be the only alkaline grain. Rice is close to millet in nutrients but cannot top millet's beneficial qualities.

Quinoa: Cook the same as the cereal and use only $2\frac{1}{2}$ – 3 cups of water per cup.

Whole Wheat Berries, Triticale, Spelt, Kamut and Whole Oats: These must be soaked in $2\frac{1}{2}$ cups of water per one cup grain for several hours or overnight before cooking. Then change the water and cook for about 45 – 60 minutes. When done, they will still be slightly chewy but not crunchy. These grains can be cooked separately or together with other whole grains. Wheat berries are especially good and come in hard red or soft yellow wheat. The soft varieties cook more quickly.

Bulgur: This is a chopped, parched wheat that is already cooked. Soak for several hours in water until soft before eating or bring one cup bulgur and two cups water to a boil together, remove from heat, cover and let sit 15 minutes until expanded. Allow to cool for about 30 minutes before using in cold recipes.

Whole Rye: Soak and cook this the same as wheat and oats above but use it sparingly because it is strong and bitter. Mix it with wheat and/or oats and cook them together using only one-sixth to one-tenth part rye. Rye adds zest to simple meals but its flavor does not appeal to everyone.

Cracked Wheat: Soak one cup cracked wheat in two cups water for two to four hours and cook them for 20 minutes or so until tender and no longer crunchy. Add extra water if needed.

Cereal Recipes

 *Muesli*

> 4 cups rolled oats
> 1 cup slivered almonds or chopped walnuts
> $\frac{1}{4}$ cup sesame seeds, ground
> $\frac{1}{4}$ cup flax seeds, ground
> $\frac{1}{2}$ cup sunflower seeds, ground
> 2 – 3 tsp carob powder or 1 tsp cinnamon
> $\frac{1}{4}$ tsp sea salt

Mix all the dry ingredients together. Refrigerate or keep in a dry, cool place until needed. Prepare this cereal like natural oats or organic oats depending on the type of oats used in this recipe or soak $\frac{1}{2}$ cup cereal in $\frac{1}{2}$ – $\frac{3}{4}$ cup very hot water for 15 – 20 minutes. Then serve with honey and milk. Note: Muesli is hard to digest for many individuals. Only those with good digestion should eat this food raw.

Granola #1

> 6 cups rolled oats
> 1 cup sunflower seeds
> 1 – 2 cups chopped nuts (almonds, cashews, filberts, or walnuts)
> 1 cup raisins or currants
> $^1/_2$ cup sesame seeds or $^1/_4$ cup teff
> $^1/_2$ cup flax seeds
> $^1/_2$ cup wheat germ or extra rolled oats or rolled rye, wheat
>   or other rolled whole grain
> Optional: $^1/_2$ cup chopped dates
> 1 – 1$^1/_2$ cups honey, maple syrup or fruit concentrate
> $^1/_2$ – $^2/_3$ cup natural oil (use more oil if more sweetening is used)
> Optional: 1 – 2 Tbsp carob powder (unsweetened) or 1 – 2 tsp cinnamon

Granola #2

> 6 – 8 cups rolled oats
> 4 – 6 cups mixed nuts and seeds and dried fruits, etc.
> 1 – 1$^1/_2$ cups honey, maple syrup or fruit concentrate
> $^1/_2$ – $^2/_3$ cup natural oil
> 1 tsp sea salt

Mix all the dry ingredients together except the salt and dried fruit. Use either recipe. Mix the oil, sweetening, and salt together in a separate large bowl. Add the dry mixture to the wet and mix everything well with a large wooden spoon or with your hands. Lightly oil two flat baking or pizza pans and spread the mixture on about $^1/_2$ – $^2/_3$-inch deep. Bake them at 350°F for 12 – 18 minutes until the top layer is golden brown. Then remove from the oven and stir or turn over all the granola. Place it in the oven for four to five minutes until top is brown and then remove and stir again. Bake granola four to five more final minutes with the added dried fruit. Remove granola from the oven and put into a large bowl. The mixture will be moist, but it will dry up and harden as it cools. The dried fruit will burn if put in the oven the entire time. Let the mixture cool before storing. Break it up every 10 minutes or so or it will harden into one lump as it cools. When cool, refrigerate or keep in a cool, dry place. Good as a snack or breakfast cereal. Can be served with milk, yogurt, apple juice, or applesauce.

Ground Toppings for Cereals

Grind nuts or seeds $\frac{1}{4}$ cup at a time in a blender at high speed or use a mortar and pestle. Keep jars of ground nuts in the refrigerator for up to two to three weeks for sprinkling on any cereals or on desserts, fruit or vegetable salads, or casseroles or any recipe. Use sunflower, pumpkin, sesame, or flax seeds. Almonds, cashews, and other nuts can also be used. Ground nuts add flavor, vitamins, and minerals to all types of foods.

Breakfast Specials

 # Pancakes & Waffles

(Serves 2 – 3)

> $1\frac{1}{4} - 1\frac{1}{2}$ *cups milk or substitute*
> $\frac{3}{4}$ *cup whole wheat flour*
> $\frac{1}{4}$ *cup pastry or unbleached white flour*
> *1 large egg, beaten*
> *1 tsp arrowroot or gluten flour*
> *Several dashes of sea salt*

Beat all the ingredients together well. Pour the batter on a grill or frying pan for pancakes or in a waffle iron. Lightly oil any cooking surface. Cook both sides of the pancakes (and waffles) until lightly browned on medium heat. Serve with syrup, fruit, and milk or yogurt. Apple or rhubarb sauce is excellent with these. For high protein pancakes, substitute soy flour for two to three tablespoons of the whole wheat flour. Cashew milk is especially good if a milk substitute is used.

♥ Wheatless Pancakes & Waffles

(Serves 2 – 3)

> 1 $^1/_2$ cups milk or milk substitute
> $^3/_4$ cup oat, millet, or barley flour
> $^1/_4$ cup buckwheat flour or amaranth flour
> 1 large egg, beaten (or 1 Tbsp powdered egg replacer
>   and 3 $^1/_2$ Tbsp milk or milk substitute)
> 1 Tbsp soy flour (or other flour)
> 1 tsp arrowroot or gluten flour
> $^1/_4$ tsp baking powder
> Salt is optional.

Preparation is same as recipe for Pancakes & Waffles.

French Toast

(Serves 2)

> 6 – 8 pieces of whole wheat or other bread (may be cut in half)
> 3 large eggs, beaten
> 3 – 4 Tbsp milk, milk substitute, or water
> Dash of sea salt

Beat the salt and liquid ingredients together well. Dip the pieces of toast fully in the egg batter and then place them on a hot grill or fry pan that has been lightly oiled. Cook each side until golden brown and no longer soggy. Serve with fruit and syrup.

Syrup Blends

1. 100% real maple syrup
2. $\frac{1}{2}$ real maple syrup and $\frac{1}{2}$ honey or fruit concentrate
3. $\frac{1}{2}$ blended cooked strawberries, blueberries, or peaches and $\frac{1}{2}$ real maple syrup (or honey)
4. $\frac{1}{6}$ to $\frac{1}{4}$ part molasses or sorghum and the rest honey or maple syrup
5. $\frac{1}{2}$ cooked cut fruit or fruit salad and $\frac{1}{2}$ honey, maple syrup, or fruit concentrate
6. $\frac{1}{3}$ to $\frac{1}{2}$ part fruit jam and the rest honey, maple syrup, or fruit concentrate

Chapter 19

Legumes – Beans, Peas, Lentils, & Tofu

Dried Legumes

In this book, dried legumes are classified into four groups based on general quality and amount of protein and vitamins.

Group 1 – Beans: (have the highest qualities) fava, soy, chick peas (or garbanzos), pinto, romano, kidney, black-eyed peas (cowpeas), black and red beans, adzuki, exotic brown or beige beans

Group 2 – Lentils and Mung Beans: (above average qualities) red lentils, brown (also called gray or green) lentils, and mung beans

Group 3 – Peas: (average quality) navy or white (pea) beans, baby or regular limas, split and whole green peas, and yellow split peas, northern beans, rice beans

Group 4 – Processed Soybean Products: tofu, tempeh and TVP (texturized vegetable protein)

All legumes are good quality proteins, only some are slightly better than others. For this reason and because each type of food has different benefits and nutritional value, a variety of legumes should be eaten regularly from each of the four main groups.

Soybeans, the "Queen of Legumes," have hundreds of uses and should be eaten once or twice a week (from Group 1 or Group 4, unless allergic) because they are the highest in protein (except for exotic fava beans, the "King of Legumes") and highest in other nutrients. Soybeans are a better quality protein than meat. If allergic to soy products, use other beans from Group 1.

Substituting Legumes

Most legumes within each group can be successfully interchanged in recipes with little or no difference in consistency or flavor. Sometimes there may be a big difference in taste, so experiments should be made before family and guests are served, unless they are adventurous types.

The following can be interchanged (in equal proportions) with little or no difference in flavor or appearance. For example, soybeans may be used in chick pea recipes or chick peas used in recipes calling for soybeans.

Exchange:

Soybeans . . . . and . . . . chick peas
Pinto, romano . . . . and . . . . kidney beans
Yellow split peas . . . . and . . . . green split peas
Navy or white pea beans . . and . . . . baby or regular limas
Red lentils . . . . and . . . . green lentils (in some recipes)
Red beans . . . . and . . . . black beans (black turtle beans)
Northern beans . . . . and . . . . baby or regular limas
Red lentils . . . . and . . . . yellow split peas
Pinto beans . . . . and . . . . adzuki beans

Note: All other beans may be interchanged, but flavor and appearance of the dishes may vary.

Main Dish Uses for Dried Legumes

For Meat Substitute Dishes: Group 1 Beans
For Chilis and Stews: Pinto, kidney, romano and some exotic beans
For Burgers and Hamburger Substitute Dishes: Soybean (and soy grits), chick peas
For Soups: All legumes are good especially split yellow peas, split green peas, red lentils, brown lentils, adzuki, kidney, and pinto beans
For Casseroles: All legumes
In Salads: Chick peas, kidney
For Sprouts: All legumes except split types and favas
For Curried Dishes: Yellow split peas, red lentils
Good by Themselves with a Few Table Seasonings: Mung, kidney, pinto, romano, adzuki, red lentils, brown lentils
Legumes that Make Their Own Gravy: Kidney, pinto, brown lentils, red lentils, split peas, adzuki, black beans
For Sandwich Spreads: Soybeans, chick peas, black beans

With Tomatoes or Tomato Sauce: Soybeans, pinto, kidney, pea beans (white or navy), lima, brown lentils

With Potatoes: Any legumes except soybeans, fava, chick peas* (*These make a bad combination with potatoes in the stomach as they are hard to digest together.)

Good Herbs and Flavorings to Use with Beans:

Savory	Thyme	Sea Kelp
Fennel	Bay Leaves	Cayenne Pepper
Basil	Oregano	Paprika
Parsley	Cumin	Tamari Soy Sauce
Dill	Curry Powder	Seasoning Salts
Chili Powder	Turmeric	
Marjoram	Sea Salt	

How to Prepare and Use Legumes

Group One and Group Three – All Whole Beans and Peas

1. Soybeans and Fava Beans:

These beans must be soaked in water for 24 hours and cooked from two to six hours until done. These are best cooked in a pressure cooker unless you are grinding or blending them.

2. All Other Beans and Peas:

Soak eight or more hours and cook 1 to $1\frac{1}{2}$ hours until done. One exception: Chick peas should be soaked 12 – 24 hours but cook easily in $1\frac{1}{2}$ – 2 hours.

How to Soak the Legumes: Beans and peas must be soaked before cooking so that they re-absorb the water they lost in drying and so they will soften enough when cooking to be easily digested. (Exception: Soaking time can be cut down or eliminated when using a pressure cooker.)

For example, $\frac{1}{3}$ cup dry beans makes 1 cup soaked beans. Soak one cup beans in three to four cups water in a jar or bowl. Leave lots of room for expansion in the container and put in enough water so beans are completely covered the entire time they are soaking. Never cover the beans with a lid while they are soaking or they will spoil quickly!

How to Cook the Legumes: After soaking the legumes, discard the water and rinse the beans thoroughly several times rubbing them together while rinsing. Cook beans (or peas) in water, 2 – $2\frac{1}{2}$ cups water to one cup beans. If possible use a pot that is double the size of the beans and the water put together. (Example: If beans and water equal three cups, the pot should be six cups, or a

$1\frac{1}{2}$-quart/litre pot.) At a maximum, beans and water can equal three-quarters of the pot but this is not recommended. Beans are apt to "froth" up. The water gets "foamy" and may rise and spill over the sides of the pot. Spills will happen less if a big pot, twice the size of the beans and water, is used, if the heat is kept low and the beans are just "bubbling." It is easiest to start beans cooking in cool water and bring them to a boil on high heat, uncovered. Then scoop off the froth and turn down the heat so they are "bubbling" (bubbling means little bubbles are forming in the water as they cook). There is no need to have them boiling furiously. Foods usually cook faster when bubbling than they do boiling, and the pot is less unlikely to boil over or burn on the stove. Keep beans covered while cooking.

Make sure water is covering all the beans by about $\frac{1}{2}$ inch or more at all times and stir once or twice during cooking so that they are all cooked evenly and completely. Always start cooking the beans in water without salt, onions, or other seasonings until the last 20 – 30 minutes or so. Adding salt too early toughens the protein. Adding salt later helps to break beans down and make them easier to digest. (When one is making soup, some non-salty seasonings can be added a little earlier.) If making a special bean dish in a sauce, it is better to make the sauce separately and add it after the beans are totally cooked. Then you can let them cook together 15 – 20 minutes longer so the flavors can mingle. When the legumes are done, they should be very soft. They must be soft in order to be digested properly and not cause gas. You should be able to mash a bean easily with a fork or with your tongue against the roof of your mouth. They should never be hard or crunchy. If they are, they need to be cooked longer.

3. Cooking Soy Grits:

These chopped, dry soybean pieces need presoaking for 10 – 15 hours or so before rinsing thoroughly and cooking for one to two hours or more until very tender. If unable to purchase them, soak whole soybeans for 15 – 24 hours; then rinse thoroughly and grind them in a food processor, homogenizing juicer, or meat grinder to make the small grits. Then cook again for one to two hours or more until tender. Do not add any seasonings to these (or any) beans until they are totally tender. Once tender, use in recipes. It is alright to reheat soy grits if a recipe requires as the proteins and minerals in beans can withstand extra cooking. Soybeans are more digestible in grit form. Chick peas can be used instead of soybeans in any recipe calling for soy grits. These two beans interchange well.

For Chick pea grits, soak whole chick peas for 8 – 12 hours, rinse, grind, and cook for one hours or more until tender. Real grits are never granular.

4. Cooking Split Peas:

The main difference in cooking these compared to other beans and peas is that you actually want the split peas to dissolve totally into soup. They must be "bubbled" approximately $1^1/_2$ hours or more. Use approximately three to four cups water per one cup beans. Do not presoak. Rinse several times before cooking to remove excess starch and gassy qualities.

Note: Amount of cooking water may vary for the preparation of legumes depending on the type of cookware used.

Group Two – All Lentils and Mung Beans

Red and brown (or green or gray) lentils and mung beans are the only legumes that do not need any soaking before cooking because they cook quickly. Actually, they should never be soaked before cooking as that alters the texture and flavor.

Red lentils are usually split. Like other legumes, they should be cooked on a low heat and "bubbled" until done. Cook them for 15 – 20 minutes in about two cups of water or less per one cup of lentils.

Brown lentils (or Green or Gray Lentils) are always whole. Bubble for 55 – 65 minutes until very soft. About $2 – 2^1/_2$ cups water per one cup lentils.

Mung Beans are always whole. Bubble for 45 – 55 minutes until soft. About 2 to $2^1/_2$ cups water per one cup mung beans.

Group Four – Processed Soybean Products
1. Tofu:

This is a wonderful meat or dairy substitute made from soy. It is low in calories and contains no cholesterol. Eight ounces (about 255g) of tofu provides: 164 calories, 17.6g protein, 292mg calcium (the same as 8 ounces milk), 286mg phosphorus, 96mg potassium and as much iron as four or five eggs.

Although tofu is bland by itself, it works wonders in recipes as it absorbs the flavors of the ingredients around it and actually extends and complements the taste of sauces, gravies, herbs, and spices. Used correctly, tofu is delicious and adds texture, protein and other nutrients to all types of dishes, including salads, main dishes, dressings and sauces, and desserts.

Store tofu completely covered by fresh water, preferably in a glass jar, in the refrigerator. Plain tofu is fresh as long as it retains its milky white color and has no scent or taste. If the tofu smells a bit, rinse it thoroughly. If no smell remains, it can still be cooked but should not be eaten "raw". If the tofu still has an odor after rinsing, discard it. Whenever the freshness of tofu is questionable or to avoid any chance of bacteria growth, lightly steam it for four to nine minutes before using it. Soft, pressed, medium, firm, or regular tofu are available. The soft tofu may be used in any dessert recipe for a less grainy texture. However, regular tofu may be used unless specified otherwise.

2. Tempeh:

Buy blocks of this fermented soybean product at natural food stores and cut it into small cubes or pieces. Add it to stir-frys for extra protein and enzymes. It may also be fried like a burger or broken up into bits and added to casseroles and sauces.

3. TVP (Texturized Vegetable Protein):

To cook TVP, add about $^7/_8$ cup boiling water to one cup of TVP and let it sit, covered, for about 10 minutes as it expands and softens. Then simply add to recipe. This can be added to soups, stews and other dishes for added protein, however if added to a recipe where it is not called for, extra liquid and seasonings are required to flavor the dish correctly and make it tasty.

How to Cook Legumes for Easy Digestion

1. Measure the amount of beans (peas/legumes) required and sort through them to remove any misshapen, discolored or damaged beans. Also remove any dirt balls, gravel, or other foreign objects and discard them.

2. Soak one cup of dry beans in three to four cups of cool or room temperature water and let the beans soak eight hours or more uncovered. Soak chick peas 12 hours or more and soak soybeans 24 hours. Soybeans usually require a pressure cooker.

3. Important: Throw away the water the beans soaked in because it contains a gas released by the beans while soaking, which in turn will give you gas.

4. Rinse the beans several times and swish them around in fresh water.

5. Put the beans in a large pot. The beans should only fill about half the pot and add fresh water until the beans are covered by one-half inch or so of water.

6. Bring the beans and water, uncovered, to a boil on high heat.

7. When the beans are boiling, a white foam or froth will generally form on top. Scoop this off and discard it. This is part of what contributes to indigestion and gas.

8. Add extra water if needed so the beans are still at least one-half inch or more under water. Turn the heat down to very low, just low enough so the beans are barely bubbling, and cover them. They cook fastest at this temperature and retain more nutrients. Cook for $1^1/_4$ – 3 hours until tender. (Most beans cook in two hours or less. Chick peas and soybeans may require two to three hours.)

9. Optional: Add one teaspoon ground fennel or preferably one teaspoon savory to the beans while cooking. This improves their digestibility. Cooking beans with sea kelp or seaweed also helps to eliminate gas, but these must be added after the beans are already tender.

10. Always chew beans slowly, never eat them fast or when under excessive stress or fatigue.

11. Have some raw foods or salad first in a meal before eating the beans, to aid in their digestion.

12. Make sure not to add any oil, salt or salty ingredients like seaweed to beans while they are cooking. These ingredients can actually toughen the beans so they stay hard. Only when they are completely tender in the cooking pot, can these ingredients be added. If oil and salt are added after the beans are soft, they help the beans become more digestible.

13. For those with excessive gas problems, bring dry beans to a boil in their soaking water, then let them cool down, uncovered, for six to eight hours (eight to twelve hours for chick peas; 12 – 24 hours for soybeans) before changing the water and cooking. (In hot weather, beans must be refrigerated after the first few hours.) Another technique to aid extreme cases of gas is to sprout the beans before cooking, but this may alter their taste. Digestive aids can be used.

14. The beans easiest to digest are lentils, adzuki beans, pinto beans, and chick peas. Those with sensitive digestion should try these first. People with poor digestion or those who are not accustomed to beans should avoid all except the lentils and occasionally cooked, mashed beans with other foods or beans blended into a soup. Cold, sweet, or marinated beans are harder to digest.

15. One cup dry beans makes about 2½ cups soaked or cooked beans.

Extra Tips about Legumes

Reheating Legumes: Unflavored peas and beans that do not make their own gravy are easy to reheat at a low temperature and seldom burn. They usually do not need stirring more than once or twice while reheating. Legumes that make gravy or are already seasoned should be reheated in a crock pot, double boiler, or on a very low heat, and stirred every few minutes or so. Casseroles and other dishes may need extra liquid or seasoning if they are dry or frozen. They can be popped in the oven frozen or defrosted. Add extra herbs to any dishes that have lost flavor during storage. Usually you can cook any legumes while frozen or defrosted.

A Quick Soaking Method for Beans and Peas: If you forget to soak beans or peas for a special dish you want to prepare today, there is a quick way to take care of the problem. Place beans in cool water (1 cup legumes to $2\frac{1}{2}$ – 3 cups water) in a partially covered pot and bring to a boil. Then turn off heat, place lid firmly on the entire pot, and let beans sit for two hours. Then rinse and cook same as usual. This method is good for all whole peas and beans except soy, fava, and chick peas. They require eight hours or more soaking after heating with this method.

Breaking Down Beans and Peas for Easier Cooking: For very tough beans, especially soy, fava, and chick peas, freezing is an excellent way to help them break down more quickly and cook faster. Soak beans as usual, then freeze for one day or more, defrost, and cook as usual.

How to Pressure-Cook Legumes: If you have never used a pressure cooker before, read the general instructions that come with the cooker. It takes most beans and peas about 25 – 45 minutes to cook if they have been soaked previously. Make sure beans and water cover only three-quarters of the cooker or a bit more, so there is room for heat to circulate and also so beans do not clog the cooker's cap and cause an explosion or eruption. Unsoaked dry beans or peas can be pressure-cooked for 40 – 75 minutes depending on their toughness. Make sure to leave plenty of room for expansion! In a $1\frac{1}{2}$-quart pot use only one cup dry beans and three to four cups water. Herbs can be added at beginning of cooking or after, by cooking them an extra 10 minutes with beans (with the lid off or the unsealed lid partially covering the pot). Cook on a medium or medium-high heat. Caution: Never remove the little pressure cap (regulator) while there is pressure in the pot. This is very dangerous. Read instructions carefully!

How to Slow-Cook Legumes: Presoak the legumes and cook them overnight in a slow cooker for eight to sixteen hours until completely tender. Use high setting.

Storage Information for Legumes

Whole Dry Legumes: Whole dry legumes will last for years (if bugs do not get to them). Store them in a cool, dry place: A high shelf in an unheated basement storage cabinet, a cool kitchen cupboard, or in the refrigerator. In winter, legumes usually store safely in the kitchen cupboard, but check them every week or so because all natural, unrefined products have the potential to become bug-infested. (Bugs are especially attracted to foods that have real food value.) In summer, legumes must be kept in a very cool place and checked every week. Usually the older the legumes, the longer time it takes to cook them because they are more dehydrated. That is one of the reasons why soybeans can take two or sometimes six hours to cook.

Soaked Beans and Peas: If you do not have time to cook soaked beans or peas when you planned to, do not fret. They last one to two days soaking on the countertop if you change the water every 24 hours, but they last only 12 – 24 hours in hot weather. If refrigerated while soaking, they last up to five to six days. Keep changing the water every 24 hours or so. Never cover beans while they are soaking, unless they are refrigerated, or they will spoil very quickly.

Cooked Legumes: Cooked legumes must be refrigerated within an hour or two after cooking, especially in hot weather. The sooner the better. They last seven to eight days refrigerated but no longer. After eight days, preferably sooner, freeze the remaining legumes or dispose of them. They become rancid or turn bad easily. (Casseroles and spreads may spoil even more quickly.)

Frozen Legumes: Freeze whole, cooked beans in water or sauce. Keep all containers or dishes covered and air-tight. They will last up to six months or more but should preferably be used up in the first three months for more flavor and vitamins. Frozen legume dishes need extra seasoning added after defrosting as they lose some of their flavor in the freezing process. Fill freezing containers loosely only about two-thirds to three-quarters full.

Bug Prevention
How to Keep Natural Foods From Becoming Insect Infested:

1. Store foods at proper temperatures (See Storage Temperature chart).

2. During cool weather bug problems are unlikely. Freeze or keep cool all grain and legume products in hot weather.

3. Wrap one to two teaspoons basil and sage and two to three bay leaves in cheesecloth and place them in each cupboard, flour bin, or large storage jar. This will discourage most bugs as they dislike the aroma of these herbs.

4. Check cupboards once a week. If bugs are found, discard all infested foods and clean the cupboards. Protect your remaining food. Bug eggs look like grains of sand the size of a pin point and are often webbed together. These turn into white worms, small beetles, and little beige and brown moths.

5. If foods are slightly infested but still appear edible, place foods in the freezer to kill all bug growth. After freezing, remove any obvious bugs and use remaining foods in well cooked dishes.

6. Protect foods that bugs infest. These are grain or legume products (whole or partial), nuts and seeds, dried fruits, red herbs and spices like red pepper, chilies, paprika, curries and rose hips. Bugs do not usually bother with milk powder, carob, green herbs, most spices, tamari soy sauce, arrowroot, agar-agar, sea kelp,

seaweed, most herb teas and coffee substitutes, and most liquid jarred items like honey. The sometimes like salt. (Usually only ants go after sweets.)

7. Keep all food in tightly closed containers, never in paper bags. Keep jars and packages wiped clean. Clean cupboards and wipe up any spills right after they happen.

8. Do not leave foods sitting out in the open, especially not uncovered. Empty the garbage regularly, especially in the summer. Keep counters, floors, and corners clean as even small amount of flour may be potential food or breeding grounds for bugs.

9. Bugs are not commonly found in homes if moderate prevention measures are taken. Check foods as you buy them to avoid picking up bugs from stores and keep your cupboards clean.

Fast Facts About Beans

Did you know that beans are high in iron, calcium, phosphorus, potassium, zinc, and several B vitamins as well as high in protein and low in fat content?

Chapter 20

Main Dishes
Using Grains, Beans, & Vegetables

 ## Greek Vegetable Briam

(Serves 6 – 8)

> 3 – 4 medium potatoes, unpeeled and sliced $^1/_2$-inch thick
> 1 medium eggplant, peeled and sliced in $^3/_4$ – 1-inch rounds
> 2 – 3 Tbsp olive oil (or other natural oil)
> 1 large onion, chopped
> 5 – 6 large tomatoes or 1 large can (28 ounces or 796ml) tomatoes,
>   drained and chopped (save juice)
> 1 cup tomato juice or juice from canned tomatoes
> 2 small zucchini, sliced in $^1/_4$-inch thick rounds
> $^1/_4$ cup freshly chopped parsley (or 1 Tbsp dried)
> 1 tsp each sea salt, basil, dill weed and thyme
> Several dashes cayenne red pepper
> 10 – 14 ounces feta cheese, crumbled
> Optional: 1 – 2 tsp mint leaves, finely chopped

Steam the potatoes until fairly tender. Bake the eggplant in a 350°F oven until tender. Sauté the onion for two minutes in the hot oil. Chop the tender eggplant and mix it with the sautéed onion and remaining ingredients except for the feta cheese. Spread mixture into a long 9-inch by 13-inch baking pan and cover with the feta cheese. Press the cheese firmly into the top of the mixture. Bake at 375°F for 55 – 70 minutes until tender throughout. Add extra liquid if needed. Serve hot with garlic bread for a tasty Greek favorite. Keeps five to seven days refrigerated. Do not freeze.

♥ *Whole Grain-Vegetable & Cheese Casserole*

(Serves 6 – 8)

> 1¹/₂ cups dry brown rice or millet
> 1¹/₂ – 2 cups cheddar cheese (medium or sharp)
>   or amber tofu cheese, grated
> 1 cup tomatoes, chopped small
> 1 medium onion, chopped
> 2 Tbsp tamari soy sauce
> 2 tsp each basil and parsley
> 1 tsp sea salt
> ¹/₂ tsp sea kelp
> ¹/₄ tsp each marjoram, thyme, and dill weed
> Few dashes cayenne
> Optional: 1 tsp vegetable broth powder
> Keep Separate:
> 1 – 2 cups mushrooms, sliced
> 2 green peppers and/or zucchini, in chunks or slices
> Optional: black olives, sliced in half
> Optional: 1 cup alfalfa, mung, or other sprouts

Toppings:

> Wheat germ or sesame seeds
> Paprika

Cook the rice and add the onions to it about halfway through the cooking time. (About 25 – 30 minutes after the rice is started.) Do not overcook the rice. When the rice is no longer crunchy, take it off the heat and pour off any excess water. While the rice is still hot, add the cheese to it and mix until the cheese melts and is spread evenly through the rice. Then add the tomatoes, herbs, and spices and mix thoroughly with the rice. Use the rice mixture immediately to make the rice loaf or refrigerate it for a day or so until you are ready to prepare the loaf. (This can also be frozen but tastes better fresh.) Add a bit of milk or water if the mixture is too stiff. To make the loaf, lightly oil one large square or two small bread-size deep baking pans. Spread a 1-inch layer of rice mixture evenly into the pan. Then layer 1-inch of raw mushrooms, green peppers, and/or other vegetables on the rice. Next add the final layer of rice, just enough to completely cover the vegetables. Press it evenly in the pan. To top it off, sprinkle sesame seeds or wheat germ and a few dashes of paprika. Bake the rice loaf for 30 – 40 minutes at 350°F to 375°F until lightly browned on top and thoroughly cooked. Keeps four to six days refrigerated and is best if not frozen.

 # *Savory Soy-Carrot Loaf*

(Serves 8 – 10)

> 2 cups carrots, grated fine
> 1^1/$_2$ cups dry soybeans or soy grits, soaked and precooked
> 1 – 2 cups milk or substitute
> 2 – 4 large eggs, beaten
> 2 onions, chopped
> 2 small cloves garlic, minced
> ^{1}/$_4$ – ^{1}/$_2$ cup cornmeal or wheat germ
> 2 Tbsp natural oil
> 2 tsp each basil, paprika, tamari soy sauce
> ^{1}/$_4$ tsp sea salt
> Few dashes each cayenne and sea kelp
> Bread crumbs
> Optional: 1 cup celery, green peppers, or broccoli, chopped small
> Optional: 2 – 4 tsp nutritional yeast

Grind the tender precooked soybeans or grits in a meat grinder, food processor, with a hand masher, or some other grinding appliance. Mix all ingredients together well except the bread crumbs. Spread the mixture in a lightly oiled loaf pan or two about two to three-inches thick and sprinkle bread crumbs on top, pressing them halfway into the loaf. Bake the loaf at 375°F for 40 – 50 minutes or until browned and thoroughly cooked. Keeps five to seven days refrigerated and may be frozen.

♥ *Hearty Vegetable Bean Stew*

(Serves 10 – 16)

1 pound dry kidney or pinto beans, soaked
2 – 3 Tbsp tamari soy sauce
1 Tbsp parsley
3 – 4 tsp vegetable broth powder
2 tsp sea salt
1 tsp basil
$1/2$ tsp sea kelp
$1/4$ tsp paprika
$1/8$ tsp or less cayenne
Optional few dashes cumin powder (cominos) or dill weed
1 pound (8 – 10) medium carrots, chopped in medium chunks
$1/2$ – 1 pound mushrooms, small ones whole, large ones quartered
    or sliced (or 1 medium eggplant, chopped)
8 – 10 stalks celery, chopped in medium pieces
7 – 10 potatoes, in one-inch chunks (leave skins on)
3 – 4 medium onions, chopped
2 – 3 green peppers, in chunks
Optional: 6 – 10 Jerusalem artichokes, chopped
Optional: 1 – 2 cups fresh or frozen corn and/or peas

Cook the kidney beans until tender. Pour off and save all the cooking juice from the beans except for two cups. Leave the two cups of juice with the beans. While the beans are still cooking and nearly finished, in a separate pot steam the hard vegetables like potatoes, artichokes, and carrots for 10 – 15 minutes. Then add the rest of the vegetables to the hard vegetables and cook them together for another 10 minutes until all the vegetables are tender but slightly crunchy. Then add the drained vegetables to the beans along with the herbs and spices. Add some of the extra bean juice if needed. Save the extra bean juice for soups or other recipes. Simmer everything together on low to medium heat for 20 – 30 minutes until the flavors mingle and enjoy. Keeps five to seven days refrigerated and may be frozen.

♥ *Lasagne Supreme*

(Serves 6 – 8)
(Makes 1 large Lasagne – 9-inch x 13-inch pan)

> 1 – 1¹/₂ pounds mozzarella cheese, grated or sliced thin
>   (A little Swiss or cheddar can be used instead of some
>   of the mozzarella for a more exciting flavor.)
> 4 – 5 cups Terrific Tomato Sauce (see recipe in
>   Chapter 22 – Sauces, Spreads, and Dressings)
> 12 ounces cottage cheese, ricotta cheese, or mashed tofu with
>   a few dashes sea salt
> 8 – 10 whole wheat lasagne noodles, boiled and cooled
> A few dashes of sea salt
> Optional: 1 – 2 cups mushrooms, eggplant, or zucchini, sliced

Bring a large pot of water to boil and then add the noodles. Turn the heat down low and cock the pot lid. Cook the noodles for 15 – 25 minutes or until the noodles are tender but not mushy. Stir the noodles occasionally so they will not stick together. When the noodles are done, drain them in a colander and run cold water over them to cool them for easier handling. Different brands of noodles require different cooking times. Lightly oil the lasagne pan. Spread a cup or more sauce on the bottom of the pan, just enough to lightly cover the bottom. Then add a single layer of noodles. Broken and small pieces of noodles can also be used. Next, spread out all of the cottage cheese or tofu and on top of this and add half of the cheese. If vegetables are used, add these as the next layer. The second and last layer of noodles comes next, followed by the rest of the sauce. The final layer is the remaining cheese. Spread all the layers evenly. Bake the lasagne at 350°F for 35 – 50 minutes until cooked through. Be sure not to overcook the top layer of cheese. On higher heat or when reheating, the cheese browns or begins to burn easily. If this happens, turn down the oven or cover the lasagne loosely with a piece of tin foil. Lasagne is delicious when reheated and can be frozen for later use. Keeps three to six days refrigerated and is best if not frozen, although it can be.

Eggplant Lasagne

(Especially good for those with wheat allergies.)
Instead of noodles, use wide slices of eggplant about $1/4$-inch thick or less. Peel one large or two small eggplants and slice them lengthwise into large flat pieces. Steam the eggplant pieces for 6 – 12 minutes until tender but still firm. Continue with instructions for Lasagne Supreme, using the eggplant in place of the noodles.

 * For a dairy free lasagne, use mashed tofu with sea salt instead of the cottage cheese and use white, Italian style tofu cheese. Sprinkle on one to two tablespoons nutritional yeast over the tofu if desired for a cheesier taste. Keeps three to five days refrigerated.

Lasagne Rice

(Serves 8 – 10)

Follow the Lasagne Supreme recipe and instructions, but instead of noodles use brown rice. Precook about $1^1/_2$ cups dry brown rice and use half of it in place of the first layer of noodles. Use the remaining rice in place of the last layer of noodles. After baking, the consistency of this dish will be slightly runny but delicious.

Elegant Eggplant Parmesan

(Serves 4 – 6)

> 2 medium eggplants or 1 very large eggplant
> 3 – 4 cups Terrific Tomato Sauce (see recipe in
>   Chapter 22 – Sauces, Spreads, and Dressings)
> $3/4$ – 1 pound mozzarella cheese, grated
> Parmesan cheese (about $3/4$ – $1^1/4$ cups)
> Optional: $1/4$ pound cheddar cheese, grated

Peel the eggplant and slice into $1/3$-inch or $1/2$-inch rounds or slices. Bake on a dry or lightly oiled baking sheet at 375°F – 400°F for 12 – 15 minutes until tender. Lightly oil a 3 or $3^1/2$-inch deep, 8-inch or 9-inch square or round baking dish. Spread about one cup or less of tomato sauce on the bottom of the dish. Then add a layer or two of eggplant, about $1/3$ of the eggplant. Then add a layer of grated or thinly sliced cheese, about $1/3$ of the cheese. Next, add one cup or less of sauce and a few sprinkles of Parmesan cheese. Add a layer of half the remaining eggplant. (Some pieces can be cut to fit corners or small spaces.) Then add half the remaining cheese, topped with half the remaining sauce. Add the remaining eggplant, then the remaining sauce topped with the rest of the cheese. As a finishing touch, sprinkle on a little Parmesan cheese according to taste. Bake at 350°F for 45 – 55 minutes until hot throughout, bubbly, and browned and serve. Keeps three to five days refrigerated. Do not freeze.

Variation: Zucchini Parmesan
(Serves 4 – 6)
Use the Elegant Eggplant Parmesan recipe but instead of eggplant use one very large or four to five small zucchini. Do not peel the zucchini or remove the seeds. In the recipe, the zucchini may be presteamed several minutes before, or used raw.

 # Soya Spaghetti

(Serves 2 – 3)

> *4 – 5 ounces whole wheat or spelt spaghetti noodles*
> *1¹/₂ – 2 cups Terrific Tomato Sauce (see recipe in Chapter 22 – Sauces,*
> *   Spreads, and Dressings)*
> *¹/₄ cup dry soy grits or TVP, cooked until tender (See Variation)*
> *Optional: Parmesan cheese*

Soya adds protein, calcium, and other nutrients to a dish that ordinarily has little nutritional value. After the soy grits are cooked very tender (see cooking instructions for grits or TVP in Chapter 19 – Legumes), mix them with the tomato sauce and heat them together until hot. While the soy grits are cooking, bring a large pot of water to boil and then add the noodles for about 10 – 20 minutes or so until tender but not mushy. Note: Different types of noodles may take more or less time. Keep the noodles cooking on a low heat with the lid of the pot cocked so they will not boil over. Stir the noodles occasionally to prevent sticking to one another or the pot. When the noodles are done, leave them in the hot water so they will stay warm. Scoop out the noodles with a fork or spaghetti spoon. Top the spaghetti with sauce and a sprinkle of Parmesan cheese. Serve the spaghetti immediately. Do not leave it sitting in the water for more than a few minutes. If the spaghetti is not to be served right away, undercook the noodles by five minutes or more and they will finish expanding without getting mushy. The addition of soy grits to the sauce makes this meal a complete protein. Keeps one to two days refrigerated. Do not freeze. Variation: Use eight ounces mashed tofu or use soy spaghetti noodles instead of whole wheat or spelt in place of the soy grits or TVP.

♥ Macaroni & Cheese Bake

(Serves 4)

8 ounces (2 cups) whole wheat soy elbow noodles
2 – 3 cups medium or sharp cheddar cheese, grated
2 large eggs, beaten
1$^1/_2$ cups milk
$^1/_2$ – 1 tsp sea salt
$^1/_4$ tsp paprika
Several dashes cayenne

Cook the noodles in unsalted, lightly boiling water for about 15 – 25 minutes until tender but not mushy. Drain and cool the noodles. You may run them momentarily under cool water. Beat the eggs, milk, and spices together and keep separate. In a lightly oiled casserole dish, place $^1/_3$ of the drained noodles and $^1/_3$ of the cheese in layers. Repeat with two more layers of noodles and cheese. (Cheese should be on top.) Then pour the milk and egg mixture over everything. Add a bit extra milk if needed so that it can be seen below or around the top layer of noodles. Bake at 375°F for 40 – 50 minutes until lightly browned and the milk has solidified. Serve hot. This recipe does not reheat well although it can be reheated with extra milk. For two people, cut recipe in half to avoid extras. May keep one to two days refrigerated. Do not freeze.

Prima Vegetarian Pizza

(Makes 2 large pizzas)

Dough:
> 5 cups whole wheat flour (fine or medium ground or mixed
>   with lighter flour)
> 2 cups warm water
> 1$^1/_2$ Tbsp baking yeast
> 1 Tbsp natural oil
> 1$^1/_2$ tsp sea salt
> Optional: 1 tsp garlic powder or vegetable powder

Add the yeast to warm water, about 102°F to 108°F, and stir it in well. Then let the yeast sit and dissolve and grow for three to four minutes. In another bowl combine flour, salt, and any extra spices. Add the dry ingredients to the yeast. Mix and then knead the dough for five minutes on a lightly floured surface. Rub the oil over the dough and knead it for a minute, and then form it into a ball. Place the dough in a lightly oiled bowl covered with a damp cloth. Keep in a warm place and let it rise for one and a half to two hours.

Pizza Toppings:
> 3 – 4 cups Terrific Tomato Sauce (See recipe in
>   Chapter 22 – Sauces, Spreads, and Dressings)
> 1 – 1$^1/_4$ pounds mozzarella cheese, grated
> $^1/_2$ pound cheddar cheese (Use extra mozzarella or Swiss cheese
>   if not available)

Choose 3 or 4 or more of the following:
> 1 – 3 cups mushrooms, sliced
> 2 – 3 green peppers, sliced or chopped
> 2 – 3 zucchini, sliced
> 2 – 3 small yellow crookneck squash, sliced
> 1 – 2 cups pineapple, drained and in chunks (delicious)
> 2 – 4 tomatoes, sliced or chopped
> 1 – 2 onions, chopped
> $^1/_2$ – 1 can of black olives, sliced in half
> Optional: Use your imagination for any other favorite toppings.

Making the Pizza:

Lightly oil two pizza pans. Be sure to cover the edges of the pan so the dough will not stick. Punch down the risen dough and divide it into two parts. Knead each part for a minute and then roll it out flat with a rolling pin, being careful to turn it over occasionally so it will not stick to the rolling surface. A bit of flour on the rolling surface will help keep the dough from sticking. Add extra flour if needed.

Then shape the dough about $1/4$-inch or less thick in the pans, filling any empty spaces with extra dough and shaping a slightly elevated crust around the outer edges. Spread on tomato sauce and then cheese. Then add the toppings. Bake the pizza at 400°F – 425°F for 20 – 30 minutes or until the toppings and crust are lightly browned. Remove from the oven and let it sit three to five minutes before serving. Keeps three to five days refrigerated. Is best if not frozen although it can be.

 # Lentils Sweet & Sour

(Serves 3 – 4)

> 2 – 2$^1/4$ cups water or vegetable stock
> 1 cup lentils, brown or green
> $1/2$ medium onion, chopped
> 3 – 4 Tbsp apple cider vinegar
> 3 – 4 Tbsp honey
> 1 Tbsp natural oil
> 1 tsp sea salt
> 1 tsp basil

Cook the lentils for a half hour and then add the onions and cook for another 15 minutes. After 45 minutes, if most of the water is not absorbed by the lentils, remove the lid of the pan and let the lentils finish cooking for another 10 – 15 minutes. Cook until most of the liquid is gone and the lentils are fully cooked and tender. Then add the oil, seasonings, and extras and cook the lentils for another five to eight minutes or so until the flavor of the spices mingles with the lentils. When finished cooking, the lentils should look like a very thick soup or stew. Add extra seasonings if desired and serve. Keeps seven to eight days refrigerated and may be frozen.

♥ Vegetable-Chick Pea Casserole

(Serves 4 – 6)

1¼ cups dry chick peas, cooked and mashed
4 – 5 (½ pound) medium carrots, grated
3 – 4 green onions or 1 medium onion, chopped
1 green pepper, chopped
1 cup broccoli or green beans, chopped
2 cups mushrooms, sliced
6 – 8 celery stalks, chopped

Dry ingredients:

½ cup wheat germ or cornmeal
1 – 2 Tbsp sesame seeds
½ cup fresh chopped parsley (or 3 tsp dried)
1½ tsp sea salt
1 tsp each basil, paprika, thyme and dill weed
⅛ tsp sea kelp
Several dashes cayenne red pepper

Wet ingredients:

1 – 1½ cups water, milk, or broth
¼ cup natural oil
2 – 3 Tbsp tamari soy sauce

Topping:

Chow mien noodles or bread crumbs

Cook the chick peas and then pour off most of the cooking water. Use just enough liquid to mash the peas with a hand masher or other appliance. Steam all the vegetables, including the carrots and onions, for about eight minutes. The vegetables may still be a little crunchy. First mix the dry ingredients separately and then mix them with the steamed vegetables. Then add the liquid ingredients and chick peas and mix together well. If the mixture is too dry, add extra liquid. Spread the mixture about 2 – 2½-inches thick in a large oiled baking pan or casserole dish. Sprinkle noodles or bread crumbs generously on top and press them slightly into the mixture. Bake for 30 – 35 minutes at 350°F until browned. Keep it warm until it is served. Keeps five to seven days refrigerated and may be frozen.

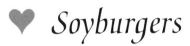 # Soyburgers

(Makes 12 Burgers)

1 cup dry soybeans (or chick peas), soaked 24 hours
1 cup cracked wheat or other cracked grain, soaked 2 – 4 hours
$^1/_2$ cup ground sunflower seeds, walnuts, or whole sesame seeds
$^1/_2$ cup whole wheat flour or other flour
1 medium onion, chopped fine
2 Tbsp tamari soy sauce
2 Tbsp natural oil
2 tsp sea salt
Optional: 1 – 2 large eggs, beaten

Put the drained soybeans through a hand grinder, food processor, or other appliance that will grind them to a fine consistency, cook them for 40 – 50 minutes and drain. Drain the water from the soaked, cracked grain and mix the grain with the cooked soybeans. Add all the other ingredients to the mixture and mix well. If the mixture is dry, add $^1/_4$ cup or so of water. Tear off 12 square sheets of wax paper. (Tin foil, dull side in, can also be used but it tends to stick to the burgers.) Divide the soy mixture equally onto the 12 sheets. Shape the soy mixture into burgers and fold them up individually in the wax paper. Place all the burgers in a plastic bag for added freshness and freeze the burgers completely before using. Frozen burgers will keep fresh for up to three months.

Cook the soyburgers as you would regular hamburgers. Heat a lightly oiled frying pan. Take the burgers directly from the freezer, unwrap them, and put them in the hot pan. Keep the frying pan covered while the burgers cook on medium-low heat. After the burgers are browned on one side, about 15 – 20 minutes, turn them over for another 8 – 12 minutes until browned on both sides. Then take the frying pan off the heat and add cheese slices if desired. Keep the lid on the burgers while the cheese melts. Then serve the burgers with natural ketchup and lettuce on whole wheat buns or bread. Keeps three to five days refrigerated after cooking. Best not to freeze.

Variation: Use chick peas, pinto, or adzuki beans instead of soybeans.

Creamed Grains & Parsley

(Serves 6 – 8)

> 2 cups millet or brown rice
> 1¹/₂ cups milk
> ³/₄ – 1 cup dried parsley
> ³/₄ cup medium or sharp cheddar cheese, grated
> 2 large eggs, beaten
> 1 medium onion, chopped
> 2 – 3 tsp sea salt
> ¹/₄ tsp each basil, paprika, and thyme
> Several dashes cayenne

Cook the grain in about four to five cups of water for about 45 minutes. Then add the onions and cook them together for another 10 – 15 minutes until most of the water has been absorbed into the grain. While the grain is still hot, mix in the remaining ingredients. Lightly oil one large casserole dish and spread the grain mixture into this about 3-inches thick. Sprinkle extra paprika on top for color. Bake at about 375°F for 30 – 40 minutes or until firm and lightly browned on top. Keeps five to seven days refrigerated. May be frozen, but is best if not.

Spinach-Potato Pie

(Makes 2 Pies – Serves 8 – 10)

> 40 ounce package frozen spinach, or
> 5 – 6 pound bunches fresh, cleaned spinach, remove
>   the bottom half of all stems
> 8 – 9 large potatoes, unpeeled and chopped in medium pieces
>   for steaming
> ¹/₂ cup milk (or more)
> 2 Tbsp butter
> Sea salt to taste
> 12 – 14 ounces medium or sharp cheddar cheese, grated

12 ounces sour cream
$^1/_2$ pound mushrooms, sliced
2 medium onions, chopped
2 Tbsp natural oil
2 tsp tamari soy sauce
1 tsp each sea salt and basil
$^1/_2$ tsp each oregano and sea kelp

Steam all the frozen spinach until it separates easily with a fork. If fresh spinach is used, steam until tender. Then drain completely and set aside in a covered pot. While the spinach is cooking, steam the potatoes until they are soft enough to be mashed. Then mash them with the milk and butter using only enough milk to make very stiff mashed potatoes. Salt them according to taste. Lightly oil two 10-inch pie pans and divide the mashed potatoes between the two pans. When the mashed potatoes are somewhat cooled, shape the potatoes in each pan into a kind of $^1/_2$ – $^3/_4$-inch thick crust covering the sides as well as the bottom of the pans. Make the crust thicker along the upper outer edge of the pan. Let the pie "crusts" sit while the vegetables are being prepared. Note: Cold potatoes do not shape well. Potatoes should be firm.

Heat the oil in a large frying pan and sauté the onions separately for two minutes. Then add the mushrooms, dry herbs, and salt. Sauté these together for two to five minutes or so until the vegetables are tender. Mix the sautéed vegetables with the well-drained spinach, tamari soy sauce, and sour cream, and mix well. Place half the spinach mixture in each pie crust and spread evenly. Sprinkle half the grated cheese on each pie. Bake the pies at about 375°F for about 35 – 45 minutes or until the tops of the pies are slightly golden brown and the cheese is melted.

Stuffed Green Peppers with Tomato Sauce

(Serves 6 – 12)

1 cup dry rice or millet
1 – 2 Tbsp natural oil
$^1/_2$ pound mushrooms, sliced
2 medium onions, chopped
6 large green peppers, cut in half lengthwise, seeds removed
1 tsp each sea salt and parsley
$^1/_2$ tsp each basil, oregano, sea kelp, and paprika
$^1/_8$ tsp or less marjoram, thyme, and savory
Optional: 1 – 2 Tbsp sesame seeds
12 ounces tomato sauce

Cook the millet or rice for 50 – 65 minutes until the grain is finished cooking and is fairly dry. In a large skillet heat the oil and sauté the onions, mushrooms and herbs until they are slightly tender. Then mix the cooked grain and sautéed vegetables together with two to three tablespoons of the tomato sauce. Place the raw green peppers in a large uncovered baking dish, cut side up. Fill the green pepper shells with the cooked grain and vegetable mixture. Fill the bottom of the baking dish around the peppers with about $^1/_3$-inch of water. Bake the peppers at about 350°F for 25 – 35 minutes until the rice is lightly browned and the peppers are tender but still a little crisp. While the peppers are baking, heat the rest of the tomato sauce on a low heat until hot. When the peppers are finished baking, spoon the tomato sauce over each serving of peppers and enjoy. Keeps two to four day refrigerated. Best if not frozen.

♥ *Stuffed Tomatoes or Peppers*

(Serves 2 – 4)

$1^1/_2$ cups brown or basmati brown rice, precooked and hot
   (about $^1/_2$ – $^3/_4$ cup dry rice)
2 – 3 tsp extra virgin olive oil (or other natural oil)
1 medium onion, chopped small
2 cloves garlic, minced
1 cup asparagus, broken into $^1/_2$ -inch lengths,
   steamed until semi-tender
1 – 2 Tbsp chopped fresh parsley (or 2 tsp dried)
$^1/_2$ tsp oregano
$^1/_4$ tsp sea salt
Several dashes cayenne red pepper
$^1/_4$ – $^1/_2$ cup crumbled feta cheese or bread crumbs
Optional: 2 – 4 Tbsp chopped nuts or pine nuts
4 very large tomatoes or 4 large bell peppers (green, red,
   yellow, purple, or orange)

Sauté the onion and garlic in the hot oil until tender. Mix the steamed asparagus, hot rice and sautéed mixture with the remaining ingredients except for the
cheese or bread crumbs and the tomatoes or peppers. Hollow out the tomatoes
leaving only $^1/_4$ of the pulp inside to keep their shape and add flavor. If peppers
are used, remove all the seeds and insides with the stem. Fill each tomato or pepper just over $^3/_4$ full with the rice vegetable mixture and top with cheese or bread
crumbs. Place the stuffed vegetables in a 1-inch deep baking dish surrounded by
$^1/_2$-inch of water. Bake in a preheated oven at 375°F for 35 – 50 minutes until hot
throughout and the cheese or bread crumbs are browned. Serve hot and enjoy.
These can be served with tamari soy sauce or yogurt if desired. Keeps four to six
days refrigerated. Do not freeze.

Stuffed Cabbage Leaves

(Serves 4 – 6)

2 cups buckwheat or kasha
2 Tbsp natural oil
1 medium onion, chopped
¹/₂ pound mushrooms, sliced or chopped
10 – 16 large green cabbage leaves, whole
2 Tbsp sunflower seeds or chopped nuts
1 tsp each sea salt and parsley
¹/₂ tsp each basil, sea kelp, paprika
¹/₈ tsp or less each marjoram and savory
Few dashes cayenne
2 – 3 cups tomato sauce, heated in a saucepan

Cook the buckwheat or kasha until tender. In a large frying pan, heat the oil and sauté the onion for a minute or two. Then add mushrooms, nuts, herbs, and spices. Sauté for another five minutes or so until the onions are clear. While the other ingredients are cooking, steam the separate cabbage leaves for five minutes or more until they are slightly tender but a little crisp. When the grains are finished cooking and the vegetables sautéed, mix them together. Fill each steamed cabbage leaf with a little of the grain and vegetable mixture while everything is still hot. Fold up the cabbage leaves and tuck them, folded side down, in a large, low-sided, lightly oiled baking dish. If the leaves will not stay folded, use toothpicks to keep them in place. Be careful to count the toothpicks and remove them all before serving the cabbage rolls. Cover the cabbage rolls with hot tomato sauce and bake them at about 325°F – 350°F for 15 – 20 minutes until everything is hot and the sauce flavors the cabbage. Serve them immediately, using extra sauce from the bottom of the baking pan as gravy. Keeps two to four days refrigerated. Best if not frozen.

♥ Sloppy Joes

1 pound dry soy grits, soaked and cooked until tender
2 – 4 cups tomato sauce
2 green peppers, chopped
2 medium onions, chopped
1 medium tomato, chopped fine
2 Tbsp tamari soy sauce
1 – 2 Tbsp natural oil
3 tsp chili powder
$1/_2$ tsp each sea kelp and cumin powder
Sea salt to taste
Few dashes each allspice, cayenne, and cinnamon
Whole grain buns or bread
Optional: $1/_4$ cup pickles, chopped fine

Drain the cooked soy grits and set them aside. In a large skillet heat the oil on medium heat and sauté the onions for two minutes. Then add the green peppers and tomato and sauté all of the vegetables until they are tender. Add the herbs and spices and the soy grits and sauté for another five minutes or so. Then add the sauce and the rest of the ingredients and simmer everything on a low heat for 40 – 60 minutes while the flavors mingle and develop. Serve the Sloppy Joes on a whole grain bun. Keeps seven to eight days refrigerated. Leftovers can be frozen.

♥ *Italian-Style Beans*

(Serves 8 – 12)

1 pound dry white pea beans or navy beans, soaked and cooked
2 cups tomatoes, chopped
1 cup celery or green peppers, chopped
2 onions, chopped
2 cloves garlic, minced
$^1/_2$ cup green olives with pimento, chopped
$^1/_2$ cup sweet pickles, chopped
2 – 3 Tbsp natural oil, virgin olive oil suggested
2 tsp parsley
1$^1/_2$ tsp sea salt
1 tsp dill weed
$^1/_4$ tsp each basil and paprika
Several dashes each cayenne and sea kelp
Parmesan cheese
Optional: $^1/_2$ – 1 cup cheddar cheese, grated

While the beans are cooking, heat the oil and sauté the onions and garlic for two to three minutes. Then add the pickles, olives, green vegetables, tomatoes, and herbs and spices and simmer for 20 minutes or more on a low heat, stirring occasionally. Keep the lid on the pan while simmering. When the beans are tender, drain them completely and mix them with the vegetable sauce and cheddar cheese, if used. Lightly oil one large or two small baking dishes and spread the bean mixture about 2-inches or 3-inches thick. Sprinkle Parmesan cheese on top according to personal taste. Bake the beans for 35 – 45 minutes at 350°F. Keeps five to seven days refrigerated or may be frozen.

♥ Incredible Chili

1 pound dry kidney beans, soaked and cooked
2 cups onions, chopped
6 – 12 ounces tomato paste (as desired)
2 medium tomatoes, chopped
1 – 2 green peppers, chopped fine
4 cloves garlic, minced
2 – 3 Tbsp natural oil
2 – 3 Tbsp tamari soy sauce
3 tsp chili powder
2 tsp sea salt
1 tsp each oregano, parsley, and sea kelp
$1/4$ tsp cumin seeds or powder (cominos)
$1/8 – 1/4$ tsp cayenne pepper
Optional: 1 tsp crushed red peppers or $1/2 – 1$ small jalapeno pepper, finely chopped

While the kidney beans are cooking, heat the oil in a large skillet and sauté the onions and garlic for two to three minutes. Then add the green peppers. Wait a minute or two before adding the tomatoes and simmer for five minutes. Add the tomato paste and remaining ingredients. Simmer the sauce on low heat for 40 – 60 minutes to develop the flavor. When the beans are ready, drain them and save the liquid. Mix the sauce and beans together and, if needed, add some of the drained liquid to bring the chili to a desired consistency. Cook the chili on a low heat for about 30 minutes or more so the flavor of the sauce will mingle with the beans. Then serve or save the chili for reheating the next day. A large batch of sauce can be made in advance and frozen in individual meal sized containers. Beans can be made fresh each time for more vitamins and flavor, but they can also be frozen with the sauce. The amount of cayenne (and optional jalapenos) determines the "hotness" of the chili. The chili can be complemented or made milder by serving with whole grains, bread, cornbread, yogurt, sour cream, grated cheese and/or avocado slices. Keeps seven to eight days refrigerated.

♥ Rice Enchiladas

(Makes 24 – Serves 8 – 10)

> 1 dozen whole grain corn and/or flour tortillas
> $^3/_4$ – 1 pound medium or sharp cheddar cheese, grated
> 1 cup brown rice or brown basmati rice, cooked
> 1 large onion, chopped
> 1 cup mushrooms, sliced
> 1 – 2 Tbsp natural oil
> 1 Tsp each sea salt and parsley
> $^1/_2$ tsp each basil, oregano, and paprika
> $^1/_8$ tsp or less each marjoram, thyme, savory, and sea kelp
> Sour cream or yogurt and/or guacamole or salsa
> Optional: 1 – 2 Tbsp sesame seeds
> Optional: Chili sauce or taco beans

Cook the rice separately and sauté the vegetables in the oil until slightly tender. Add the herbs and sauté another couple minutes. Then mix it all together. The tortillas can be made or purchased at most supermarkets and natural food stores. There are three ways to soften the tortillas:

1. Dip each tortilla in water before using.
2. Heat about $^1/_3$-inch of oil in a skillet and keep it hot while lightly cooking a tortilla for about five seconds on each side until softened. (Let the tortillas drain on paper before using.)
3. Warm each tortilla on a hot, dry iron griddle for about 45 – 60 seconds on each side

Fill each tortilla with about $^1/_2$ or $^3/_4$ cup of the rice mixture and roll it so it is as tightly closed as possible with the ends open. Place the folded tortilla, fold side down, on large, low-sided, lightly oiled baking pans. Cover the enchiladas with chili sauce, taco beans and grated cheese. Bake at 325°F – 350°F for about 20 – 30 minutes or until cheese melts. Top each serving with sour cream or yogurt and/or guacamole or salsa.

♥ Mexicali Tacos

(Serves 6 – 10)

1 dozen taco shells or corn flour tortillas
$^1/_2$ – $^3/_4$ pound medium or sharp cheddar cheese, grated

Use all or a few of the following:
Lettuce, shredded
Sprouts, any kind, alfalfa are best
Onions or chives, chopped
Green peppers, chopped
Cucumber, chopped
Avocado, chopped
Tomatoes, chopped
Taco beans (see following recipe)
Optional: Tomato sauce, chili sauce or salsa (picante sauce)

Begin by filling the taco shells with a layer of taco beans and either a little chili sauce or salsa, followed by layers of any favorite vegetables. Top it with sauce, grated cheese, and, as a special treat, guacamole and/or sour cream. Variation: Use whole wheat chapatis or pita bread instead of taco shells or tortillas. Only prepare enough food for each meal. Extras may keep for one day but are better fresh.

♥ Pinto Taco Beans

2 cups dry pinto beans, soaked and cooked
1 – 2 medium onions, chopped
2 – 3 Tbsp tamari soy sauce
2 – 3 tsp chili powder
1 tsp sea salt
$1/_8$ tsp or less cayenne
Few dashes sea kelp
Optional: a bit of honey to mellow the flavors

Cook the pinto beans and onions together until tender. Drain and save most of the water from the beans. While the beans are still hot, mix in the herbs and spices. Mash about half of the beans (leave some whole but do not separate) with a little of the drained liquid from the beans. Discard the rest of the liquid or save for other recipes or soups. Serve the beans hot as a side dish with enchiladas or use them in tacos. Keeps seven to eight days refrigerated and freezes well.

Variation: Chili Tacos
Instead of taco beans or tomato sauce, use warm chili in the Mexicali Taco recipe. Be sure to use chili with a thick consistency.

Variation: Refried Beans
Heat taco beans in a lightly oiled frying pan for 10 – 15 minutes or until warmed. Keep them on a low heat so they will not burn.

♥ Mexican Tamale Pie

(Serves 8)

3¹/₂ – 4 cups precooked pinto or kidney beans (about 1¹/₂ – 1³/₄ cups dry)
Crust:
1 cup whole cornmeal, fine or medium ground
2¹/₂ – 3 cups water
2 large eggs, beaten
¹/₂ – ³/₄ tsp sea salt
1 – 2 cups medium or sharp cheddar cheese or
    amber tofu cheese, grated
Filling:
2 – 3 tsp natural oil
1 large onion, chopped small
2 – 3 cloves garlic, minced
4 – 5 large ripe tomatoes, chopped
¹/₃ – ¹/₂ cup chopped green pepper
¹/₂ cup sliced, pitted black olives or green olives with pimento
1¹/₄ cups tomato sauce
1 Tbsp tamari soy sauce
3 – 4 tsp chili powder
¹/₂ – ³/₄ tsp sea salt
Several dashes cayenne red pepper

Over medium heat, use a wire whisk to stir the cornmeal into the water until thickened. Continue to stir and cook the mixture until it thickens and loses its grittiness. Then stir in the sea salt and well-beaten eggs. Lightly oil a large, deep, cast iron skillet or a 9-inch by 9-inch by 3 or 4-inch casserole dish. Spread half the cornmeal mixture over the bottom and sprinkle with ¹/₂ – 1 cup of one of the cheeses (if desired.) For the filling, heat the oil in a frying pan on high heat and sauté the onion and garlic until semi-tender. Add the remaining filling ingredients and simmer on low heat for 10 minutes, covered. Add the tender, hot, drained beans and mix them with the other filling ingredients. Spread the filling evenly over the crust and top with an even covering of the remaining crust. Sprinkle on the remaining grated cheese and bake for 30 – 40 minutes at 350°F until hot throughout and the cheese is browned. Keeps six to eight days refrigerated.

♥ Middle Eastern Falafel Spread

1 cup dry chick peas, soaked and cooked
$1/3$ – $1/2$ cup sesame tahini
1 – 2 cloves garlic, minced
2 tsp tamari soy sauce
2 tsp parsley
1 tsp cumin seeds or powder (cominos)
1 tsp onion, grated or chopped fine
1 tsp chili powder
$1/2$ – 1 tsp sea salt
$1/4$ tsp each sea kelp and celery seed
Several dashes cayenne to taste

Cook the chick peas until tender, then drain and save the liquid. While the chick peas are still very hot, mash them together with the garlic and remaining ingredients. Herbs and spices may be changed according to personal taste. Use the falafel spread as a sandwich spread or in the following falafel recipes. Leftover spread can be refrigerated up to seven or eight days or frozen in small containers. Make three to four batches at once and stock your freezer as this is a great weekly meal or snack. This can be stuffed into celery or tomatoes, or served cold with vegetables sticks as well as in the following recipes. The spread is tastiest when hot. Add extra liquid if needed.

Variations: Use less liquid and make the mixture dryer. It can be rolled in balls, then in flour and deep-fried or formed into patties like burgers and grilled and served on a bun.

Cold Falafel Sandwiches

(Makes 8, Serves 4)

> 4 pita or pocket breads (also called Greek or Bible bread)
> $1^1/_2$ – 2 cups falafel spread
> $^1/_2$ – $^3/_4$ pound cheddar cheese or tofu (amber) cheese, grated
> 2 – 3 medium tomatoes, chopped or sliced in thin wedges
> 2 green peppers, chopped or sliced
> 1 cucumber, chopped
> 8 – 12 lettuce leaves or 16 – 24 large spinach leaves, shredded
> Optional: 1 – 2 avocados, chopped

Cut the round, flat breads into half moons and open their pockets. Spread a layer of falafel spread along the inside of one of the sides of the pocket. Then layer the pocket with vegetables and top it with cheese. Serve and enjoy. For both the cold and hot recipes, only prepare enough for one meal to ensure freshness.

Hot Falafel Sandwiches

(Makes 8, Serves 4)

> 4 pita or pocket breads
> $1^1/_2$ – 2 cups falafel spread
> $^1/_2$ – $^3/_4$ pound cheddar cheese or tofu (amber) cheese, grated
> 2 – 4 medium tomatoes, chopped or sliced
> $^1/_2$ cup mushrooms, sliced thin
> $^1/_2$ small zucchini, sliced in $^1/_4$-inch or thinner rounds
> 2 green peppers, cut in thin strips
> Optional: 1 – 2 avocados, sliced thin or chopped

Cut the round, flat breads into half moons and open their pockets. Spread a layer of falafel spread along the inside of one of the sides of the pocket. Layer the pocket with vegetables and top with cheese. Place sandwiches down on a dry, flat baking sheet and bake in a preheated oven at about 350°F for 7 – 12 minutes until the bread is crispy, the cheese melted and the vegetables tender. Serve hot.

♥ Mexi Falafel Sandwiches

(Makes 8, Serves 4)

4 pita or pocket breads (also called Greek or Bible bread)
1 1/2 – 2 cups falafel spread
1/2 cup or more salsa (spread over the falafel layer -
    1 – 2 Tbsp per sandwich)
1/2 – 3/4 pound Monterey jack, jalapeno, cheddar cheese
    or tofu cheese, grated
2 – 4 medium tomatoes, chopped or sliced
2 green peppers, cut in thin strips
Optional: 1 cup cooked corn kernels

Follow the directions for the Hot Falafel Sandwich. Serve with corn chips, extra salsa, and yogurt if desired.

Greek Falafel Sandwiches

(Makes 8, Serves 4)

4 pita or pocket breads
1 1/2 – 2 cups falafel spread
1/2 – 3/4 pound Feta cheese, crumbled
2 – 4 medium tomatoes, chopped or sliced
1/2 small zucchini, sliced in 1/4-inch or thinner rounds
2 green peppers, cut in thin strips
1/2 cup pitted green or black olives, sliced in half lengthwise
Optional: 1/2 cup mushrooms, sliced thin

Follow the directions for the Hot Falafel Sandwich. Serve with fresh parsley and yogurt if desired.

♥ East Indian Dahl

(Serves 4)

> *3 – 4 cups water*
> *1 cup dry red lentils or dry yellow split peas*
> *1 onion, chopped*
> *2 Tbsp butter or natural oil*
> *2 – 3 tsp honey to balance the flavors*
> *1 tsp each sea salt and curry powder*
> *1 tsp turmeric*
> *$1/2$ tsp each ground coriander and cominos (ground cumin powder)*
> *$1/16$ – $1/8$ tsp each cayenne, cinnamon, and ground cloves*

Begin cooking the lentils or peas in the water. Lentils will take 15 – 25 minutes to cook fully. The smaller red lentils usually cook in 15 minutes and the larger split red lentils may take 20 – 25 minutes. The yellow split peas will take 45 – 60 minutes in about three cups of water or so. Do not cook them until they fall apart, just until they are tender. About 15 minutes before the legumes are finished cooking, add the onions and other ingredients and cook everything together until legumes are tender and absorb the flavor from the herbs and spices. Correct the spices according to personal taste. Add extra water for a sauce. Keeps seven to eight days refrigerated and may be frozen.

Variations: Add $1/2$ – 1 cup fresh green peas or 1 – 2 cups chopped, steamed cauliflower to the dahl during the last 10 minutes or so of cooking time.

Curried Grains & Vegetables

(Serves 4)

> 1 cup dry brown rice *
> $^1/_2$ cup dry wheat berries, buckwheat, or barley
> 1 – 2 cups mixed vegetables per person, chopped and steamed
>   (mushrooms, carrots, peas, peppers, broccoli, onions, or others)

Curry Sauce:

> $3^1/_2$ cups milk
> 6 Tbsp whole wheat flour
> 4 Tbsp butter
> 1 – 2 tsp curry powder
> 1 tsp each turmeric and sea salt
> Several dashes cayenne red peppers or to taste
> Optional: bit of honey or other sweetening to balance flavors
> Optional: 1 – 2 tomatoes and/or avocados, sliced in strips or wedges

Cook the rice and other grain separately until they are tender. When the grains are about half cooked, begin steaming the cut vegetables and make the curry sauce. For the sauce, heat the butter on medium-high heat in a frying pan. When it melts, add the flour and stir mixture on low heat until it is browned and crumbly. Then add the seasonings and milk and stir it on a medium-to-low heat with a wire whisk until it thickens into a sauce. Mix the two grains together and serve them on individual plates or one large platter. Cover the grains with the cooked vegetables and top it all with curry sauce. A few fresh tomatoes cut in wedges and avocado slices on top of this makes it extra tasty and attractive. Sauce keeps five to seven days refrigerated or my be frozen. Prepare other ingredients fresh for each meal.

  * Try other whole grains instead of rice like basmati brown rice, millet, or quinoa.

The Best Baked Beans

(Serves 6 – 8)

> 2 cups dry white pea or navy beans
> $^1/_2$ cup Barbados molasses or sorghum
> $^1/_3$ cup tomato paste
> 1 medium onion, chopped
> 2 Tbsp tamari soy sauce
> 2 tsp apple cider vinegar
> $^3/_4$ – 1 tsp sea salt
> 1 tsp each curry powder and dry mustard
> $^1/_2$ tsp sea kelp

Cook the beans until very tender. Drain off all the water except $1^1/_2$ cups. Mix all the ingredients with the beans and water. Scoop all the mixture into a 1 or $1^1/_2$-quart oiled baking dish. Bake for an hour at 250°F – 275°F and serve. Leftovers keep five to seven days and may be frozen.

Molasses & Beans

(Serves 6 – 8)

> 2 cups dry pinto beans
> $^3/_4$ – 1 cup molasses or sorghum
> $^3/_4$ cup natural ketchup
> 1 large onion, chopped
> 3 – 4 Tbsp tamari soy sauce
> $^1/_2$ tsp dry mustard
> $1^1/_2$ tsp sea salt or to taste

Cook the beans in water by themselves until they are very tender. Drain off any excess liquid but keep one or two cups liquid within the beans. Add the remaining ingredients and mix well. Simmer the mixture for 20 – 30 minutes over low to medium heat so the flavors can mingle and the onions can cook. Serve hot as a main or side dish. Keeps six to eight days refrigerated and freezes well.

♥ Tempting Tempura

(Serves 4)

Use 5 to 10 different vegetables from the following (Use 1 – 2 cups per person):

Carrots, thick slices or strips
Broccoli, 1 to 2-inch flowerettes
Mushrooms, small whole or cut in half
Green, red, yellow or orange and/or purple peppers, cut in strips
Zucchini, sliced or in chunks
Cauliflower, 1 – 2-inch flowerettes
Onions, sliced in rounds or rings
Small yellow squash, sliced or in chunks
Celery, in medium-sized chunks or strips
Edible pea pods, whole
Small turnips, in $1/4$-inch thick slices or strips
Eggplant, in $1/2$-inch chunks or $1/4$-inch thick strips
Jerusalem artichokes, in $1/2$-inch chunks
Corn on the cob, in 1-inch rounds
Green onions, in 1 to 2-inch pieces
Yam, in $1/2$-inch chunks or $1/4$-inch slices, presteamed until tender

Batter:
1 cup whole wheat flour
$2/3$ cup cold water
2 large eggs, beaten
2 Tbsp tamari soy sauce
1 tsp sea salt
4 ice cubes
Oil for frying
Optional: Tofu chunks or Tofu Cutlets à la Jim

Heat about two to three inches of oil in a frying pan or wok until very hot but not smoking. Keep it on medium-high heat so the oil will not burn. Mix all the batter ingredients together thoroughly with a wire whisk, except the ice cubes. Add the ice cubes to the batter to keep it cold. Stir it occasionally to keep it cold and well mixed. If the batter gets too watery, remove the ice. Using chop sticks or tongs, dip each vegetable in batter and then drop it in the hot oil. Several vegetables at a time can be cooked this way, but be careful not to add so many vegetables that the oil gets cool. Vegetables should "sizzle" all the time that they are frying. Keep the vegetables in the hot oil for a minute or two until they get crispy and golden. Turn them over if necessary. Replenish the oil if it gets low, giving it a chance to get hot before adding more vegetables. The tempura should be eaten immediately as it cools in minutes. Have the rest of the meal prepared before starting to cook the vegetables. Note: If oil is not hot enough vegetables will be greasy. But make it only hot enough that it keeps bubbling. Served best with a whole grain and tamari soy sauce for dipping.

♥ Danish Vegetable Nutloaf

(Serves 6)

1½ cups raw pecans or fresh, raw walnuts: 1 cup chopped small
   and ½ cup ground
1 cup buckwheat or amaranth flour
3 – 4 small turnips (¾ pound or 350g), chopped small
1 – 2 Tbsp natural oil
1 large leek or 1 medium onion, chopped small
2 cloves garlic, minced
1 Tbsp parsley
1 tsp sea salt
½ tsp each sage, thyme, and paprika
Several dashes cayenne red pepper
1 cup milk or substitute
4 large eggs, beaten
2 Tbsp tamari soy sauce

Chop and crush the nuts and mix them with the flour. Steam the turnips until very tender. Sauté the leek or onion and garlic in hot oil until semi-tender. Add sea salt and herbs and cook for another minute and remove from heat. Then mash the turnips while still hot and mix mashed turnips and remaining ingredients with the sautéed mixture. Spread the mixture into a lightly oiled loaf pan and bake at 350°F for 45 – 55 minutes until firm and thoroughly cooked. Enjoy hot or cold with extra soy sauce on top. Leftovers are delicious hot or cold. Keeps four to six days refrigerated. Best if not frozen.

♥ Vegetable Quiche

(Makes 2 Pies – Serves 8 – 12)

> 2 – 9-inch or 10-inch pie crust shells
> 12 – 16 ounces Swiss cheese, grated (or $^1/_2$ Swiss cheese
>   and $^1/_2$ cheddar cheese)*
> 4 large eggs, beaten
> $^1/_2$ pound mushrooms, sliced (about $1^1/_2$ - 2 cups)
> 2 cups chopped broccoli
> $1^1/_2$ - 2 cups milk *
> 1 large onion or 6-8 green onions, chopped fine
> 2 green peppers, chopped
> 2 Tbsp natural oil
> 2 tsp tamari soy sauce
> $1^1/_2$ tsp sea salt
> 1 tsp parsley
> $^1/_8$ tsp each basil and paprika
> Several dashes cayenne red pepper

Heat the oil and sauté the onions and vegetables until slightly tender. Add the salt and herbs and sauté another couple of minutes. Pour off any excess liquid or let it evaporate. When the vegetables are tender, mix them with the tamari soy sauce and set them aside. Heat the milk. (Use more milk if more cheese is used.) Take the milk off the heat before it comes to a boil. Spread half the cheese evenly in the pie crust shells. Stir the sautéed vegetables and spread most of them in the crust over the cheese. Add the second layer of cheese and top with remaining vegetables. Mix the beaten eggs into the hot milk and pour them over the vegetables in the pie shell. Do not leave the eggs in the hot milk for more than a minute or two, or the eggs will harden. Bake immediately in a preheated oven at 350°F for 35 – 45 minutes or until the pie is slightly golden and firm. Cool a few minutes before slicing. Keeps five to seven days refrigerated and may be frozen.

* Tofu cheese and a milk substitute can be used instead of dairy products. This recipe is delicious with or without a pie crust. See desserts for crust recipe.

♥ Shish Kebabs

Use ½ – ¾-inch thick pieces about 1 to 2-inches long of several of the following vegetables and foods: (Use 2 cups per person.)

Pineapple chunks
Citrus slices, peeled and seeded
Green peppers, in chunks
Zucchini, sliced in rounds or chunks
Mushrooms, whole or large ones cut in half
Potato chunks (presteamed 10 minutes)
Broccoli flowerettes (presteamed 5 minutes)
Cauliflower flowerettes (presteamed 5 minutes)
Tomato wedges
Tofu or tofu cutlets, in chunks
Onion wedges or chunks
Edible pea pods, whole

Use one or more of the following sauces:
French dressing
Barbecue sauce
Tomato sauce mixed about half and half with tamari soy sauce
*   or dark miso*

Use two or more skewers about one foot long per person. Bamboo * or stainless steel skewers (spears) may be used. Use a variety of vegetables and other foods. Place the foods on the spears alternately, filling each spear completely. Use a cooking brush to baste the kebabs with the sauce(s). Use plenty of sauce. Broil the kebabs for 5 – 10 minutes until tender and juicy. Serve immediately before they cool. Time varies depending on type of broiler and distance from heat source.

* If an outdoor barbecue is used for grilling, bamboo skewers must be soaked in water for an hour or so before using.

♥ Myboulie - (My Taboulie)

(Serves 4)

1¹/₂ cups dry bulgur, soaked until soft and drained*
   (see Chapter 18 – Whole Grains)
1 cup green onion tops or chives, chopped
1 green pepper or 2 celery stalks, chopped fine
¹/₃ cup dry chick peas, soaked and cooked until tender, then drained
3 – 4 small tomatoes, chopped small
1 – 2 carrots, sliced paper thin
Optional: ¹/₂ cup tofu or tofu cutlets, crumbled or mashed
¹/₄ cup natural oil
3 – 4 Tbsp apple cider vinegar or lemon juice
2 – 3 Tbsp each parsley
1 – 2 Tbsp tamari soy sauce
1 – 1¹/₂ tsp sea salt or 2 tsp vegetable or sesame salt
1 tsp each basil, paprika, and oregano
¹/₄ tsp each thyme and sea kelp
Several dashes cayenne red pepper
Optional: ¹/₄ tsp or less dill weed, cominos, or chili powder.

Mix oil, vinegar, and all herbs and spices together well. Mix the remaining ingredients together in a separate bowl. Then mix everything together well and chill for one to two hours or more before serving. Stir every half hour or so. Keeps one to two days refrigerated. Do not freeze.

Variations: Add 2 – 3 cups chopped lettuce or spinach to the mixture to make it a salad. Add other chopped, raw vegetables as desired.

Short cut: Use 2 – 3 tablespoons of the Herb Mixture (see recipes in Chapter 14 – Herbs, Spices, Condiments, and Natural Oils) with the tamari soy sauce and eliminate all the other herbs and spices in this recipe.

* Two cups cooked millet, quinoa or brown rice may be used instead of bulgur if desired.

♥ Stir-Fried Vegetables

(Serves 4)

$1/4$ pound (about 1 cup) mushrooms, sliced in trees (from cap to stem)
$1/2$ head or less Chinese cabbage, chopped fine
    (can also use regular cabbage or kale)
4 stalks celery, $1/4$-inch thick, sliced on a long slant
2 – 3 green onions, chopped in small, slanted pieces
2 – 3 large carrots, 1/8-inch thick, sliced on a long slant
1 green pepper or 1 stalk broccoli or other vegetable,
    chopped in long, thin pieces
1 – 2 cloves garlic, peeled and sliced lengthwise into 3 – 4 pieces
$1/2$ cup bean stock or water or broth
$1/8$ cup tamari soy sauce
2 – 3 Tbsp natural oil
2 – 3 tsp arrowroot powder
Optional: 1 cup edible pea pods and/or large, white mung bean sprouts
    (whole) and/or a few sliced water chestnuts and/or tofu chunks
Optional: A dash or two of finely grated ginger root or $1/4$ cup peeled,
    sliced ginger

An Oriental wok is preferred for this recipe, but a large iron skillet or frying pan can be used instead. Heat the oil in the wok with the garlic and sliced ginger (if any) and be sure the sides of the wok are also oiled. Use chop sticks or tongs to lift vegetables and to stir. When the oil is sizzling, add all the vegetables and grated ginger (if any) except the mushrooms, pea pods, and sprouts and cook until almost tender. Stir the mixture often to coat and cook the vegetables completely. Keep the pan hot enough so the mixture sizzles continually. This way the vegetables stay coated rather than saturated with oil. This protects their nutrients and flavor. Add the remaining vegetables and continue to stir. When the vegetables are bright in color and nearly transparent (about 10 minutes or less), add enough stock and tamari soy sauce so there is $1/3$ to $1/2$ cup liquid with the vegetables. Keep hot. Separately mix together well two to three teaspoons arrowroot with $1/4$ cup of extra, cool broth or water. Then mix it all together with the vegetables, heat everything another minute or two, and serve immediately over rice, millet, or chow mien noodles. These vegetables will have a delicate yet rich flavor. If desired, all the extra liquid ($^1/_2$ cup or more) and arrowroot can be eliminated, just use tamari soy sauce. Black beans sauce or other Oriental sauce may be used for a different flavor. Prepare only enough for one meal. Does not store or freeze well.

 # Easy Tofu Cutlets

(Serves 8 – 12 – Prepare in few hours if tofu prefrozen)

> $2^1/_2$ – 3 pounds frozen pressed tofu, purchased or home-made
> 4 cups water
> $^2/_3$ cup tamari soy sauce
> 2 Tbsp chili powder
> 1 Tbsp onion powder
> 1 Tbsp garlic powder
> $^1/_2$ tsp sea kelp
> Several dashes cayenne red pepper

Defrost the tofu in a large bowl of hot water. Change the water a few times if necessary or defrost it at room temperature earlier if time permits. Gently hand-press the excess water from the tofu. Slice it into $^1/_4$-inch thick pieces and press them dry with paper towels. Mix the water and spices together in a large pot and bring it to a boil. Lower the heat and simmer the sauce for 15 – 20 minutes or so before adding the tofu pieces. Add the tofu and simmer all together for 30 minutes or more. Turn and baste the tofu pieces regularly while simmering. Then drain the tofu and store in jars or freeze in bags or containers for later use. Use the serving suggestions from the following recipe: Tofu Cutlets à la Jim. Note: Prefreezing changes and improves the texture of the tofu. It releases excess water and strengthens the tofu.

♥ Tofu Cutlets à la Jim

(Serves 8 – 12 – Prepare several days before needed)

2¹/₂ – 3 pounds regular tofu
4 cups water
²/₃ cup tamari soy sauce
2 Tbsp chili powder
1 Tbsp onion powder
1 Tbsp garlic powder
¹/₂ tsp sea kelp
Several dashes cayenne red peppers

Equipment:
2 boards covered with plastic bags
Paper toweling
Books or bottles for weights
Pot for cooking
Bags for storage

Cut each block of tofu into four pieces. Prop one board up on a small slant and cover it with six to eight pieces of paper toweling. Then place all the tofu pieces on the board at least 1-inch apart. Top this with more paper toweling and the second piece of board. Put heavy weights on top of the last board to help squeeze the excess water from the tofu. Keep pressing the tofu for two hours or more. After pressing, freeze the tofu in bags for one or more days. Pressing and freezing helps develop the texture of the cutlets. After freezing, defrost the tofu pieces in warm water until thawed and rinse thoroughly. Then using the boards and weights, press the tofu again for two hours or more. Then remove the tofu pieces and slice into ¹/₄-inch thick slices or strips. Mix the four cups water and all the spices and herbs together in a large pot and bring it slowly to a boil, stirring occasionally. When it boils, lower the heat to a simmer and add the tofu pieces. Simmer for 30 minutes or more, stirring the liquid occasionally and turning the tofu pieces. Then drain the tofu pieces and store in containers in the refrigerator (keeps up to ten days) or freeze. This nutritious high protein and calcium food is a great snack or meal (¹/₄ pound can keep you energized for hours). Also, try it in: shisk kebabs, spaghetti sauce, tempura, casseroles and stir-frys. Freeze it in double baggies for individual servings if desired. Delicious hot or cold. For exceptional flavor, try broiling pieces for several minutes on each side. Also, serve the same as hors d'oeuvres in little chunks on toothpicks.

 # Herb Tofu Cutlets

(Serves 8 – 12)

> $2^1/_2$ – 3 pounds frozen pressed tofu, purchased or homemade
> 4 cups water
> $2/_3$ cup tamari soy sauce
> 2 – 3 Tbsp dried parsley flakes
> 2 tsp basil
> 1 Tbsp onion powder
> 1 Tbsp garlic powder
> $1/_2$ tsp sea kelp
> Several dashes cayenne red pepper and ground marjoram and/or thyme

Follow directions for the Tofu Cutlets à la Jim or Easy Tofu Cutlets.

Main Dish Recipes Found in Other Chapters:
Chapter 16 – Vegetable & Vegetable Salads: Three- and Four-Bean Salads, Perfect Potato Salad, Rice Salad
Chapter 24 – Sandwich Ideas & Lunchbox Specials: Hummus, Soyspread, Miso-Soy Spread

♥ *Chapter 21*

Soups

A delicious blend of herbs, vegetables, whole grains, legumes, miso, and other ingredients are used to create these hearty, taste tempting soups that nourish and satisfy. There are quick, cold blender soups for summer or for side dishes, and robust soups that can be enjoyed as a main dish. Enjoy these pleasing soups and see my other books, especially *Hearty Vegetarian Soups and Stews* and *Vegan Delights*, for dozens of additional recipes.

How to Make Vegetable Soup Stock
Three Methods
1. Leftover water from steaming vegetables may be used as stock.
2. Odd leftover vegetables, especially broccoli, cauliflower, corn, zucchini, celery, carrots, mushrooms, turnips, yams, and cabbage can be covered in water, brought to a boil on high heat, and then simmered on low heat for 20 – 60 minutes. After simmering, cool and strain the mixture. Save the liquid for stock. Avoid using potatoes, beets or tomatoes for stock. The former is too starchy and the last two may dye the water and alter the color of the soup.
3. Leftover cooked vegetables, like the ones suggested above, can be puréed and used as stock. Use one cup vegetables for every five to six cups water.

Blender Soups
A delicious treat! Use leftover grains and/or beans and/or steam one or more vegetables such as beets, carrots, turnips, broccoli, potatoes, or tomatoes. Use the Herb Mixture or herbs from other recipes or choose your own. Add water, stock,

milk, yogurt, or sour cream and blend thoroughly in the blender. Add a few green onions, a small clove of garlic or one to two teaspoons raw chopped onion before blending and heating the soup for extra flavor.

Soups can be eaten cold or heated. Do not boil. Serve immediately after cooking. It is not recommended to reheat this type of soup, especially if leftovers are used. (One half to one teaspoon prepared horseradish may be used instead of onions or garlic if desired.)

Soup Recipes

 Gazpacho Delight

(Serves 2)

> 4 large ripe tomatoes (may be peeled or seeded if desired)
> 1 cup milk, tomato juice, or broth
> $1/4$ cup mayonnaise, yogurt, or sour cream
> $1/2$ medium green pepper, chopped
> 1 – 2 tsp tamari soy sauce
> $1/2$ – 1 tsp onion or a bit of chives, chopped
> $1/2$ or less clove garlic, minced
> $1/4$ tsp each basil and dill weed
> Vegetable salt to taste
> Several dashes each sea kelp and cayenne

Blend everything together and serve cold or heat up to boiling and serve. Use milk or water for pink gazpacho and use tomato juice for red gazpacho and fuller flavor. Keeps two to three days refrigerated. Do not freeze.

Cold Cucumber Yogurt Soup

(Serves 4 – 6)

> 4 cups fresh cucumber, peeled, seeded, and chopped
> 2 cups yogurt, plain
> $1/4$ cup cold water or ice cubes
> 6 – 8 green onion tops (not white part), chopped
> 1 – 2 cloves garlic, minced
> 8 – 10 fresh mint leaves (in a pinch use $1/2$ – 1 tsp
>   dried peppermint leaves)
> 1 tsp sea salt
> $1/2$ – 1 tsp dill weed
> Optional: 1 – 2 tsp parsley

Blend everything thoroughly and chill for about two hours or more. Garnish with unpeeled, thinly sliced cucumber rounds, whole mint leaves, or chopped fresh parsley and serve. Keeps two to three days refrigerated. Do not freeze.

Cold Red Bell Pepper Soup

(Serves 2 – 4)

> 2 cups chopped red bell peppers (about 2 medium)
> 1 cup yogurt, plain
> 2 green onions, white part only, chopped
> $1/4$ tsp sea salt
> Few dashes cayenne red pepper
> 1 small red bell pepper, finely chopped
> 1 cup alfalfa sprouts with hulls removed or grated zucchini

Blend the first five ingredients thoroughly in a blender. Strain and chill the mixture if desired. Mix the extra chopped red pepper into the soup and top each bowl with a handful of sprouts or grated zucchini. Serve and enjoy. Keeps two to three days refrigerated. Do not freeze.

♥ Split Pea Soup

(Serves 8 – 12)

> 1 pound split green peas
> 7 – 9 cups water or stock
> 2 medium onions, chopped small
> 2 – 3 Tbsp natural oil or butter
> 3 – 4 tsp tamari soy sauce
> 3 tsp parsley
> 1 – 1$^1/_2$ tsp each sea salt and dried, crushed mint leaves
> 1 – 2 tsp honey or other natural sweetener to balance flavors
> $^1/_2$ tsp each basil, sea kelp, and thyme
> $^1/_4$ tsp each marjoram, oregano, and savory
> Few dashes cayenne red pepper
> Optional: 1 – 2 potatoes and/or carrots, chopped small and presteamed

Rinse the peas in fresh water several times to remove gassy starches. Bring split peas and water to a rolling boil on high heat and discard the water. Add more fresh water and bring to a boil again. Cook the split peas and water in a large pot for about 1$^1/_4$ – 1$^1/_2$ hours on medium-to-low heat. Then add the onions, herbs, spices, and vegetables, and cook over a medium-to-low heat for about 30 minutes more or until the peas totally dissolve into liquid. Use more water if a thinner soup is wanted. Stir the soup occasionally so it will not stick or burn. If the soup begins to boil over, turn the heat down and cock the lid of the pan. Keeps six to eight days refrigerated and may be frozen.

♥ Tomato-Lentil Soup

(Serves 8 – 10)

> 7 – 8 cups water or stock
> 2 cups brown or green lentils
> 12 – 13 ounces tomato paste
> 3 – 4 medium tomatoes, chopped
> 3 – 4 stalks celery, chopped
> 1 medium or large onion, chopped
> 2 – 3 Tbsp natural oil or butter
> 2 – 3 tsp tamari soy sauce
> 2 tsp parsley
> 1 – 2 tsp honey or other natural sweetener to balance flavors
> 1 tsp each sea salt, basil, and oregano
> $1/2$ tsp each sea kelp, marjoram, and thyme
> Several dashes cayenne red pepper

Cook the lentils and water for 45 minutes in a large pot on medium-low heat. Then add the onions, tomatoes, and vegetables and cook these all together for another 20 – 25 minutes. Then add the remaining ingredients. Continue cooking everything on a low heat for about 20 – 30 minutes or until the tomatoes have turned into liquid, the vegetables are tender, and the lentils are soft. Stir the soup occasionally. Keeps up to seven days refrigerated and may be frozen.

♥ Hearty Vegetable Soup

(Serves 8 – 10)

6 – 7 cups water or stock
1 cup peas or chopped green beans
1 cup mushrooms, sliced
4 – 6 large tomatoes, chopped
2 potatoes, chopped, unpeeled
2 – 3 stalks celery or 1 green pepper, chopped
2 carrots, sliced thin
1 large onion, chopped
Optional: 1 cup corn (can be sliced off the cob)
1 – 2 Tbsp natural oil or butter
2 – 3 tsp each parsley and tamari soy sauce
2 tsp vegetable broth powder or 2 vegetable bouillon cubes
$1^1/_2$ tsp sea salt
$^1/_2$ tsp each basil, sea kelp, and oregano
Few dashes cayenne
Optional: 1 – 2 tsp honey or other natural sweetener

Steam the hard vegetables, potatoes and carrots, for 5 – 10 minutes before making the soup. Sauté the onions and mushrooms in the oil in a large soup pot until the onions are slightly transparent. Then add the water, steamed vegetables, and remaining ingredients. Cook the soup on a low to medium heat for 40 – 60 minutes until all the vegetables are tender but not mushy, and the flavors develop. Add a bit of honey if necessary to help balance the flavors. Correct the spices according to personal taste and add extra water if needed. Serve it hot and let leftovers cool before refrigerating Keeps five to seven days refrigerated. Best if not frozen.

Vegetable Barley Soup
Use the Vegetable Soup recipe but instead of potatoes use $^1/_2$ cup dry pot barley. Add a little extra water if needed and be sure the grain is fully cooked before serving the soup. (One to two cups precooked pot barley may also be used.)

Alphabet-Vegetable Soup or Noodle-Vegetable Soup

Use the Vegetable Soup recipe, but instead of potatoes use $^3/_4$ – 1 cup noodles or alphabet noodles. Add a little extra water if needed and be sure not to overcook the noodles. Add noodles for the last 30 – 35 minutes of the soup's cooking time.

 # Miso-Seaweed Soup

(Serves 6 – 8)

> 6 cups water or stock
> $^1/_3$ – $^2/_3$ ounces dried seaweed (wakame or kombu are best)
>   or 4 – 6 ounces fresh, edible seaweed, rinsed and chopped
> 2 carrots, sliced thin
> 2 stalks celery, chopped
> 1 large onion, chopped
> 1 vegetable bouillon cube
> 1 Tbsp natural oil
> $^1/_2$ tsp each salt and parsley
> Few dashes sea kelp
> $^1/_3$ cup dark miso, keep separate

Sauté the onions and vegetables in oil in a large pot. Use a pot big enough to hold all the soup. When the vegetables are tender and slightly transparent, add the water, seaweed, and other soup ingredients except the miso. Let the soup cook on low heat for 25 – 35 minutes to develop the flavors. Then take the soup off the heat and keep it covered and hot. Remove one cup of broth from the soup and mix it with the miso. When the miso is dissolved into the broth, mix it with the rest of the soup and let the soup sit covered for about 5 – 10 minutes. Do not cook the miso, that will destroy valuable vitamins and enzymes. Serve the soup immediately when ready. Leftover soup can be reheated slightly but never let the soup come to a boil. Keeps five to seven days refrigerated and should not be frozen.

♥ *Beautiful Brown Bean Soup*

(Serves 10 – 12)

> 2 cups dry pinto beans, kidney beans or adzuki beans
> 10 – 12 cups water or stock
> 1 large onion, finely chopped
> 2 – 3 Tbsp tamari soy sauce
> 2 Tbsp dried parsley or $^1/_4$ – $^1/_3$ cup finely chopped fresh parsley
> 2 Tbsp butter or natural oil
> 4 tsp vegetable broth powder
> 2 vegetable bouillon cubes
> $^1/_2$ – 1 tsp sea salt or vegetized sea salt
> $^1/_2$ – $^3/_4$ tsp sea kelp
> Cayenne red pepper to taste
> Optional: 1 – 2 tsp honey or other natural sweetener
> Optional: 2 – 3 cups chopped vegetables (carrots, broccoli, peas)
> 3 – 4 Tbsp dark miso (keep separate)

Cook the beans until tender and add enough extra water to bring the total up to 10 – 12 cups of liquid. Add the onion and cook another 20 minutes, covered. Then add the remaining ingredients and vegetables, if any, (except the miso) and cook another 20 minutes more on medium heat. Take three to four cups of beans and liquid from the soup and blend or process it with the miso and return it to the soup. The blended beans will add extra flavor. Serve hot and enjoy. Keeps six to eight days refrigerated or may be frozen.

♥ Wild Rice & Mushroom Soup

(Serves 3 – 4)

1 – 2 Tbsp natural oil or butter
2 cups sliced mushrooms
3 cups water or stock
3 cups precooked wild rice (about 1 cup dry rice)
1 – 2 cloves garlic, minced
2 – 3 Tbsp tamari soy sauce
³/₄ – 1 tsp vegetized sea salt
Several dashes cayenne red pepper

Sauté the mushrooms in the hot oil or butter until tender. Then put the sautéed mushrooms and remaining ingredients into a blender and blend thoroughly until smooth. Heat the soup in medium-low heat for 20 minutes or more until hot throughout and flavors mingle. (Make sure garlic taste is subtle.) Add extra sea salt if desired. Serve hot and enjoy.

Curried Wild Rice & Mushroom Soup
Add ¹/₂ – 1 teaspoon curry powder, ¹/₈ – ¹/₄ teaspoon cumin powder (cominos) and 1 – 2 teaspoons honey or other natural sweetener to the Wild Rice Mushroom Soup recipe. Use cayenne red pepper to taste.

♥ Greens & Garnishes Soup

(Serves 3 – 4)

2 cups broccoli (about 1 – 2 small stalks), chopped
2 cups zucchini (about 1 medium zucchini), chopped
2 bunches spinach, washed and chopped
$1/2$ – 1 cup fresh parsley, finely chopped
2 – $2^1/2$ cups milk or milk substitute
2 – 3 tsp tamari soy sauce
1 tsp basil
$1/4$ – $1/2$ tsp sea salt
$1/4$ tsp each thyme, paprika, and dill weed
1 – 2 tsp raw onion, finely chopped
1 clove garlic, minced
Cayenne red pepper to taste
Optional: 1 tsp honey or other natural sweetener

Steam the first three ingredients until tender. Purée everything in a blender. Heat the soup on medium heat, covered, for 20 – 30 minutes or so. Stir occasionally and keep simmering until the sharp edge is off the onion and garlic and the flavors mingle. Serve hot and enjoy. Garnish with chopped chives, green onion tops, or sprigs of parsley or dill weed. Yogurt may be used instead of milk for a flavor variation or serve yogurt with the soup. This delicious healing soup is high in chlorophyll.

 *Chapter 22*

Sauces, Spreads, & Dressings

Sauces

 *Natural Ketchup*

> *12 ounces tomato paste or sauce*
> *2 – 3 Tbsp apple cider vinegar*
> *2 tsp honey*
> *1 tsp parsley*
> *$\frac{1}{8}$ tsp each basil, paprika, and tamari soy sauce*
> *Few dashes each cayenne and sea kelp*
> *Sea salt to taste*

Mix well and chill before using so flavors can mingle. Ketchup made from sauce will pour. Ketchup made from paste must be spread. Keeps six to eight days refrigerated. For longer lasting ketchup, simmer everything on low heat, covered, with $\frac{1}{4}$ cup water for 15 minutes. Stir and chill before using. This heated version keeps fresh two to three weeks or more.

 Cocktail Sauce

3/4 cup ketchup
1/4 cup pickles, finely chopped
2 – 3 Tbsp lemon juice
1 tsp honey or other natural liquid sweetening
1 tsp tamari soy sauce
Sea salt to taste

Add one to two teaspoons extra honey if tart pickles are used. Mix well and chill before using. Keeps five to seven days refrigerated and may be frozen.

 Tangy Tartar Sauce

1 cup mayonnaise
1/4 cup pickles, chopped (add 1 – 2 tsp honey if tart pickles are used)
2 tsp chives or green onion tops, finely chopped
1 – 2 tsp lemon juice
1 tsp prepared mustard (not dry)
Few dashes each cayenne and basil
Sea salt to taste

Mix well and chill before serving. Keeps three to six days refrigerated. Do not freeze.

Terrific Tomato Sauce

(Makes approximately one batch of Lasagne plus two or more Pizzas)

12 – 13 ounces tomato paste
1 – 1$\frac{1}{2}$ cups water
4 large tomatoes, finely chopped (2$\frac{1}{2}$ – 3 cups)
2 medium onions, chopped
1 small eggplant or 1 cup mushrooms, chopped
Optional: 1 small green pepper, chopped
2 – 4 cloves garlic, minced
3 bay leaves
2 – 3 Tbsp tamari soy sauce
2 Tbsp natural oil
2 – 3 tsp parsley
1$\frac{1}{2}$ tsp each basil and oregano
1 – 1$\frac{1}{2}$ sea salt
1 tsp honey or other natural sweetener
$\frac{1}{2}$ tsp each marjoram, thyme, sea kelp, and rosemary
$\frac{1}{8}$ tsp or less cayenne red pepper

Heat the oil in a large frying pan or sauce pot on fairly high temperature. When the oil is hot, add chopped onions, garlic, and eggplant or mushrooms and sauté until they are tender and the onions look clear. Then add the tomatoes, reduce the heat to medium-low and cook covered until tomatoes liquefy (about 15 – 20 minutes). Add the tomato paste and water, and mix everything thoroughly. Lastly add the herbs and spices and simmer covered on low heat for 45 minutes or more, with the lid covering the pan, stirring occasionally. A little extra water may be added for a thinner consistency. Correct the spices if needed. When the sauce is finished, remove the bay leaves. Then use the sauce in recipes or refrigerate it no longer than seven days or freeze it for later use. The recipe can be doubled or tripled for larger batches.

Cheddar Cheese Sauce
(for steamed vegetables or grains)

1 cup milk
³⁄₄ cup mild or medium cheddar cheese, grated
2 Tbsp butter
2 Tbsp whole wheat flour (or 1 Tbsp each rice and millet flour)
¹⁄₄ tsp sea salt
¹⁄₄ tsp paprika
Several dashes cayenne red pepper

On a low heat, melt the butter in a saucepan and stir in the flour until mixed and crumbly, about one to two minutes. Then slowly stir in the milk. When the milk is hot, make sure the mixture is put on the lowest heat possible. Add the rest of the ingredients and stir continually until the cheese melts and thickens. Do not overcook or the sauce will separate. Serve immediately over steamed vegetables or cooked grains and enjoy. Prepare only enough for one meal. May keep one to two days refrigerated. Do not freeze.

Mock Cheese Sauce

¹⁄₂ cup engevita yeast or other yellow nutritional yeast
3 Tbsp whole wheat, kamut, millet, or quinoa flour
4 tsp arrowroot powder
¹⁄₂ tsp sea salt
1 cup water
1 Tbsp natural oil
1 – 2 tsp prepared Dijon or yellow mustard or ¹⁄₂ – 1 tsp dry mustard

Mix the first four ingredients together. Then add the water and oil and mix thoroughly with a wire whisk. Stir or whisk over medium to medium-high heat until the mixture thickens and begins to bubble. Stir in the mustard and heat another 30 – 60 seconds. Serve instead of cheese sauce over vegetables and/or whole grains. Keeps one to two days refrigerated. Do not freeze.

Parmesan Pesto Sauce

3 large bunches fresh basil (3 packed cups), stems removed
$^1/_2$ – $^3/_4$ cup fresh parsley, finely chopped
$^1/_2$ cup pine nuts
6 – 8 Tbsp parmesan cheese, finely grated
$^1/_2$ – $^2/_3$ cup extra virgin olive oil
3 – 4 cloves garlic, chopped
$^1/_2$ – $^3/_4$ tsp sea salt

Combine all ingredients in a food processor or blender until smooth. Toss gently with favorite pasta and serve with garlic bread and vegetables. Keeps three to five days refrigerated. Do not freeze.

Easy Vegan Pesto Sauce

2 – 3 bunches fresh basil leaves
$^1/_2$ cup pine nuts
$^1/_3$ – $^1/_2$ cup virgin olive oil
$^1/_4$ cup engevita yeast or other yellow nutritional yeast
1 – 2 cloves garlic, lightly chopped
$^1/_2$ tsp sea salt

Use a food processor or blender to mix ingredients thoroughly. Chill and serve with pasta and accompaniments. Keeps two to four days refrigerated.

Ginger Nut Sauce

2 Tbsp natural oil
2 medium onions, chopped small
3 – 4 cloves garlic, minced
2¹/₂ – 3 cups water
1 cup almond butter, cashew butter, sesame tahini or other nut butter
4 – 5 Tbsp fresh lemon juice
3 – 4 tsp ginger root, peeled and finely grated
¹/₂ – 1 cup raw, chopped almonds, cashews or other nuts
4 tsp honey, maple syrup, or other natural liquid sweetener
4 tsp apple cider vinegar
1 Tbsp tamari soy sauce
¹/₂ – ³/₄ tsp sea salt
Cayenne red pepper to taste

Heat the oil and sauté the onions and garlic until slightly tender, about two to three minutes. Add all the remaining ingredients and mix thoroughly. Simmer on the lowest possible heat for 30 – 35 minutes, stirring occasionally. Serve over vegetables or whole grains and enjoy. This sauce can be spicy or mild depending on how much cayenne is used. Keeps five to seven days refrigerated. May be frozen.

Mock Meat Gravy

2 cups pinto, kidney, or adzuki bean's cooking juice
2 – 3 Tbsp tamari soy sauce
1 Tbsp natural oil
¹/₃ – ¹/₂ cup whole wheat, kamut, spelt, millet, or quinoa flour
¹/₄ – ¹/₂ tsp chili powder, curry powder, or vegetable broth powder
¹/₄ tsp sea salt
¹/₄ tsp sea kelp
Several dashes cayenne red pepper
Optional: ¹/₂ – 1 tsp onion or garlic powder

Use previously stored, frozen, or refrigerated bean juice, or cook $\frac{1}{2}$ – 1 pound (225g – 450g) beans until tender and drain off and save two cups of the "muddiest" part of the liquid for this recipe. Use the beans in another recipe or freeze them for later use. Combine the remaining ingredients with the cooled bean juice and stir over medium-low heat until thickened and thoroughly hot. Use a wire whisk or blender to mix well. Correct the seasonings to taste, and serve the gravy over vegetables, potatoes, casseroles, burgers, or whole grains. Keeps six to eight days refrigerated and may be frozen.

 # Mushroom Gravy

1 cup mushrooms, sliced thin (any kind, shiitake are especially tasty)
1 Tbsp natural oil
2 cups water or stock
$\frac{1}{2}$ cup whole wheat, kamut, spelt, millet, or quinoa flour
2 – 3 Tbsp tamari soy sauce
1 – 2 tsp vegetable broth powder or 1 – 2 bouillon cubes
Several dashes each cayenne red pepper and sea kelp
Optional: 1 – 2 tsp honey or natural sweetening to balance flavors

Sauté the mushrooms in the oil. Add the flour and stir constantly over medium-low heat for two minutes in order to brown the flour for added flavor. Add the remaining ingredients and stir with a wire whisk until the sauce is well mixed and there are no lumps. Stir constantly over medium heat until hot. Reduce the heat and cover, cooking on the lowest possible heat for 12 – 15 minutes more until the sauce thickens. Stir occasionally while its thickening. Serve hot over vegetables, potatoes, whole grains, burgers, and casseroles. Keeps three to six days refrigerated and may be frozen.

 *Basic Cranberry Sauce*

> *¹/₂ pound fresh or frozen cranberries*
> *1 cup water*
> *¹/₄ – ¹/₂ cup honey or other natural liquid sweetener (or to taste)*
> *Optional: few dashes sea salt*

Heat the water and berries in a covered pan on a medium-low heat for 10 – 15 minutes or until the berries break down and mix with the water. When the berries are cooked and the sauce is still hot, add the honey to taste. Chill thoroughly before using. Delicious with breads, soyloaves, and mock meats. Blend or strain existing sauce for a finer consistency. Keeps one to two weeks refrigerated.

Variation: Add one finely chopped, fresh, preferably organic, small lemon to the mixture before heating and blend everything lightly before chilling and serving. (Remove seeds but include rind, if the lemon is organic.)

 Mayonnaise

> *2 egg yolks*
> *3 – 4 Tbsp apple cider vinegar or fresh lemon juice*
> *2 tsp honey or other natural liquid sweetener*
> *1 tsp sea salt*
> *¹/₄ tsp dry mustard*
> *Few dashes cayenne red pepper*
> *1¹/₄ cups natural oil*

Mix all ingredients except oil together and beat well or blend slowly. Add the oil, little by little, while blending slowly or beating continuously. For thicker mayonnaise add up to ¹/₂ cup more oil. Chill before using. Use a wire whisk if a blender is not available. Keeps four to eight days refrigerated. Do not freeze. Caution: Use only very fresh eggs.

Better Butter

> 1 pound (2 cups) butter
> 2 cups natural oil (canola, sunflower, or safflower are best)
> Optional: Several dashes sea salt
> Optional: 2 – 3 Tbsp flax seed oil (if butter is used up within one week)

Leave the butter in large bowl at room temperature until soft. Use a hand mixer to slowly mix in the oil, about ¼ cup at a time. Once the oil is completely blended, put the mixture into covered containers and refrigerate. Keeps one to three weeks refrigerated or longer if kept bacteria-free and well covered. Once refrigerated it solidifies like butter but unlike butter, this spread cannot be left out of the refrigerator or it may become rancid. This recipe reduces cholesterol amounts per serving and is better for you than margarine—it costs less too. Herbs and flavorings like parsley, dill weed, and garlic can be added to this blend for specialty butters.

Veggie Butter

> ½ pound (225g) soft butter or lecithin spread,
>   or 6 ounces regular tofu plus 2 Tbsp natural oil
> ½ small green or red bell pepper or 2 stalks celery, chopped small
> 5 Tbsp tomato paste
> 1 – 2 Tbsp white or yellow onion, minced
> 1 clove garlic or 1 tsp garlic powder
> 1 Tbsp dried parsley leaves
> 1 tsp each oregano and dill weed
> ½ tsp basil
> Sea salt or vegetable sea salt to taste

Combine all ingredients in a blender or food processor. (A food mill or homogenizing juicer may be used as well.) Chill well before serving. Keeps refrigerated for one to two weeks, only four to seven days if tofu is used. This delicious spread extends or replaces butter and enlivens vegetables, breads, and other foods. The best West Coast natural food restaurants serve this tasty spread. May be frozen.

Dressings

Most homemade oil-based salad dressings will last up to one month or more. Some creamy dressings or dressings made with cut vegetables will last only a few days up to two weeks. Date your dressing bottles (use masking tape) and discard leftovers if they smell or taste odd. However, it is unlikely you will have to discard anything because homemade dressings get eaten up in a flash.

 ## *Yogurt Dressing*

> *1 cup plain yogurt*
> *$1/4$ cup chives or green onion tops, chopped small*
> *Optional: 1 small clove garlic, crushed*
> *$1/8$ – $1/4$ tsp sea salt or $1/2$ – 1 tsp tamari soy sauce*
> *$1/2$ tsp paprika*
> *6 – 8 dashes cayenne red pepper*

Mix well and chill. Do not blend. Add a bit of honey if the yogurt is too bitter. Especially tasty with leafy green salads.

 ## *Yogurt Dill Dressing*

> *1 cup plain yogurt*
> *1 – 2 tsp dill weed*
> *2 tsp fresh lemon juice*
> *Several dashes cayenne red pepper*

Mix well and chill. Do not blend. Serve with leafy green or sprout salads.

Blended Cucumber Dressing

1 cup mayonnaise, sour cream, natural oil, or yogurt
    (or a blend of half of two of these)
1 medium cucumber, peeled, seeded, and chopped
$^1/_2$ – 1 small green onion or 1 tsp chopped onion
1 tsp lemon juice
$^1/_2$ tsp salt or 1 tsp tamari soy sauce
Few dashes each of sea kelp and cayenne
Optional: 1 small clove garlic, crushed

Chop the vegetables and mix all the ingredients in a food processor or blender until smooth. Chill before serving.

Mixed Cucumber Dressing

1 cup mayonnaise, sour cream, natural oil, or yogurt
    (or a blend of half of two of these)
1 medium cucumber, peeled, seeded, and grated fine
    (save the juice for dressing)
1 tsp white or yellow onion, chopped fine or crushed with garlic press
Optional: 1 small clove garlic, crushed
1 tsp lemon juice
$^1/_2$ tsp sea salt or 1 tsp tamari soy sauce
Few dashes each sea kelp and cayenne red pepper

Thoroughly mix all ingredients except the cucumber juice. Use just enough cucumber juice to bring dressing to desired consistency. Chill and serve.

Zesty Tomato Dressing

1 cup peeled tomatoes or tomato juice
$^1/_2$ cup natural oil
1 small green onion, chopped
1 Tbsp apple cider vinegar or 1 – 2 tsp lemon juice
1 – 2 tsp honey
1 tsp sea salt or to taste
$^1/_2$ tsp each paprika and parsley
$^1/_8$ tsp each basil and oregano
Few dashes sea kelp and cayenne

Blend all ingredients until smooth and chill.

 # Oil & Herb Dressing

$1^1/_4$ cups natural oil
2 – 4 Tbsp apple cider vinegar or 1 – 2 Tbsp lemon juice
1 tsp each parsley and paprika
1 tsp each sea salt and tamari soy sauce
$^1/_2$ tsp basil
$^1/_4$ tsp marjoram, thyme, sea kelp, and dill weed
Few dashes cayenne red pepper
Optional: $^1/_2$ – 1 tsp vegetable broth powder, vegetized sea salt,
    or Gomashio

Mix well using a fork or wire whisk and refrigerate for a couple hours so herbs and flavors can mingle.

Variations: Blend in one of the following: 2 – 3 stalks chopped celery, 1 small green onion, 1 – 2 cloves garlic, or green pepper, half peeled and chopped.

♥ Sweet Citrus Dressing #1

(For Fruit Salads only)
$^1/_3$ cup orange juice
2 – 3 tsp honey or maple syrup, or 2 – 3 Tbsp pineapple juice

Sweet Citrus Dressing #2

(For Fruit Salads only)
$^1/_4$ cup lemon juice
2 Tbsp honey or maple syrup

For both Sweet Citrus dressing recipes, mix these ingredients with the salad to add flavor and to prevent the salad from spoiling.

Citrus Dressing

$^3/_4$ – 1 cup natural oil
$^1/_2$ cup orange juice
$^1/_2$ cup lemon juice
2 – 3 tsp honey
1 tsp sea salt

Mix well and serve. This dressing is delicious on vegetable or fruit salads.

♥ Thousand Island Dressing

1 cup cottage cheese or tofu
$1/4$ cup milk or nut milk
2 – 3 Tbsp pickle relish or chopped pickles
2 Tbsp each natural ketchup and apple cider vinegar
$1/2$ – 1 tsp tamari soy sauce
$1/2$ tsp onion, grated or minced
Dash or two cayenne

Blend lightly until all ingredients are mixed. May add a bit of honey.

Easy Thousand Island Dressing

1 cup mayonnaise
1 – 2 Tbsp tomato paste
2 – 4 tsp apple cider vinegar or fresh lemon juice
$1/3$ cup relish or pickles, finely chopped
Several dashes each sea salt and cayenne

Beat ingredients together and adjust flavorings as desired. Chill before serving.

French Dressing

1 cup natural oil
$1/3$ cup apple cider vinegar
$1/3$ cup ketchup
1 Tbsp honey
1 tsp each sea salt and paprika
Few dashes cayenne

Mix well and refrigerate before using. Variation: For Garlic French Dressing, follow the French Dressing recipe, add 1 – 2 small garlic cloves, finely chopped or crushed.

♥ Avocado-Nut Dressing

1 avocado, peeled and pitted
1 – 2 small green onions, chopped
$^1/_2$ cup water
$^1/_4$ cup raw cashews or almonds, chopped
1 – 2 tsp lemon juice
1 tsp dried parsley
$^1/_2$ tsp sea salt
Few dashes cayenne
Optional: 1 tsp honey or other natural liquid sweetener

Blend all ingredients until smooth or, if desired, until the nuts are slightly crunchy. Chill before serving.

♥ Creamy Onion Dressing

1 cup cottage cheese or tofu
$^1/_4$ cup yogurt, mayonnaise, or tofu mayonnaise
1 – 2 small green onions, chopped fine
2 tsp tamari soy sauce
1 – 2 tsp lemon juice
1 tsp parsley
$^1/_4$ tsp each sea salt, basil, and paprika
Optional: 1-2 Tbsp blue cheese

Blend all ingredients lightly and chill before serving. If tofu is used, add extra seasonings such as $^1/_2$ – 1 teaspoon of the Herb Mixture, curry powder, or other seasonings to taste and/or $^1/_4$ – $^1/_2$ cup steamed broccoli or asparagus. May add a bit of honey or other natural sweetener.

♥ *Special Italian Dressing*

1 cup natural oil
¹/₄ – ¹/₃ cup apple cider vinegar
2 – 3 green onions, chopped or 2 tsp onion, chopped fine
¹/₄ green or red bell pepper, chopped
1 sprig parsley or 1 tsp dried parsley
1 – 2 cloves garlic, minced
1 Tbsp lemon juice
1 tsp sea salt or vegetable sea salt
¹/₂ tsp each basil, marjoram, and dill weed
¹/₄ – ¹/₂ tsp anise seed
¹/₈ tsp cayenne

Combine the ingredients together in a food processor or blender and mix for two minutes, until everything is smooth. Serve either chilled or at room temperature.

Chapter 23

Dairy Products, Eggs, & Substitutes

About Dairy Products and Eggs

About one-fifth or less of your daily food intake may be dairy products. Dairy products may have a place in the diet but they are not necessities. Substitutes can be made and are now required or preferred by many individuals. More than 70% of North Americans have at least partial food allergies or intolerances to some dairy foods.

Dairy products provide protein and some vitamins and minerals such as calcium, phosphorus, and vitamins A, B, and D (the latter are added to milk). Once dairy products are heated or pasteurized they lose many of their vitamins and helpful digestive enzymes which is why some vitamins are added after pasteurization.

Dairy products make a good protein snack and add flavor to many recipes. They are good for you in small amounts, but in large amounts, dairy products can clog the digestive system, create too much mucus in the body, and contribute to food allergies, indigestion, and other diseases. Dairy substitutes will be discussed in this chapter.

Milk

Raw cow's milk is preferable to pasteurized cow's milk because of its high content of vitamins, minerals, and helpful digestive enzymes. As long as the cows are inspected regularly for disease, and conditions are sanitary, raw milk is the best cow's milk on the market. Buy only certified raw milk when and if it is available. Raw milk is easier to digest. Often those with dairy allergies can tolerate raw milk. Unfortunately, even certified raw milk is illegal in many areas. Check at your local natural food store.

Goat's milk is even easier to digest than cow's milk. Goat (and sheep) milk is the most similar to human milk of all the animal milks. It can be purchased in canned or powdered form in most health food stores and a few supermarkets. In some places it can be bought fresh, raw, and certified.

Goat's milk contains no cholesterol. Those who are allergic to all forms of cow's milk can sometimes tolerate goat's milk. Ask your health practitioner for advice if you have an allergy.

Milk Powder

Non-instant milk powder has more flavor and vitamins than instant milk powder, but must be beaten well when mixed with liquids. Instant milk powder is generally lower in quality but mixes instantly in liquids. However, instant milk powder tends to get lumpy when used with dry ingredients. Non-instant milk powder is best for use in frostings, sauces, spreads, puddings, and cookies. To make milk from milk powder, mix about 3 – 3½ cups water with one cup milk powder. (Use a wire whisk or blender to mix non-instant milk powder into water or other liquids.) Add a bit more or less milk powder or water according to taste. Many nutritionists feel that a half-and-half mixture of milk made from milk powder and regular milk is the most healthful type of milk available for the average person.

Cheeses

Avoid processed cheeses made with artificial ingredients, flavorings, colorings, and preservatives. Natural cheeses are more nutritious and often easier to digest. Raw milk cheeses are the best, but sometimes hard to find. Also, cheese made with pectin is healthier and easier to digest. Pectin is a natural ingredient derived from fruit which helps the cheese harden. Vegetable rennet is also a natural cheese hardener. Cheese made with vegetable rennet or pectin is harder to find and sometimes more expensive.

The average hard cheese is made with animal rennet instead of pectin. Animal rennet, listed simply as rennet on labels, is an enzyme found in a calf's stomach. It helps the calf to digest milk. However, the enzyme itself is indigestible for humans and either clogs the system or passes through slowly, unable to be useful.

Generally, imported cheeses are better quality and contain fewer additives but some American and Canadian brands are good quality, including several Wisconsin and Canadian brands.

Some soft cheeses such as cream cheese, cottage cheese, sour cream, and some farmer's cheeses do not contain rennet but may legally contain several additives that do not have to be listed on the package. Exceptions to this can include feta, quark, or ricotta, which are often foreign made. These are almost always high quality cheeses.

All varieties of raw milk cheeses are excellent for snacks and sandwiches. But, the lower quality raw milk cheeses can often cause a cooked dish to taste moldy or spoiled after refrigeration or freezing. So, use these cheeses for cooking that will not be refrigerated or frozen and the higher quality, more expensive raw milk cheeses for salads, sandwiches, and large batch cooking.

Eggs

Fertilized eggs laid by free-range chickens are the healthiest and most nutritious. Vegetarians, of course, should avoid fertilized eggs. Rounded yolks of a golden color with thick whites are the highest grade. Eggs bought directly from a local farmer or reliable distributor tend to be the freshest. Two to four eggs are recommended weekly for the average, non-allergic individual. Dairy products or other protein may be eaten instead of eggs if desired. See the Substitution Chart at the back of the book for egg alternatives in recipes.

The best way to hard-boil eggs is to bring them to a rolling boil, and let sit in the water covered, for 20 minutes or so. (This keeps the eggs from overcooking and avoids a blue rim around the egg yolk.) Then run them in cold water and refrigerate. Serve whole or in egg or potato salads.

Yogurt

Yogurt (also spelled yoghurt or yoghourt) is by far the best of all dairy products. Yogurt is a living food. It is easy to digest and, when eaten with other foods, it makes them easier to digest. Yogurt can be digested in one hour and it may cut down the digestion time of many foods by half. Some of the helpful enzymes in yogurt remain in the stomach to assist later digestion.

Fermented milk or yogurt is eaten throughout the world and is claimed to be a major factor in promoting and maintaining good health. It is also low in calories, unless high-calorie sweeteners, sweetened fruits, or other foods are mixed with it. Low fat and no-fat yogurt varieties are also available.

Enjoy yogurt several times a week, up to five or six days weekly. Yogurt can be eaten by itself, with tart or acid fruits, with vegetables, in desserts, dressings, breads, and hundreds of other recipes. It can be used instead of sour cream (for $1/3$ the calories), sour milk, or buttermilk in most recipes, and sometimes instead of mayonnaise.

How to Make Yogurt
Yogurt #1

Thoroughly mix two cups skim or whole milk powder very slowly into $2^1/_2$ cups of lukewarm water. Add two cups of boiling water. Check the temperature of the mixture with a waterproof yogurt, candy, or meat thermometer (one that starts at least at 100°F). The ideal temperature is 105°F. Add hot or lukewarm water accordingly to keep temperature between 103°F and 107°F. Be careful not to add more than $^1/_2$ cup of extra water, bringing the total mixture to $7 - 7^1/_4$ cups. Next mix in $^3/_4 - 1$ cup room temperature plain yogurt from an older batch or from purchased yogurt. Do not use sour tasting or smelling yogurt for your culture. Mix the yogurt into the milk mixture gently with a wire whisk/whip or hand beater. Incubate.

Yogurt #2

Mix the two cups milk powder with five cups lukewarm water together well and, on low heat, cook very slowly until it reaches about 105°F. Test it with the thermometer. If it overheats, let it cool down to the right temperature and then with a wire whisk, gently mix in about one cup plain yogurt and incubate.

Yogurt #3

Mix $6^1/_4$ cups whole milk with $^3/_4$ cup milk powder or six cups skim milk with one cup milk powder. Heat the milk to a boil to kill bacteria in the milk that would be harmful to the yogurt culture. Cool the milk to about 103°F to 107°F and then with a wire whisk, gently mix in about one cup plain yogurt and incubate.

Yogurt #4

Make yogurt from a special package culture, and follow the instructions provided. Some examples are acidophilus or Bulgarian cultures.

How to Prepare the Yogurt for Incubation

Yogurt recipes #1 to #3 make about eight cups of yogurt. Yogurt #4 has its own separate proportions and instructions.

All the bowls, jars, and pans used in making yogurt should be exceptionally clean and rinsed in boiling water before use. External bacteria can kill the yogurt. Place the eight cups of yogurt culture in two quart or liter jars with lids or one pot with a lid for incubation.

How to Incubate the Yogurt

Once everything is mixed, the yogurt must be incubated, that is, kept at one steady temperature until the yogurt bacteria grows or reproduces. This usually takes from two to six hours until the yogurt forms a soft custard-like texture that will solidify as it chills. There are dozens of ways to incubate the yogurt. Basically, it should be kept at about 100°F to 105°F during incubation. Some incubation techniques are as follows:

1. Use a heating pad set on low or medium. If medium is too hot and low is too cool, put the pad on medium and put a few layers of towels between the yogurt containers and the pad. Cover the tops of the jars with towels to keep everything warm. Better yet, put the pad, yogurt, and towels in a cardboard box and cover it to keep it insulated. Occasionally test the mixture's temperature with a thermometer.

2. Keep the yogurt in a pot with a lid and set it on a pilot light if you have a gas stove. Cover it with towels on top only. Test mixture occasionally.

3. If your refrigerator top is warm from the motor, place the jars directly on top and cover them with towels. Test occasionally.

4. Put an oven on 200°F for 10 – 15 minutes and turn it off. Put the yogurt in the oven and close the door. If the yogurt does not reproduce in two hours, take it out of the oven and heat the oven again for five to ten minutes. Then turn the heat off and put the yogurt back in until it is done. Test every hour.

5. Put water in your electric frying pan and leave it on the lowest heat possible (simmer). Put jars of yogurt on a thin metal rack or resting on jar lids in the water. Cover the top with towels. Test occasionally.

6. On very hot days, set the yogurt to incubate in the sun. Be sure to put it in an opaque container. Test often.

7. Put the jars or pots of yogurt into a bath tub of very warm but not hot water. Test often and add warm water as needed.

8. Buy and use a special yogurt incubator that keeps yogurt at just the right temperature at all times, while preparing.

There are many other methods. Use one of the above or find one that suits your needs. Check the yogurt every hour while it is incubating to make sure it does not get too hot or too cold. Adjust each method accordingly.

After Incubation

Chill the yogurt for several hours before serving. Do not let the mixture sit out after it turns to yogurt or it will turn sour and become strong tasting. Properly made yogurt is mild and slightly sweet. The minute the yogurt is ready, refrigerate it.

Tips About Yogurt

1. If the yogurt turns out too thick for your taste, add less milk powder next time. If the yogurt is too loose or runny, add more milk powder next time or allow for a longer incubation period.

2. If the yogurt is underheated and does not thicken or "yog", reheat the milk mixture to the right temperature and add new yogurt culture.

3. If the yogurt overheats and separates completely into curd (solid) and whey (liquid), strain the curd and make homemade cottage cheese. See following recipes.

4. If just a little extra whey forms on top of the yogurt, it can be poured off or mixed with the yogurt after it is chilled.

5. After it yogs, stir the yogurt only when absolutely necessary or it will damage the yogurt bacteria. Do not let saliva or perspiration come in contact with the yogurt before you eat it. Saliva and perspiration bacteria can sour the yogurt too quickly. As it sours, it loses freshness, nutrients, and eventually becomes inedible.

6. Store yogurt in covered jars. Scoop or pour yogurt, but make sure whatever touches the yogurt is clean.

7. Instant or non-instant milk powder can be used for making yogurt. Be careful not to use old milk. If the milk powder smells strongly like milk it may be old and the yogurt will not yog properly.

8. Use plain yogurt or a package yogurt for culture to make new yogurt with. Buy plain yogurt or yogurt with fruit on the bottom. (Do not use the fruit part.) Good brands include Dannon, Columbo, Mountain High, Naja, Maya, Brown Cow, Knudsen, Breyers, Nancy's, and a few others in the US. Good brands in Canada include Olympic, Lifestream, and Lucerne.

9. Yogurt can be frozen for up to one year. Defrost slowly in the refrigerator so it does not separate.

10. Non-instant skim milk powder is best for use in yogurt making.

How to Eliminate Dairy and Egg Products from the Diet

For those who wish to reduce or eliminate dairy products for health, economic, spiritual or ecological reasons, follow these guidelines:

1. Have at least one serving of each of these foods five to seven days per week: (Best served warm.)

    Legumes (soybeans, pinto, kidney, chick peas, adzuki beans, or black beans)
    Whole grains (rice, millet, oats, quinoa, amaranth, barley, buckwheat, or teff)

2. Have at least three servings of any of these foods every day:

Tofu or soy milk	Cashews	Sunflower butter
Soybeans	Hazelnuts (or filberts)	Sesame Tahini
Chick peas	Almonds	Peanut butter
Pinto beans	Sunflower seeds	Nut butter
Adzuki beans	Sesame seeds	Nut or seed milk
Black beans	Peanuts	
Kidney beans		
Warmed, cooked whole grains		

3. Have at least two servings of any of these green vegetables every day:
(preferably one raw and one cooked, one of these should be leafy)

Spinach	Broccoli	Deep green lettuces
Watercress	Asparagus	Globe artichokes
Mustard greens	Brussels sprouts	Alfalfa sprouts
Exotic greens	Chard	Sunflower sprouts
Beet greens	Kale	Wheatgrass

4. Have two to four servings of each of these foods every week:
Spirulina, chlorella, blue-green algae, or barley green (about $1/4$ tsp minimum)
Molasses (unsulphured, 1 tsp per serving) or dried fruit
Orange vegetables (carrots, orange yams, winter squash)

5. Include all the foods needed for every day (or week) listed in Chapter 4 - Meal Planning except dairy and egg products.

Egg & Yogurt Recipes

 Scrambled Eggs Special

(Serves 2 – 3)

> 6 eggs
> 6 Tbsp milk or water
> $1/2$ tsp parsley
> $1/8$ tsp each of basil and paprika
> $1/4 – 1/2$ tsp tamari soy sauce
> Several dashes sea salt or vegetable salt
> Few dashes each of sea kelp and cayenne
> Natural oil
> Optional: chopped green pepper, sliced mushrooms, grated cheese,
>   or tomato chunks.

Use a wire whisk, blender, or electric mixer to beat all the ingredients except the vegetables and cheese together well. Blend until the egg mixture is light and fluffy. Lightly oil a frying pan and put on low heat until the oil is hot. If vegetables are used, use at least two to three teaspoons of oil. Once the oil is hot, add the veggies and sauté until they are slightly tender. Then pour in the egg mixture and add cheese, if any. Cook the mixture on a medium-low heat, stirring occasionally, for about five to seven minutes until the eggs are somewhat solid. Do not overcook the eggs or they will become rubbery. Serve immediately or, if necessary, cover to keep hot. Best if eaten fresh and not stored.

Asparagus Omelet

(Serves 2)

> *8 ounces asparagus, broccoli, or avocado, cut in 2 to 3-inch spears*
> *or slices*
> *4 large eggs, beaten until foamy*
> *4 Tbsp water*
> *1 – 2 Tbsp natural oil or butter (or mixture of the two)*
> *$1/2$ tsp each sea salt and parsley*
> *$1/8$ tsp each paprika, basil, and dill weed*
> *Several dashes cayenne red pepper*
> *4 ounces medium cheddar or Swiss cheese, grated*

Steam the asparagus or broccoli or sauté in one to two teaspoons oil until tender. Keep them warm and covered until needed. If avocado is used, leave it raw. Beat the eggs, water, and seasonings with a wire whisk or hand mixer until light and foamy. Preheat the oven broiler on high and place a rack four to six inches below. Heat the oil and/or butter in a stainless steel or iron frying pan on medium-high heat. When hot, pour in the egg mixture and cook (do not stir) on medium heat until brown underneath. Check under the edges by lifting with a spatula. It is okay to let some of the runny egg mixture from the top of the omelet run under the omelet. When lightly browned underneath, sprinkle on the cheese and place in the hot oven so the top of the omelet can cook. The green vegetables can be added with the cheese or when removed from the oven. When the top is cooked and the cheese melted (about two to three minutes), the omelet is ready. If the vegetables have not been added yet, place them over half of the omelet. Use a spatula or turner to lift one half of the omelet and fold it over the other forming a half moon with the vegetables inside. Serve immediately and enjoy with sauce, salsa, or yogurt.

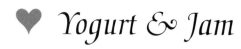 Yogurt & Jam

(Serves 1)

Mix $\frac{2}{3}$ cup plain yogurt with $\frac{1}{4}$ – $\frac{1}{3}$ cup favorite jam or preserves. Stir them together and add extra honey if desired. (The jam or preserves have already been cooked, so any variety may be used and still follow food combining rules.)

 Fruit & Yogurt

(Serves 1)

1 cup fruit, sliced peaches, pears, kiwis, or apples
  and/or whole strawberries or blueberries
$\frac{1}{2}$ cup plain yogurt
Optional: 1 tsp or less honey or other natural sweetener

Mix or top your favorite tart or acid fruit with yogurt and either dribble the honey or other natural sweetener over the yogurt or mix with the yogurt first. Proportions vary according to taste.

Cucumber Yogurt or Raita (Rata)

(Serves 1)
>   **2 cups plain yogurt**
>   **1 cucumber, grated (save juice)**
>   **$^1/_2$ – 1 tsp paprika**
>   **Bit of honey if yogurt is tart**

Mix the grated cucumber and its juice with the yogurt and paprika. Serve it as a snack or side dish with a meal. Best served with vegetable meals and spicy foods.

Variations: Instead of cucumber try chopped green onions and/or tomatoes, or chopped green peppers.

 # Yogurt Cottage Cheese

If yogurt overheats and separates into curds and whey, drain off all the whey and save it for soup stock or dressings. Drain the remaining curds in doubled or tripled cheese cloth by hanging it over a sink or pot for one hour or more. Mix the drained curds, or cheese, with chives or green onion tops, herbs and spices, sea salt, tamari soy sauce, and a bit of honey. Eat as is or use in cooking in place of cottage cheese. This mild, easy-to-digest cheese can be prepared intentionally by overheating the yogurt slightly about one hour or so after incubation.

Yogurt Recipes
Other yogurt recipes are throughout this and other natural food cookbooks. Yogurt can be used in all kinds of main dishes, side dishes, breads, and desserts.

Chapter 24

Sandwich Ideas &
Lunchbox Specials

About Lunches

Box lunches provide a never-ending challenge for new ideas and interesting foods that will make a packed lunch appealing. If you or your family trade lunches at school or work, discard them in favor of bought lunches, or even skip the meal altogether, then try these interesting and delicious alternatives.

Enjoy your lunch! It should be a full meal. The energy from lunch should carry you until supper, even a late one, and keep you feeling active, alert, and cheerful for the remainder of the day.

A complete lunch should include one main dish or sandwich that includes a whole grain and a protein (meat or dairy product, or legume or nuts) and a vegetable or fruit. Lunch desserts are optional.

Here are some sandwich, stew, and soup ideas plus extras for lunches. Some dessert suggestions are also given. For sample menus, see Chapter 4 – Meal Planning.

Lunchbox Equipment:
1. Lunchbox or reusable lunchbag
2. Thermos
3. Glass or Plastic containers and/or a reusable lunch bags
4. Reusable cloth napkins or paper napkins (recycled paper is best)
5. Silverware
6. Sea salt or extra seasonings
7. Optional: frozen "ice pack"

Lunchbox Menu:
1. Sandwich or main dish (must include a whole grain and/or a protein)
2. Vegetable or fruit
3. Mixed nuts or other munchies
4. A natural beverage
5. Optional: dairy product
6. Optional: dessert

Lunchbox Tips
1. Sandwiches can be prepared and frozen ahead of time. Take sandwiches early that morning from freezer to lunchbox so they will defrost by lunchtime or defrost them overnight in the refrigerator first. Most sandwiches will stay fresh frozen up to one month. Use masking tape and a marker to date and label the packages. Add lettuce, if any, to sandwich after it has defrosted.
2. Use "ice packs" to keep lunches cold in the lunch boxes. Freezer ice packs can be purchased or you can fill sturdy plastic containers with water, about three-quarters full, and freeze them. For double protection wrap the ice container in a plastic bag before putting it in the lunch pail.

Delicious Menus for Lunchboxes and Picnics
Some of the recipes for the following Lunchbox Specials can be found in Chapter 15 – Appetizers, Snacks, and Party Foods: Nut Butters, Guacamole, Stuffed or Deviled Eggs, Swiss Cheese Spread, and Sweet Appetizers including dates stuffed with cream cheese, date candies, fruit-nut balls, and peanut butter balls.

Other recipes can be found in Chapter 20 – Main Dishes & Chapter 21 – Soups: Falafels, Sweet and Sour Lentils, Incredible Chili, Kidney Bean Stew, and soups.

Lunches with Dairy or Eggs:
(Omit the bread with dairy product or eggs if desired for food combined meals.)
- Extras Included -
1. Cheese and alfalfa sprouts with butter or mayonnaise on whole grain bread or in pita bread. Serve with salad or vegetable sticks and munchies.
2. Vegetable salad with grated cheese, cream cheese, or feta cheese in pita bread. Serve with mixed nuts and seeds and dessert.
3. Egg salad and lettuce or spinach on bread. Include an apple for before lunch and cake for dessert.

4. Swiss Cheese Spread on crackers or bread with lettuce. Serve with vegetable sticks or salad.

5. Avocado slices with tomato, cheese, and sprouts on whole grain bread or in pita bread. Serve with munchies and/or dessert.

6. Hard-boiled eggs with bread and butter or a sandwich and a vegetable salad with dressing.

7. Falafel or Hummus Spread in pita bread with chopped lettuce, tomatoes, and cheese on top. Guacamole or avocado slices are optional. Serve with yogurt or pudding and munchies.

8. Cream cheese, cucumber slices, and alfalfa sprouts on bread or crackers. Ground nuts or seeds can be sprinkled on top. Serve with soup, stew, or lentils.

9. Cheese, guacamole, and lettuce on bread. (See Chapter 15 – Appetizers, Snacks, and Party Foods for Guacamole recipe.) Serve with salad and cookies or munchies. Try some sunflower seeds or pumpkin seeds.

10. Celery stuffed with cream cheese and peanut butter served with crackers or bread and butter. (See Chapter 15 – Appetizers, Snacks, and Party Foods for recipe.) Serve with sandwich or fruit salad.

11. Deviled eggs and a vegetable salad with bread or crackers.

12. Perfect Potato Salad with cut vegetables.

13. Tomato slices and cream cheese on whole wheat or rye bread. Choose your favorite extras or serve with a salad.

14. Swiss (muenster or cheddar) cheese, lettuce, and sliced or chopped black olives on rye bread. Serve with soup or salad. Try cake for dessert.

15. Cream cheese, sesame tahini, ground nuts, and lettuce on bread. Serve with salad and munchies.

16. A large fruit salad with cheese and nuts or seeds with a sandwich or bread and butter. Apple juice adds a nice touch.

17. Yogurt with added fruit, nuts, and seeds with a sandwich or bread and butter.

18. Tofu Cutlet Sandwich with lettuce and/or tomato. Serve with yogurt or milk and an apple with munchies.

19. Rainbow Roll-Ups served with a vegetable salad.

20. Veggie Nut Dip served with bread and vegetable sticks and optional cheese slices.

Vegan Lunches:

1. Soy or Hummus Spread with lettuce on bread. Can be served with tofu cheese and munchies.
2. Soy or Hummus Spread with lots of raw vegetable sticks and chunks for dipping, like celery, carrots, cauliflower, broccoli, or green peppers. Serve with bread or cookies.
3. Tofu Spread and lettuce or spinach on bread on in pocket pita bread. Chopped or sliced tomatoes add a delicious touch. Serve with pudding or cake.
4. Peanut butter and sliced bananas on bread. A little honey may be added to the peanut butter. Serve with an apple and munchies like nuts and seeds or popcorn.
5. Nut and Date Butter Sandwich: Spread date butter on one piece of bread and nut butter on another and place together for a super sandwich. Serve with a dairy-free Greek salad or other hearty salad.
6. Miso-Soy Spread and lettuce on bread. Serve with salad or half an avocado stuffed with nuts or nut butter.
7. Sesame tahini or sesame butter with apple or other fruit butter on bread, similar to peanut butter and jelly. Serve with vegetable sticks or salad.
8. Hot soup in a thermos along with crackers, rice cakes, or bread. (See soup recipes.) Serve with vegetable sticks.
9. Hearty Vegetable Bean Stew in a wide-mouth thermos. Serve with vegetable salad and crackers or munchies.
10. Chili in a wide-mouth thermos served over or with plain cold rice or crackers served with vegetable sticks or stuffed celery.
11. Sweet and Sour Lentils served hot or cold along with crackers or bread and veggie butter. Include a salad with dressing or an avocado.
12. Vegetable salad mixed with cold rice or millet and salad dressing. Mixed nuts with crackers or bread. Choose a light dessert such as cookies.
13. Falafel or Hummus Spread in pita bread with chopped lettuce, tomatoes, and avocado slices with pudding or munchies such as popcorn or nuts.
14. Vegetable salad with sunflower seeds and dressing in pita bread. Tahini and crackers and dessert.

Tasty Snacks:

1. Celery filled with:
    a. Cream cheese (sprinkle paprika on top)
    b. Soy Spread
    c. Peanut butter or other nut butter

    d. Falafel or Hummus spread (sprinkle paprika on top)

    e. Veggie Nut Butter

2. Dates stuffed with cream cheese or nuts (recipes in Chapter 15 – Appetizers, Snacks, & Party Foods).

3. Nut Butter Balls (recipe in Chapter 15 – Appetizers, Snacks, & Party Foods).

4. Fruit-Nut Mixture: Dried fruits mixed with nuts and seeds. Use some of the following, raisins, shredded coconut, dates, dried peaches, apricots or pears, sunflower seeds, pumpkin seeds, cashews, almonds, walnuts, and/or filberts. A delicious snack. (Only for those with good digestion.)

5. Sliced vegetables like carrots, celery, broccoli, cauliflower, green peppers, and whole cherry tomatoes with dip. (See Chapter 15 – Appetizers, Snacks, & Party Foods).

6. Whole fruit or vegetable slices or pieces.

7. A fruit or vegetable or sprout salad.

8. Soynuts, peanuts, almonds, or other nuts or popcorn.

9. Dry granola or granola and milk.

10. Cottage cheese with chopped avocado or chives.

11. Yogurt, cheese, or milk.

12. Fruit or vegetable juices.

    Also, see both Chapter 16 – Vegetables & Vegetable Salads and Chapter 25 – Desserts for snack ideas.

Outdoor Cooking Menu Ideas

Soyburgers: Can be cooked on the grill on tin foil. Lightly oil the tin foil before placing burgers on it and cover burgers loosely with another piece of foil.

Shisk Kebabs: Can be broiled directly on the grill. See recipe in Chapter 20 – Main Dishes.

Potatoes: Whole or cut, unskinned potatoes can be wrapped twice in foil and roasted in hot coals or on the grill for 15 – 30 minutes, depending on the size of potatoes and the heat of the fire.

Corn on the Cob: Roast in hot coals or on the grill. Wrap husked corn twice in foil. The corn cooks in eight to fifteen minutes. Zucchini, eggplant, turnips, squash and other vegetables can be cut in $1/2$-inch thick, long slices, dipped in water, milk, egg or milk substitute, then in flour or batter and grilled.

    Do not forget the extras: try Perfect Potato Salad or Three-Bean Salad, Baked Beans, Myboulie, breads, and beverages.

Sandwich Spread & Butter Recipes

 Egg-Salad

> *4 eggs, hard-boiled*
> *2 – 3 Tbsp mayonnaise*
> *Few dashes each paprika, cayenne, and sea kelp*
> *Vegetable salt to taste*
> *Optional: Bit of chopped celery, green pepper or spinach*

Mash the hard-boiled eggs together with the mayonnaise and spices until the eggs are mashed and the spices blended. Chill and use as a sandwich or cracker spread along with lettuce or alfalfa sprouts. Keeps two to four days. Do not freeze.

 Mock Egg Salad (Tofu Spread)

> *12 ounces regular tofu*
> *2 – 3 stalks celery or $1/2$ green pepper, chopped fine*
> *1 small tomato, chopped fine (drain excess juice and remove seeds)*
> *$1/4$ – $1/2$ tsp onion or garlic powder or lots of chopped chives*
> *1 tsp parsley*
> *$1/4$ tsp each paprika and basil*
> *Several dashes each cayenne and sea kelp*
> *Vegetable salt to taste*
> *Optional: $1/4$ tsp turmeric for a yellow color*

Drain the tofu and mash it together with all the spices and salt. Drain the tomato on paper towels and mix with the celery or green pepper. Use as a sandwich spread on bread or in pita bread or as a dip for crackers. Tofu is high in protein and calcium. The tofu can be used raw if rinsed and very fresh, or it can be steamed in chunks for five minutes to kill bacteria, especially if it is more than a few days old.

♥ Hummus - Chick Pea Spread

1 cup dry chick peas, soaked and cooked (save the water)
$^1/_3$ – $^1/_2$ cup sesame tahini
$^1/_2$ small onion or 1 – 2 green onions, chopped fine
2 – 3 cloves garlic, minced
3 – 4 Tbsp lemon juice
2 – 4 tsp tamari soy sauce
1 – 2 tsp parsley
$^1/_2$ tsp each parsley and paprika
Few dashes each cayenne and sea kelp
Vegetable salt to taste
Optional: 2 stalks celery or $^1/_2$ green pepper, chopped fine

Mash the cooked chick peas (or use a food processor) using only about one cup of their cooking water or more for desired consistency. Mix or blend the onion, garlic, lemon juice, tamari soy sauce, and herbs and spices along with a few table-spoons of cooking water from the chick peas in a food processor or a blender. (Onions and garlic may also be chopped and cooked with the chick peas.) Add tahini to mixture and then add mixture to the chick peas and mash everything together while the chick peas are still hot. Add chopped celery or green pepper for texture and flavor. Use the spread in sandwiches, on crackers, as a celery stuffer, or as an appetizing vegetable dip. (Also called humous or humus.) Keeps seven to eight days refrigerated and may be frozen.

 *Soy Spread*

>1 cup soybeans*
>1 cup chopped carrots or orange yams, steamed and mashed
>1 medium onion, chopped
>2 cloves garlic, minced
>1 – 2 tsp tamari soy sauce
>2 tsp parsley
>1 tsp sea salt
>$^1/_2$ tsp each vegetable powder and paprika
>$^1/_4$ tsp each basil and thyme
>Several dashes each cayenne and sea kelp
>Optional: 2 stalks celery or $^1/_2$ – 1 green pepper, chopped fine
>Optional: 1 – 2 tomatoes, chopped and drained of excess liquid and seeds

Soak the soybeans overnight and cook them until tender in a pressure cooker. When the beans are finished, cook them without pressure for 15 – 20 minutes more with the onion and garlic. Then drain all of the liquid from the beans except for 1 to 1$^1/_2$ cups and mash the remaining liquid with the beans. Mash in the herbs, spices, and yams or carrots with the vegetables that are to be used. Use as a sandwich or cracker spread. A food processor can be used for a finer spread. *Chick peas may be used instead of soy without using a pressure cooker.

 Miso-Soy Spread

Use the Soy Spread recipe and mix it half and half with miso or mix $^3/_4$ soy spread to $^1/_4$ miso. Makes a good sandwich or cracker spread. Chick peas and chick pea miso can be used instead of soy.

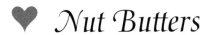# Nut Butters

Nuts or seeds
Sesame or sunflower oil

Nut butters can be made with blenders, food processors, and some juicers. Follow the instructions for butters or peanut butter provided with your juicer or processor. Blender peanut butter is described in Chapter 12 – Food Preparation Tips & Tricks. Juicers do not require the use of oil, but it may be added as needed.

Butter can be made with sesame and sunflower seeds, cashews, almonds, filberts, and peanuts. These are the tastiest and most popular kinds, although any type of nut can be used. (Sesame seed butter does require the use of oil.)

Date Butter

2 cups dates, pitted
1 cup water
1 Tbsp lemon juice
1 tsp lemon rind
Dash of sea salt

Heat the water and dates in a saucepan on low-to-medium heat. When the water starts to boil, turn the heat down low and cook the mixture until the dates dissolve into the water. Once the dates break down, mix in salt and lemon and stir. Use the mixture on or in desserts or as a bread or cracker spread. In some recipes it can be used instead of honey or other sweeteners. Can be used instead of jellies and jams.

 *Chapter 25*

Breads

Types of Flours and Their Qualities
Whole Wheat Flours
Hard Wheat or Bread Flours: Ground from hard red wheat kernels also called wheat berries. Different grades of flour can usually be found in fine, medium, and coarse grinds. Use medium and fine ground flour for most baking and cooking purposes. Coarse flour should generally be mixed half and half with medium or fine ground flour or with one-quarter to one-sixth part unbleached white flour or fine pastry flour. Since most flours are not marked fine, medium, or coarse, one must learn to tell the difference by the look and feel of the flour. Avoid flours that smell like molasses or cinnamon as they make poor bread and give an unwanted heavy or sweet flavor. Hard wheat flour contains more gluten (protein) than any other flour. This is the source of gluten flour.

Soft Wheat, Cake, or Pastry Flour: Ground from soft wheat berries. It gives a more tender, crumbly texture to pastry. It is usually found in a fine or medium grind. A mixture of soft wheat flour and hard wheat flour is recommended for most pastry. Use half and half or slightly more pastry flour. This type of flour can be whole wheat or white flour.

Graham Flour: Whole wheat flour with part of the outer bran layers removed.

Kamut Flour: A variety of wheat flour that about 50% of people who are allergic to wheat can tolerate. Whole grain kamut is whiter than whole wheat flour, has a lighter flavor, but it is just as versatile. Use it instead of whole wheat in almost any recipe. For a darker color and more whole wheat flavor, use about $1/4$ cup rye, buckwheat or amaranth flour per each cup of kamut flour used in a recipe.

Spelt Flour: This is another variety of wheat flour that is easy to digest. This is a redder, heavier flour and only $7/_8$ cup should be used in place of 1 cup of whole wheat flour. Be sure to use some lighter flours with spelt flour. This is a good pasta flour. Many with wheat allergies can tolerate spelt.
Other whole wheat flours include durum, farina, and bolted wheat.

Other Flours

Stone Ground Flour: Any flour that is milled by using stone rollers or stone grinders. This flour is usually heavier and coarser than other flours and usually must be mixed with lighter flours.

Unbleached White Flour: Flour made from only the inner part of the wheat called the endosperm. The bran and germ are removed, but unlike white flour this flour is not bleached and no chemical additives are used. This is the part of the wheat that contains the gluten.

Gluten Flour: The high-protein part of the whole wheat flour that works with the yeast or baking powder to help bread or other baked goods rise and keep their shape. A small amount of gluten flour, about one to three teaspoons per loaf, can be added to whole wheat flour to increase the rise in the bread. For cakes, see recipes in Chapter 26 – Desserts. Never use gluten flour with all white flour.

Semolina Flour: A cream colored, high-gluten white flour used to make pasta and noodles. It helps pasta keep its shape.

Rye Flour: A heavy, strong flavored flour that is generally not used by itself. Mix half and half with whole wheat flour or use slightly more whole wheat or rye. Use a little rye mixed with more wheat flour for some main dish or bread recipes. Contains gluten. Fine ground whole rye may be used alone in some bread recipes.

Oat Flour: A mild flour that helps keep pastry and breads light and fine-textured. Mix it with whole wheat flour in almost any proportions. Excellent for use in wheatless breads also. (contains gluten)

Buckwheat and Barley Flours: These are heavy yet flavorful flours that should be mixed with larger proportions of other flours. Good in pancake mixes, veggie burgers, and casseroles. While barley contains gluten, buckwheat is basically gluten-free.

Rice Flour: A mild, light-textured flour. It does not rise well or bond well by itself, so it should be used with larger proportions of whole wheat, oat, or other flours. Basically gluten-free.

Millet Flour: A medium grade flour, golden in color. Nutritious and flavorful if fresh. It can be bitter if old. Especially good in wheatless breads as a main flour. Basically gluten-free.

Soy Flour: This is a heavy flour, made from soybeans. It is usually ground very fine. High in protein and with a strong flavor. It comes in regular or low fat varieties. Add to breads about one-eighth to one-half cup per loaf. Grain-free.

Chick Pea Flour: Another heavy flour that is high in protein content. May also be used to add protein to breads, one-eighth to one half cup per loaf. Good in vegetarian burger mixes. Gluten- and grain-free.

Lentil Flour: A heavier, high protein flour made with brown or green lentils. Often used to make East Indian pappadum breads which are comparable to large round corn chips. Use the same as soy and chick pea flours, up to half a cup per loaf of bread for extra protein. Gluten- and grain-free.

Other Bean Flours: These include black bean flour, green and yellow pea flours, pinto bean flour, red lentil flour, and white bean flour. Use these like the other bean flours above. Do not use too much in each recipe or they could contribute to gas.

Potato Flour: Use this flour as a thickener in some sauces or in bread making. Use about $1/4 - 2/3$ cup per loaf of bread or use to taste. Gluten- and grain-free.

Cornmeal or Corn Flour: The flour is ground finer but both may be used in breads and cereals. They can be used by themselves or with other flours. A fairly heavy yet flavorful flour. Basically gluten-free. The corn flour sometimes contains added wheat.

Amaranth Flour: A rich, dark, gluten-free flour (from seeds) that is perfect for grain-free diets. It works best mixed with a lighter flour like brown rice flour and especially good mixed with grain-free tapioca flour or arrowroot powder. Use about $1/4$ cup amaranth to $1/4$ cup lighter flour in a recipe. Do not substitute these directly for whole wheat or other gluten flours, exchange ratios vary with each recipe. See Substitution Chart in Part IV or recipes.

Quinoa Flour: A medium weight flour essentially gluten-free. There are two basic types of quinoa flour, one lighter which can be used like millet flour and one darker which can be used like amaranth flour.

Tapioca Flour: A very light, gluten- and grain-free flour that is best mixed with a heavier flour as tapioca has minimal nutritional value. Tapioca is a binding agent that compliments heavier flours like amaranth, buckwheat, rye, soy, chick pea, and other bean flours. (This can also be used instead of milk powder in bread recipes and in Nut Butter Balls.)

Teff Flour: A medium-light flour that mixes well with light or heavy flours. This gluten- and grain-free flour is especially good in place of white flours, rice flour, millet flour, and quinoa flour in recipes. (Recipe will need altering when this is used to replace white flour.)

Gluten Allergies:

Those allergic to gluten should avoid all flours except the following:

Amaranth	Cassava	Potato
Arrowroot	Chick pea	Quinoa
Bean flours	Cornmeal (not flour)	Rice
(pinto, black bean, etc.)	Lentil	Soy
Buckwheat	Millet	Tapioca
Carob	Nut	Teff

Grain Allergies:

Those allergic even to minute amounts of gluten or grain should avoid all flours except the following:

Amaranth	Cassava	Potato
Arrowroot	Chick pea	Soy
Bean flours	Lentil	Tapioca
(pinto, black bean, etc.)	Nut	Teff
Carob		

Bread Making

The Purpose of Each Ingredient Used in Bread Making:

Water: Acts as a binder for flour and other ingredients. Allows a medium for the yeast to grow and expand.

Milk or Milk Powder: Adds flavor and a bit of sweetness to bread. Makes a smoother textured bread.

Yeast: Active dry yeast is a growing bacteria or fungus that makes the bread rise. It creates carbon dioxide bubbles in the dough. (Gluten in the flour keeps the bubbles whole, while the bread rises and bakes.)

Flour: Is the basic ingredient in bread. It contains most of the vitamins in the bread plus gluten (protein), fiber, and carbohydrates.

Sweeteners: These feed the yeast. They help the yeast grow and develop. Sweeteners also give the bread a pleasant flavor and texture. Liquid sweeteners act as a natural preservative to keep bread fresh longer.

Salt: Helps to balance out the flavors in bread. Brings out the taste of the sweeteners used. (Slightly hinders rising which is why in yeast bread salt is added later.)

Oil: Adds to the flavor and texture of bread. Helps bind the bread together. Helps to keep the bread moist for a longer period of time. Increases shelf-life of baked goods.

Lecithin: Adds vitamins and minerals. Acts as a natural preservative. Is a good binding agent and improves the texture of the bread.

Eggs: Give bread a lighter texture, act as a binder, help bread rise and keep its shape. They give bread a rich flavor and golden color.

Baking Powder: Used in quick-bread recipes instead of yeast to make bread rise and give it a lighter texture.

Sourdough: Used as leavening agent. A natural replacement for yeast-free diets instead of baker's yeast.

 # Six-Hour Basic Yeast Bread Recipe

(4 Loaves)

> 5 pounds medium or fine ground hard wheat or bread flour, OR
>   3 pounds regular or coarse whole wheat flour and 2 pounds pastry flour,
>   OR 4 – 4$^1/_2$ pounds coarse or medium whole wheat flour and $^1/_2$ – 1
>   pound unbleached white flour
> 6 cups water
> $^2/_3$ cup honey (or $^1/_2$ cup honey and 2 Tbsp molasses)
> $^1/_2$ cup natural oil
> 2$^1/_2$ Tbsp baking yeast
> 2 Tbsp sea salt
> Optional: 1$^1/_2$ – 2 cups milk powder
> Optional: $^1/_4$ cup gluten flour
> Optional: 2 – 3 tsp liquid lecithin

Basic Timetable:
  $^1/_2$ hour basic mixing
  1 – 1$^1/_2$ hrs foam or sponge rising
  $^1/_2$ – $^3/_4$ hour adding extra ingredients and kneading
  1$^1/_2$ hrs dough rising and oiling and flouring the bread pans
  $^1/_4$ hour dividing dough into balls, kneading , shaping, and placing in
    pans
  $^1/_2$ hour or less letting loaves rise, heating oven
  1 hour or less baking
 Tip: Beginners measure very carefully!

Twenty-Two Steps to Great Yeast Breads

1. Start with six cups of very warm water about 100°F – 107°F in a 6 – 10 quart bowl, pan, or bucket. Use a cooking thermometer to test the water if needed.

2. Add the 2½ tablespoons of yeast and mix well with a wire whisk or spoon.

3. Let the water and yeast sit together for two to four minutes undisturbed to help the yeast develop.

4. Then add ⅔ cup honey or ½ cup honey and two tablespoons of molasses, and liquid lecithin if any.

5. Mix it thoroughly and let it sit another two to four minutes while the sweetener helps the yeast grow.

6. Add milk powder if desired and beat it into the mixture completely before adding flour to prevent lumps. (If milk powder is improperly mixed, there will be pockets of dry powder in the finished bread.)

7. Add six to seven cups whole wheat flour plus ¼ cup gluten flour if desired to aid the bread's rising. Beat the flour in completely with a wire whisk or wooden spoon. (Two cups of the flour should be pastry or unbleached white.)

8. Remove the stirring utensil from the batter and scrape the sides of the bowl with a knife so that none of the batter is wasted. Set the batter in a warm place such as on top of a refrigerator, in a slightly warmed oven turned off, or on a warm heating pad. Cover the bowl or other container with a large, damp piece of paper towel or a damp clean dish towel. (Paper towel is best as it can be discarded. Doughy towels are hard to clean.)

9. Let the batter sit undisturbed for 1 – 1½ hours until the foamy batter or sponge rises to about twice its previous size.

10. Then remove the cloth from over the sponge. (Scrape and save any dough on the toweling.) Scatter the salt and oil over the sponge and slowly stir them in together. Do not use a wire whisk. Be careful not to tear or cut through the batter. Just fold it over carefully to mix in the oil and salt.

11. Carefully fold in four to six cups more flour until the batter becomes too hard to stir.

12. Use a large table or board for kneading. Thinly spread three to four cups of flour over this surface. Then pour out the batter or dough and thinly cover it with two to three cups more flour. This will keep your hands from sticking to the dough while kneading.

13. Carefully press or knead the flour into the dough by pressing it with the palms of your hands, turning the dough and overlapping it as needed to mix in the flour.

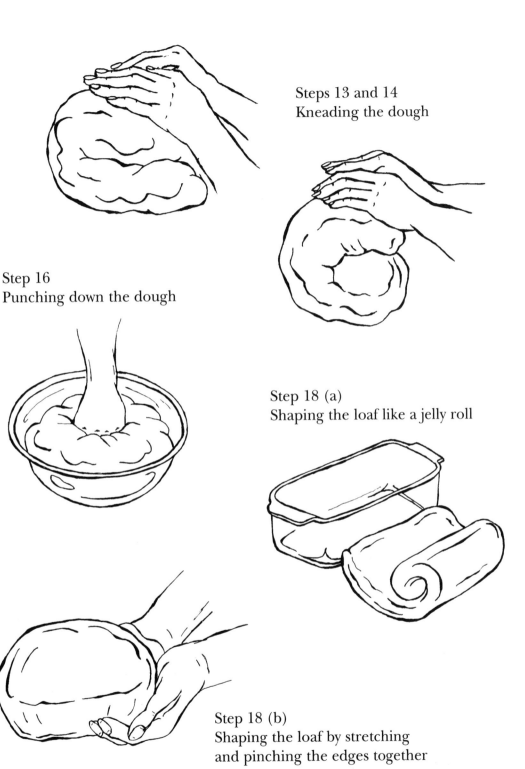

Steps 13 and 14
Kneading the dough

Step 16
Punching down the dough

Step 18 (a)
Shaping the loaf like a jelly roll

Step 18 (b)
Shaping the loaf by stretching
and pinching the edges together

14. Keep kneading the dough until four pounds or more flour has been used in the complete recipe so far. The dough will feel somewhat heavy when enough flour has been added. The dough will remain slightly sticky and should be handled carefully. The less flour is added, the lighter the bread texture will be. In all about $4\frac{1}{4} - 4\frac{3}{4}$ pounds flour is used.

15. Wash the pan or bowl that was used for the sponge rising. Dry it and lightly oil it so the dough will not stick to it. Place the dough back in the bowl, and turn it over so all sides of the dough are lightly oiled. (Use less than 1 tablespoon.) Cover the bowl once again with a clean damp cloth or damp toweling.

16. Let the dough rise $1\frac{1}{2}$ hours or more until it comes close to doubling in size. Then punch it down with your fists. You may let it rise and punch down one or two more times if you are busy with other projects or it can be prepared now, after punching down the first time.

17. When the dough is almost through rising, oil and flour four bread pans for baking. Lightly coat each pan with $\frac{1}{2}$ teaspoon or more oil and then shake flour in each pan until it coats the bottom and sides. Do not oil and flour non-stick pans.

18. Pour the risen dough onto a clean surface and divide it into four parts or balls. Knead each part for a minute or two, adding a little flour if the dough is too sticky to handle. Then shape each one into a loaf and place it in the oiled and floured pans.

There are several ways to shape the loaf:

    a. Roll it out into a rectangle, the width of the rectangle being the same as the length of the pan. Then roll it up like a jelly roll, pinch the ends together and pinch the bottom crease and place in the pan.

    b. Shape the loaf by stretching the dough into shape. Make sure all ends and edges are pinched together or the bread may split along the sides of the loaf.

19. Cover the pans of dough with a lightweight piece of damp cloth or toweling to keep them moist. Let them rise for 15 – 25 minutes until the dough nearly doubles in size. Do not worry if it does not completely double, it will continue to rise in the oven. While the bread is rising in the pans, heat the oven to 350°F. Adjust the temperature slightly if needed. (If glass pans are used, lower the temperature 25°F.) Note: The bread may fall in the oven if you let it rise more than 30 minutes before putting it in the oven. (If it has risen more than 30 minutes, punch it down, knead and reshape it and place it in a newly oiled and floured pan or in a non-stick pan to rise again.)

20. Place the pans in the oven as far apart from one another and the sides of the oven as possible. Close the oven door and bake for 50 – 60 minutes until the bread is a golden dark brown. It should be very firm on top when done.

21. When the bread is done, take it from the oven. Make sure all the loaves have baked completely.

To test the bread:

1. Knock on it to make sure the top of the bread is hard. It should not give when knocked and should make a hollow sound.

2. Remove one bread from the oven and take it out of the pan. The bottom of the bread should be brown (not black or very light gold) and firm. If it is too spongy, it is not finished yet. Loosen the finished breads from the pans by sliding a knife around the inside edges of the pans. Then place the hot loaves right side up on a cooling rack or bread board until they are cool.

22. Bread is delicious hot with butter, but it will still be somewhat doughy inside. The bread will harden more inside as it cools. Wait until the bread cools completely before making sandwiches or wrapping and storing, or it will get soggy. If you are in a rush to go out, leave the bread on the table an hour or two to cool. If you will be gone several hours, cover the bread with dry dish towels.

Bread Storage

Refrigeration: It will keep up to seven days or more. Refrigerate all bread within one day of baking or keep it in a cool, dry place at 55°F or less. Never leave it out in hot weather.

Freezing: Freeze extra bread after wrapping it securely in double plastic bags or special single freezer bags. It will keep fresh frozen up to six or eight weeks or more. Unrisen bread dough can also be frozen. Shape it into loaves and freeze it in plastic bags before it rises. Let dough thaw and rise before baking in the same way as fresh, unfrozen dough. Also try freezing dough in a plastic bag and shape into loaves after it defrosts. With a napkin or toweling, lightly dab up any excess water from the dough as it thaws. Note: Defrost dough slowly at room temperature. Never place on a hot surface to thaw or it will ferment and spoil the yeast.

Defrosting: Defrost bread at room temperature for a few hours and then refrigerate. Defrosted bread will keep as long as fresh bread in the refrigerator.

Yeast Bread Recipe Variations

(4 Loaves)

Follow the basic recipe for whole wheat bread making the following changes:

1. Raisin, Nut, and Honey Bread: Double the honey in the first mixing stage. Mix one or more cups of raisins and nuts into the batter right after the sponge stage along with the oil and salt. Another way is to add these ingredients just before putting the bread dough in the pans to rise. Roll the dough like a jelly roll. Before rolling, spread a thin layer of honey, nuts, and raisins. Be sure that the loaf ends are securely pinched together or the honey will spill out and the bread will burn.

2. Sweet Bread: Double the amount of honey and make sure one-quarter to one-half the flour used is pastry flour and the rest regular whole wheat. Be sure to use milk powder for a sweeter flavor and good texture.

3. Cinnamon or Spice Bread: As in raisin, nut, and honey bread, add spices just before rolling the dough like a jelly roll. Do not mix the cinnamon with the batter or dough or it will hinder rising and change the texture of the dough.

4. Eggbread: Add eggs after adding milk powder in the first mixing stage of bread making. Use four to eight well-beaten eggs per four loaves of bread. Decrease the original amount of water used by three to four tablespoons per each egg used. Five minutes or more before bread is ready to come out of the oven, use a brush to paint the top of the bread loaves with an "egg wash." This adds flavor and gives the bread a shiny, golden crust. Use one or two well-beaten eggs to cover four loaves. Milk or melted butter can also be used in place of eggs on top of the bread. Continue to bake the bread for five more minutes.

5. Bread Made with Milk: Use milk in place of water in the recipe in the same proportions. Milk must be scalded (boiled) at 150°F or more and then cooled down to 100°F to 107°F. Unscalded milk has bacteria that would hinder the growth of the yeast. Exclude the 1½ – 2 cups milk powder from the recipe and add more flour instead.

6. Rolls, T-Rings, and Coffeecakes: Use about half bread flour and half pastry flour for lighter-textured bread for rolls and T-rings. Use more sweetening for pastry-type breads.

7. High Protein Bread: Add one to two cups soy flour per four loaves. Also be sure to include one to two tablespoons lecithin and ¼ – ½ cup gluten flour. Eggs and milk powder are optional but will add extra protein and flavor.

8. Caraway-Rye Bread: Use ⅓ cup molasses and ⅓ cup honey. Use half rye flour and half wheat flour mixed equally each time flour is used in the recipe. Add two to four tablespoons of caraway seeds when the oil and salt are added. For wheat-less rye use one-half to three-quarters rye and the rest millet or oat flour and a little soy flour.

9. Surprise Bread: Use two to four cups of any kind of unusual flour in place of some of the whole wheat flour in the recipe. Use only one type of extra flour plus the wheat flour so the new taste can be distinguished. One-quarter cup gluten flour may also be added to aid rising if heavy flours are used.

10. Sprouted-Wheat Bread: Sprout about $^1/_2$ cup whole wheat berries. (Makes more than 1 cup of sprouts.) Grind the mature wheat sprouts in a hand grinder, food processor, or a little bit at a time in a blender. Add the ground sprouts to the bread just after the sponge rising with the salt and oil. Be sure to use some gluten flour or some extra-light flour to aid rising this heavier bread.

11. Cracked-Wheat or Other Cracked-Grain Bread: Soak one to two cups any cracked grain in twice as much water and let soak for two to four hours until soft. Add the cracked grain after the sponge rising. Gluten or other light flour may also be added to the bread.

12. Rolled-Oat Bread: Add one to two cups dry rolled oats before the sponge rising. Be sure to add one to two cups less flour also because of the extra oats.

 # Garlic Bread

> $^1/_4$ – $^1/_2$ *cup melted butter or natural oil*
> *4 – 6 cloves garlic, minced*
> *1 tsp onion, minced*
> $^1/_8$ *tsp sea salt or to taste*
> *Optional: 1 – 2 tsp parsley*

Blend these ingredients in a blender to make the garlic spread. Use one or two loaves of basic whole wheat bread. Slice the loaves and use a pastry brush to apply the garlic spread on one side of each piece of bread. Wrap the loaf or loaves in tin foil and warm them in the oven for 15 – 25 minutes at 350°F – 400°F until the bread is hot. Serve and enjoy.

♥ Zwieback

This is bread that is baked two times to make a crunchy snack for adults or a biscuit for teething babies. This bread has very little mucus and is much easier to digest than fresh bread. Use any kind of whole grain bread. Slice the bread and lay it flat on the oven racks. Bake it in a very slow oven at 200°F for one hour or slightly longer until it is dry and crispy. A little honey and cinnamon can be baked on the bread during the last 10 – 15 minutes for a sweet zwieback if desired.

Quick Bread Recipes

♥ Oat or Oatmeal Bread

(Makes 1 loaf)

1 – $^1/_2$ cups milk or substitute (cashew milk is nice)
1 cup rolled oats
1 cup oat flour
$^3/_4$ cup rice flour
$^1/_2$ cup honey or other natural liquid sweetener
$^1/_4$ cup soy or oat flour
2 Tbsp natural oil
4 tsp baking powder
1 Tbsp arrowroot
1 Tbsp liquid lecithin
1 tsp sea salt
$^1/_4$ tsp cinnamon (to add flavor)
Optional: 1 – 2 tsp gluten flour or 1 tsp xanthan or guar gum

Mix the wet and dry ingredients separately and then mix everything together well. The batter should be very stiff but stirrable. Scoop the batter into a lightly oiled loaf pan and smooth it into place. Bake at 375°F to 400°F for 1 – 1$^1/_4$ hours until lightly browned. If the top gets too dark before the inside is baked, cover the bread loosely with a tent-shaped piece of tin foil for 10 – 15 minutes of the baking time. Remove the foil 10 minutes or so *before* the bread comes out of the oven.

Millet-Rice Bread

(Makes 1 loaf)

Follow the instructions for the oat bread except for the rolled oats and oat flour. Instead of a two cup total of oats and oat flour, use $1\frac{1}{2}$ to $1\frac{3}{4}$ cups millet flour. Note: Millet and rice flour may taste a little bitter at times unless milk or a milk substitute is used in the recipe.

 # Cornbread or Muffins

(Makes 1 loaf or $1\frac{1}{2}$ dozen muffins)

> *2 cups cornmeal*
> *1 cup milk or milk substitute*
> *1 large egg, beaten*
> *2 Tbsp natural oil*
> *1 – 2 Tbsp honey or other natural liquid sweetener*
> *1 Tbsp baking powder*
> *$\frac{1}{2}$ – 1 tsp sea salt*
> *Optional: 1 – 2 tsp gluten flour or 1 tsp guar or xanthan gum*

Mix the wet and dry ingredients separately. Mix everything together and beat well. Make sure the mixture is very thick but pourable. Adjust wet and dry ingredients slightly if needed. Oil a loaf pan and pour in the batter. Bake at 400°F for 25 – 35 minutes until golden and a toothpick comes out fairly clean.

Sweet Loaf Variations

 *Golden Banana Bread*

(Makes 1 large loaf)

> *2 cups whole wheat flour, fine or mixed*
> *2 very large bananas (or 3 small)*
> *$1/2$ cup honey or maple syrup*
> *$1/3$ – $1/2$ cup milk or substitute*
> *$1/4$ cup natural oil*
> *3 – 4 tsp no-alum baking powder*
> *1 tsp real vanilla*
> *$1/4$ tsp sea salt*
> *Optional: $1/2$ cup chopped nuts or raisins*

Cream the oil and honey together. Mash the bananas separately and beat them into the oil and honey. In a separate bowl, sift all the dry ingredients together and add them to the wet mixture. Add nuts or raisins, $1/3$ cup milk, and vanilla and beat well. Add extra milk only if the batter is too stiff. Batter should be very thick but stirrable. Scoop mixed ingredients into an oiled and floured pan and bake at 350°F for 50 – 60 minutes until nicely browned on top and a toothpick comes out fairly clean. As with yeast breads, these breads become less doughy as they cool.

Use these instructions for the following four sweet loaf recipes.

Pumpkin Bread

(Makes 1 large loaf)

> 2 cups whole wheat flour, fine or mixed
> 1 cup pumpkin, cooked and mashed
> 1 cup honey or maple syrup
> $1/3 - 1/2$ cup milk or substitute
> $1/4$ cup natural oil
> 3 – 4 tsp no-alum baking powder
> 1 tsp real vanilla
> 1 tsp cinnamon
> $1/8$ tsp each nutmeg and ginger
> $1/4$ tsp sea salt
> Optional: $1/2$ cup chopped nuts or raisins

Follow instructions for Golden Banana Bread.

Raisin-Nut-Date Bread

(Makes 2 small loaves)

> 2 cups whole wheat flour, fine or mixed
> $3/4$ cup honey or maple syrup
> $1 - 1 1/4$ cup milk or substitute
> $1/2 - 1$ cup dates, chopped
> $1/2$ cup walnuts or pecans, chopped
> $1/2$ cup raisins
> $1/4$ cup natural oil
> 3 – 4 tsp no-alum baking powder
> 1 tsp real vanilla
> 1 tsp cinnamon
> $1/4$ tsp sea salt

Follow instructions for Golden Banana Bread.

Apple-Raisin Bread

(Makes 1 large loaf)

> 2 cups whole wheat flour, fine or mixed
> 1 cup homemade applesauce or stewed apples
> $1/2$ cup honey or maple syrup
> $1/3$ – $1/2$ cup apple juice
> $1/4$ cup natural oil
> 3 – 4 tsp no-alum baking powder
> 1 tsp real vanilla
> $1/4$ tsp sea salt
> 1 tsp cinnamon
> Dash or two of nutmeg and ginger
> $1/2$ cup raisins

Follow instructions for Golden Banana Bread.

Zucchini or Carrot Bread

(Makes 1 large loaf)

> 2 cups whole wheat flour, fine or mixed
> 1 cup of small zucchini squash or carrots, grated fine
> $3/4$ cup honey or maple syrup
> $1/3$ – $1/2$ cup milk or substitute
> $1/4$ cup natural oil
> 3 – 4 tsp no-alum baking powder
> 1 tsp real vanilla
> $1/4$ tsp sea salt
> Optional: Add $1/2$ cup pineapple, crushed and drained

Follow instructions for Golden Banana Bread.

♥ *Baking Powder Biscuits*

(Makes 1 dozen)

> 1¹/₂ cups whole wheat flour, fine or mixed
> ¹/₃ cup milk powder
> ¹/₃ cup wheat germ
> 3 – 4 tsp no-alum baking powder
> 1 tsp sea salt
> ²/₃ cup milk
> ¹/₃ cup natural oil

Sift the dry ingredients together in a bowl. Mix the oil and milk separately. Add the wet ingredients to the dry and mix them together with a fork or pastry blender. Knead the dough for a few minutes and roll it out about ³/₄-inch thick. Cut the biscuits with a biscuit cutter or overturned plastic cup or glass. Place the biscuits on an oiled cookie or pizza pan and bake for 10 -- 14 minutes at 450°F until golden brown.

Muffins

Any quick bread recipe can be used for muffins. Bake muffins for 15 – 25 minutes at 400°F until browned. Each loaf makes about 1¹/₂ – 2 dozen muffins. Fill baking cups or oiled muffin tins about two-thirds full. Fill empty, leftover muffin pan containers with water, while baking, so the empty cylinders do not scorch.

Quick Bread and Muffin Variations

Substitute ¹/₂ cup whole wheat flour in any recipe for any other light or heavy flour, including soy, barley, or rice.

Use water or fruit juice instead of milk in almost any recipe.

Use one part molasses or sorghum to two parts honey in any recipe.

Use maple syrup or fruit concentrate instead of honey.

Egg replacer may be used instead of eggs. Use about one tablespoon powdered egg replacer per egg with 3¹/₂ tablespoons water or other liquid.

Two to three teaspoons of liquid lecithin can be added per loaf to act as a preservative and binder.

Doubling most of the above sweetbread recipes will make three small or medium-sized loaves.

If extra nuts and other ingredients are added to the recipe, one loaf may stretch into two, and two small loaves may stretch into two large or even three loaves. Note: All bread and cake recipes in this book call for baking powder with no alum. If low-alum baking powder like Rumford is used, decrease the amount of baking powder in these recipes by one-quarter. If high-alum powder from a supermarket is used, decrease the amount used in these recipes by one-third.

 # *Blueberry Muffins or Bread*

(Makes 2 – 2^1/$_2$ dozen muffins or 1 large loaf)

> 2 cups whole wheat flour, fine or mixed
> 4 tsp no-alum baking powder
> ^{1}/$_2$ tsp sea salt
> ^{1}/$_3$ – ^{1}/$_2$ cup honey or maple syrup
> ^{1}/$_2$ – ^{3}/$_4$ cup milk or milk substitute
> ^{1}/$_4$ cup natural oil
> 2 large eggs, beaten
> 1 cup fresh blueberries (whole frozen may also be used, defrosted)
> Variation: Use 1^1/$_2$ cups flour and ^{1}/$_2$ cup wheat germ or bran

Mix wet and dry ingredients separately. Mix everything together well and add the blueberries. Spoon the mixture into baking cups or muffin tins (oiled). Fill about two-thirds full. Bake at 400°F for 20 – 25 minutes until browned.

Bran Muffins
(Makes about 2 dozen)

> 1 cup whole wheat flour, fine or medium
> $^1/_4$ cup unbleached white flour
> $^3/_4$ cup bran
> 4 tsp no-alum baking powder
> 1 tsp sea salt
> $^1/_3$ – $^1/_2$ cup honey or maple syrup
> $^1/_2$ – $^3/_4$ cup milk or milk substitute
> $^1/_4$ cup natural oil
> 2 large eggs, beaten
> $^1/_2$ – 1 cup raisins or currants

Mix wet and dry ingredients separately. Then mix everything together well. Spoon mixture into baking cups or muffin tins (oiled). Fill about two-thirds full. Bake at 400°F for 20 – 25 minutes until browned.

Bread Sticks

(Makes 1 dozen)

> 1 cup unbleached white flour
> 1 cup whole wheat flour
> 1 Tbsp gluten flour or 1 tsp baking powder
> Optional: sesame seeds (to roll dough in)
> $^3/_4$ cup cold water
> 3 Tbsp natural oil
> 2 Tbsp honey or other natural liquid sweetener
> $^1/_4$ tsp sea salt

Mix the liquid and dry ingredients separately. Then mix together and knead for about five minutes. Roll the dough into sticks about 6-inches to 10-inches long and $^1/_2$-inch thick. Then roll each one in sesame seeds. Place the sticks on an oiled cookie sheet and bake at 350°F or 375°F for 20-30 minutes until golden brown.

 *Chapter 26*

Desserts

Dessert Recipes

 Carob Frosting

Sift together:
> *¹/₂ cup milk powder (non-instant is best)*
> *¹/₂ cup roasted carob powder*
> *Optional: 2 – 3 tsp instant coffee substitute (for a more chocolatey flavor)*

Add:
> *¹/₃ – ¹/₂ cup honey or maple syrup*
> *6 Tbsp milk*
> *2 Tbsp natural oil*
> *1 – 2 tsp real vanilla*
> *4 – 6 drops peppermint extract*
> *Optional: ¹/₄ – ¹/₃ cup coconut, shredded and unsweetened*
>   *to sprinkle on top of cake*

In one bowl, mix the carob powder with the non-instant milk powder. In another bowl, mix all the wet ingredients and slowly add dry mixture to them. Mix thoroughly until smooth. (If non-instant milk powder is not available, mix instant milk powder separately with the milk. Then add rest of the wet ingredients and mix. Lastly, add carob powder. Instant milk powder tends to stay lumpy when mixed differently.) Add extra milk if a thinner consistency is wanted. Frosting will thicken and harden as it chills. Chill frosting for one to two hours before applying to cake. Keeps refrigerated five to seven days.

Carob Fudge Topping

$2/_3$ *cup milk, nut milk, or rice milk*
$1/_3$ *cup honey, maple syrup, or fruit concentrate*
$1/_4$ *cup carob powder, dark roasted or regular*
2 tsp arrowroot powder
Few dashes sea salt
1 tsp real vanilla

Blend all ingredients together and bring just up to a boil on medium-high heat. Immediately turn heat down to medium-low and simmer for four to five minutes. Stir constantly until the mixture thickens. Remove from heat, chill, and use for cakes, ice cream or other desserts. Keeps refrigerated five to seven days.

 # Cream Cheese Frosting

16 ounces cream cheese
$1/_2$ – *1 cup honey or other natural liquid sweetener, to taste*
2 tsp real vanilla
Optional: coconut to sprinkle on top

Leave the cream cheese at room temperature for one to two hours until very soft. When the cake is done and cooling, the cream cheese should be soft enough to whip. Use a mixer and slowly mix the honey and vanilla into the cream cheese until smooth. Chill the frosting for an hour or so and then frost the cake. Sprinkle coconut on top if desired. Keeps six to eight days refrigerated.

Tapioca Frosting

> *2 cups tapioca flour*
> *1 – 1¼ cups maple syrup or honey*
> *3 – 4 tsp real vanilla*
> *4 Tbsp arrowroot powder*
> *Few dashes sea salt*

Combine all the ingredients in a food processor and thoroughly blend. Chill slightly before spreading on a cool cake. This is a thick, rich frosting, a bit like a glaze. Keeps refrigerated up to seven to eight days.

 # Tofu Whipped Cream

> *6 – 8 ounces very fresh, soft tofu*
> *4 – 5 Tbsp maple syrup or other liquid sweetener*
> *1 – 2 tsp real vanilla flavoring*
> *Optional: 1 – 2 dashes cinnamon and/or dash of sea salt*

Rinse and dry the tofu. Use a food processor or blender to mix with other ingredients until smooth. Adjust flavorings to taste. Chill and serve. Keeps two to five days refrigerated.

 # Carob Cake

(Makes one - 9-inch x 13-inch or one - 2-layer 8-inch round cake)

Wet Ingredients:

1½ cups honey or maple syrup
1 – 1½ cups milk or milk substitute
½ cup light oil or softened butter
3 large eggs, beaten or egg substitute
2 tsp lemon or orange rind
2 tsp real vanilla
1 – 2 tsp liquid lecithin

Dry Ingredients:

2½ cups whole wheat flour, half pastry, half regular
½ – ⅔ cup roasted carob powder
2 – 4 ounces walnuts or pecans, chopped
3 – 4 tsp low or no-alum baking powder
½ tsp sea salt
Optional: 1 – 2 Tbsp gluten flour
Optional: 3 – 4 tsp instant coffee substitute (for a more chocolatey flavor)

Mix all the wet ingredients together with a fork or wire whisk. Begin by using only one cup of milk and add the extra ½ cup only if the batter is too dry. In a separate bowl mix the dry ingredients by sifting them together once and stirring. Mix wet and dry ingredients together. The mixture should be thick but able to be poured into the baking pan(s). Beat the cake batter 100 – 200 strokes until smooth and then mix in the nuts. Lightly oil and flour the pan(s), pour in the cake batter, and bake at 325°F for 45 – 60 minutes until lightly browned and a toothpick comes out clean. Cool the cake before removing it from the pan and adding frosting. Frost with Carob Frosting for the best tasting cake, although Carob Fudge Topping or cream frosting may also be used. (See Chapter 12 – Food Preparation Tips & Tricks for cake techniques.)

24 Karat (Carrot) Cake

(Makes one - 9-inch x 13-inch or one 2 or 3 layer 8-inch round cake)

Wet Ingredients:

6 medium carrots, grated fine (about 2 cups)
$1^1/_2$ cups honey or maple syrup
$^3/_4$ – 1 cup milk or milk substitute
$^1/_3$ cup natural oil
3 large eggs, beaten or substitute
2 tsp real vanilla

Dry Ingredients:

$2^1/_2$ cups whole wheat flour, half pastry, half regular
2 – 4 ounces walnuts or pecans, chopped
3 – 4 tsp baking powder
1 tsp cinnamon
$^1/_2$ tsp nutmeg
$^1/_2$ tsp sea salt
Optional: 1 – 2 Tbsp gluten flour

Mix the wet ingredients together thoroughly. In a separate bowl mix the dry ingredients together. (May be sifted.) Add the dry mixture to the wet and beat 100 – 200 strokes. Then mix in the nuts. Lightly oil and flour the pan(s) and scoop the thick mixture into the pan(s). Bake at 350°F for 50 – 60 minutes until golden brown. Cool the cake before removing from pan(s) and frosting. Frost with Cream Cheese Frosting or Tapioca Frosting.

Happiness Cake (oil-free cake)

(Makes 1 - 9-inch x 9-inch cake)

> 2 cups sprouted wheat berries, ground
> 1 cup honey or other natural liquid sweetener
> 1 cup whole wheat flour
> 1 Tbsp baking powder
> 1 tsp cinnamon
> $1/2$ tsp sea salt
> $1/4$ tsp each ginger and nutmeg
> Few dashes allspice

Use a hand grinder or other appliance to grind the wheat berries and then mix them with the sweetening. In a separate bowl, mix all dry ingredients. Lightly oil and flour a small pan. Mix the separated ingredients together completely and press them into the pan. Bake at 325°F for 35 – 50 minutes or until lightly browned. This cake is delicious by itself or topped with whipped cream, dribbled honey, Cream Cheese Frosting, or Tapioca Frosting. Enjoy it in happiness and health.

 Cashew Pudding

(Serves 3 – 4)

> 2 cups milk
> $1/2$ cup raw cashews, ground
> $1/3$ – $1/2$ cup honey or maple syrup
> 2 Tbsp butter
> 3 – 4 Tbsp arrowroot powder
> $1/8$ tsp sea salt
> Optional: coconut, shredded and unsweetened to sprinkle on top
> Optional: $1/2$ tsp guar gum or xanthan gum

Blend all ingredients together in a blender except the coconut. In a saucepan, heat the mixture on medium heat. Stir constantly until a thickened, pudding texture forms and remove it from the heat. A double boiler can be used to avoid burning the pudding. Pour the pudding into separate bowls or cups and refrigerate it until it hardens. Coconut can be sprinkled on top before serving. For a firmer pudding, add the guar or xanthan gum to the pudding before chilling.

 # Carob Pudding

(Serves 3 – 4)

Use Cashew Pudding recipe but instead of using cashews, use $^1/_3 - {}^1/_2$ cup roasted carob powder. Coconut may be blended into this pudding or sprinkled on top. Also add two to three teaspoons instant coffee substitute to recipe for richer flavor.

 # Pumpkin Pudding

(Serves 4 – 6)

> 2 cups cooked pumpkin, baked or boiled until soft, peeled and seeded
> 1$^1/_2$ cups milk
> $^1/_2 - {}^3/_4$ cup honey or maple syrup
> 2 large eggs
> 2 – 3 Tbsp milk powder
> 1 – 2 Tbsp molasses
> 2 tsp arrowroot
> 1 – 2 tsp real vanilla
> $^1/_2$ tsp each cinnamon and ginger
> Few dashes each nutmeg and sea salt

Blend ingredients and taste mixture. Make any changes according to taste. Lightly oil one or two baking dishes and pour mixture in about 1$^1/_2$ to 2 inches thick. Bake pudding at 325°F for 30 – 45 minutes until it becomes firm and turns golden brown. Chill pudding before serving. Can be eaten plain or topped with whipped cream.

Pumpkin Pie

Use any favorite single pie crust recipe from this or another book. Use the pumpkin pudding recipe as the filling and bake the same as the pudding. One pudding recipe makes two or three pies. Serve it by itself or topped with whipped cream, Tofu Whipped Cream, or with ice cream on the side.

 Apple Pie

(Makes 1 pie)

> *8 – 10 baking apples, cored and sliced thin (may or may not be peeled)*
> *$^1/_4$ – $^1/_3$ cup water*
> *$^3/_4$ cup honey or other liquid sweeteners (more if apples are sour)*
> *3 Tbsp arrowroot powder*
> *2 – 3 Tbsp fresh lemon juice*
> *2 tsp cinnamon*
> *$^1/_4$ tsp sea salt*
> *Optional: $^3/_4$ cup raisins or currants*

Use Rome, MacIntosh, Jonathan, Spartan, or Lodi apples for pies, never Red Delicious. Cook the apples and raisins, if any, about 8 – 10 minutes in $^1/_4$ – $^1/_3$ cup water. Use about $^1/_4$ cup or less water from the apples, cooled, and mix it with the arrowroot and salt and heat it in a small saucepan until it thickens. Remove from heat and mix in the cinnamon, lemon juice, sea salt, and honey. Mix well and then combine with the drained apples. Use a double pie crust recipe. Spoon the apple mixture into the bottom pie crust and cover it with the top crust. Be sure to use a fork to prick holes in the bottom crust. Use a knife for slits in the top crust and flute the outer edges of both crusts together before baking. Bake at 425°F for 30 – 40 minutes or until golden brown. Serve pie hot or chilled.

Dessert Pie Crusts

Add one teaspoon honey to any of the following recipes if they are to be used for dessert recipes.

 # *Double Pie Crust Recipe*

(Makes one 10-inch double crust or two single crusts)

> *2 cups sifted whole wheat flour, at least half pastry flour*
> *1 tsp sea salt*
> *²⁄₃ cup natural oil*
> *¹⁄₄ cup cold milk or cold water*
> *1 – 2 tsp liquid lecithin*

Mix the wet and dry ingredients separately. Add the dry ingredients to the wet and use a fork or pastry blender to mix. Knead the dough for a couple of minutes and divide it into two parts. Roll one part between two pieces of wax paper. Roll the dough until it is about ¹⁄₈-inch thick and 11 – 12 inches in diameter. While rolling out the dough be careful to turn it upside down once in a while and occasionally lift the wax paper on each side so it will not stick permanently to the dough. Lightly oil the 10-inch pie pan. Remove one layer of wax paper from the rolled dough and turn it upside down over the pie pan. Gently remove the top, last layer of wax paper and shape the pie crust to the pan. Push the dough into the corners of the pan, but do not stretch the dough or it will shrink while the pie is baking. Use a fork to poke air holes in the dough. After shaping the bottom crust, fill with pie filling and cover with the second rolled-out pie crust. Flute the edges together, make a few slits in the top crust, and then bake at 425°F for 30 – 40 minutes until golden and flaky. Serve pie hot or chilled. The single pie crusts can also be used as double pie crusts. Used for pies or quiche.

Single Pie Crust #1

(Makes two single or one double crust)

> 2 cups sifted whole wheat flour, at least half pastry flour
> 1 stick butter, softened but not melted
> $^{1}/_{4}$ cup cold water
> 1 – 2 tsp liquid lecithin
> 1 tsp sea salt

Single Pie Crust #2

(Makes two single or one double crust)

> 2 cups sifted whole wheat flour, at least half pastry flour
>   or 1$^{1}/_{4}$ cups millet flour, $^{2}/_{3}$ cup rice flour, and 1 Tbsp arrowroot
> $^{1}/_{2}$ stick butter, softened but not melted
> $^{1}/_{4}$ cup natural oil
> $^{1}/_{4}$ cup cold water
> 1 – 2 tsp liquid lecithin
> 1 tsp sea salt

Add the mixed flour and salt to the butter and lecithin, and mix thoroughly with a fork or pastry blender. Add the water and continue mixing. Knead a few minutes and then prepare the single pie crust the same as the double crust recipe except use two pie pans and make two single crusts. Also, bake the crust five to six minutes at 325°F before adding the filling and then bake it together according to the filling recipe. Use this for pies or quiche. Note: Crusts made with butter tend to shrink a bit, so be careful not to stretch the dough.

Oat Crumb Crust

(For Date Squares and Apple Crisp)

Mix:
>$^3/_4$ – 1 cup honey, maple syrup, or fruit concentrate
>$^1/_2$ cup natural oil

Mix separately:
>$2^1/_2$ cups rolled oats
>1 cup whole wheat flour
>2 Tbsp lemon rind, grated fine
>$^3/_4$ tsp sea salt

Add the dry ingredients to the mixed wet ingredients. Mix well. Press the crust into a lightly oiled pan. Add filling and follow the Date Squares or Apple Crisp recipe instructions before baking. To bake crust with another recipe, bake at 350°F for about 30 – 45 minutes or until golden brown with filling.

# Date Squares

(Makes 1 - 9-inch x 13-inch pan)

> 2 batches crumb crust recipe
> 2 pounds dates, pitted
> 2$\frac{1}{2}$ cups water
> 2 Tbsp lemon juice
> 2 Tbsp lemon rind, grated fine
> Few dashes sea salt

Mix the dates, water, and lemon ingredients together in a saucepan and cook on a low heat until the dates break down and mix easily with the water. When the date mixture can be stirred into a paste, remove from heat and let it cool before using with the crumb crust. Press one of the batches of crumb crust into the bottom of a 9-inch x 13-inch lightly oiled pan. Add a thick layer of date filling. Use the second batch of crumb crust on top as a third layer. Spread everything evenly. Bake around 375°F for 30 – 45 minutes until the top is light brown. Let it cool 15 minutes before cutting into squares and removing from the pan. Do not let the top layer harden in the oven or it will cool and become as hard as a rock. It should remain tender like a cookie until it cools. Before it cools completely, cut it into small pieces or it will become difficult to cut later. A rich dessert.

Apple Crisp

(Makes 1 - 9-inch x 9-inch or 10-inch x 10-inch pan)

> $\frac{2}{3}$ – 1 batch crumb crust recipe
> 1 filling from apple pie recipe

Spread most of the crumb crust on the bottom and halfway up the side of the lightly oiled baking pan. Put in the apple filling mixture and sprinkle the rest of the crumb crust lightly and evenly over the top. Bake at 400°F for 35 – 45 minutes until the crust is golden and apples fully baked. Be careful not to overbake. Crust should be very tender when done as in the Date Squares.

Mom's Baked Apples & Honey

(Serves 4)

> 4 large baking apples, whole and cored, peeled around the
>   top and bottom only
> $^1/_2$ – $^3/_4$ cup honey or other natural liquid sweetener
> $^1/_2$ cup orange juice (or apple juice)
> 4 tsp butter (can be optional)
> Raisins
> Chopped walnuts or pecans
> Cinnamon
> Few dashes each nutmeg and sea salt

Use Rome, MacIntosh, Spartan, Stayman, or other baking apples for baking, never Red Delicious. Sit the apples upright in a small oil baking dish and stuff the centers of the apples with mixed raisins and nuts, topped with one teaspoon butter each. Pour the orange juice equally over the apples and then do the same with the honey. Sprinkle on lots of cinnamon and a dash of salt and nutmeg on each apple. Bake at 400°F for 30 – 45 minutes or until the apples are completely tender. Serve these before, during, or after a meal. They may even be served with a vegetable meal as apples are a somewhat neutral fruit, especially when cooked.

 # Fruit & Whipped Cream

Serve a favorite fruit salad or single cut fruit with whipped cream and honey for a treat. Whip the cream with an electric mixer (never in a blender) until it gets stiff and peaks form. Top the fruit with the whipped cream and dribble honey or a little maple syrup over the top. It is best not to mix the honey beforehand with the whipping cream or it will not whip properly. The whipped cream can also be used to top jello, cakes, or pies. For non-dairy topping, see Tofu Whipped Cream recipe.

Fruit & Sherbet or Ice Cream

Top a favorite fruit salad or single cut fruit slices with any kind of sherbet or vanilla, butter pecan, or other light-tasting ice cream or non-dairy ice cream. Chopped nuts or coconut can be sprinkled on top.

 # Applesauce

(Serves 4 – 6)

> 10 – 12 very large baking apples, peeled or unpeeled, cored
>   and chopped in $1/_2$-inch chunks
> $1/_2$ cup water
> Optional: $1/_4$ – $1/_3$ cup honey or other natural liquid sweetener
>   (or add honey to taste)
> Optional: 1 – 2 tsp cinnamon
> Optional: $1/_8$ tsp sea salt
> Optional: Few dashes each nutmeg and ginger

MacIntosh or Spartan apples are especially good for applesauce. Heat the apples and water together in a saucepan on high heat for one minute then turn to low heat for an hour or more until tender. Stir them occasionally and watch them carefully so they will not overcook. When the apples break down completely, add the honey and spices and cook everything together for two to three minutes more on low heat. Then turn the heat off and keep the sauce covered until it cools and can be refrigerated. If needed, use a hand masher or food processor to make the applesauce finer. Applesauce can be served hot or cold, but do not reheat it unless cooked in another recipe. Use it as a side dish, dessert, or dessert topping.

Rhubarb Sauce

Prepare this the same way as applesauce except that sweetening is required. Use six to eight cups chopped rhubarb instead of apples. Rhubarb sauce can be used just like applesauce and can be easily interchanged with it in most recipes. Use extra honey according to taste. Rhubarb sauce tastes best cold and can be served over ice cream, in and over cakes and breads, or by itself.

Fruit Jello - Vegetarian

(Serves 6 – 10)

> 1 cup cool water
> 1 – 1$^1/_2$ quarts fruit juice, try papaya, grape, strawberry, cherry,
>   apricot, peach or apple but avoid citrus juice
> $^1/_4$ ounce (about 6 – 7 Tbsp) agar-agar flakes or 1$^1/_2$ – 2 Tbsp
>   agar-agar powder

Heat the agar flakes or powder in the water and bring it to a boil, stirring as it heats. Once it boils, turn down the heat and simmer until most of the agar is dissolved. Make sure the fruit juice is at room temperature or slightly warmed. Pour the fruit juice in a bowl and strain the agar mixture into it. Stir and mix everything well. Chill until it hardens. When jello is partially set in about 30 – 40 minutes or more, add cut fruits if desired. Jello is ready to eat in 1$^1/_2$ – 3 hours. Some juice may settle to the bottom of the bowl when the jello is spooned out, this is natural for agar jello. Note: Most citrus juices do not "set well" with this jello recipe so avoid them or use only a small amount mixed with other juices.

Bread Pudding

(Serves 8 – 12)

> 3 – 4 cups cubed whole grain bread, old or fresh
> 2 cups milk
> $^3/_4$ cup honey or other natural liquid sweetener
> $^1/_2$ cup milk powder, non-instant
> $^1/_4$ cup brown date sugar or other natural granular sweetener
> 2 large eggs, beaten
> 1 Tbsp whole wheat flour
> 1 tsp each cinnamon and real vanilla
> $^1/_8$ tsp sea salt

Beat or blend the milk powder into the milk until smooth. Mix in the remaining ingredients except for the bread. Add the bread last. Put the pudding in a lightly oiled, square baking dish about 2 – 2$^1/_2$-inches thick. Bake at 350°F for 30 – 50 minutes until firm.

Granola Bars

> 1 batch of raw granola including the honey and oil
>   (see granola recipes in Chapter 18 – Whole Grains)

Extra ingredients besides granola:
> $^1/_2$ – $^3/_4$ cup honey
> $^1/_4$ cup whole wheat flour or oat flour
> $^1/_4$ cup natural granular sweetener (brown date sugar
>   or natural raw sugar)
> Optional: $^1/_2$ – 1 cup plain yogurt
> Optional: extra nuts or dried fruit

Mix the extra ingredients with the batch of raw granola. Shape the mixture into 2-inch x 5-inch bars about $^1/_2 - ^3/_4$-inch thick on an oiled cookie sheet and bake at 350°F for 20 – 30 minutes or until lightly browned. Keep the bars flat until they cool and harden. Use the bars for snacks, desserts, or quick breakfasts.

 # Easy Cheesecake

(2 - 9-inch or 10-inch pans)

> 40 ounces cream cheese, very soft
> $1^1/_2$ cups honey or maple syrup
> $^1/_4$ cup milk
> 6 large eggs, beaten
> 3 Tbsp whole wheat flour
> 1 – 2 Tbsp grated orange or lemon peel
> 2 tsp real vanilla
> $^1/_8$ tsp sea salt
> Optional: $^1/_2$ tsp cinnamon

Make sure the cream cheese sits out on a counter for about $1^1/_2$ hours or more until it is very soft. Mix the honey, cream cheese, and vanilla together with an electric mixer until they are smooth. Then add the rest of the ingredients and mix once again until smooth. Lightly oil two cake or pie pans and pour in the batter. Bake at 375°F for about 20 minutes or until slightly firm in the middle of the cake. The top of the cake may be dusted with cinnamon if desired. Topping is optional. Try strawberry or other fruit topping, Applesauce or Rhubarb Sauce if desired.

Tofu Cheesecake

(1-9-inch or 1-10-inch round cake)

> 1¹/₂ pounds (750 g) soft tofu
> 1 cup maple syrup or fruit concentrate
> ¹/₄ cup natural raw sugar or other natural granular sweetener
> 3 Tbsp natural light oil
> 4 Tbsp arrowroot powder
> 3 Tbsp grated lemon or orange rind
> 2 tsp guar gum or xanthan gum
> 1 Tbsp real vanilla extract
> ¹/₄ – ¹/₂ tsp sea salt
> Optional: 8 – 14 drops natural lemon or orange flavoring
> Optional: 1 pie crust shell

Mix all ingredients together, except the pie crust, in a food processor or homogenizing juicer. Line a 10-inch pie plate with the crust or, if no crust is used, oil a 9-inch pie plate. Preheat the oven to 350°F. Spread the tofu mixture evenly in the crust or the oiled pie plate, and smooth out the top so the cheesecake will be even. Bake for about 45 minutes or until the cake is "set" and turns a medium golden color. Chill thoroughly and serve with Strawberry Topping. If desired, the topping can be spread over the cool cake and chilled to add a fruit layer to the cheesecake, or the topping can just be spooned on before serving each piece.

Strawberry Topping

(For cheesecake, cakes, or ice cream)

> ¹/₂ pound fresh or frozen unsweetened strawberries, sliced
> 1 cup water
> 3 Tbsp arrowroot powder
> 2 – 3 Tbsp honey or other natural liquid sweetener

If fresh strawberries are used, add $^1/_4$ cup extra water. In a small pot, mix the arrowroot and water together with a wire whisk. Then cook them on a low heat until the arrowroot thickens slightly (about 7 – 12 minutes). Add the strawberries and honey and cook together another five to seven minutes. Let the mixture cool down slightly before using on cheesecake. Make sure the cheesecake is cool and firm before adding this as a topping. This topping can also be used with Happiness Cake. Chill it completely for use on ice cream. Instead of strawberries, use blueberries, peach slices, or raspberries.

 # Deluxe Carob Brownies

(Makes 1 - 9-inch x 9-inch or 10-inch x 10-inch pan)

> $1^1/_4$ *cups honey, maple syrup, or fruit concentrate*
> *1 cup roasted carob powder*
> *1 cup whole wheat flour*
> *1 cup pecans or fresh walnuts, chopped*
> $^3/_4$ *cup pastry or unbleached white flour*
> $^1/_3$ *cup natural oil*
> $^1/_4$ *cup milk or milk substitute*
> $^1/_4$ *cup milk powder, non-instant (or soy milk powder)*
> *2 large eggs, beaten or substitute*
> *2 tsp real vanilla*
> *1 – 2 tsp molasses or sorghum*
> *1 – $1^1/_2$ tsp no-alum baking powder*
> $^1/_4$ *tsp sea salt*
> *Optional: 2 – 3 tsp instant coffee substitute (for chocolatey flavor)*

Mix the wet and dry ingredients separately. Sift the carob powder and milk powder together to dissolve any lumps. Mix everything together well. Spread the mixture in an oiled 9-inch or 10-inch pan. Bake for 35 – 45 minutes or until a toothpick comes out fairly clean. Bake at 350°F – 375°F. For thinner, chewier brownies use one teaspoon baking soda instead of the baking powder and use a bigger pan.

Rich Carob Ice Cream

> 2 cups water or milk
> ¹/₂ cup carob powder (dark roasted or regular is best)
> ¹/₂ cup ground raw cashew pieces or ground blanched almonds
> ¹/₃ – ¹/₂ cup maple syrup, honey, or fruit concentrate
> 3 Tbsp arrowroot powder
> 1 – 2 tsp real vanilla
> 1 tsp slippery elm powder, guar gum, or xanthan gum
>   or 1 egg, beaten until foamy
> Several dashes sea salt
> Optional: 10 – 16 drops peppermint flavoring
> Optional: 1 tsp instant coffee substitute

Follow the directions for Rich Vanilla Ice Cream.

Fabulous Fruit Ice Cream

> 2¹/₂ – 3 cups one type of fruit, try blueberries, strawberries,
>   raspberries, peaches, mangos, kiwis, bananas
> 20 ounces soft tofu
> ¹/₃ – ¹/₂ cup honey, maple syrup, or fruit concentrate
> 2 tsp real vanilla
> 1 tsp slippery elm powder, guar gum, or xanthan gum
>   or 1 egg, beaten until foamy
> Several dashes sea salt

Mix everything together using a food processor, blender, or hand mixer. Freeze solid, then process again or break up in a food processor or homogenizing juicer. (Blender or hand mixer will not work here!) Freeze a second time and enjoy. The second freezing adds more air and makes a lighter, smoother ice cream. Remove from freezer several minutes before serving to soften slightly. Keeps frozen many weeks. Delicious and high in calcium, phosphorus, potassium, and protein!

♥ Rich Vanilla Ice Cream

2 cups water or milk
³/₄ cup ground raw cashew pieces or ground blanched almonds
¹/₃ cup maple syrup or honey
3 Tbsp arrowroot powder
3 tsp real vanilla
1 tsp slippery elm powder, guar gum, or xanthan gum
  or 1 egg, beaten until foamy
Several dashes sea salt

Blend all the ingredients thoroughly in a blender until smooth. Freeze the mixture solid. Cut into pieces and use a food processor or homogenizing juicer to soften it for a smoother, more uniform texture. Refreeze the ice cream and remove it from the freezer several minutes before serving. Enjoy by itself or with cooked fruit or Carob Fudge Topping. If making ice cream with milk, ¹/₂ – 1 cup cream can be substituted for some of the milk for a very rich dairy ice cream. An ice cream maker can also be used for the recipe if dairy ice cream is being made. Follow the directions given with the machine.

♥ Popsicles

Use any of the fruit drink recipes in Chapter 27 – Beverages, but use only half as much water (if any). Add 1 teaspoon or so extra honey or sweetener and freeze in popsicle containers or ice cube trays.

 *Rice Pudding*

(Makes 1 - 9-inch x 9-inch casserole pan)

> 2 cups cooked brown rice (plain, leftover rice can be used or
>   sweet rice if it is available)
> 1¹⁄₂ cups milk, nut milk or sweet fruit juice (such as apple, peach,
>   or apricot juice)
> ¹⁄₂ – ³⁄₄ cup honey or other natural liquid sweetener
> 2 large eggs, beaten or use variation
> 2 – 3 tsp lemon or orange rind, grated fine
> 2 tsp real vanilla
> ¹⁄₈ tsp sea salt
> Optional: ¹⁄₂ – 1 cup raisins, currants and/or chopped nuts
> Optional: 1 – 1¹⁄₂ tsp cinnamon

Mix all the ingredients together. Pour them into a lightly oiled casserole and cover it. Bake it covered for 45 – 55 minutes at 325°F. Serve hot or cold.

   Variation: Instead of eggs, use 2 tablespoons powdered egg replacer or ¹⁄₂ teaspoon guar or xanthan gum along with 1 tablespoon arrowroot powder. Add ¹⁄₃ – ¹⁄₂ cup extra milk or milk substitute with either of these variations.

 Walnut-Anise Cookies

(Makes 1¹⁄₂ – 2 dozen)

> ¹⁄₂ cup honey or maple syrup
> ¹⁄₄ cup natural oil
> ¹⁄₄ cup brown date sugar or other natural granular sweetener
> 1¹⁄₂ cups whole wheat flour, half pastry
> ³⁄₄ cup fresh walnuts, chopped
> ¹⁄₂ cup raisins, currants, or chopped dates
> ³⁄₄ – 1 tsp anise seeds
> ¹⁄₈ tsp sea salt

Optional: $^1/_4$ – $^1/_2$ cup coconut, shredded and unsweetened
Optional: 1 – 2 tsp gluten flour (for lighter cookies)

Mix the oil and liquid sweetening together well. Mix the other ingredients separately and add them to the wet mixture. Mix well. Use about one or two tablespoons of the mixture or so per cookie. Place the cookies on an oiled cookie sheet and bake at 400°F for 9 – 12 minutes until lightly browned.

 # Carob Chip-Nut Cookies

(Makes about 4 – 5 dozen)

Mix together:
> $^2/_3$ cup honey, maple syrup, or fruit concentrate
> $^1/_2$ cup (1 stick) butter, softened or substitute
>   (see Peanut Butter Cookies)
> $^1/_2$ cup brown date sugar or other natural granular sweetener

Add and mix in well:
> 1 cup whole wheat flour
> $^3/_4$ cup carob chips
> $^1/_2$ cup whole wheat pastry or unbleached white flour
> $^1/_2$ cup fresh walnuts, pecans, or almonds, chopped
> $^1/_4$ cup milk powder, non-instant
> 1 large egg, beaten
> 2 tsp gluten flour or arrowroot powder
> 1 tsp real vanilla
> $^1/_4$ tsp sea salt

For each cookie drop a spoonful or two of batter on a lightly oiled cookie sheet. Bake for 10 – 12 minutes or until lightly browned at 375°F. These cookies (or any other in this book) can also be made into bar cookies by spreading the batter about $^1/_2$-inch thick on a cookie sheet and baking at 350°F for 15 – 20 minutes. Then cool a few minutes and cut into squares or bars. Natural chocolate chips may be used instead of carob if desired.

Peanut Butter Cookies

(Makes about 4 dozen)

Mix together:

> *¹/₂ cup butter, softened or use variation*
> *¹/₂ cup brown date sugar or other natural granular sweetener*
> *¹/₂ cup honey, maple syrup, or fruit concentrate*
> *1 – 2 tsp molasses or sorghum*

Add:

> *1 cup peanut butter, smooth or crunchy*
> *1 cup whole wheat flour*
> *¹/₂ cup pastry or unbleached white flour*
> *¹/₄ cup milk powder, non-instant (or soy milk powder)*
> *2 tsp arrowroot powder or gluten flour*
> *1 tsp real vanilla*
> *¹/₂ tsp no-alum baking powder*
> *¹/₄ tsp sea salt*

Mix the dough together well. It should not be too dry. Add a bit of extra milk, water, or sweetening if needed. Roll the dough into little balls about 1-inch or more thick. Press the balls flat and, with a fork, make a crisscross design on the cookies. Bake at 400°F for 12 – 16 minutes.

Variations: Sesame tahini, almond butter, cashew butter, or another nut butter may be used instead of peanut butter. Instead of butter, use ¹/₂ cup natural oil and 1 teaspoon liquid lecithin added to the wet ingredients plus 2 extra tablespoons arrowroot added to the dry ingredients.

Oatmeal Cookies

(Makes 4 – 5 dozen)

Mix together:
> $^2/_3$ *cup brown date sugar or other natural granular sweetener*
> $^1/_2$ *cup (1 stick) butter, softened or use variation*
> $^1/_2$ *cup honey or molasses or $^3/_8$ cup honey and $^1/_8$ cup molasses*
> *or sorghum*

Add:
> *2 cups rolled oats*
> *1 cup whole wheat flour*
> $^1/_2$ *cup pastry or unbleached white flour*
> *2 large eggs, beaten*
> *1 tsp cinnamon*
> *1 tsp real vanilla*
> $^1/_2$ *tsp baking powder (no-alum)*
> $^1/_4$ *tsp sea salt*
> *Few dashes nutmeg*
> *Optional: 1 – 2 tsp gluten flour*

Mix the dry ingredients separately and gradually add them to the wet ingredients. Make sure the batter is fairly stiff and hard to stir. Add a bit more honey or flour if needed. Drop a spoonful or two of batter per cookie on an oiled cookie sheet. Make sure cookies are one-inch or more apart. Bake at 400°F for 10 – 14 minutes or until lightly brown.

Variation: Instead of butter use $^1/_2$ cup natural oil and 1 teaspoon liquid lecithin added to the wet ingredients plus add 2 tablespoons arrowroot powder added to the dry ingredients.

Oatmeal-Raisin Cookies

Follow the oatmeal cookies recipe but use only 1½ cups rolled oats and add 1 cup raisins.

Oatmeal-Coconut Cookies

Follow the oatmeal cookies recipe but use only 1½ cups rolled oats and add ½ cup shredded, unsweetened coconut.

 # Almond Heart Cookies

(Makes about 18 cookies)

Wet Ingredients:
½ cup honey, maple syrup, or fruit concentrate
3 Tbsp almond oil (or substitute another natural oil)
1 Tbsp almond butter
1 – 2 tsp pure vanilla

Dry Ingredients:
¾ cup whole wheat flour and ½ cup whole wheat pastry flour
   or unbleached white flour OR ¾ cup kamut flour and
   ½ amaranth flour
¼ cup natural granular sweetener
¼ cup sliced or chopped almonds
2 Tbsp ground almonds
1 tsp each: baking powder and cinnamon
½ – 1 tsp almond extract
⅛ tsp sea salt

These delicious cookies can be made into heart shapes. Preheat the oven to 375°F. Combine the wet ingredients thoroughly. In a separate bowl, sift together the dry ingredients. Add the dry ingredients to the wet and mix well. Flatten a handful of batter to half inch or less of thickness and use a heart shaped cookie cutter for each cookie. Use a spatula to lift the cookie onto a lightly oiled cookie sheet. Bake 12 – 15 minutes and let the cookies cool on wire racks. Whole almonds or natural candies can by used to decorate each one if desired.

Eggless, Butterless, or Milkless Cookies and Cakes

Note: Not every variation works with every recipe. See substitution charts for more information.

1. Instead of each egg called for, add 2 teaspoons arrowroot powder and $1/2$ teaspoon guar gum, xanthan gum, or baking powder, 1 teaspoon liquid lecithin, and $3^1/_2$ tablespoons water or milk.
2. Instead of milk powder, use soy milk powder or tapioca flour.
3. Instead of butter, use 7 tablespoons oil and 1 tablespoon liquid lecithin per 1 stick (4 ounces) of butter. (In cake recipes or cookies, add 2 tablespoons arrowroot powder.)
4. Instead of milk, use soy, rice, coconut, or nut milk. Recipe turns out more flavorful if a milk substitute is used rather than water. Sometimes sweet fruit juice like apple, pear, or peach can also be used instead of milk.

Wheatless Cookies and Cakes

Note: Not every variation works with every recipe. See substitution charts for more information.

Instead of 1 cup whole wheat flour use:

1. $1/2$ cup oat flour, $1/4$ cup rice flour, $1/4$ cup millet flour, plus $1/2$ teaspoon baking powder (no-alum)
2. $3/4$ cup oat flour, $1/4$ cup millet or potato flour plus $1/2$ teaspoon baking powder, guar gum or xanthan gum
3. $1/2$ cup oat flour, $1/2$ cup millet flour plus $1/2$ teaspoon baking powder, guar gum or xanthan gum
4. $7/8$ cup millet or oat flour, $1/8$ cup arrowroot flour or soy flour.
5. $1/2$ cup oat flour, $1/2$ cup barley flour plus $1/2$ teaspoon baking powder, guar gum or xanthan gum
6. $3/4$ cup millet flour, $1/4$ cup rice flour plus $1/2$ teaspoon baking powder, guar gum or xanthan gum
7. $3/4$ cup amaranth or quinoa flour and $1/4$ cup tapioca or rice flour plus $1/2$ teaspoon baking powder, guar gum or xanthan gum

8. $^7/_8$ cup spelt flour and optional: 1 tablespoon arrowroot powder
9. 1 cup kamut flour, finely ground
10. $^3/_4$ cup kamut flour, $^1/_4$ amaranth flour or buckwheat flour

   Similar combinations are acceptable. See Chapter 25 – Breads and be sure to mix a light and heavy combination of flours plus arrowroot, baking powder, or one of the gums. Be sure to use a wheat-free baking powder.

Instead of one tablespoon gluten flour use:
1. $2^1/_2$ teaspoons arrowroot and $^1/_2$ teaspoon baking powder
2. 1 teaspoon light flour (like rice), $1^1/_2$ teaspoons arrowroot, and $^1/_2$ teaspoon baking powder
3. $2^1/_2$ teaspoons flour (any kind) and $^1/_2$ teaspoon guar gum or xanthan gum

Extras to Add to Almost Any Cookie or Cake Recipe:
1. 1 – 3 teaspoons grated lemon or orange rind
2. $^1/_4$ – $^1/_2$ cup ground or chopped nuts
3. $^1/_4$ – $^1/_2$ cup sesame or sunflower seeds
4. $^1/_2$ – $^3/_4$ cup raisins, currants or chopped dates
5. $^1/_2$ – $^2/_3$ cup coconut or carob powder
6. 1 mashed banana (add $^1/_4$ cup or more extra flour)
7. $^1/_2$ teaspoon or so cinnamon, anise, cloves, nutmeg
8. (a) $^1/_2$ cup milk powder or soy milk powder
   (b) Add extra liquid or liquid sweetening
9. Honey or other liquid sweetener (add extra flour to balance)
Note: Sea salt or salt can be excluded in any recipe, but it will detract slightly from the flavor of the dessert. Sea salt can be substituted with $^1/_4$ or less the amount of potassium chloride in many recipes.

Chapter 27

Beverages

Beverages

Fluids are essential to our bodies, which are made up of about 70% water. Our bodies require a minimum of three to four glasses of water a day (up to double that amount in hot weather) plus other liquid foods and beverages equaling about three to four glasses or more. A total of about $1^1/_2 - 2$ quarts or liters of liquids (three to four quarts or liters in hot weather) should be had each day. (Amounts vary depending on each individual's needs and activities as well as weather conditions.) Naturally, more liquids are needed in summer to replenish what we lose in hot, dry weather from perspiring. Avoid heavily sweetened or sugared drinks of all kinds, especially those with artificial coloring, flavoring, or other added chemicals.

Water

Water is the most important of all beverages. Bottled, tested spring water is said to be one of the healthiest for human consumption. Tested spring water is a large step up from tap water. It may contain some minerals, but usually not excessive or harmful amounts. The minerals it contains are generally considered helpful to the body. This is the most natural type of water, but must be tested as polluted springs are becoming more common.

Distilled water with minerals added is also considered to be one of the better types of drinking water. Only helpful and necessary minerals are added for flavor and to benefit the body. With today's pollution levels, distilled water is now the water of choice. If plain distilled water is drunk regularly, be sure to take a mineral supplement and enjoy a high-nutrient diet of natural foods.

Fluoridated hard water or tap water is the real danger. It has been proven to contain chemicals and cancer-causing substances, often including some of the following, asbestos, aluminum, sulphur, copper, lead, chloroform, and/or carbon tetrachloride. Since the original laboratory tests were made to prove fluoridation helpful, later tests have proven it to be of slight value in prevention of tooth decay. Factors such as using good growing soils for food, eating a wholesome diet, and regular brushing have been proven more effective as preventative measures against tooth decay. People who still wish to use fluoride may use a fluoride toothpaste instead of drinking it or get fluoride treatments from a dentist.

Bottled mineral waters may be had, but only in moderation. Bubbling or sparkling bottled waters like Perrier must be drunk within about 24 hours after they are opened or they lose their natural carbonation. They lose it even faster if not kept tightly covered until use. Many sparkling waters are high in mineral content that may lead to constipation for some individuals. Club soda has the opposite effect and actually helps to loosen the bowels, however it is acidic and can contribute to dental cavities if over-consumed. Only occasional use of either is recommended.

Beverage Ideas and Recipes

Some of the following recipes are large, for parties, and some are small, for one or two people. All recipes can be cut down or made larger as needed. Most of the fruit-juice-based drinks will keep five to ten days in the refrigerator. Milk-based drinks will keep one to three days refrigerated. Unsweetened cocoa powder may be used in place of carob powder if desired.

 Tropical Fruit Punch

> *2 quarts fresh orange juice*
> *1 quart pineapple juice, unsweetened*
> *$^1/_2$ – $^3/_4$ pounds strawberries (about 1 pint or more)*
> *4 bananas or $^1/_4$ – $^1/_3$ cup honey or other natural liquid sweetener*

Blend well and chill. Float lemon, orange, or strawberry slices in the punch bowl.

Hawaiian Cooler

>2 cups pineapple juice
>$1/_2$ cup coconut juice or 1 Tbsp grated coconut
>$1/_2$ cup or more strawberries
>Optional: 1 – 2 tsp honey other natural liquid sweetener
>Optional: 2 ice cubes

Blend all ingredients except the ice until drink is smooth. Add ice and blend until it gets crushed into fine ice.

 # Papaya Delight

>1 cup papaya juice
>1 cup of berries (strawberries, raspberries, or blueberries)
>2 ice cubes
>Optional: 1 – 2 tsp honey other sweetener if needed

Blend all ingredients until smooth. Serve with fresh mint leaves and extra ice cubes for added color and flavor.

 # Watermelon Cooler

>1 cup seeded watermelon chunks
>1 cup fresh orange or pineapple juice
>1 – 2 tsp honey or other sweetener

Blend and serve chilled or with ice.

♥ Fruit Slushes

1 cup fruit juice
4 – 5 ice cubes
Optional: 1 – 2 tsp honey or other sweetener or to taste

Blend all ingredients in the blender until the ice is chopped fine.

♥ Black or Blue (Berry) Bottoms

1 cup blackberries or blueberries
1 cup milk
2 – 3 tsp honey or other natural liquid sweetener
$\frac{1}{2}$ – 1 tsp real vanilla

Blend all ingredients until smooth. Serve chilled or with a little ice.

♥ Yogurt Divine

1 cup yogurt (plain)
1 cup papaya, apricot, or peach juice
1 banana
1 – 2 tsp honey or other natural liquid sweetener
Few dashes cinnamon

Mash the banana and beat all the ingredients together or blend everything for a smoother textured, more flavorful drink. Simply heavenly!

 # Lemonade

Slightly less than 1 quart water
1 cup hot water
Juice of 2 fresh, large lemons (or 3 – 4 small)
3 – 4 Tbsp honey or other natural liquid sweetener

Mix the honey into the water until the honey dissolves. Add lemon juice, ice cubes, and cold water until the mixture equals one quart. Stir and serve. If ice is not available, use all water and chill before serving.

 # Pink Lemonade

Follow the directions for lemonade and blend in $\frac{1}{2}$ – 1 cup fresh or frozen strawberries. Add a bit more honey if needed.

 # Fruit Surprise

1 cup any fruit juice
1 – 2 pieces fresh fruit (use one type of fruit out of the following fruits, peaches, mangoes, pears, bananas, apricots, kiwi, pineapple slices, watermelon chunks, cantaloupe)
1 – 2 tsp honey or other natural sweetener
2 – 3 ice cubes

Blend all ingredients together well except the ice. Add ice and blend until lightly crushed. Variation: Substitute milk for fruit juice.

 Orange Julia's

>1 cup fresh orange juice
>1/4 cup cream or milk
>1 large raw egg (very fresh) or variation
>1/2 – 1 tsp real vanilla
>1 – 2 tsp honey, maple syrup, or fruit concentrate

Blend and chill or serve with ice. Variation: Instead of the egg, use 1/2 small banana or 2 teaspoons liquid lecithin.

 Nectar of the Gods

>1 quart Lemonade (see recipe)
>1 quart pineapple juice
>1 – 2 cups strawberries

Blend and chill or serve with ice.

 New Wine

>1 1/2 pints. sparkling spring water or club soda (about 1 large bottle)
>1 1/2 pints grape juice (or apple juice or cider)

Enjoy this new light-flavored, non-alcoholic wine. Similar to wine in flavor without the strong taste. Add more juice for flatter, less bubbly wine. Add a twist of lemon or lime for accent.

Hot Apple Spice

> **1 cup apple juice or cider**
> **$^1/_2$ tsp fresh lemon juice**
> **Few dashes cinnamon**
> **Dash of nutmeg**

Mix all ingredients and heat and simmer for about three to five minutes. Do not boil. Serve it hot.

Variations: Omit lemon juice and serve the hot drink with a lemon slice or wedge. Use cinnamon sticks instead of powdered cinnamon and remove them before serving.

 Eggnog

> **2 cups milk**
> **2 large raw eggs (very fresh)**
> **2 – 3 tsp honey or other natural liquid sweetener**
> **$^1/_8$ tsp cinnamon**
> **Dash ginger**
> **Dash nutmeg**
> **Optional: $^1/_8$ tsp real vanilla**
> **Optional: 8 – 10 drops natural rum or butterscotch flavoring**

Mix well or blend and serve chilled. Heat if desired and serve hot.

Red Berry Splash Punch

(Christmas Special)

> 1 quart cranberry juice
> 1 quart apple juice or cider
> $^1/_2$ – $^3/_4$ pound strawberries or raspberries (about 1 pint or more),
>   fresh or frozen
> 2 – 4 Tbsp honey or other sweetener, or to taste
> *Optional:* raspberries or strawberries to float in punch, fresh or frozen

Blend all ingredients except extra berries to be floated. Instead of the other berries, cranberries can be threaded on a string and tied in a small ring and floated on top as a decoration only.

 # Ice Cream Punch

> 1 cup any kind of fruit juice (prechilled)
> 1 scoop ice cream
> 2 – 3 ice cubes

Blend lightly and serve immediately.

 # Carob-Coffee Shake

> $^3/_4$ – 1 cup milk
> 2 tsp roasted carob powder
> 1 – 2 tsp honey or other natural sweetener
> 1 tsp instant substitute coffee

Mix well or blend and serve chilled.

Tiger by the Tail Shake (Carob Shake)

> 2 cups milk or milk substitute
> 3 tsp roasted carob powder
> 2 – 3 tsp honey or other natural sweetener
> 1 large banana
> 1 tsp real vanilla flavoring
> Optional: 2 – 3 ice cubes
> Optional: 1 – 2 tsp liquid lecithin, nutritional yeast, or protein powder

Blend everything together well and serve immediately. A filling snack.

Carob Malt

> 2 cups milk or milk substitute
> 1 – 2 scoops vanilla or carob ice cream
> 3 tsp roasted carob powder
> 2 tsp honey or other natural sweetener
> Optional: 1 large raw egg (very fresh) or 2 tsp liquid lecithin

Blend all ingredients lightly until smooth and bubbly. Serve immediately.

Hot Carob Milk

(Hot Chocolate Substitute)
> 2 cups milk
> 2 Tbsp roasted carob powder
> 2 scant Tbsp honey or other natural liquid sweetener
> Optional: $1/2$ – 1 tsp real vanilla

Mix all ingredients well except honey. Heat mixture slowly until hot. Do not boil. Add honey to hot carob milk and mix well. Serve hot. Tip: Never use milk powder and water in hot drinks. They separate when heated.

Cold Carob Milk

(Chocolate Milk Substitute)

> 2 cups milk
> 2 Tbsp roasted carob powder
> 2 Tbsp honey

Mix these ingredients together well with a wire whisk or in a blender. If mixed improperly, carob and milk will separate and require stirring while drinking.

 # Carob "Smash"

(High-Protein Energy Shake)

> 1 cup milk
> 1 large, fresh raw egg (can be omitted)
> 3 tsp honey or maple syrup
> 2 tsp carob powder
> 1 – 2 tsp lecithin (any kind)
> 1 – 2 tsp nutritional yeast and/or protein powder
> $\frac{1}{2}$ tsp real vanilla
> 2 – 3 ice cubes

Blend everything together and serve immediately. This drink makes a filling snack or a small meal. Use a good tasting, yellow nutritional yeast such as engevita.

Sesame Milk

> 1 cup cold water
> $1/_3$ cup sesame seeds, hulled or unhulled
> 1 – 2 tsp honey or maple syrup or 3 – 4 pitted dates
> Optional: 1 – 2 tsp roasted carob powder
> Optional: 1 – 2 ice cubes for a colder drink

Blend the sesame seeds and cold water in the blender for about one minute. Strain the mixture twice through a fine strainer or cheesecloth. After straining, blend in honey (or dates) and carob powder and ice if any and serve chilled.

Almond or Cashew Milk

> 1 cup cold water
> $1/_3$ cup almonds or cashews, blanched
> 1 – 2 tsp honey or maple syrup or 3 – 4 pitted dates
> Optional: 1 – 2 tsp carob powder
> Optional: 1 – 2 ice cubes

Soak the nuts in one cup of very hot water for 15 – 30 minutes. Drain the water from the nuts and blend them in the blender with the cold water. Strain twice through a fine strainer or cheesecloth. Add honey (or dates) and carob powder and ice if any and blend again. Serve chilled.

Variation: Use sunflower seeds instead of nuts.

Easy Nut Milk #1

(for drinking alone or beverage recipes)

Use the Almond or Cashew Milk recipe. Use ground nuts instead of whole nuts. Do not soak the ground nuts, merely blend them with the other ingredients. There is no need to strain these ingredients.

 *Easy Nut Milk #2*

(for recipes such as breads)

>   1 cup water
>   3 – 4 Tbsp blanched almonds or cashews, whole or ground

Blend thoroughly for two to three minutes. Strain, if needed, and use in recipes where unsweetened milk substitutes are desired. If whole nuts are used, straining may be required. Ground nuts make a smoother, whiter milk. Do not use this recipe in beverage recipes or to drink by itself.

 Soy Milk

>   1 cup cold water
>   1 – 2 Tbsp soy milk powder
>   1 – 2 tsp honey or maple syrup or 3 – 4 pitted dates
> $^1/_4$ tsp real vanilla
>   Optional: 1 – 2 tsp carob powder
>   Optional: 1 – 2 ice cubes

Blend all ingredients until smooth. Serve chilled. Soy milk powder can be purchased at most health food stores.

♥ Juicer Vegetable Drinks

Use a juicer to make the following juices and juice combination drinks.

1. carrot juice
2. 3 parts carrot juice, 1 part beet juice
3. 3 parts carrot juice, 1 part celery or cucumber juice
4. 2 parts celery or cabbage juice, 1 part spinach or parsley,
    1 part beet juice
5. 2 parts carrot juice, 2 parts beet juice
6. tomato juice
7. 2 – 3 parts tomato juice, 1 – 2 parts celery or green pepper juice
8. 3 parts tomato juice, 1 part parsley or spinach juice

Make your own delicious combinations using almost any vegetables. Add a dash of salt, sea kelp, vegetable salt, or honey for flavoring if you wish. See appendixes to find what vitamins and minerals are found in each type of vegetable. For added chlorophyll and nutrients, $^1/_2$ – 1 ounce wheatgrass juice or preferably $^1/_4$ – $^1/_2$ teaspoon barley green powder can be added to almost any juice combination. One garlic clove can also be added for those who like the healing effects and can tolerate the strong taste.

 *Chapter 28*

Herbal Teas

Why Herbal Teas?

So what is wrong with the average black, green, and orange pekoe supermarket teas? Caffeine! And, in some brands and special blends, dyes are added for color, or aroma is sprayed on to enhance the senses. Also, some of these teas also contain more caffeine than many brands of coffee, and they have little nutritional value. Yet, nothing beats the taste of a nice hot cup of tea. There are tasty alternatives found in herbal teas. These teas are natural, do not contain caffeine, and are rich in many vitamins and minerals. Hundreds of varieties of herb teas are available in natural flavors. There are different varieties and combinations to please everyone.

Two Types of Herbal Teas

There are two categories of herbal teas, pleasure teas and medicinal teas. All herbal teas have some medicinal effect, but some are too potent to drink regularly while others can be drunk all day long without any unpleasant effects. These teas can be bought as loose or bulk teas or in tea bags.

Pleasure Teas

The most popular pleasure teas are:

Peppermint: Aids digestion, a very mild natural stimulant

Spearmint: Aids digestion, good for gas or nausea

Chamomile: Aids digestion and menstruation, soothes nerves, mild relaxant

Rose Hips: Good for colds, high in vitamin C

Lemon Grass: Good for eyes, high in vitamin A

Other Pleasure Teas:

These have more common flavors. They are often blended with other teas to make a more exciting flavor, but they are also tasty by themselves or with honey.

Raspberry Leaves: High in vitamin C, good for female organs

Strawberry Leaves: High in vitamin C

Fenugreek: For internal healing, good for intestines

Alfalfa: High in many vitamins and chlorophyll, good for arthritis

Catnip: Soothing, relaxant, very mild, especially good for infants and children, helps prevent nightmares

Fennel: Good for digestion, cramps, and gout, helps eliminate gas

Medicinal Teas

Medicinal teas should always be used sparingly and with proper directions, at proper times. For proper use of these teas, one should have sufficient information from the "herb bible", *Back to Eden* by Jethro Kloss, or from a reliable herbalist. These teas are not cures. They are simple aids to assist the body in healing itself. Your physician or naturopathic doctor should be consulted for any severe problems or illnesses.

Herbs work slowly and gradually. It takes a long time to get sick, so do not expect herbs to give you overnight cures or miracle remedies. Many medicinal teas taste strong or slightly unpleasant and, therefore, should be mixed with the popular pleasure teas for a more pleasant flavor. Licorice Root and Sassafras are delicious by themselves but should be used only as needed. Caution: Do not purchase, use, or gather your own herbs without sufficient information. Misuse of some herbs may be harmful. The few medicinal teas listed here are somewhat mild and may be taken a few times a week or more, or a couple times a day, only when needed. Drinking these herbs too often can make your body resistant to their effects. Only drink medicinal teas when they are needed.

Common Medicinal Teas:

Comfrey: Good for coughs, lung inflammation, hemorrhage, and asthma, high in chlorophyll

Red Clover: Blood purifier

Licorice root: Laxative, very effective, yet gentle

Hopps or Skullcap: Relaxant, helps induce sleep

Yarrow: Helps stop internal and external bleeding, for fever or wounds

Sassafras: Purifies blood, good for digestive organs, may be served only a few times a month as a pleasure tea

Eucalyptus: For fevers and asthma

Cornsilk: For kidney and bladder problems

Goldenseal: Blood purifier, promotes healing, for flus; use carefully

Slippery Elm: Good for sore throats, throat ailments, breaking up mucus

Senna: Good laxative when used with equal parts of flax seed

Myrrh: Use with goldenseal as a strong tincture for toothaches and teething babies. Swish tea in mouth or apply with cotton swab.

Ginseng: Stimulant, strengthens heart and nervous system, increases body manufacture of hormones. This is not a drug but a vitamin-rich mineral food. Use sparingly as needed. North American varieties are best for North Americans. Women should use Dong Quai varieties, not regular ginseng, as it stimulates too many male hormones.

Important Tips About Teas

1. If you have hay fever problems, avoid flower herb tea varieties such as lavender, hibiscus, chamomile, and clover teas.

2. Warm or hot teas are more potent and have more medicinal value than cold teas.

3. Bulk teas added to water and strained or used in a tea ball are more beneficial than tea bags.

4. Freshly made tea is more beneficial than reheated tea.

5. After steeping bulk tea, strain it as soon as possible and drink it shortly after to avoid a bitter flavor.

6. Strain leftover tea right after steeping and refrigerate it as soon as possible.

7. Use leftover tea for iced tea or make it into ice cubes to be added to other beverages or iced tea. To water house plants occasionally, use leftover unsweetened mint, chamomile, alfalfa, and other mild leaf teas, watered down. Vitamins and minerals from these herb teas are good for plants. Use one part tea per three to four parts water.

8. Drink herb teas by themselves or with added honey or other natural sweeteners, never with sugar or artificial sweeteners. Sugar defeats the purpose of these useful herbs and may counteract their good effects.

9. Honey is soothing for the throat and a good food for the body, so it is great for use in herb teas. If you have blood sugar problems avoid honey or use it infrequently. Also, avoid honey (or other sweeteners) with evening and sleep teas, as the natural sugars in the honey may keep you awake.

10. Avoid root and bark teas for everyday use. They are strong and potent and should be used only as needed.

11. Pleasure teas are safe and beneficial for frequent use by everyone unless one is allergic or as otherwise specified. Frequent use is three to four times a day or less.

12. Children may generally drink all pleasure teas. Caution: Only use medicinal teas that are recommended for children or very mild green leaf herb teas. This does not include twig, bark, root, or other medicinal teas unless recommended by a qualified herbalist or naturopathic doctor.

13. Do not gather your own herbs unless you are positive of what they are. The wrong herbs may be poisonous. Improper storage and drying of teas may also be detrimental.

14. Avoid caffeinated teas such as maté and Labrador tea that are often sold in special herb tea blends.

15. All teas should be covered while steeping or boiling to prevent loss of vitamins, minerals, and flavor. Use good quality enamel or Corningware pots for boiling water for medicinal teas as metal pots may interfere with the medicinal properties of some teas.

16. Most leaf and flower teas can be eaten, especially pleasure teas, with no troublesome effect. Sometimes this is even more beneficial than just drinking tea. Therefore, do not be concerned if there are some leaf or flower particles floating in the tea.

17. Use medicinal teas carefully. Misuse of there herbs may be harmful!

How to Make Herb Teas

Leaf or Flower Tea (and powdered rose hips)
Use one teaspoon of loose tea per cup. Steep only. Boiling makes these teas bitter and kills valuable vitamins and enzymes. To steep: Boil the water. When it becomes a bubbling boil, turn off the heat, pour into a tea pot, add the tea, and cover the pot. Then let it steep for 10 – 12 minutes. Strain and drink. A tea ball may be used for leaf and flower teas only.

Seed or Twig Teas (and crushed and broken rose hips)
Use one-half to one-quarter teaspoon loose tea per cup. Bring water and tea to a boil together and let it boil on just a low bubble for 5 – 10 minutes. Then let it steep for another 10 minutes off the heat. Strain and drink.

Root or Bark Tea (and whole rose hips)
Use one-quarter teaspoon root or bark, broken or chopped into small pieces per cup. Make sure tea is broken up as much as possible. Prepare the same as seed

and twig tea except that it should be on a low bubble for 15 – 20 minutes instead of five to ten. Follow with steeping for 10 minutes. Strain and drink.

Powdered Root or Bark Tea
Use one-tenth to one-sixteenth teaspoon powdered tea per cup. Mix the tea well in the water before heating. Then bring it to a boil and keep it on a low bubble for 20 – 30 minutes. Let it steep for two to three minutes, then stir and drink.

All Herb Tea Bags
Each herb tea bag can be used to make two to three cups of herb tea. For the first cup of tea add the tea bag to the hot water so the flavor will not be too strong or bitter. For extra cups from the same bag, pour hot water over the tea bag for full flavor. If the tea bag is fragile, do not pour the hot water directly on the bag but rather a little off to the side of it so the bag does not break and spoil the tea. If the tea bag should break, strain the tea with a small bamboo or stainless steel strainer. For tea pots, add the tea bag to two to three cups of hot water and cover pot while tea steeps.

Herb Tea Recipes and Ideas
Special Flavorings for Teas
The following is a list of a few teas or flavorings that can be added to either pleasure or medicinal teas to give them a delicious and exciting extra flavor. Unless otherwise specified, these extras should be boiled on a low heat (bubbled) for five to ten minutes with bark, twig, and root teas or boiled separately for two to five minutes before adding leaf or flower teas. Add one-eighth to one-half teaspoon per cup of one or two of the following:

    Orange or lemon peel, from undyed, natural fruits
    Anise seeds
    Cinnamon sticks or powder
    Lavender flowers, steep only
    Ginger root, peeled and finely grated
    Carob powder, roasted powder is best
    Wild rose petals, must be from wild, unsprayed bushes, steep only
    Allspice, use a dash only

How to Make Herb Tea Combinations

When making an herb tea combination, special care must be taken not to over-cook the teas. For example, when making a combination of twig and leaf tea, one cannot boil the leaf tea with the twig tea or the tea will become bitter and lose vitamins. Leaf tea should never be boiled. The twig tea should be low boiled by itself and the leaf tea should be added to the boiled twig tea during the steeping time only. (See How to Make Herb Teas.) The same idea holds for root and other teas. Never heat a type of tea longer or differently than the directions call for, give or take a minute or two. All kinds of different tea combinations are possible, but for general use, use only one or two teas at a time. Combinations of three to five types of tea are all right a few times a week or so, but they should be avoided because certain teas when combined may cancel the benefits of each other.

Herb Tea Combinations

1. Steep all three of these teas together: Peppermint or spearmint, lemon grass, catnip. Use equal portions of each of the three ingredients.
2. Heat crushed rose hips and cinnamon sticks on a low bubbling boil for five to ten minutes. Then add red clover and let it steep. Use about one small cinnamon stick per two teaspoons each of the other ingredients.
3. Heat anise seeds and natural orange peel on a low bubbling boil for five to ten minutes. Then add chamomile and ground rose hips and let steep. Use one part anise seeds to two parts each of all the other three ingredients.

Other Herb Tea Combinations:

1. Peppermint, Alfalfa, Chamomile
2. Raspberry Leaves, Peppermint, Lemon Grass
3. Rose Hips, Strawberry Leaves, Orange or Lemon Peels
4. Lemon Grass, Red Clover, Comfrey
5. Spearmint or Peppermint, Alfalfa or Comfrey, and Lemon Grass
6. Alfalfa, Catnip, Anise
7. Rose Hips, Chamomile, Mint
8. Chamomile, Spearmint, Cinnamon
9. Peppermint, Rosehips, Slippery Elm powder
10. Create new combinations!

Special Touches for Iced Tea or Other Beverages

1. Use ice cubes made from leftover herb tea or fruit juice (try pear, apple, or strawberry).

2. Use ice cubes made from citrus juice such as orange, lemon, grapefruit, pineapple, or lime. Add honey to the ice cube mixture to sweeten it if the juice is too bitter.

3. Put a ring or wedge of lemon or other citrus fruits on the edge of each glass. For punches, float citrus fruit slices for added flavor and eye appeal.

4. Float a few fresh mint leaves in the beverage for added zingy flavor.

5. Use sparkling spring water, mineral water or club soda to add natural carbonation to your favorite iced tea or punch.

6. Add fresh fruit purée to your favorite teas to create new flavors.

7. Mix iced teas half and half or three-quarters and one-quarter with chilled fruit juices or fruit juice blends for exciting beverages and party punch ideas.

 ## Sun Tea

Use tea bags or bulk leaf or flower tea and lukewarm water in a glass jar with a lid. Stir the tea well to mix it with the water. Place the jar in the sun for 20 – 50 minutes or until it becomes tea. The outside temperature should be 75°F – 21°C or higher. This method prevents the tea from overheating and becoming bitter. The tea will be fresh and pleasant-tasting and retain its natural vitamins. Use only leaf or flower teas.

 ## Iced Tea

Make one quart or liter of herb tea using two tea bags or one to two tablespoons of bulk tea. Use less tea if twig or seed tea is used. Do not use bark or root tea for iced tea. Strain tea if necessary. Mix in two to three tablespoons honey while tea is still hot. Chill for several hours and serve. For one gallon iced tea use six to eight tea bags or five to six tablespoons bulk leaf or flower tea and $1/2 – 3/4$ cup honey. In a hurry? Use three to four cups of boiling hot water per two to three tea bags. Let it steep the full time, strain, and mix in the honey. Then add ice cubes until the amount of ice and tea equals one quart or liter or eight cups. In ten minutes or less you will have instant iced tea as the ice cubes will melt quickly in the hot water.

 # Tropical Iced Tea

2 quarts iced tea
1 – 2 quarts pineapple-coconut juice (or other tropical juice such as papaya or mango-strawberry)

Mix the juices and tea well and chill. Serve with ice or ice tea cubes. Can be used as a punch. For punch, float pineapple chunks, strawberries, or other fruits if desired. Garnish with mint sprigs and/or lemon or lime wedges.

 # Mock Caffeinated Tea

Steep raspberry tea leaves half and half with comfrey leaves and serve with a squirt or wedge of lemon.

Part Four

Charts, Tables, Glossaries, & Guides

Food Weights and Measures
One pound equals the following in cups

Item	Cups	Item	Cups	Item	Cups
Whole Grains		**Dry Legumes**		**Dry Fruits**	
Barley	$2^1/_2$	Chick Peas		Coconut	
Buckwheat	$2^3/_4$	(garbonzoa)	3	(fine shredded)	8
Corn	$2^1/_3$	Fava	3	(coarse shredded)	6
Kasha	$2^3/_4$	Kidney	$2^1/_2$	Apricots	$3^1/_2$
Millet	$2^1/_2$	Lentils (brown)	$2^1/_2$	Dates and Figs	$2^1/_2$
Oats	$2^3/_4$	Lentils (red)	$2^1/_2$	Peaches and Pears	3
Rice (brown)	$2^2/_3$	Mung	$2^3/_4$	Prunes	$2^1/_2$
Wheat	$2^1/_2$	Peas (split)	$2^1/_4$	Raisins	3
		Pinto	$2^1/_4$		
Cereals		Soy	$2^1/_2$	**Liquids**	
Bran	4	White Peas Beans (navy)	2	Honey	$1^1/_4 - 1^1/_2$
Bulgur	3			Maple Syrup	2
Cornmeal	3	**Nuts**		Milk	2
Cracked Wheat	3	Almonds	$3^1/_2$	Molasses	$1^1/_2 - 1^3/_4$
Oats (rolled)	$5 - 6$	Brazil	$3^1/_2$	Oil	$2^1/_2$
Rice polish	2	Cashews	$3^1/_2$	Sorghum	$1^1/_2$
Rye Flakes	5	Chestnuts	3	Tamari Soy Sauce	$2^1/_2$
Wheat Flakes	$4^1/_2$	Filberts (hazelnuts)	$3^1/_2$		
Wheat Germ	4	Peanuts	3	**Miscellaneous**	
		Pecans	4	Arrowroot Powder	3
Flours		Pine Nuts (pignolias)	4	Carob Powder	5
Buckwheat	4	Walnuts	4	Date Sugar (brown)	3
Corn	$4^1/_2$			Dry Milk Powder	4
Graham	4	**Seeds**		Yeast Flakes	$5 - 7$
Millet	$4^1/_2$	Alfalfa	$2^1/_4$	Nut Butters	2
Oats	$4^1/_2$	Falx	3	Regular Butter	2
Rice	$4^1/_2$	Sesame	3	Eggs (4 large)	1
Rye and Soy	4	Sunflower	4	Lemon (1 medium)	
Unbleached White	$4^1/_2$	Pumpkin	4	. . . 4 Tablespoons juice	
Whole Wheat	$3^1/_2$			Agar-Agar	
				(1 oz. flake)	1 cup
				(1 oz. granulated)	$^1/_2$ cup

Conversion Tables
Capacity (liquids)

American Measure				Metric Equivalent	
1 tsp	=1/3 Tbsp	= 1/6 fl. oz.		= 0.5 cl.	
1 Tbsp	= 3 tsp	= 1/2 fl. oz.		= 1.5 cl.	
1 oz.	= 2 Tbsp	= 6 tsp		= 2.9cl.	
1 cup	= 1/2 pt.	= 8 fl. oz.	= 16 Tbsp	= 2.37 dl.	
1 pt.	= 2 cup	= 16 fl. oz.		= 4.73 dl.	
1 qt.	= 2 pts.	= 32 fl. oz.	= 4 cups	=9.46 dl.	=.946 liter
1 gal.	= 4 qts.	= 128 fl. oz.	= 16 cups	= 3.79 liter	

British Measure (Imperial)				Metric Equivalent	
1 tsp	= 1/3 Tbsp	= 1/5 fl. oz.		= 0.6 cl.	
1 Tbsp	= 3 tsp	= .63 fl. oz.		= 1.7 cl.	
1 oz.	= 1.6 Tbsp			= 2.9 cl.	
1 cup	= 1/2 pt.	= 10 fl. oz	=16 Tbsp	= 2.84 dl.	
1 pt.	= 2 cups	= 20 fl. oz.		= 5.7 dl.	
1 qt.	= 2 pts.	= 40 fl.oz.	=4 cups	= 1.1 liter	
1 gal.	= 4 qts.	= 160 fl. oz.	=16 cups	= 4.5 liter	

100 centiliters = 10 deciliters = 1 liter

American Measure	British Equivalent
6 tsp	= 5 tsp
1 1/3 Tbsp	= 1 Tbsp
1 1/4 oz.	= 1 oz.
1 1/4 cups	= 1 cup
1 1/4 pts.	= 1 pt.
1 1/4 qts.	= 1 qt.
1 1/4 gal. or 1 gal. and 1 qt.	= 1 gal.
1 Tbsp	= 4/5 Tbsp
1 cup	= 4/5 cup
1 pt.	= 4/5 pt.
1 qt.	= 4/5 qt.
1 gal.	= 4/5 gal.

Weights (Solids)

American & British Measure	Metric Equivalent
1 oz.	= 28 grams
3½ oz.	= 100 grams
2.2 lbs.	= 1000 grams
2.2 lbs.	= 1 kg.
1 lb.	= 450 grams

Oven Temperatures

Slow.	300 degrees
Moderately slow	325 degrees
Moderate.	350 degrees
Moderately hot	400 degrees
Hot	450 degrees
Very Hot	500 degrees

Storage Temperatures

Grains and Beans	62° or less
Flours and Meals.	55° or less
Vegetables and Fruits	35° – 55°
Dried Fruits.	65° or less
Dairy Products	33° – 45°
Frozen Foods	0° – 22°
Natural Oil Products.	35° – 45°

Chart Abbreviations

fl.	=	fluid
oz.	=	ounce
lb.	=	pound
c.	=	cup
pt.	=	pint
qt.	=	quart
gal.	=	gallon
cl.	=	centiliter
dl.	=	deciliter
kg.	=	kilogram

Abbreviations for Recipes

tsp	=	teaspoon
Tbsp	=	tablespoon
oz.	=	ounce
lb.	=	pound
pt.	=	pint
qt.	=	quart
gal.	=	gallon
doz.	=	dozen
min.	=	minute
hr.	=	hour

Recipes in this book are based on American measurements.

Food Storage Charts

Refrigerate or Keep in a Cool, Dry Place
about 65° or Less

- ■ Whole grains
- ❙ Whole grain flours or meals
- ❙ Whole grain crackers, noodles, and other products
- ❙ Natural cookies and candies
- ● Dried fruits
- ● Lecithin granules or powder
- ❙ Vegetable bouillon cubes
- ■ Beans, peas, and lentils
- ❙ Granola and muesli
- ● Nuts and seeds
- ▲ Nut and seed meals
- ■ Tamari soy sauce
- ● Peanut butter
- ❙ Protein powders
- ● Coconut - shredded (dried) or chopped
- ■ Natural molasses
- ■ Sorghum

May be Frozen

- ❙ Ice cream (must be frozen)
- ❙ Breads and rolls
- ❙ Yogurt
- ❙ Tofu
- ● Natural ketchup
- ❙ Fruit and vegetable juices
- ❙ Herb tea drinks (pleasure only)
- ❙ Dairy products (defrost these slowly in refrigerator)
- ● Sauces
- ❙ Soups and stews
- ❙ Cooked grains and beans
- ● Blanched vegetables and fruits
- ❙ Miso

May Be Frozen Raw for Later Cooking Use

- ❙ Unrisen bread dough
- ❙ Whole bananas
- ❙ Whole tomatoes
- ● Whole or halved green peppers
- ● Whole or sliced avocados
- ❙ Whole grain nut or bean burgers
- ❙ Cranberries
- ● Strawberries

Code for Storage Times:
- ▲ Stores safely for 2 weeks or less
- ❙ Stores safely for 3 months or less
- ● Stores safely for 6 months or more
- ❙ Stores safely for 1 year or more
- ■ Stores safely for years.

These products will store for the above stated times
only if wrapped carefully and stored as directed.

- ▮ Gooseberries and others
- ▮ Chopped rhubarb stalks
- ▶ Some sliced fruits (peaches, pears, apricots)

Shelf Storage
- ▮ Herbs and spices
- ▮ Herbs teas
- ▮ Honey
- ● Apple Cider Vinegar
- ▮ Carob powder
- ▮ Arrowroot powder
- ▮ Agar-Agar
- ▮ Seaweeds
- ▮ Skim milk powder
- ▮ Sea kelp
- ▮ Coffee substitutes
- ▮ Vegetable broth powder
- ▮ Most vitamin pills
- ▮ Baking powder
- ▶ Potatoes
- ▶ Onions and garlic
- ▶ Pumpkins and squashes
- ▲ Bananas
- ▲ Unripe avocados
- ▲ Unripe fruit
- ▶ Whole coconuts
- ▲ Sprouts - while growing

Refrigerator Storage
- ● Wheat germ
- ● Bran
- ● Rice polish
- ▶ Diary products
- ▶ Eggs
- ● Acidophilus
- ▶ Tofu

- ▲ Most vegetables
- ▲ Most fruits
- ▮ Yeast - baking or nutritional
- ▶ Products containing natural oils that are not in airtight, prepackaged containers
- ▲ Whole grain breads
- ▶ Most whole grain flours
- ▲ Ripe fruit
- ▲ Sprouts, full grown
- ● Whole milk powder
- ▮ Miso
- ▶ Root vegetables

Shelf Storage - Refrigerate When Opened
- ▶ Natural oils
- ▮ Liquid ginseng
- ▶ Salad dressings
- ▶ Mayonnaise
- ▶ Natural ketchup
- ● Natural peanut butter
- ● Sesame tahini
- ▶ Nut and fruit butters
- ▶ Natural jams and jellies
- ▮ Real maple syrup
- ▲ Fruit and vegetable juices
- ▲ Mineral waters
- ▮ Liquid lecithin

Above column is for items that are packed airtight. They may be shelved until the air seal is broken. These items stay fresh about 6 months or more unopened. Code indicates refrigerator storage time after opening.

Substitutions for More Nutrition & Special Diets

What Not to Use	Why Not to Use	Use Instead	How Much to Use
Baking powder with alum (most market brands)	Alum (aluminum) is claimed to be a contributing factor in causing cancer. It also affects the brain.	Baking powder, natural (low-alum or no-alum); Rumford is low-alum.	1½ tsp natural per 1 tsp regular alum powder
Brown sugar	Same as below for Sugar	Molasses with honey or natural granular sweetener or date sugar	¹⁄₁₀ to ¼ cup molasses and the rest honey or the rest ½ honey and ½ date sugar per 1 cup brown sugar
Butter or margarine	Butter and margarine are saturated fats, natural vegetable and seed oils are not. For special diets also.	Natural oils	1 cup oil and ⅛ teaspoon salt per 2 lbs. of butter or margarine OR Better Butter or Veggie Butter
Cocoa and chocolate	Cocoa and chocolate contain caffeine, which is a stimulant. Also, it is high in fats. Chocolate mixed with milk makes the calcium in milk unusable.	Carob powder, dark, roasted. Carob is a fruit, tasty, and full of vitamins. Good for those with chocolate allergies.	Equal amounts
Coffee	Coffee contains caffeine, which damages the nervous system and disturbs the emotions, brain, and spinal column. Addictive - has withdrawl symptoms.	Coffee substitutes: Soya coffee, Pero, Pioneer, Bamboo, Caf-lib, dandelion and grain coffees.	Equal amounts

Substitutions for More Nutrition & Special Diets

What Not to Use	Why Not to Use	Use Instead	How Much to Use
Cornstarch or baking soda	Cornstarch and soda destroy vitamin C and other vitamins in the body.	Arrowroot powder. Arrowroot works just as well as a thickening agent. Guar gum may be used to help things rise or as a binder.	Equal amounts
Eggs	For vegetarians or those on special diets who wish to avoid eggs.	Arrowroot powder, agar-agar flakes, liquid lecithin, powdered egg replacer (sometimes guar gum may be used $1/2$ to 1 tsp at a time).	Per egg: 3 Tbsp water plus 1 Tbsp lecithin; or 1 tsp arrowroot, 2 tsp lecithin, and 3 Tbsp water; or 2 tsp agar-agar dissolved in 3 Tbsp boiling water (mix then heat and cool); or 1 Tbsp egg replacer plus 3 Tbsp water
Flours – whole wheat or unbleached	For those with wheat allergies.	Wheatless flours: millet, oat, soy, potato, almond, or other flours	Equal amounts (see Chapter 25 – Breads and Chapter 26 – Desserts)
Gelatin	For vegetarians. Gelatin is from animal bones, usually cows.	Agar-agar. Agar-agar is seaweed.	See Fruit Jello and dessert recipes.
Gluten flour	For those with gluten allergies.	Arrowroot powder or xanthan or guar gum	Equal amounts for arrowroot, for gums use 1 – 2 tsp for baking powder recipe

Substitutions for More Nutrition & Special Diets

What Not to Use	Why Not to Use	Use Instead	How Much to Use
Meat	Use these foods instead of meat sometimes.	Legumes, nuts, grains, dairy products, and eggs	About 1 – 3 servings a day
Milk, dairy	For special diets or allergies.	Nut milks, soy, cashew, or other, sometimes goat milk	Equal amounts for recipes (see recipes)
Milk powder, instant	Non-instant milk powder is usually better quality and contains more vitamins and minerals.	Milk powder, non-instant	Equal amounts, beat well into liquids
Molasses, sulphered, a sugar by-product	Sulphur damages kidneys and blood cells and causes aches and nausea. Also, avoid sulphured dried fruits.	Molasses, unsulphured or sorghum	Equal amounts
Nuts, salted and roasted in oil	Roasting kills vitamins and makes nuts harder to digest. Salted (and chopped) nuts become rancid more easily.	Nuts, raw and unsalted. Raw nuts are full of calcium, iron, protein, B vitamins, and oils.	Equal amounts
Oils – supermarket oils or commercial oils and animal fats	Supermarket oils have no food value and are processed with chemicals.	Natural oils (from beans, nuts, and seeds). Natural oils may be only partially refined and are still full of nutrients, especially vitamin E.	Equal amounts

Substitutions for More Nutrition & Special Diets

What Not to Use	Why Not to Use	Use Instead	How Much to Use
Pepper, black or white	Black and white pepper irritate the stomach lining.	Cayenne or red pepper. Red pepper (a vegetable, not a spice) is beneficial for the body and helps it to heal.	$^1/_{10}$ to $^1/_4$ tsp red pepper per 1 tsp black or white pepper
Rice, white	This affects the body like refined foods. White rice also has the rice polish removed along with vitamins and flavor. It is often precooked.	Rice, brown (or wild)	Equal amounts or $^3/_4$ cup brown per 1 cup white rice
Salt, earth (regular table salt)	Earth salt contains additives like sugar and chemicals. It is harder to digest than sea salt.	Sea salt	About $^3/_4$ to $^7/_8$ tsp sea salt per 1 tsp earth salt
Shortening or lard	Use natural oil and lecithin in place of animal fats and chemically processed oils and shortenings. The latter are saturated fats and may help increase cholesterol levels.	Natural oils and liquid lecithin or butter or Better Butter	3 ounces or 6 Tbsp oil plus 2 Tbsp lecithin per $^1/_2$ cup shortening, equal amounts for butters
Sugar – any kind	All natural vitamins are killed in these refined sugars. They are poison to the system. (See Chapter 7 – Sweets for the Sweet)	Date sugar, brown, or natural granular sweetener is especially important in cookie recipes and some cakes	$^1/_2$ cup date sugar or natural granular sweetener and $^1/_2$ cup honey per 1 cup sugar, increase recipe's dry ingredients $^1/_3$ cup or so

Substitutions for More Nutrition & Special Diets

What Not to Use	Why Not to Use	Use Instead	How Much to Use
Sugar or brown sugar	Same as above for Sugar.	Honey Note: Quality of honey determines amount needed to exchange.	$1/2 - 3/4$ cup honey per 1 cup sugar and increase the flour $1/4$ cup or decrease the liquid $1/4$ cup in the recipe.
Sugar (can also be used in place of honey)	Same as above for Sugar.	Maple syrup (use less if sweeter variety used)	$1/3$ to $2/3$ cup syrup and the rest of a cup milk per 1 cup honey OR rest of the cup natural granular sweetener per 1 cup sugar.
Teas, black or green commercial or supermarket	Commercial teas contain caffeine.	Herbal teas (see Chapter 28 – Herbal Teas)	Equal amounts
Vinegar - any kind	Some nutritionists claim that all types of vinegar lead to anemia and are unhealthy. Apple cider vinegar is the best of all vinegars.	Lemon juice	$1/2$ cup or less lemon juice per 1 cup vinegar (good only in some recipes). Use apple cider vinegar when vinegar is required.
Vinegars – white wine, rice or other	Vinegars are harmful to the body and may contribute to anemia and clog the system.	Apple cider vinegar. Apple cider vinegar is claimed to promote healing, help regulate weight, remove toxins, and improve the metabolism of the body.	Equal amounts or slightly less apple cider vinegar

Glossary of Cooking Terms

Bake: Cooking with dry heat, usually in an oven.

Baste: Moistening foods during cooking with a sauce, other liquid, or pan drippings. This adds flavor to the food and helps prevent it from drying out.

Beat: Using a rapid stirring motion to mix or add air to a food with a spoon or electric mixer.

Blanch: Loosening skins, setting colors, or removing colors from a food by pouring boiling water over it or by boiling for a couple of minutes.

Blend: Mixing two or more ingredients until they are smooth. Usually the foods are combined or blended to make liquids, sauces, or spreads.

Boil: Cooking a liquid at a high temperature while air bubbles are forming and dissolving in the liquid.

Bubble: Cooking a liquid at a low or moderate temperature while small air bubbles are forming and dissolving in the liquid.

Chop: Cutting into pieces with a knife or other cutter.

Cream: Stirring, mixing, or mashing with a spoon until a mixture is soft and smooth.

Cut: Separating food into pieces with a sharp knife, scissors, or other cutting tool.

Dice: Cutting or chopping a food into very small pieces or cubes.

Fold: Adding an ingredient to one or more ingredients by pressing it into the main ingredients and working them together.

Fry: Cooking in one or two-inches or more of hot oil or fat. For stir-fry, see Sauté below.

Garnish: Decorating a dish with pieces of small, colorful food.

Glaze: Coating a food with a liquid sweetener to add color and flavor.

Grate: To shred, usually cheese, fruit, or vegetables, in small, uniform, noodle-like strips about one-inch long or shorter.

Knead: Pressing and working dough with the hands and occasionally turning or folding it over.

Marinate: Letting a food stand in a liquid, usually oil and vinegar, until it softens and the liquid has partially soaked into the food, adding flavor.

Melt: Using heat to liquefy.

Mince: Cutting or chopping into very tiny pieces, smaller than dicing.

Mix: Combining ingredients, usually by stirring.

Pare: Cutting off the skin of a food.

Peel: Removing the outer skin of a food, not always by cutting.

Pit: Removing pits from fruits.

Sauté: Cooking in a very small amount of oil, usually just enough to lightly cover the bottom of a pan, about one to two tablespoons. Heat oil until hot, then add food and stir occasionally over medium heat until food is tender or cooked as desired. Keep food sizzling while sautéing so the food does not become saturated by the oil, but rather the oil coats it and seals in nutrients while cooking.

Scald: Bringing a liquid to a temperature just below boiling point.

Scallop: Baking a food with a sauce or other liquid such as milk, usually in a casserole.

Shred: Cutting in long, narrow pieces.

Sift: Putting dry ingredients through a sieve or flour sifter once or twice.

Simmer: Cooking slowly over a low heat.

Steam: Cooking food in a tightly covered pot wherein food is suspended on a rack or basket with holes in it. Boiling water is beneath the rack but does not touch the food. The food is cooked by hot steam rising from the water.

Steep: Extracting color, flavor, and vitamins from a food, often to form a liquid such as tea, by letting it sit in hot water that is just below the boiling point, usually for about ten to fifteen minutes.

Sterilize: Destroying microorganisms in food by cooking, usually at a very high heat. Or rinsing kitchen equipment in boiling water.

Stew: Mixing ingredients with a spoon as they are cooking on a stove.

Toss: Lightly mixing ingredients together as in tossing a salad.

Whip: Adding air to a mixture by beating rapidly.

Glossary of Natural Foods

Acerola: A tropical cherry-like fruit that is very high in vitamin C. It is similar in flavor to a crab apple or raspberry. Usually found in tablet form, sometimes with added rose hips. It is a main ingredient in making natural vitamin C.

Acidophilus: A special type of friendly bacteria that is especially helpful to the body. It puts flora into the intestines that are an aid to digestion and cleanse the system. It can be purchased in yogurt, in a dry package for self-preparation, as a bottled beverage, or mixed in milk. (Also in capsule form.)

Agar-agar: (In flakes, powder, or bars.) A gelling agent used instead of animal gelatin in making jellos, jams, puddings, pies, and other desserts. It is a white seaweed with almost no calories. See the Substitution Chart in Part IV and recipes for more information on its use.

Alfalfa: (In seeds or leaves.) Alfalfa is high in all kinds of vitamins. The tiny seeds are golden brown and green. The plant leaves are inedible, raw or cooked, as they are hard to digest and upset the stomach, but the small green leaves are excellent as an herbal tea and can be steeped. The seeds can be sprouted or slightly boiled (bubbled) for tea. (See Herb Tea and Sprouting sections for preparation information) When sprouted, the seeds are very high in protein and chlorophyll as well as in vitamins. In some cases, if alfalfa is taken regularly two to four times a day, as tea or tablets, over a period of a couple months or more, it is helpful in relieving some of the pains and problems of arthritis. Alfalfa flowers are edible in salads.

Aloe vera: (Gel or juice.) A succulent plant with astringent qualities that can be soothing to stomachs and may assist in the healing of ulcers. The pure gel can be used in small amounts internally or externally to bathe wounds, help heal dry or damaged skin and speed healing of sunburns, other burns, cuts, rashes(including diaper rash), blisters, and even warts. Drink one to four ounces daily unless a healing reaction occurs, then reduce intake or avoid. Keep refrigerated.

Amaranth: (Seed, flour, or puffed.) Made from a tiny grain-like seed of a tall plant native to Mexico, but now grown in the US and Eastern Canada. The ancient Aztecs were nourished on this high-energy food, which is considered a complete protein, high in calcium and other nutrients. This is not a grain. Use it in grain-free baking recipes with tapioca, arrowroot, or other starchy flours to lighten baked goods. It has a robust, pleasant, nutty flavor and is smaller than a straight pin head.

Amazake: Rice culture sweetener made from koji (aspergillus oryzae) added to rice. It is easy to digest, and is a mild but flavorful sweetener usually found in liquid form. Use in place of honey or maple syrup in recipes but adjust the amount as its sweetness varies and is usually less sweet.

Apple cider: Pure apple juice that is not watered down, refined, or preserved. No sugar should be added. The best and freshest apple cider is unpasteurized and highly perishable. It lasts only a few days to a week refrigerated but surpasses other juices in quality, vitamins, and flavor. Keep free from perspiration, bacteria, and saliva for longer freshness.

Arrowroot: (In powder form) This is a thickening agent high in minerals. It is used in soups, cakes, and other desserts as a more healthful replacement for cornstarch or baking soda in equal amounts. It is made from the dried root of a tropical plant. (See the Substitution Chart and recipes.)

Baking powder: This is a leavening agent. Buy baking powder that has no unnecessary additives and no alum or low alum. Alum (aluminum) makes for higher-rising baked goods but is claimed to be a detriment to health. Use about $1\frac{1}{2}$ times the amount of natural baking powder in place of alum baking powder. Also, use about one teaspoon gluten flour or $\frac{1}{4}$ teaspoon guar or xanthan gum for every one to two teaspoons of baking powder to help baked goods rise high naturally. Those with wheat allergies should purchase special wheat-free baking powder.

Baking yeast: (In granules.) This is a living fungus (before baking). Use as a leavening agent in breads and baked goods. One tablespoon yeast equals one individual packet or square. Avoid brands that contain chemicals like BHA and BHT and other preservatives. Yeast will naturally last six months to a year or more if it is refrigerated in a closed jar or package. Avoid baking yeast for most yeast allergies and Candida albicans diets.

Barbados molasses: This molasses is sweeter than blackstrap, but lower in iron content. This is the best variety to use in all recipes including baked beans, puddings, cookies, and pumpkin pies. An unsulphured, natural molasses superior to table or cooking varieties.

Barley: (In pearl or pot varieties) One of the four main gluten grains, used mainly in soups, casseroles, and vegetable burgers. Since the outer layers of barley are so tough and indigestible, some of them must be removed, so it is partially refined. Pot barley is small, oblong, and brown white in color. The brown color denotes more vitamins. As little of the outer layers are removed as possible for this type. Pearl barley is refined down to a small round white bead. It has less vitamin content, flavor, and color. Therefore, pot barley is preferable. Note: These two types of barley are sometimes mislabeled and names interchanged incorrectly.

Barley green: (Grass, powder or tablet.) A high nutrient and chlorophyll-rich food grown the same as wheatgrass but is more easily tolerated. The grass can be used in salads or juiced and the powder can be sprinkled on food or mixed with juices or water. Best to use about $^1/_4 - ^1/_2$ teaspoon serving at a time with other foods. Extremely high in potassium.

Barley malt: (Powder or syrup.) Used as a mild sweetening agent. Good for wheat-free diets, but it does contain gluten.

Bee pollen: (Comes in granules.) Bee pollen is extremely high in vitamins, minerals, and protein. It may be successfully used by some as a hay fever preventative if one to two teaspoons are eaten (mixed in food or in a blender drink) once to twice a day beginning several months before hay fever season starts.

Besan: Chick pea flour. Same as chana flour.

Blackstrap molasses: This sweetening agent is higher in nutrients and iron than regular table or Barbados molasses but with a more bitter taste. It is sometimes mixed with honey or another sweetener to improve the flavor. Use unsulphured. Good for cereals and as an iron supplement taken by the spoonful.

Blue-green algae: (Powder or tablets.) A single celled plankton (plant) that has been growing in the oceans for thousands of years and is food for whales and sea creatures. One of the most complete foods, 70 – 80% percent protein, high in beta carotene, chlorophyll, iron and other nutrients. Contains digestible saponins that help combat high blood pressure, hardening of the arteries and helps remove cholesterol and heavy metals from the body. Also good for Chronic Fatigue Syndrome and high or low blood sugar diets. One of the highest non-meat sources of vitamin B12.

Bone meal: (In tablets or powder.) The ground bones of calves, which are very high in calcium. This makes strong teeth. Use in breads, blender drinks, and main dishes. Good supplement if you are non-vegetarian.

Bran: Bran is the outer layer of the wheat berry (or wheat kernel) or other kind of grain. This is the coarse part of the grain and is high in vitamins, especially B vitamins.

Brewer's yeast: A nutritional yeast usually found in tablets or powder form, often a by-product of the brewing industry and beer making. This raw, edible food yeast is not used for leavening but as a food supplement, high in B vitamins and protein. It can be added to many different raw or cooked foods but should be used in small amounts until you acquire a taste for its strong flavor. Good for vitamin/protein blender drinks. See nutritional yeast. Avoid for yeast-free diets.

Buckwheat: A small white-brown-green triangular grain. It is used mainly in soups, casseroles, and vegetable burgers. This is essentially a gluten-free grain and does not contain wheat. Toasted buckwheat is called kasha.

Bulgur: Parched, toasted cracked wheat used in cereals and main dishes. It can be soaked overnight or for several hours in water, and eaten raw as a cereal or cooked in breads and casseroles. A main ingredient in taboulie.

Butters: (Nut and fruit butters.) Nut butters are nuts ground into a spread. They may be raw or roasted nuts and may have salt and/or oil added. Fruit butters are pureed fruits, sometimes strained but preferably with nothing removed. Honey is sometimes added. Butters are used on bread or crackers. Fruit butters can top desserts and nut butters can be used on celery, in dressings, or sandwich spreads. Some examples are: apple butter, date butter, peanut butter, almond butter, and sesame butter or tahini.

Carob: (Comes in powder or pods in raw or roasted form.) Otherwise known as Honey Locust and St. John's Bread, this powder is used as a chocolate substitute. The roasted powder resembles chocolate more in flavor. The raw powder has a more fruity taste, since carob is a fruit of sorts. (Actually, it is a member of the legume family although it grows on a tree like fruit.) Carob is good for people with chocolate allergies. It is high in vitamins and minerals and has over ten times less fat than chocolate. The roasted pods can be eaten as they are. (Do not eat seeds.) They are crunchy, sweet, and have a malt-like flavor. Carob powder can be used in equal proportions instead of cocoa powder. Like cocoa powder, carob needs extra sweetening in cooking recipes. Carob is also a very mild laxative, but can be used quite often without troublesome effects. Unlike chocolate, carob contains no caffeine or oxalic acid and does not make the calcium in milk unusable.

Carrageen: Also called Irish moss. A seaweed used as a thickening agent in many packaged foods. It can be slightly irritating to some stomachs.

Cashews and cashew milk: Nuts high in calcium, protein, and fats. These are used as dairy substitutes. Like all nuts, they are hard to digest whole and are best used in milks, butters or ground for use in recipes. Buy the raw type. Technically, all cashews must be cooked slightly to make them edible. A cashew is not a true nut. It is in the same food family as the mango and pistachio.

Cassava flour or root: From a starchy tropical root vegetable which is also the main source of tapioca. The precooked woody root is also available frozen in specialty markets and may be boiled and mashed like potatoes. This is especially good for the diets of those who have multiple food allergies.

Cayenne: Same as red pepper. Tastes stronger than black pepper but is actually mild on the stomach, unlike white and black pepper, and very beneficial and healing to the body. Red peppers are a vegetable. Cayenne, or capsicum as it is sometimes called, is good for the heart, circulation, ulcers, and a variety of other health concerns.

Chana flour: Chick pea flour or besan.

Chia seeds: This is a very small, round, gray-black seed, about the size of a head of a pin. Used for sprouting. Some North American Indian tribes are said to have used this as an endurance food or for strength. Add a bit to blender drinks.

Chick peas: (Also called garbanzos.) This is a type of bean very high in protein. It is light golden brown in color and is similar in size to a soybean, only it is not completely round. It is somewhat bumpy and curved in texture. Chick peas can be used like soybeans as a meat substitute or used in soups, stews, sandwich spreads, casseroles, burgers, and other main dishes. These are higher in fat than other beans, but still much lower in fat than most meats.

Chick pea flour: (Chana, besan) A bit ($1/4 - 1/2$ cup per recipe) can be used to add protein to bread recipes. Used commonly in East Indian foods like chipatis.

Chlorella: (Powder or tablet.) A green, single celled algae similar to spirulina with generally a bit less B12 and other nutrients. It is one of the highest sources of chlorophyll and may contain up to ten times as much as alfalfa and about twice as much as spirulina for the same volume.

Chlorophyll: (Liquid or tablets.) The substance that makes plants green. It promotes healing and is good for external sores or rashes. Eliminates unfriendly bacteria in the stomach and aids those with stomach disorders.

Cilantro: Mexican or Chinese parsley. I think it has a bit of a "soapy" taste and is not liked by everyone. Used like parsley to garnish and flavor foods.

Cornmeal: A coarsely ground corn used in breads and as a cereal. Make sure it is true cornmeal and that the "germ" is included in the meal for more vitamins. Cornmeal spoils easily and must be kept in a cool place. It is somewhat bitter and must be sweetened. If the flavor is extremely strong, the cornmeal may be rancid and should be discarded. Keep no longer than six months. Best kept in freezer for freshness. (Cornmeal used for cereal should not be refrigerated or it may become damp and taste like wet cement.) Corn flour may contain wheat, although not always, and it is more finely ground.

Cornstarch: May contribute to constipation, diarrhea, or digestive troubles and may rob the body of vitamin C and other nutrients. Arrowroot may be used as a more wholesome substitute in equal proportions in recipes.

Couscous: A precooked Moroccan grain dish made from semolina wheat. It can be steamed for about 10 minutes or more until tender or heat one cup couscous in $2\frac{1}{2}$ to $3\frac{1}{2}$ cups of water or broth until it comes to a boil, then turn heat off and let it set, covered, five minutes before serving. Serve with butter and salt along with vegetables and legumes. A partial grain that is not especially nutritious but can be enjoyed occasionally.

Cracked wheat: This is wheat berries cracked into smaller pieces for easier cooking in soups, cereals, and other recipes. Cracked wheat does not usually need soaking and can be cooked immediately. This is not precooked and must be cooked before eating, not just soaked, like bulgur.

Date sugar: This is sugar made from dates. The coarse brown date sugar is a good sugar substitute but it is not nearly as sweet as sugar and must be mixed with honey, molasses, or other sweetener for sweeter recipes. The small, white, granulated date sugar should be avoided as it is refined and is little better for you than cane sugar.

Dulse: (In whole, flaked, or powdered form.) The dried seaweed is similar to kelp. It can be dried and powdered and used as seasoning in foods or eaten fresh or dried and cooked in soups or vegetable dishes. It is high in vitamins and minerals especially iodine, calcium, and traces of iron.

Eggs: Buy free-range or organic eggs when possible. Quail, duck or other eggs can be substituted for those allergic to hen's eggs. One hen's egg is about $1/4$ cup liquid, so measure other eggs accordingly for recipes. (See Chapter 23 – Dairy Products, Eggs, and Substitutes.)

Egg substitutes: Packaged egg substitutes may be purchased. Follow the directions or use the substitutes suggested in many of this book's recipes or the Substitution Chart.

Engevita yeast: A good tasting, edible, yellow nutritional yeast that can be used to flavor popcorn, patés, or other recipes. Used in many recipes for a cheesy flavor or as a cheese substitute. Avoid for yeast-free diets.

Fava beans: Very large beans with more protein than any other beans, including soybeans, and a flavor similar to potatoes cooked in their skins. Fava beans are shaped like lima beans, but are brown in color and more than twice their size. The texture is bumpy. This "King of legumes" is hard to cook and often requires pressure cooking. These are also high in a variety of vitamins and minerals.

Fenugreek seeds: These are used in sprouting or as a pleasure or a medicinal herb tea, good for ulcers and fevers. The small seeds look like gravel and are gold, brown, and black. The aroma of the tea resembles the smell of chicken soup, but the taste is mild and pleasant.

Flax: (In seed, meal, or oil form.) Flax is high in vitamins and minerals and is as excellent as gelatin for growing strong, hard nails and beautiful shining hair. The flax seeds, or linseed, should be cooked or ground into meal to make sure the vitamins are able to be assimilated. Use seeds in casseroles, soups, or cooked cereals. Use the raw meal to sprinkle on cereals, salads, or casseroles for even more nutritional value. The unhulled seeds are flat and pointed on the ends and brown in color. The hulled seeds are golden in color and have less nutritional value. Meals should be ground fresh every week or two. The raw oil is used as a supplement to help replenish natural oils and provide Omega 3 and 6.

Flours: See Chapter 25 – Breads.

Food yeast: See Brewer's yeast and Primary yeast, Engivita yeast and Torula yeast.

Fruit, dried: High in iron and natural sugars. Use unsulphured varieties, as sulphur is known to agitate the liver and kidneys and cause indigestion. Do not eat before bedtime or leave on teeth as they may contribute to cavities.

Fruit concentrate: A natural liquid sweetener that may be used in place of honey or maple syrup, in about equal proportions. This specially manufactured sweetener is a highly concentrated fruit product not to be confused with fruit juice concentrate. It looks like honey but has a slightly fruity taste.

Garbanzos: See Chick peas

Gluten grains and flours: Technically speaking, all true grains contain at least a small amount of gluten. However, most people allergic to gluten grains can tolerate everything except the four high-gluten grains, wheat, rye, barley, and oats. Spelt and kamut also contain more gluten as they are a form of wheat. Durum, farina, bolted wheat, graham, semolina, cake, pastry, bread (soft or hard), and gluten flours are all types of wheat fours that include gluten.

Gluten-free grains and flours: Grains containing only minute amounts of gluten. These include buckwheat (kasha), rice, millet, corn, and, some say, quinoa. Also see Grain-free flours.

Goat cheese and milk: More than 50% percent of people allergic to cow's milk products can tolerate goat dairy products. Goat milk is closer to human milk in quality, is easier to digest, and generally lower in fats and cholesterol. Goat products are mild tasting if male goats are kept separate from the female goats.

Gomashio: Same as sesame salt. Toasted sesame seeds mixed with sea salt. See recipe in Chapter 14 – Herbs, Spices, Condiments, & Natural Oils.

Grains (whole): The small hard seeds of a cereal type of grass. Whole grains are hulled but do not have their outer layers removed (not refined), so they retain more vitamins and flavor. These include: wheat, barley, oats, rye, corn, buckwheat (kasha), rice, millet, and some say quinoa.

Grain-free flours: Those who cannot eat any grains should use these flours: amaranth, arrowroot, carob, cassava, potato, tapioca, and teff. Also seed, nut and legume flours which include soy, lentil, chick pea, pinto bean, black bean, split pea, sunflower seed, sesame seed, almond, cashew, filbert/hazelnut, and other flours and meals.

Granola: A toasted, rolled oats cereal with sweetening and sometimes nuts or dried fruit added.

Grits: (Soy grits or rye grits.) A bean or grain chopped into small pieces for easier preparation and shorter cooking time. Used as a cereal or in soups or stews or to add protein to almost any main course dish. True grits are not granular.

Groats: (Oat or barley groats.) A hulled grain chopped into pieces bigger than grits. Groats sometimes refers to the whole grain.

Guar gum powder: A thickener and binder used to help gluten-free baked good keep their rise. Can be mixed into cold or hot foods to thicken foods such as salad dressings, puddings and casseroles. Derived from an East Indian seed, guar gum can be used instead of eggs, liquid lecithin, or arrowroot in some recipes. (Should not be used in yeast breads.) Good as a mild laxative, for ulcers and as an appetite suppressant in very small amounts.

Gums: See Guar gum and Xanthan gum.

Haricots: (Also called white pea beans and navy beans.) Legumes used most often in pork and beans. They are in the lower protein group with peas and limas.

Hato mugi: See Job's tears.

Herb teas: Derived from leaves, flowers, bark, roots, and seeds of plants. The majority of natural herb teas contain no caffeine. (See Chapter 28 – Herbal Teas and Substitution Chart in Part IV.)

Honey: A natural liquid sweetener produced by bees from flower nectar. Honey is a food rich in flavor, vitamins, and minerals. There are various types, qualities, and tastes of different honey. (See Chapter 7 – Sweets for the Sweet.)

Honeyleaf: (Also called stevia, sweet leaf, and sweet herb.) A potent South American herb sweetener also grown in the Orient. A few drops are as sweet as tablespoons of other liquid sweeteners. It mixes easily in hot or cold foods and has one-three-hundredth the calories of sugar. Experiment with it in beverages, breads, and desserts. About one to three drops sweetens one cup liquid. Available in tablets or powder. Poorer qualities have a bit of a bitter licorice after taste.

Job's tears: (Hato mugi) Although it is sometimes called pearl barley, this unique grain is not at all like the small, white, round, refined pearl barley available in many stores. It is really not barley at all. It looks somewhat like puffed brown rice and is the seed of an annual wild grass. This biblically named seed has been used for thousands of years. One macrobiotic sourcebook claims Job's tears will counteract the effect of eating animal proteins and fats, and that it is a "cooling" off food, good for cancers and other growths like warts and moles. Use the seeds in soups and stews, with brown rice, or instead of barley. It is a robust seed with a pungent flavor. Gluten- and grain-free.

Kamut: (pronounced ka-moot, grain or flour.) A Mediterranean unhybridized wheat, which until recently has been almost ignored in favor of commercial quality wheat. Interest in the grain has revived because many people allergic to common wheat can tolerate kamut (about 50% or so) with no allergic reaction. Maybe because kamut has not been overprocessed as much as common wheat and therefore contains 40% more protein and sixty-five percent more amino acids and is more digestible. Kamut has superior flavor, slightly sweet and nutty. Use this large, soft, white wheat as regularly as standard wheat in recipes. Kamut is also a good flour and pasta grain. For extra nutrients and flavor, add amaranth flour, one-quarter to one-tenth part, with kamut flour in recipes.

Kasha: This is buckwheat, lightly toasted until it is brown in color. It makes any main dish recipe more tasty and has a soft nutty flavor. Cooks more quickly than buckwheat.

Kefir: (In milk or yogurt form.) A cultured milk product full of helpful stomach and digestive enzymes and nutrients. It can be used as a beverage, put in blender drinks, or non-cooked recipes to retain its value. It can also be bought in a form like yogurt only less solid. This is good for dips and dressings and some yogurt recipes.

Kelp or sea kelp: (In fresh, ground, or tablet form.) A seaweed that is usually dried, ground, and sprinkled on food to add vitamins, minerals, and flavor. Like most seaweed, kelp contains iodine as well as high amounts of magnesium, calcium, phosphorus, potassium, and trace B vitamins, plus sodium. In tablet form, it is used to help the thyroid and for some weight-loss diets.

Kidney beans: Oblong kidney-shaped red beans from the legume family, high in protein and vitamins and very flavorful even with very little seasoning. They make their own gravy while being cooked. Use mainly in chilis and stews. (Tastes similar to pinto beans, but are a little "gassier" – see Pinto beans.)

Kombucha: (kom-boo-cha) A medicinal tea grown from a mushroom fungus and claimed to help digestion, eliminate toxins, and support the immune system.

Kudzu or Kuzu: (In powder, chunks, or noodles) A starchy extract of the kudzu root used like arrowroot or agar-agar. Adds flavor and medicinal qualities to foods. Good for digestive disorders. In Asia, the chopped root is used for tea and the powder is made into noodles. It is also a plentiful and sometimes troublesome weed in the Southern US.

Lecithin: (In granules, liquid, powder, or tablet form) It is usually derived from soybeans. Among its many benefits, it helps dissolve cholesterol, controlling cholesterol levels in the body. It is also a helpful immunity against infections, viruses, diseases, hardened arteries, and heart or other major organ problems. Lecithin is also a natural energizer and preservative used in cooking and can be used in part as an egg or shortening replacement. Liquid lecithin is not too tasty but can be used best in baking, pie crusts, and blended drinks. As granules it can be sprinkled on foods or be used in cooking. Use in moderation, not daily.

Lecithin spread: A processed butter or margarine substitute with a rather oily taste. Some tolerate its flavor while others find it necessary to mask it in recipes, like the delicious Veggie Butter in this book. Not available everywhere.

Legumes: Usually are pod types of vegetables that may be broken down into three basic categories, beans, lentils, and peas. They are often called protein foods and are generally high in protein, calcium, iron, zinc, and other nutrients. (See Chapter 19 – Legumes – Beans, Peas, Lentils, & Tofu)

Legume flours: Non-grain, high protein bean flours that include soy, chick pea, pinto bean, black bean, split pea, lentil, and others . These do not contain gluten.

Lentils: Easy-to-cook legumes. There are two main types. One kind of lentils are brown-green in color and often called either brown lentils or green lentils, occasionally grey lentils. They are small, round, and flat, about $\frac{1}{4}$-inch in diameter. Some organic varieties are one half this size. The second type of lentils are called red lentils although they are actually orange in color. They are almost always split in half and are round and flat like a dime, about $\frac{1}{8}$-inch or more in diameter. Lentils are delicious in any main dish recipe, and green or brown lentils make excellent sprouts. Lentil flour is used for East Indian chipatis (crisp, fried breads), allergy baking recipes, and to add protein to other main dishes and breads. Another less common type of lentil is the French green lentil. These are actually whole, small, more rounded, black lentils which cook up in about 25 minutes.

Macadamia nut: A delicious nut similar to filberts or brazils in flavor. They are round and $\frac{1}{2}$ to $\frac{3}{4}$-inch in diameter. The shell is extremely hard and must be broken with a hammer or strong pliers. This evergreen-tree nut originated in Australia but is now mainly produced in Hawaii. When shelled, they are one of the tastiest, but most expensive nuts.

Malt: (In nuggets, powder, or syrup.) Generally made from sprouted barley and baked or toasted until crisp and dark brown in color. Homemade powdered malt can be made by baking sprouts one or two hours in a 200°F oven, cooling and grinding. Other cereal grains such as wheat and rye may also be used. Malt is naturally sweet and may be eaten in the crunchy nugget form or ground into powder and used with honey in dessert recipes. The syrup is less sweet than honey but can be used as a substitute in some recipes.

Maple sugar: Made from maple syrup that is cooked until it becomes granulated. It is light golden-brown in color and looks somewhat like brown sugar. Like all other refined sugars, maple sugar is very sweet and affects the body like white sugar, so it should be avoided or used very infrequently. It does have richer flavor and more nutrients than white sugar.

Maple syrup: The boiled sap of the maple tree used for sweetening pancakes and desserts. Though it is not as processed as maple sugar, it should still be used infrequently because of its sweetness. Buy 100% maple syrup and avoid artificial varieties, pancake syrups, or those with chemical additives.

Meals: Meals are any kind of nut or seed coarsely ground, like flaxseed meal, sunflower, pumpkin, sesame, almond, or cashew meal. These are delicious and nutritious and usually make the vitamins in the seeds or nuts more digestible. They are excellent sprinkled on cereals, mixed in casseroles, veggie burgers or other main dishes, and in desserts or toppings. They are most beneficial eaten raw and should be ground fresh every week or two and kept refrigerated.

Milk powder: This is usually spray-dried milk and comes in instant and non-instant. Non-instant is preferable as it is less processed and has more vitamins and fewer additives. Instant stirs quickly into water and non-instant must be beaten or blended into water. Use only non-instant in pudding and frosting recipes, as the instant will bead up and remain in granular form unless stirred into a liquid. Soy milk powder and tapioca flour can sometimes be used as substitutes.

Milk substitutes: Includes nut, seed, rice, or soy milks and sometimes coconut milk. Choose any of the first four when a recipe calls for milk substitute. Buy them at the store or make them at home. (See recipes.)

Millet: Higher in vitamins and minerals than most other grains, rice included. It has a tasty, nutty flavor, similar to rice, and can be used instead of rice or half and half with rice in any recipe calling for rice. Millet is considered the only alkaline grain and is very mild on the stomach. It is especially good for babies and people with ulcers or food allergies. Poor quality millet is somewhat white in color. As the quality of millet improves, the color is more golden. The best quality millet is golden brown.

Miso: A dark or light golden soybean paste, high in minerals and enzymes. Used in soups, spreads, and other main dishes. Chick pea miso is also available in some areas and is a good substitute for those with soy allergies.

Molasses: A by-product of sugar cane. It is much less refined than sugar and contains many vitamins and minerals, especially iron. It is one of the highest sources of iron. Avoid the sulphured and "table" or "cooking" molasses varieties. Some of the better brands are made specially and are not by-products of sugar making. See Barbados and Blackstrap Molasses.

Muesli: A cereal similar to granola only it is made from raw ingredients instead of toasted. Made with rolled oats, dried fruits, and nuts and seeds. See recipes.

Mung beans: These legumes are similar to lentils in protein value, they do not need presoaking and are easy to cook. Mung beans taste a little like potatoes when cooked and can be used in many main dish recipes or can be sprouted. These are one of the most popular sprouts sold, especially in Chinese restaurants as bean sprouts. As a bean they are small, oval-shaped, and grass green in color.

Navy beans: See Haricots

Nigari: A natural solidifier made from the salts of seawater and used in the making of tofu.

Northern beans: Similar to dry limas in their white color and flavor but shaped like kidneys. Use like haricots. Lower nutrient, higher carbohydrate type of legume.

Nutritional yeasts: Varieties include brewer's, engevita, torula, primary and a number of other yellow, good tasting, edible yeasts. Edible yeasts can be eaten raw, without cooking or used in recipes. These are high in many nutrients, especially B vitamins. Brewer's and torula are often used in blended protein drinks, while other golden varieties of yeast are better for recipes or can be sprinkled on popcorn for added nutrients and a cheesy flavor. Those with Candida albicans and certain other allergies should avoid all types of yeast. Nutritional yeasts are not leavening agents to be used in baking.

Nuts: Nuts are edible, hard-shelled seeds that can be stored. Pecans, walnuts, chestnuts, almonds, brazil nuts, filberts, macadamias, cashews, and peanuts are all considered to be nuts.

Oats: (In whole, groats, or rolled form) One of the four main gluten grains, whole oats are a long grain, rather grayish-green in color. They can be cooked whole as a cereal or main dish grain. Groats can be used as cereal or in quick cooking recipes. Rolled oats are round and paper thin, golden-white in color. They are used mainly in cereals like granola and oatmeal and in dessert recipes.

Oils, natural: Natural liquid oils, unlike supermarket varieties, are pressed without chemicals or solvents. They retain much of their original coloring, flavoring, and vitamins. (See Chapter 14 – Herbs, Spices, Condiments, & Natural Oils.)

Peas: (In split or whole form; dried or fresh) Dried split yellow or split green peas are very common and are mainly used in soups and casseroles. Whole green dried peas are sometimes available and useful when soaked and cooked for stews and other main dishes. They are a legume in the lower protein group and tend to be a bit gassy. Both used in East Indian cooking.

Pepitas: These are hulled, roasted pumpkin seeds, green and white in color and oblong and flat in shape. They are slightly bitter, yet flavorful, and are high in zinc and good for dispelling some intestinal parasites. See Pumpkin Seeds.

Pepper: See Cayenne red pepper

Pignolias: (Also called pine nuts) Edible seeds or nuts from certain North American pine trees. They are delicious small, oblong nuts with a woodsy, slightly bitter flavor. Used in pestos and ethnic cooking.

Pine Nuts: See Pignolias

Pinto beans: Legumes shaped like kidney beans only more rounded. They are cream-colored with brown splashes of color, are similar to kidney beans in flavor, and can be used interchangeably in recipes. They are used mainly in Mexican dishes but are delicious in any main dish. They are less gassy than kidney beans and more digestible. They are higher in protein and calcium than most beans.

Primary yeast: An edible food yeast, similar to Brewer's yeast, but often higher in quality with more vitamins. A type of nutritional yeast. Avoid for yeast-free diets.

Protein powder or liquid: These protein supplements usually contain soybean powder, edible food yeast, lecithin, sweetening, and other ingredients. They are meant to be an added protein supplement and should not be relied on as a main source of nourishment. The powder or liquid is terrific in blender drinks, milk, or baked in recipes. Use only occasionally, not daily as these can be hard on the digestive tract for many individuals. These sometimes contain egg powder.

Pumpkin seeds: (In hulled or unhulled form) The white unhulled seeds must be roasted to be eaten, but even then they are not easy to digest and must be chewed well. The green hulled seeds are large and flat and are often called pepitas. They are an excellent snack and are good in meals, cereals, and some main dish recipes. Like many nuts and seeds, they are slightly expensive. Pumpkin seed oil is full of nutrients and may be beneficial for those with prostate problems. Use the oil raw, like flax oil, on salads and in dressings. See Pepitas.

Quinoa: (Pronounced keen-wah) A quick-cooking essentially gluten-free, high-protein grain, excellent for allergy diets. The mother grain of the Incas is grown in South and North America. It is not a true grain, but is excellent used in place of rice or millet as a cereal or main dish grain. It is naturally protected by an agitating substance called saponin which is often removed by a dry process and home washing. Delicious quinoa is high in amino acids, protein, and other nutrients.

Rice and brown rice: Besides refined white rice that comes from polished, long-grain brown rice, there are other types of rice, all brown rice and all natural and unrefined. (Some black and red rices are also included here.) They are as follows:
Black and Red Thai Rices: These colorful rices are uniquely flavored and different from other rices. Unfortunately, they are hard to digest and cause allergic reactions for many individuals.
Basmati Rice: These come in brown or white varieties and both are more nutritious than regular white rice and very flavorful, digestible, and quick-cooking.
Long Grain Brown Rice: A long, thin, white-brown grain with much more flavor and vitamins than white rice. Brown rice is better because the rice germ or inner kernel and the brown outer layers called rice polish are left on the rice. These are removed from the white rice, leaving it with fewer vitamins and mostly starch.

Short Grain Brown Rice: Like long-grain in color and content, only shorter and plumper. Said by some to have slightly more vitamins than long-grain brown rice.

Sweet Brown Rice: A naturally sweet-flavored rice, similar in shape and color to short-grain but with a smooth, shiny surface. It is used mainly as a sweet cereal or in desserts like rice pudding.

Wehani Rice: A tasty, nutritious, natural red rice sold separately and in mixed rice blends.

Wild Brown Rice: A very-long-grain rice, very dark brown black in color. It has a wild flavor and is used mainly in turkey stuffing, casseroles, and special rice dishes. It is usually mixed with another rice as it is expensive. Not a true rice.

Rice bran: The outer layers of brown rice that are discarded to make white rice. It is especially high in niacin, some B vitamins, iron, phosphorus, and potassium. Good in soups, breads, cereals, and some dessert recipes.

Rice cakes: Round, flat biscuits made from pressed, puffed rice. Good with melted cheese and sesame seeds on top or plain with peanut butter or other spreads and toppings.

Rice polish: The inner layers of the rice bran. It is also high in B vitamins and some claim vitamin A. Use the same as rice bran.

Rice syrup: A natural sweetener made from rice that is used as a honey substitute, although not quite as sweet.

Rolled oats: Whole oats pressed thin as paper, round and flat, golden and white in color. They are mainly used in cereals, oatmeal, granola, muesli, and in desserts, usually in cookies, breads, and as crusts.

Rolled rye, rice, or barley: Sometimes available in health food stores. Use instead of rolled oats in some recipes including granola.

Rose hips: (Can be fresh or dried in whole, crushed, or powdered form) This is the base of the wild rose blossom, the part that holds the petals. When the rose petals fall, this part turns red. It is ripest and reddest after the first frost and can be harvested only from wild roses because they are higher in vitamins and have no chemicals used in their past or present growth process. The dried rose hips make an excellent tea. The whole fresh rose hip, minus the hard, rocklike seeds, is edible raw or can be cooked in soups or stews as some Europeans do. They are delicious and especially high in vitamins when raw. One of the highest natural sources of vitamin C. (See Chapter 28 – Herbal Teas)

Rye: A whole grain similar in looks to oats. A very strong-tasting, somewhat bitter grain. It is best when mixed with another grain, one part rye to four parts some other grain, usually wheat. When mixed with other grains it adds extra tangy flavor to breads, cereals, and soups. One of the four high gluten grains. Rye bread may contain wheat.

Sea salt: Derived from vacuum-dried seawater. Contains all the natural minerals found in salt that are usually refined out of earth salt. Earth salt is harder to digest and contains sugar in the form of dextrose, and additives to help preserve it, keep its color, and retard moisture. Sea salt has none of these unnecessary extras and is more easily digested. Also, it does not cause the body to retain as much water as earth salt. Sea salt is finer and can generally be used in smaller amounts than earth salt.

Seaweed: (In fresh, dried, powdered, or flaked form) Seaweed can be eaten as a cooked vegetable in soups, casseroles, Oriental dishes, by itself, or eaten fresh in salads. Powdered or flaked, it can be used for flavor and minerals like sea kelp on all main dishes and soups and vegetables. It has a slightly salty flavor and is especially high in minerals, including iodine. Some kinds, like agar-agar, can be used as thickening agents. Seaweed ranges in color from white to red, gray, black, and green. Some varieties are nori, kombu, hijiki, wakame, kelp, and dulse.

Semolina: A high-gluten, protein-rich flour, made from durum wheat. It is used mainly in commercial pasta to help the noodles keep their shape. Also used in making couscous, a Moroccan grain dish. A partial grain.

Sesame butter: Same as tahini only it is usually made from raw seeds that are often unhulled, and therefore it can be slightly bitter, though more nutritious.

Sesame salt: Same as gomashio. Toasted sesame seeds, generally ground and mixed with sea salt.

Sesame seeds: The small seeds are high in vitamins, proteins, and oils. A very good source of calcium and vitamin E. The unhulled seeds are brown and slightly bitter. They can be ground or used in cooked foods. The hulled seeds are white and milder-tasting and can be used in sesame salt, raw cereals, salads, and ground into meal. Both kinds can be used whole in baking or cooking but are more easily digested when ground.

Sesame tahini: A nut butter made from roasted, ground sesame seeds, oil, and sometimes salt. Used in spreads, dressings, dips, main dishes, and in some desserts. More digestible and less bitter than sesame butter.

Slippery elm: The white bark of a tree which works as a great thickening agent, can be made into tea or lozenges. Soothing to the throat. Used in some natural ice cream recipes. (See Chapter 28 – Herbal Teas)

Sorghum: A syrup made from a grain that is similar to Indian corn. It is largely unrefined and used as a natural sweetener. Can be used instead of molasses in most recipes. Commonly used in the southern USA.

Sourdough: A fermented dough used as a leaven in bread making instead of yeast or baking powder. Good for some yeast-free diets.

Soybeans: Dried, they are round, golden-brown legumes. When fresh or soaked, they more than double in size and become oblong and golden in color. This is the "Queen of legumes" and surpasses all beans (except fava) in high protein content. It is as frequently used by vegetarians and natural food lovers as hamburger is by others. Besides being used in main dishes and veggie burgers, they make a great meat substitute or can be made to taste and even look like real meat. Soybeans can also be made into flour, milk, cheese, oil, margarine, and sprouts. They are rather bland until other flavorings are used with them, but then they become deliciously versatile. By themselves, soybeans are considered to be a complete protein. Soy products include: tofu, tempheh, tamari soy sauce, miso, TVP (texturized vegetable protein), and others.

Soy grits: Bits of chopped up dry soybeans. Although there is a granular soy product called soy grits, true soy grits are small chunks of soybean pieces used for stews, burgers, or Sloppy Joes.

Soy milk: Milk made from soybeans or soy flour, water and added natural flavorings.

Soy sauce: See Tamari soy sauce

Spelt: (Nicknamed dinkle) A European grain closely related to wheat. Although high in gluten, many allergic to wheat can tolerate it well because of its high quality, protein and enzymes which make it more digestible. Use a bit more liquid or less flour when using in place of wheat in recipes. This pasta grain looks similar to wheat but is softer, redder in color, and a bit heavier. (See Chapter 25 – Breads)

Spirulina: (Powder and tablets or capsules) A microscopic plant made from the interaction of sunlight and water (photosynthesis). It is a complete protein and a very high source of vitamin B12. High in many vitamins and minerals. Sprinkle the powder on foods or mix it with blender drinks or vegetable juices.

Sprouts: Seeds, beans, and grains that are soaked and watered regularly for three to seven days until a little sprout or green stem appears. Then they become living food. When eaten raw, they are powerhouses of protein, vitamins, and minerals. Sprouts vary in type, size and color. They are delicious in salads and sandwiches, sprinkled on soups, or cooked in casseroles, breads, and Oriental dishes. (See How to Make Sprouts in Chapter 16 – Vegetables & Vegetable Salads)

Stevia: See Honeyleaf

Sugars: Used as sweeteners mainly in desserts and beverages. (See Chapter 7 – Sweets for the Sweet for detailed information.)

Sunflower seeds: The seed of a flower, high in oils and vitamins. A food source of vitamin D and very high in calcium, iron, phosphorus, potassium, and some B vitamins. A delicious little gray seed used for sprouting, oils, and meals, nut butters, or eaten raw or roasted as a snack. Great in cereals, desserts, and main dishes such as casseroles, veggie burgers, and mock meat loaves.

Tahini: See Sesame tahini

Tamari Soy Sauce: A natural soy sauce, fermented and aged without chemicals or added extras. (Sometimes aged six months or longer in wood.) Only salt and sometimes wheat and alcohol are used in the process. Much higher quality than most soy sauces and with a better flavor. Used in all kinds of main dish recipes, especially rice, millet, and other grain dishes, and on cooked vegetables and soups. Some Asian tamaris are actually the thickest part of the soy sauce scraped from the wooden barrels. Most supermarket soy sauces are not real tamaris. They are not aged or natural and may contain BHA, MSG, and caramel coloring and artificial flavoring. Kikoman is real but not as thick as some other tamaris. Wheat-free varieties are made by: Eden, San-J, and Amano.

Tapioca flour: A gluten-free, grain-free flour usually derived from cassava root. Tapioca is a starchy, slightly sweet, white, powder-like flour that mixes well with amaranth. It can be used instead of milk powder in some recipes. Use about $1/4$ – 1 cup per recipe to sweeten breads, cakes, frostings, and other desserts. Even those who dislike tapioca pudding enjoy the taste of the flour in recipes.

Teff: (Seeds or flour) An Ethiopian seed whose name translates as lost, a consequence of dropping this smallest of grains. One grain of wheat weighs about the same as 150 grains of teff. This seed ranges in color from ivory or tan to brown and reddish varieties. It contains five times the iron, calcium and potassium of any grain, is high in protein and fiber and is gluten and grain-free. Teff has been used for thousands of years to bake Injera, a delicious Ethiopian flat bread. Use whole teff as a cereal, in cookies, or main dishes. Half a cup can also be used instead of one cup sesame seeds in many cooked or baked recipes. The flour can be used in place of other grain flours and is especially good for allergy cooking.

Tempeh: A high-protein main dish made from soybeans. It is made by natural culturing like cheese or yogurt. It is easy to digest and can be used in a variety of ways. It can be broken into chunks and added to stir-frys and casseroles. It is usually purchased at natural food stores rather than homemade.

Tofu: A cheese-like curd made from soybeans, usually from soy flour. Comes in white blocks similar in consistency to feta cheese only softer. A rather bland, tasteless food but excellent mixed with other flavorings in spreads and main dishes as it absorbs flavors easily from sauces and seasonings. High in calcium, phosphorus, iron, and protein. One-half pound is about 164 calories.

Tofu cheese: A basically non-dairy cheese substitute available in cheddar (amber), mozzarella (Italian-style), Monterey Jack and jalapeno flavors. Great for most dairy-free diets, except these usually contain casein, a protein dairy derivative used to harden the cheese. There are non-casein varieties but they are sorely lacking in flavor and quality. The casein varieties taste similar to cheese, grate and melt like cheese, are a good substitute for most recipes that contain cheese, and are generally tolerated for most dairy allergies.

Torula yeast: A concentrated food product derived from microscopic plant cells. About 50% protein plus B vitamins. A somewhat strong tasting, non-yellow, nutritional yeast that can be used like Brewer's yeast. Avoid for yeast-free diets.

Treacle: Another name for molasses.

Triticale: A whole grain that is a hybrid cross between whole wheat and whole rye that is higher in protein.

TVP (Texturized Vegetable Protein): A quick cooking, dehydrated soybean product that is often fortified with vitamin B12. Not as nutritious as whole beans but a convenient source of protein. Occasional use recommended, as TVP is often considered the "fast food" of natural foods.

Vegetized or vegetable sea salt: Sea salt with dried powdered vegetables added to extend the salt and add extra flavor. Usually dried, ground celery, spinach, parsley, and sometimes green pepper and/or alfalfa leaves in a pale green-white powder.

Vinegar: There are many types of vinegar from different sources such as apple cider, white, wine, and rice. Most vinegars are said to be harmful to the body, often leading to anemia. Only apple cider vinegar is said to be good for you. Apple cider vinegar aids digestion and healing. Also, it helps regulate your weight and is good for soaking sore or dry skin.

Vitamins: See Chapter 6 – Vitamins and Minerals

Wheat or wheat berries: This whole grain is one of the most common and frequently used grains in North America. Used mainly as flour in breads, pastry, crackers, and pasta. High in vitamins and flavor. In whole or cracked form it makes delicious cereals or can be added to soups or other main dishes. There are many types of wheat usually found in two categories, either hard wheat or soft wheat. Whole hard wheat is darker brown or red in color and is used as bread flour. It is a heavier and usually coarser flour. Hard wheat may be sold as coarse, medium, or fine whole wheat flour. Whole soft wheat is golden in color. Soft wheat is used as pastry flour and is usually very fine and powdery. (See Chapter 25 – Breads)

Wheat germ: The inner kernel or core of the wheat berry. The best type is golden yellow and is one of the highest sources of vitamin E, especially in oil form. It is best eaten raw but can be used in cooking. Highly perishable, so it must be refrigerated to preserve the vitamins and prevent rancidity.

Wheatgrass: Wheat berries are planted in long wooden flats about one-quarter-inch deep in two to four inches of soil. In seven to twelve days a thin grass will have grown two to three inches high. Snip the grass with scissors and juice it or use it in salads. A delicious, nutritious food, high in chlorophyll, vitamin C, and a wide variety of nutrients. Used for cancer therapy and for other medicinal purposes.

Whey: (In liquid or powder form) A nutritious, natural milk sugar that is easy to digest. Full of helpful stomach and digestive enzymes. It is the cloudy liquid that separates from yogurt or milk when heated. Some individuals may be allergic to whey.

Xanthan gum: A corn derived thickener and emulsifier. It improves the texture of baking powder breads and acts as a good binder and thickening agent in puddings and dressings. Also used in the commercial packaging of meat and poultry. Those with corn allergies should use guar gum instead. (See Guar gum)

Yeast: See Brewer's, Baking, Engevita, Nutritional, Primary or Torula yeast.

Yogurt: A living bacteria culture that can be grown in milk. It is easy to digest and actually helps digest other foods eaten with it. A delicious food eaten raw or substituted in any recipe calling for sour cream. Great used in spreads, dips, and desserts. Buy plain yogurt or yogurt with fruit on the bottom if you want higher quality, real yogurt. Without the living yogurt or culture present, a product is not real yogurt. A dairy product. (See Chapter 23 – Dairy Products)

Yucca: (Herb, gel, or tablet.) A very versatile desert plant that can be used for food, fabric, soap, or medicinal purposes. Good for rheumatism and arthritis.

Zest: Finely grated lemon, orange, or other citrus rind. Also, the energy you get from eating wholesome, natural foods!

Guide to Vegetables

Artichokes, Globe

Special Information: These hard-to-grow vegetables are not always available and can be expensive. Can be found mainly in spring and early summer. They are considered a special vegetable, and artichoke hearts are included in many gourmet recipes. Chock full of vitamins and especially healing for the liver.

Selection: Choose small or medium sized fresh artichokes with tight, closed leaves. Globe artichokes are an olive green with dark edges. Avoid artichokes with fuzzy or purplish leaves. Artichoke hearts may also be purchased canned in water or marinated.

Storage: Keep in the crisper section of your refrigerator or wrap them in plastic. Keep them dry until used. They store up to six days or longer.

Serving: Rinse the artichokes and cut off most of the stem and one-inch off the top of the globe. Snip one-half-inch or more off all the remaining leaf tops except the tiny ones at the stem end, which can be removed. Place the globes upside down in the vegetable steaming rack and steam for 40 – 50 minutes until the entire globe is tender. Serve the artichoke with a sauce for dipping. The most popular sauce is as follows, $\frac{1}{4}$ cup melted butter, several dashes salt, and lemon juice to taste. Parsley or soy sauce can be added. Try mayonnaise and lemon as another sauce. Cheese sauces are good with these. Eat the artichoke by taking a leaf at a time, dipping the stem end in sauce, and scraping the base part of the leaf between the teeth and eating only the tender fleshy parts. The leaves get more tender toward the center. When the leaves are gone you will come to a fuzzy, stringy part called the choke, which is scraped off with a spoon and discarded. The rest of the artichoke, called the heart, is a delicacy, the sweetest part. Eat this with or without the sauce. Fresh, tender artichokes are delicious. However, like avocados, one may have to acquire a taste for them.

Artichokes, Jerusalem

Special Information: Also called sun chokes. These are high in vitamins and low in starch. Especially beneficial for people with high or low blood sugar as these help balance blood sugar levels and promote healing. Contain high amounts of potassium and thiamin.

Selection: These small root vegetables resemble ginger roots only they are smaller and rounder. Buy fresh, firm unwrinkled roots.

Storage: Keep up to one to four weeks in a cool, dry place but are best if refrigerated in the crisper section.

Serving: Scrub them with a good vegetable brush and grate the whole thing raw into a salad, or chop them and steam or bake until tender. Good for soups, stews, and casseroles or cooked with other steamed vegetables.

Asparagus

Special Information: These are a delicacy. They are delicious and often expensive. Asparagus contain a variety of vitamins especially A, B and C, potassium, and zinc.

Selection: Available mostly in the first half of the year. Choose firm, thin stalks with tight, close tips. Avoid those with white ends or wrinkled stalks.

Storage: For best storage and longer freshness, cut a thin layer off the bottom of the stalks and store upright in a tall plastic container, like a juice container, with an inch or so of water at the bottom. Try wrapping wet toweling around the bottom of the stalks and store in a plastic bag. Keep refrigerated. They keep fresh for four to eight days, sometimes longer if very fresh when picked or purchased and stored and wrapped properly. If eaten within two to three days, no special wrapping is required.

Serving: Cut off the top two-thirds of each stalk and steam them whole or cut into two-inch pieces. Discard all white parts. Steam eight to twelve minutes or until tender. Eat them plain with butter, salt, and herbs or favorite sauce. For the remaining one-third of each stalk, peel off the outer skin and eat the inner part raw, like celery, or peel, chop, and add them to a salad, or peel and cook with the top part of the asparagus.

Beans, Yellow or Green (Snap, String, or Wax)

Special Information: High in protein and many vitamins and minerals including good quantities of vitamin A and the B vitamins, calcium, and potassium.

Selection: Available most of the year. Choose firm, unmarred bean pods, unwrinkled and bright in color.

Storage: Keep in a cool, dry place. Refrigerate if possible. Fresh beans keep for a week or two if wrapped in plastic.

Serving: Trim off the very tips of the beans and use whole or cut into pieces. Should be marinated or cooked. Fresh, tender beans can be chopped small for salads. Steam for 15 – 25 minutes or until tender.

Beets

Special Information: Especially high in iron and potassium and a variety of vitamins. The beet greens are exceptionally high in vitamin A with good amounts of calcium. The red beets are a treat for the liver.

Selection: Choose firm, dark red, small or medium-sized beets with small tail roots. Avoid storage beets that are dull colored, marred, and have an old, musty basement smell. These are not good tasting cooked and definitely not fresh eaten raw or juiced. If beets have top leaves, pick fresh green-red unblemished leaves. Avoid leaves with holes or yellow or black marks or coloring.

Storage: Beet greens last three to six days. Fresh beets may last for several weeks, or even months. Use the beets before they get soft and spoiled. Store beets in a cool, dry place or refrigerate. Always refrigerate beet greens or keep very cold.

Serving: Scrub beets with a scrub brush. Do not peel. Grate them raw into salads. They are delicious and full of many vitamins this way. Remove as little as possible from the top and tail of the beet. Wash the beet greens thoroughly and chop and steam for 15 – 25 minutes until tender. Eat both with salt and herbs or in a favorite recipe or stir-fry. Fresh grated beet is tasty mixed with lemon juice which turns them sweet.

Broccoli

Special Information: Especially high in vitamins C and A. It contains more than twice the amount of vitamin C than the same amount of oranges. Also high in calcium and potassium.

Selection: Available all year round but may be poor quality during some of the summer months. Choose those with full, dark green heads and slim stalks. Avoid those with yellow or dark purple heads and thick, tough stalks. Choose firm, not limp stalks without a hole in the base.

Storage: Refrigerate. Good for about five to eight days if fresh and wrapped before storing in a vegetable crisper. Very fresh, crisp, or garden broccoli can be stored in water in a cool place. Use a large pan or bucket and fill with one or two inches of water. Cut a small slice off the bottom of each stalk and place them close together, standing up in the water like trees. They will stay fresh for six to twelve days. Recut stalk ends and change water every few days. Then freeze or use fresh. (Home garden broccoli must be soaked in saltwater for one half hour or so to expel worms.)

Serving: Eat the top one-half of the stalk raw with a vegetable dip or steam or bake it. Cut the top part of the stalks lengthwise into long trees for eating raw or cooking. Peel the remaining half of the stalk if tough. Then slice it into small, round quarter-inch thick pieces and steam these together with the top section of the broccoli. It is better to save the bottom half of the broccoli for cooking only. Steam for eight to twelve minutes or until tender. (Use a potato peeler or knife to peel the bottom stalk.)

Brussels Sprouts

Special Information: Contain a variety of vitamins but especially high in vitamin C. Like broccoli, they have more than twice the amount of vitamin C than the same amount of oranges.

Selection: Available mainly in fall and winter. They are usually at their best in fall. These miniature cabbage-like vegetables often come prepacked. Choose those with little heads, bright green in color. Avoid sprouts with yellow leaves or black specks on them. Avoid those that have big, woody-looking stem ends (the base where the cabbage is connected to the plant).

Storage: Refrigerate. Keep two to six days.

Serving: They should be cooked before eating. Brussels sprouts can be steamed by themselves or with other vegetables. Cut a little off the base end of the sprout and remove a few outer leaves. Then steam whole or cut in half or quarters for faster cooking. Steam 10 – 14 minutes until tender if cut, 15 – 25 minutes if whole.

Cabbage

Special Information: Cabbage is low in calories and has a good amount of vitamin C and a few trace vitamins and minerals. The main types of cabbage include:

Chinese: A green long-stemmed cabbage that looks like a cross between celery and romaine lettuce but has a white stem and veins in the leaves and bright, dark green leaves that cover the sides of the stalks about one-half to two-thirds of the way up.

Savoy: A tasty, pale green, crinkly-leafed head cabbage.

White: A whitish green, smooth leafed, heavy head variety.

Red: A purplish-red, smooth leafed cabbage similar to white cabbage with white veins and insides. The white and red cabbage are the most common and popular.

Selection: Pick firm, heavy heads. Avoid those with rust spots, limp leaves, or other signs of spoilage. Small heads are more tender.

Storage: Refrigerate and keep wrapped. Generally keep seven to fourteen days or more. Store whole.

Serving: Remove and discard a couple of the outer leaves. Eat raw or cooked. Pull off leaves one by one and chop or grate them for eating raw in salads or steaming alone or with other vegetables. Pulling off the leaves, rather than chopping off the cabbage head, keeps the remaining cabbage fresh longer. If all the cabbage is being used or will be in the next couple days, cabbage can be chopped or grated for salads. Steam seven to ten minutes or until tender.

Carrots

Special Information: Very high in vitamin A, betacarotene. Good for eyesight and cancer prevention. Although younger carrots are tastier, older, larger carrots are higher in vitamin A content. (Homegrown plump carrots are an exception and are usually flavorful.) Carrot juice is healing and easier to digest than raw carrots, therefore, more nutritious. Sip it slowly for best absorption of nutrients.

Selection: Choose firm, thin or medium-thick, long carrots with bright colors. Younger, fresher carrots usually have more flavor. Avoid very plump, bruised, or soft carrots when purchasing and buy organic whenever possible.

Storage: Keep in a very cool place or refrigerate. They store longest in the crisper section of the refrigerator, up to several weeks. If the carrots have tops, discard them or dry them for use in soups. Tie and hang carrot tops near a ceiling or in a dry place out of direct sunlight. When thoroughly dry, store them in jars or tins to be used a tablespoon or so at a time in soups and stews.

Serving: Delicious raw or cooked. Use carrots raw, grated or sliced thin, in salads or sticks as finger food with a dip. Chop them for cooking in round slices or one to two-inch pieces for steaming. Do not boil. Steam 10 – 14 minutes or until tender. Use grated in casseroles, veggie burgers, or carrot cakes. Slice for soups, stews, and other main dishes. Steam and purée them for casseroles, sauces, veggie burgers and dips. Juice them for blender drinks, beverages, or to serve with plain yogurt.

Cauliflower

Special Information: Contains vitamin C and a variety of other vitamins and minerals. Can be hard to digest and a bit gassy eaten raw.

Selection: Choose white, unblemished heads with healthy leaves. Avoid dark spoiled spots on heads. Although they are harmless and may be cut right off, these indicate lack of freshness.

Storage: Refrigerate and keep wrapped. Lasts five to ten days or more.

Serving: May be eaten raw or cooked. Use chopped in salads or use the small flowerettes as finger food with dip. Break or cut into large flowerettes for steaming. Steam 10 – 14 minutes or until tender. Cauliflower is especially delicious with melted cheese sauce. Use in soups, stews, casseroles, stir-frys, and with other vegetables for steaming.

Celery

Special Information: Low in calories. It has a few vitamins but is a good bulk, fiber food.

Selection: Choose wide, thin, crisp stalks that are whitish and pale green in color. Narrow, thick, dark green stalks are tough and stringy. Avoid celery with rust spots, yellow leaves, and other blemishes.

Storage: Store wrapped in the refrigerator. Keeps one to three weeks.

Serving: Serve chopped in salads or raw as finger food with dip or stuffed with cream cheese, falafel, or peanut butter. Use it chopped and cooked in casseroles, soups, stews, stir-frys, and chili. The leafy green top part of the celery can also be used in cooking only.

Celeriac

Special Information: Contains a few vitamins and minerals. This globe shaped root grows below the ground.

Selection: Choose small, firm globular roots.

Storage: Keeps one or two weeks in the refrigerator.

Serving: Peel, chop, and cook, bake, or steam for 10 – 15 minutes or until tender and use in stews and casseroles. A good substitute for potatoes.

Chives

Special Information: A mild, onion-flavored green, sometimes called an herb. Trace vitamins and minerals.

Selection and Storage: Sometimes these cannot be bought except in seed or as a potted plant. May be sold in small bunches. Can be easily cultivated all year round indoors and will return year after year outdoors. Grow your own and snip off the grasslike greens to use as needed. Do not overwater the plant. Snip off flowers whenever they appear or the plant will go to seed.

Serving: Use like green onion tops. Are more flavorful when used raw but may be cooked. Chop for use in salads, with cottage cheese, sprinkle on bowls of hot soup or casseroles, vegetables and whole grain dishes. A great garnish.

Corn

Special Information: Contains a basic variety of vitamins and minerals. This is also considered a grain and can be used instead of rice or another grain with legumes. Can be hard to digest for many individuals or agitate allergies.

Selection: Choose long, medium-thick or thin ears with pale yellow, small kernels as the darker yellow the corn, the less sweet it is. Peel back the top section of the corn when selecting to check for worms or other defects. Avoid ears with irregular rows or missing kernels.

Storage: Keep refrigerated for one or two weeks or more.

Serving: Remove the outer husk and corn silk. Steam the whole corncob 12 – 18 minutes or until tender above boiling water. Overcooking makes corn tough. Or slice corn off the cob and use it in casseroles or raw in salads. For barbecues, wrap husked ears in double foil and place on hot coals or hot stones in the fire. Turn the corn occasionally and cook about 20 minutes.

Cress

See watercress

Cucumber

Special Information: These contain an average of amount of vitamins and minerals and a better than average amount of vitamin C. Can cause gas for many individuals. English cucumbers are easier to digest.

Selection: Try to buy unwaxed cucumbers. Waxed skins are filmy and slipper-feeling and look shiny. Choose firm, medium green cukes with no wrinkles in the skin. Avoid cukes with lots of yellow on the skin as they may taste vinegary. English cucumbers are about twice as long, thinner and firmer. Choose organic whenever possible.

Storage: Can be refrigerated up to one or two weeks.

Serving: Generally served raw. Peel waxed cucumbers and discard the skins. Try not to remove the inner green beneath the skin as it contains many vitamins. A potato peeler is the best tool for this. Do not peel unwaxed cucumbers or English cucumbers. Just wash carefully with a brush. Slice or wedge cucumbers for finger food. Slice or chop for salad. Or grate them and save the juice and use both in plain yogurt for East Indian Raita with paprika. This is delicious and cooling especially with hot spiced foods. (See recipes)

Eggplant

Special Information: A member of the nightshade family along with tomatoes, potatoes and peppers. These can be slightly toxic and hard to digest for sensitive or allergic individuals. Occasional consumption is fine. Sautéed, eggplant is a good mushroom substitute. Contains trace vitamins and minerals. Do not eat these raw.

Selection: Usually available all year round. Choose dark, firm eggplants that are very light in weight. The lighter they are, the riper they are. Mature eggplants should have seeds throughout and not be green under the skin. Unripe eggplants may be eaten, but they are less flavorful. Small banana shaped Chinese eggplants are also available.

Storage: Can be refrigerated for five to ten days or more, depending on firmness.

Serving: Peel off only the outer skin, if desired, and discard. When properly cooked and seasoned, eggplant has a pleasant taste and special texture that makes it perfect for use in cooking. It can be used in place of mushrooms or meat in many dishes such as chili, tomato sauces, and stews, or is delicious in Elegant Eggplant Parmesan or eggplant casseroles. It can be steamed by itself or with other vegetables seven to ten minutes or until tender. Especially tasty when broiled. Can also be baked in $1/2$-inch slices for 10 – 15 minutes without oil for use in recipes.

Endive, Escarole, and Radicchio

Special Information: High in vitamins and minerals, especially vitamin A. Endive and escarole are curly-leafed, whitish, pale green salad plants that have a tangy, robust flavor. Radicchio is reddish-purple with white veins and tastes a bit like cabbage.

Selection: Choose fresh, crisp, unblemished greens. Avoid yellow or blackened leaves.

Storage: Keep six to ten days wrapped in the refrigerator.

Serving: Serve raw in salads to add zestful flavoring and vitamins. Do not cook these.

Garlic

Special Information - A pungent vegetable, more often considered an herb. Contains trace minerals. Beneficial for cleansing, purifying, and strengthening the body. Ancient peoples used it as a medicine to cure infections. Helps kill bacteria and parasites. Good for healing, and colds and flus. Organic garlic is more beneficial. Large, elephant garlic in not true garlic and has less flavor and medicinal value.

Selection: Garlic is sold in small bulbs about the size of a small onion. Each bulb breaks up into separate sections called cloves. Buy bulbs for their firmness and large sizes. Those with a slight purplish tint to them are the most nutritious. Buy organic garlic when possible.

Storage: Can be kept at room temperature for approximately two to four weeks. Store in a cook dry place away from strong light.

Serving: Mostly used in cooking. Garlic is easier to peel if cut in half lengthwise first. Remove and discard the outer paperlike skin from each individual clove and chop or mash the clove into small pieces. Used especially in hot spicy foods. Use about two to four cloves per average recipe. Garlic can be used raw but has a very strong flavor and causes bad breath, which may be offensive to many people. It can be crushed and used raw in salads, dressings, dips, and on garlic bread or cooked into main dishes, sauces, soups and stews.

Greens

Special Information: High in many vitamins and minerals, especially iron. Greens include beet, turnip, radish, kohlrabi, collard, mustard, exotic, and wild greens, also spinach, kale and Swiss chard.

Selection: Choose crisp, green, bright leaves free from blemishes and yellow leaves.

Storage: Keeps three to seven days or longer in the refrigerator.

Serving: Many raw exotic and wild greens, spinach, and kale may be torn and added to salads. All greens except lettuces may be steamed or baked. Cook most greens 10 – 25 minutes or until tender. Cook tough greens like kale, beet, and turnip greens, twenty to thirty-five minutes or until tender. Greens and other vegetables can be topped with the same garlic butter used for the garlic bread recipe or try one of the other sauces for Chapter 22 – Sauces, Spreads, & Dressings.

Green Onions

Special Information: These mild-flavored onions are also called bunching onions or scallions. They are a type of scallion. Extremely high in vitamin A, with good amounts of potassium and calcium.

Selection: These are long, round, small onions with a green top and small white tip. They are sold in bunches of about eight to fourteen onions. Choose fresh, firm onions. Avoid those that are wilted or blemished.

Storage: Can be kept wrapped six to ten days in a cool part of the refrigerator.

Serving: Use raw in salads or as finger food. Use the entire onion, both green and white parts. They can be cooked in specialty dishes like quiche or in casseroles.

Jicama (pronounced he-ka-ma)

Special Information: A Central American brown vegetable similar to turnips in form and nutrients, with dark skin and flesh.

Selection: Choose firm, unmarred jicamas of uniform color.

Storage: Keep refrigerated up to one or two weeks.

Serving: Peel and grate raw into salads or steam or bake like potatoes. Delicious raw when peeled, sliced, and dipped in lime juice. Plain, raw or cooked, they taste a bit like water chestnuts.

Kohlrabi

Special Information: Sometimes called cabbage turnips. High in calcium and vitamin C.

Selection: These are similar in flavor to cabbage. They look like root vegetables but grow above the ground. Choose small, firm, pale green, unblemished kohlrabi globes.

Storage: Keeps one to two weeks refrigerated.

Serving: Grate raw into salads or chop and steam 15 – 20 minutes until tender. Can be baked 15 – 20 minutes in thick slices. Cook alone or with other vegetables. Serve with butter and other seasonings. Peeling is optional.

Leeks

Special Information: A mild-flavored member of the onion family. A type of scallion.

Selection: These big, thick, green stalks with white tips are sometimes slightly expensive but have a special flavor that makes them worth the little extra cost above onions. Choose unblemished, firm leeks.

Storage: Keep seven to ten days in cool section of refrigerator.

Serving: Use like onions or greens. Use raw, finely chopped, or cooked. Especially good in Oriental and ethnic cooking. Chop finely and steam or bake for 20 minutes or until tender. Use the white and $\frac{1}{2} - \frac{3}{4}$ of the green part except for the top ends in all kinds of soups and main dishes.

Lettuce

Special Information: See pictures for varieties. Lettuce usually comes in heads or loose leaves. The darker green the lettuce, the more vitamins and minerals it contains. The whiter the lettuce, the fewer vitamins and the higher the water content. Lettuce, like most vegetables, is a bulk, fiber food. Most types are high in vitamin A, with some vitamins and potassium. Crisphead, iceburg, or head lettuce has very few nutrients, is hard to digest, agitating to allergies and may be sulphured to preserve it, especially in restaurants. This type is best avoided. Enjoy Boston, bibb, romaine, red, leaf, exotic greens, and other varieties instead.

Selection: Choose fresh, bright green, firm leaves. Avoid wilted leaves, rust spots, and other blemishes.

Storage: Keeps three to ten days in the refrigerator. Store wrapped and unwashed to prevent spoiling. In most cases, do not remove the core until the lettuce is used.

Serving: Use raw only, in salads. Tear, do not cut, the leaves for longer freshness and unblemished edges.

Mushrooms

Special Information: Rich in potassium, zinc and B vitamins, especially niacin. The shiitake mushrooms are high in germanium and said to be good for cancer.

Selection: Choose unblemished mushrooms that are uniform in color. Smaller mushrooms are sometimes more tender. Avoid mushrooms with bits of white mold on them. Pick button mushrooms with tops that are closed all around the stem, not open. Most store-bought mushrooms are the button type, but occasionally other types are available that do not have closed tops around the stems. This is especially true of many mushrooms gathered in the wild. (Do not pick your own as many are poisonous.) Other types include shiitake, oyster, and Chinese mushrooms.

Storage: Keep three to seven days in the refrigerator.

Serving: Slice like little trees into salads or marinate or eat them raw with dip. Cook them whole or chopped with rice or vegetables, in casseroles, soups, and stews, and use them in specialty dishes or sautéed for rich, delicious flavor. Cook or steam five to ten minutes or more. (Avoid most mushrooms, especially raw ones if you have Candida albicans problems.)

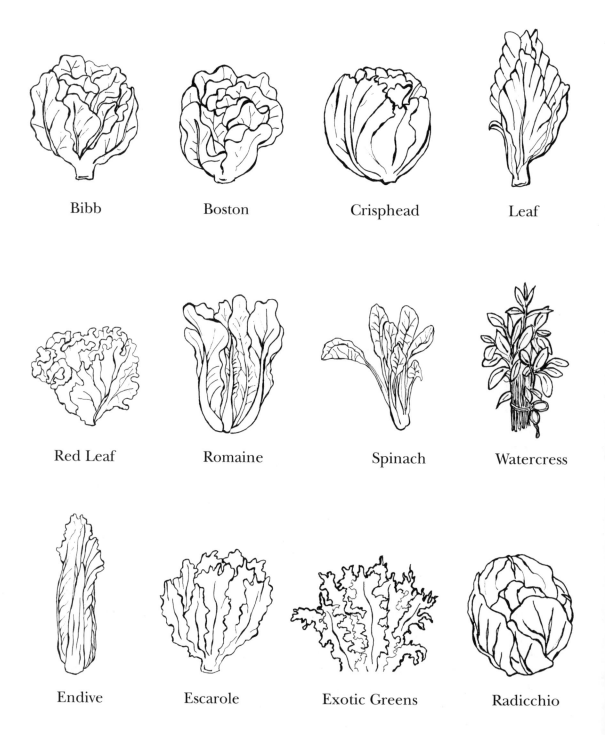

Bibb　　Boston　　Crisphead　　Leaf

Red Leaf　　Romaine　　Spinach　　Watercress

Endive　　Escarole　　Exotic Greens　　Radicchio

Okra

Special Information: Also called gumbo. A southern US favorite. Contains good amounts of potassium, phosphorus and vitamin A.

Selection: Available mainly in summer. Choose fresh, green pods that are bright-colored and unwrinkled. Three to four-inch pods are the most tender and flavorful.

Storage: Store wrapped not more than one to two weeks in the refrigerator.

Serving: Used steamed, cooked, or baked in soups, stews, or vegetable dishes. Cook 10 – 15 minutes or until tender. Cook in stainless steel, Corningware, or enamelware to avoid bad flavors or discoloration.

Onions

Special Information: Contain trace vitamins and minerals and some vitamin C. Considered cleansing and strengthening for the body. Onion varieties include white, yellow, and red types. The red have a milder, sweeter flavor and are often eaten raw. Stronger-flavored onions usually keep the longest. Many individuals have trouble digesting raw onions but easily tolerate and enjoy cooked ones. Chew parsley to get rid of the onion breath, and rub hands with salt or lemon and wash to remove the onion odors. (Same for garlic.)

Selection: Choose firm onion with thin skins. Avoid buying moist, soft onions with green tops growing from them. Slightly soft onions can be used but they are not the freshest. Fresh onions should be dry and topless.

Storage: Store at room temperature in a dry, cool place away from strong light. They spoil more easily if kept refrigerated.

Serving: Chop raw onions sparingly into salads or dressings. Use them plentifully in all kinds of cooked main dishes including whole grains, legume, and other vegetables. They are especially good sautéed. Cook 15 minutes or more. To minimize tears while chopping onions, refrigerate them for several hours before using. Also, rinse the onion in cold water after peeling and again after quartering. When one onion is chopped, keep it in a covered dish while chopping the other onions, and say good-bye to tears.

Parsnips

Special Information: They look like white carrots and taste similar to turnips with a bit of cinnamon flavor. Very high in calcium, phosphorus, and potassium.

Selection: Choose small or medium, firm, crisp parsnips.

Storage: Can be kept wrapped for one to two weeks or more in the refrigerator.

Serving: Chop and then steam 20 minutes or until tender. For baking, slice into one to two-inch pieces and bake 30 – 40 minutes. Use in soups, stews, and vegetable dishes. Can be used as a substitute for potatoes or grated raw into salads or eaten like carrot sticks.

Peas (fresh)

Special Information: High in a wide variety of vitamins and minerals including A, B's, C, and protein.
Selection: Fresh peas are available mainly in summer. Choose unblemished, bright green pods. Avoid wrinkled pods.
Storage: Keep seven to ten days or more in the refrigerator. Use as soon as possible for sweetest, freshest flavor.
Serving: Eat peas shelled from their pods, raw, in salads or steamed eight to ten minutes. Cook by themselves or with other vegetables or in stews and casseroles.

Pea Pods (Snow Peas)

Special Information: These smaller, flat pea pods are also called Chinese snow peas or edible pea pods. High in a variety of vitamins and minerals.
Selection and Storage: Same as peas.
Serving: Pull off the ends and the vein by pulling the string spine off before cooking. Eat the entire pod raw in salads or steam five to nine minutes. Especially good in Oriental recipes and stir-frys.

Peppers

Special Information: Types include sweet green, purple, orange, yellow and red bell peppers and hot peppers like cayenne, jalapeno, and serrano. Very high in vitamins C and A with other trace nutrients.
Selection: Choose firm, unwrinkled peppers with no soft spots or marring.
Storage: Can be refrigerated for six to ten days.
Serving: Chop or slice raw into salads. Cook, steam, broil, sauté or bake in stews, chili, stuffed pepper recipes, stir-frys, quiche, and specialty dishes.

Potatoes and Sweet Potatoes

Special Information: High in starch content. High in phosphorus and potassium. Contain an average amount of vitamin C and a few other vitamins and minerals. Most vitamins are in the skins. Sweet potatoes are high in vitamins A and C and are pale yellow to golden inside. The orange kind are called yams. Potatoes are part of the nightshade family and slightly toxic. Eat in moderate amounts.

Selection: Choose firm, unwrinkled potatoes with small unsprouted eyes and no green tinted spots.

Storage: Keep in a cool, dry place away from strong light. They keep two weeks to one month or more. Best if not refrigerated.

Serving: Grate small, raw, new potatoes into salads. Scrub the potato skins with a good brush but leave the skins on when steaming or baking and even for mashed potatoes for more vitamins and flavor. Steam chopped potatoes 15 – 20 minutes. Steam whole potatoes 40 – 50 minutes or until tender. Bake whole potatoes 40 – 60 minutes until tender inside. Prick potatoes with a fork several times before baking or steaming whole. Sweet potatoes can be sliced or chopped and baked with honey, oil, and sea salt. Do not eat potato sprouts or eyes as they may be poisonous.

Radishes

Special Information: The most common types are red or white. They contain small amounts of vitamins and minerals. The white are Japanese daikon.

Selection: Choose small, firm, unblemished radishes.

Storage: Keep refrigerated about one to three weeks or more.

Serving: Generally used raw. Slice in salads or use as finger food. Healthy-looking radish greens may be steamed 15 minutes or more or used sparingly in raw salads. White radishes have a stronger flavor and are often grated and served with Oriental and macrobiotic main dishes; however, the red ones may also be cooked. The green tops of red radishes can be steamed or cooked if fresh and firm.

Rutabagas

Special Information: A member of the turnip family, this large, yellow and pale purple vegetable is high in vitamin A, calcium, and other vitamins and minerals. Some individuals have trouble digesting these.

Selection: Choose medium, firm, unblemished rutabagas.

Storage: Keep one to three weeks or more in the refrigerator.

Serving: Although it is considered edible, avoid eating the heavily waxed outer skin of this vegetable. Peel, then slice or chop the rest of the rutabaga roots and bake about 30 minutes or steam 15 – 20 minutes until tender. Do not eat raw. The cooked flesh can be mashed like potatoes and used as a potato substitute.

Scallions

Scallions include green onions, leeks, and shallots. See these individual listings for more information.

Shallots

Special Information: These are onions with a mild garlic flavor. These resemble garlic in every way. They grow in bulbs with individual cloves like garlic, only the cloves are larger and have brown skin.
Selection: Choose firm, unblemished bulbs.
Storage: Keep in a cool, dry place away from strong light, like onions and garlic. Can be refrigerated. Keep up to a couple weeks or more.
Serving: Use the same as green onions for special cooked dishes.

Spinach

Special Information: High in many vitamins and minerals, especially A, C, and iron. There are three main types of spinach: large, smooth leafed (pictured page 400), the crinkle-leafed, and small velvety-leafed New Zealand spinach.
Selection: Choose fresh, crisp leaves. Avoid yellowed or wilted or blemished leaves.
Storage: Keeps in the refrigerator, when wrapped, five to ten days or more.
Serving: Wash the fresh leaves carefully to remove grit. Swish the leaves in a pan of cool water and keep changing the water until all the grit is removed. Spinach is sometimes sold prewashed, so this type need not be washed unless desired. Tear raw spinach into salads or steam it five to eight minutes or until tender. Delicious and one of the most nutritious of all vegetable greens.

Sprouts

Special Information: Extremely high in protein and contain more vitamin C than tomatoes. Have a large variety of vitamins including A, B's, C, D, E, and minerals and enzymes. Nutrients are doubled, tripled, and more when seeds, grains, or legumes are sprouted.
Selection: Generally only a few types of sprouts are available for purchase in supermarkets, health food stores, or Oriental markets. These are bean sprouts, alfalfa sprouts and sometimes lentil or sunflower sprouts. Bean sprouts are mung bean sprouts used commonly in Oriental dishes. These are one to two inches long and look like little white roots. They actually are little roots, or small seedlings. Choose firm, not limp, mung bean sprouts. Avoid brown spots or other blemishes. Alfalfa sprouts are green and white and one to two inches long. They are most

often sold overripe with brown rootlets. Avoid those with brown or spoiled roots and overgrown, large, dark green leaves. Other varieties may be available in health food stores. Fresher sprouts can be grown at home. (See Chapter 16.)

Storage: Can be refrigerated for two to eight days. If sprouts smell, rinse them. If they still smell after rinsing, discard them. Use sprouts as soon as possible for more nutritional value and freshness.

Serving: The entire sprout is edible. Use mung bean and/or lentil sprouts steamed a few minutes or cooked in Oriental recipes, casseroles, stews, soups, or with vegetables. Use homegrown mung bean or lentil sprouts raw in salads or as a snack. Use alfalfa or sunflower sprouts raw in salads, sprinkled over soup, as a raw snack, cooked in casseroles, or in sandwiches in place of lettuce. Other types of seed and grain sprouts may be eaten raw. Bean and pea sprouts should be cooked or steamed 15–20 minutes before eating. Sesame salt is delicious on sprouts.

Squash (Summer)

Special Information: Contain a variety of vitamins and minerals including calcium, phosphorus, and vitamin A. These squash include pattypan (also called cymling or scallop squash), yellow squash (crookneck and straightneck) and also small zucchini squash, golden zucchini, and chayote squash. Summer squashes grow quickly and are eaten immaturely.

Selection: Choose small, well-shaped squash with firm, unblemished skins.

Storage: Can be refrigerated for about one to two weeks.

Serving: Tender young yellow and zucchini squash are delicious sliced, grated or chopped and eaten raw in salads or as a finger food. Just scrub the outer skin and cut off the ends. Eat the remaining vegetable skin, seeds and all. They are a good replacement for cucumbers in raw dishes, can be grated raw into salads with or instead of lettuce, but are also delicious cooked in casseroles, on pizzas, and in numerous other dishes. Steam alone or with other vegetables for 12 – 15 minutes. Bake or broil sliced about 20 – 30 minutes. Pattypan and chayote can be boiled whole 15 – 20 minutes until tender. Scoop out the seeds and inner pulp and peel it. Eat it with herbs and butter or stuff the hollowed-out raw squash with cooked rice and other vegetables and bake for 45 minutes or until tender.

Squash (Winter)

Special Information: Extremely high in vitamin A. Contain a variety of other vitamins and minerals. These include hubbard, nugget, buttercup, butternut, acorn, banana, turban, dumpling, delicata, spaghetti, and large zucchini squash.

Selection: Choose hard, heavy squash that sounds slightly hollow when knocked.
Storage: Whole squashes keep at room temperature for about one to three months. Store opened squash and large zucchini in the refrigerator for up to three to five days.
Serving: Wait a few days or so before cooking to make sure they are fully ripe. They will continue to ripen as they sit at room temperature. They are best boiled whole or baked, in pieces or halves. To bake in halves, cut them and scoop out the inner seeds and pulp. Fill the squash cup with butter, honey, and salt and bake for 45 – 60 minutes until tender. Generally, skins are not eaten. Whole squash can also be cleaned out and stuffed with cooked rice and vegetables and baked one-and-a-half to two hours. They can also be boiled whole. Then discard the seeds, pulp, and skin and mash the rest of the squash with butter and herbs and serve alone or use it in a pie, casserole, or soup.

Tomatoes

Special Information: Contain fairly high amounts of vitamins A and C. Varieties include yellow acidless tomatoes, red tomatoes like beefsteak, field and hothouse, red Italian pear-shaped tomatoes called roma, and red cherry tomatoes.
Selection: Choose firm, bright-colored tomatoes. Red tomatoes should be red, not pink. Avoid those with soft spots, bruises, and blemishes.
Storage: Refrigerate ripe tomatoes. Unripe tomatoes may be kept on a windowsill or countertop until ripe or placed in a plastic bag with holes in it for a few days to speed ripening. Green tomatoes may be wrapped in newspaper and kept in a cool, dry place to ripen slowly over a period of weeks or months. Check wrapped tomatoes every few days and remove the ripe ones to refrigerate or freeze.
Serving: Eat the entire tomato raw by itself or in salads. Cherry tomatoes are great finger food. Slice these in half for salads so they do not splatter. Green tomatoes may be sliced, dipped in batter, and fried in a few drops of oil. Fresh red tomatoes may be stewed 15 – 20 minutes until a sauce forms and eaten with herbs and salt or cooked into main dishes. All tomatoes can be washed and frozen whole in freezer bags or double bags. No precooking is necessary. Later, they can be chopped while still frozen and used in soups, sauces, stews, or other dishes. Run hot water over these while still frozen and the skins will slip off easily.

Turnips

Special Information: High in starch content. They contain a small variety of vitamins and minerals and high potassium amounts.

Selection: Choose firm, unblemished small white turnips with light, purplish tips and fresh greens if greens are attached.

Storage: Keeps two to four weeks in the refrigerator. Greens keep three to six days.

Serving: Grate whole fresh turnips raw into salads. Chop them and steam or cook them by themselves or with other vegetables for 15 – 20 minutes until tender. Bake them whole for 40 – 60 minutes at about 350F until tender. A delicious change from potatoes. Turnips can be used instead of potatoes or sweet potatoes in many recipes. Chop them like french fries and bake with a light coating of oil and sea salt on a lightly oiled flat pan for 15 – 20 minutes until tender and crispy.

Watercress and Cress

Special Information: High in vitamin A and other vitamins and minerals and sometimes includes iodine. The three main varieties of cress are watercress, which grows in streams and along stream banks, garden cress or pepper grass, and upland or winter cress, which grows in cooler climates (pictured page 400).

Selection: Choose fresh, bright green, unblemished leaves.

Storage: Keep wrapped two to six days in the refrigerator.

Serving: Eat raw in salads or as a sandwich green or steam lightly five to seven minutes as a vegetable. Use in soups or casseroles.

Wheatgrass

See Glossary of Natural Foods

Yams

Special Information: A variety of sweet potatoes but sweeter, and they are orange inside, and more nutritious than the yellow sweet potatoes.

Selection and Storage: Same as sweet potatoes. See Potatoes and Sweet Potatoes.

Serving: Delicious steamed or baked and topped with butter and sea salt. (Sometimes the yellow potatoes are called yams and the yams are called sweet potatoes in markets.) Like turnips, these can also be prepared like French fries or can be mashed like potatoes.

Yellow Squash

These include crookneck and straightneck varieties. See Squash (Summer).

Zucchini

For small zucchini, see Squash (Summer). For large zucchini, See Squash (Winter).

Guide to Unusual Fruits

Apples, pears, peaches, plums and bananas along with other common fruit are not included here as most people know how to pick out a good apple or chop a banana. See glossary for other books on fruits and vegetables.

Avocado

Special Information: These are technically fruits but are usually eaten as vegetables as they are easy to digest and combine well with vegetables. North American avocados are mainly grown in California and Florida. There are two main varieties: One is green, pear-shaped, and smooth-skinned; the other is oval-shaped, black, and has a very rough surface; both types are green inside. They are high in protein, vitamins, natural oils, and are delicious. They are mild-flavored and can be eaten with fruits or vegetables. Avocados are generally expensive except in late winter or early spring. There are approximately 138 calories per average one-half avocado. Although considered high in fats, avocados are a wonderful food and can be enjoyed two to three times per week. Especially good for those on special diets, including those with allergies or Candida.

Selection: They are generally available all year round. Choose avocados that are fairly soft, but not so soft that they may already be bruised. Avoid those that are very wrinkled or have many black spots.

Storage: Store hard avocados on the kitchen counter for a few days or even a week if necessary until they are quite soft. Refrigerate ripe avocados and eat them within three or four days. Never cut an avocado until it is ripe and ready to be eaten. Once cut, it stops ripening and must be eaten shortly, in a day or so. Ripe avocados can also be frozen whole for a few weeks and defrosted in the refrigerator and then eaten raw if desired.

Serving: Quarter a ripe avocado and peel off the outer skin, remove the pit, and chop the avocado into pieces for salads, or cut it in half, remove the pit, and eat it with a spoon out of its skin. The texture of a ripe avocado should be soft and smooth like soft butter, never hard or crunchy. Soft avocados are easier to digest, higher in vitamins, and more flavorful. They are best eaten raw although they may be cooked into casseroles and other dishes.

Berries

See Wildberries

Coconuts

Special Information: They are mainly grown in Florida for North American use. The coconut flesh contains 30% or more natural oils.

Selection: Shake the coconut and listen for a splashing noise of coconut milk. If there is no milk, the coconut is old and may be spoiled. Avoid coconuts with deep cracks in them. The average coconut is about the size of a cantaloupe only oblong with brown stringy skin.

Storage: They can usually be kept up to two to three weeks on a shelf or counter at room temperature, or they may be refrigerated. They will stay fresh as long as the milk lasts in them. If the coconut is cracked or opened, it must be refrigerated. After being cut, it lasts about seven to ten days.

Serving: To open a coconut, hold it with one hand over a bowl to catch the milk. Use a hammer with the other hand and give it a few good whacks until it cracks and the milk runs out. Then put the milk aside and give the coconut another whack or two until it splits in half. Use a round-edged table knife to pry out the inner white flesh of the coconut for munching. Do not use a pointed knife as the tip usually breaks and gets wedged into the coconut. Carve out a square of coconut and then pry it loose from underneath. The thin brown skin attached to the white pieces of coconut is also edible. Drink the milk or use it in a fruit drink or salad. Munch on the whole pieces of coconut or grate them into salads or desserts. Discard the outer coconut shell or, because it is waterproof, use it as a planter.

Currants

Special Information: Varieties are white, red, yellow, and black. Red are the most common. Most of these berries are edible raw. Some black types must be cooked first. Eat only cultivated varieties. These are high in vitamin C. Dried currants are high in iron.

Selection: Usually fresh berries must be home-grown. Dried currants, similar to raisins in color and texture but smaller and sweeter, are often available in stores. Some currants are tart and some are sweet.

Storage: Store dried currants in a cool, dry cupboard, or refrigerate them. Fresh berries should always be refrigerated.

Serving: Use dried currants like raisins or instead of raisins. Eat them from the box as a snack or use in cakes, breads, or other desserts. Use fresh currants as a snack, in a fruit salad, or with sweetening in a dessert.

Guavas

Special Information: These are high in vitamin C and contain vitamin A and some B vitamins. Usually grown in Hawaii and Florida. Guavas come in all sizes and shapes with green to yellow skin and white to red flesh. They can be sweet or sour. They are called pear guavas, apple guavas, etc., according to their shape and flavor.
Selection: Choose ripe, unblemished fruit. In many areas only canned guavas are available and sometimes guava jelly.
Storage: Refrigerate fresh fruit and opened cans or jars of fruit.
Serving: Remove the seeds and skin and eat the ripe fruit fresh or make it into juice. The juice can be mixed with others for an exotic drink or punch. They are excellent for making jams or jellies because of their natural high pectin content.

Kiwi

Special Information: These little oblong fruits are not much bigger than eggs. They have furry brown skins and are lime green inside with black seeds. They have many vitamins and are delicious and moderately priced in most areas of North America. They are very high in potassium. Two little kiwis have as much potassium as a banana.
Selection: Choose uniformly tender kiwis with unblemished skins. Kiwis should not be too soft or too firm and unripe. Should not be crunchy or mushy.
Storage: Can be refrigerated up to three to six days or more.
Serving: Remove the outer brown skin and eat the entire insides, including the little black seeds, which taste as good as the banana seeds do in bananas. Some people like to cut an unpeeled kiwi in half and scoop out and eat it with a small spoon. Kiwis are especially delicious and can be eaten alone or in fruit salads, puddings, pies and fruit flans.

Kumquats

Special Information: These are tropical fruits that are a little like a citrus in quality and flavor. They contain better than average amounts of vitamin C.
Selection: Fresh fruits are generally not available in many areas. The fruit is small and round, like a miniature orange in color and shape and about an inch or smaller in diameter. Canned and jarred kumquat jellies and jams are sometimes available.
Storage: Refrigerate fresh fruit up to a few days. Refrigerate opened cans or jars.
Serving: Eat the skins of the fresh fruit, which have a spicy flavor, as well as the insides. The pulp is usually sweet and juicy. They can also be used in a fruit salad. Good fruit for making jams and jellies.

Lychee Nuts

Special Information: Also called litchi, lichee or lichi. A popular fruit in China and other Asian countries. Now grown in South America, Hawaii, California, and Florida. Available fresh, mainly in summer. High in vitamin C and potassium.

Selection: These rough, brown, round little fruits are about the size of melon balls. They have a scaly, bark-like covering that should be firm, unbruised, and still on their stems when purchased fresh. Avoid tiny bits of white or greenish mold on the outer skin. Dried, large, raisin-like lychees or canned lychee nuts are more readily available than fresh. Often available in Oriental markets.

Storage: Fresh ones keep for one to three weeks refrigerated.

Serving: Peel these juicy little white fruits by digging your fingernails into the rough skin and gently pulling it away. Although tough looking, the skin is thin and easier to remove than an orange's skin. The pearly inner flesh has a grape-like texture and tastes like a cross between red grapes, honeydew melon, and rose petals. A real delicacy. Chew the white flesh around the almond like seeds and discard the seeds. Cut for fruit salads, blender drinks, puddings, ice creams, and exotic recipes. Use canned ones similarly. Used dried lychees in baking.

Mangos

Special Information: Mangos are grown for North America in Florida, California, and Hawaii. The unripe fruit is green in color. Ripe fruit is partially green and yellow with splotches of bright red. The fruit, which is full of vitamins, is large and oblong with a large pit inside.

Selection: Choose mangos with multicolored skins that feel slightly soft to the touch. Avoid bruised and blemished fruits. Choose ripe fruit for a more delicious flavor. If picked when unripe, the fruit may never fully mature.

Storage: Slightly unripe, firm mangos may be placed on a windowsill or counter for a day or two before refrigerating. Refrigerate all ripe fruit, which will keep for about two to six days.

Serving: Peel off the outer skin and slice the juicy orange mango pieces off the large, flat pit inside. Discard the skin and pit. Fresh mangos are delicious and sweet eaten by themselves, or they can be used in fruit salads or in special fruit recipes. They are perfect for jams, fruit salads, ice cream, dessert toppings, and pies.

Melons

Special Information: Melons are mainly a summer and fall fruit. Watermelons are sometimes available in early spring. They are delicious, cool, and soothing.

Melons include: Cantaloupes, casabas, crenshaws, honeydews, honey rocks, Persian melons, Santa Claus melons, and watermelons. Their outer skins range in color from green to gold to green and white or yellow. Their delicious inner flesh can be golden, peach, green, or red. Enjoy them all. Melons are best eaten by themselves, raw.

Selection: Choose melons with firm outer rinds that sound slightly hollow when knocked. Cantaloupes and similar melons should have outer rinds that feel slightly soft to the touch and be soft at the round stem end. Avoid those with mold near the stem ends. Melons with a nettinglike rind, like cantaloupes, are riper when lighter in color. Avoid those with a dark green netting. Most melons are riper and sweeter when heavy in weight. When choosing melons that are already sliced, choose those that have bright-colored inner flesh. Select ripe honeydew melons, as they will not continue to ripen at home like other melons.

Storage: If space is limited and a melon is not overripe, unopened melons may sit on a counter or in a cool basement for a day or two. Melons can also be refrigerated. Ripe or opened melons must be refrigerated right away and will keep fresh from three to seven days.

Serving: Melons are best eaten alone raw, but can be served with dairy products or nuts. They are especially good in a variety melonball salad that may be served a little before mealtime. When a melon is first opened, remove and discard all the seeds (except in watermelons) to prevent the melon from spoiling. Eat only the sweet, tender inner flesh of melons. Discard the seeds, skin, and inner white rind.

Papaya

Special Information: These fruits are high in vitamins A and C and some B vitamins. Papayas are also called tree melons and resemble cantaloupe in flavor. They are a valuable aid to digestion. Papaya fruit and/or powder helps to break down proteins and can be eaten with meats, poultry, or dairy products. The dried powder is used as a meat tenderizer.

Selection: Papayas are shaped like large pears. The skin is yellow-green when ripe, and the flesh is pale orange or peach colored. Choose slightly tender, unblemished papayas.

Storage: May be kept in the refrigerator for about two to six days.

Serving: Do not eat the seeds. Discard them with the outer skin of the fruit. Eat tender, ripe papayas by themselves or in a fruit salad or cooked dessert recipe. They are especially favored as a juice or in preserves and jellies. One-half a papaya with a scoop of ice cream in the center is a special treat.

Passion Fruit

Special Information: Also called granadilla. This fruit gets its name from the way the flowers are said to represent the Passion (crucifixion) of Christ. Passion fruit is also considered an aphrodisiac or passion enhancer. Grown in South America and the US tropical states. High in vitamin A, C, phosphorus, potassium and calcium.

Selection: This oblong fruit has three basic types: the giant variety with yellow-green skin and purple, sweet-acid pulp, the sweet variety with orange-brown skin and white flesh, and the least common purple variety with tough purple skin and orange pulp. Ripe passion fruit is about three to four inches long, soft and yields to gentle pressure.

Storage: Keep refrigerated for several days to one week.

Serving: Discard the skin but eat the little seeds. The fruit can be cut in half and eaten with a spoon like a melon or baked in cakes, breads or used in ice creams, puddings, jellies, or blender drinks.

Persimmons

Special Information: Very high in vitamins A and C.

Selection: Persimmons are bright red-orange and sometimes black-speckled when ripe, and are very soft to the touch. They are somewhat egg sized and shaped but have one flat end with a top knot stem similar to eggplants.

Storage: Unripe fruit may be left on a counter a day or two until ripe. Ripe fruit may be kept in the refrigerator for about three to seven days.

Serving: Persimmons are sweetest when ripe. Eat the outer skin and inner flesh and the small seeds. They are best eaten fresh. Recipes for them include puddings, jams and jellies, or they may be experimented with in fruit recipes or used in fruit salads. Inside it looks like a tomato but is deliciously sweet.

Pineapple

Special Information: Generally from Hawaii or Florida. Pineapples are high in vitamin C and phosphorus, and have good amounts of vitamins A, B1, B2, and calcium.

Selection: Choose ripe pineapples as they ripen soon after picking. Fragrant pineapples with a golden meat are usually ripe and sweet. The outer skin should feel slightly soft when squeezed. Red or greenish looking, very hard-skinned pineapples are usually hard inside and unripe. Avoid those with dark spots that indent easily when pressed, these parts are overripe and spoiled inside. A pineapple's leaves will easily pull out if its ripe.

Storage: They may be kept on the counter a few days if they are not totally ripe. Refrigerate when fully ripe or when cut open. Will keep from three to seven days refrigerated.

Serving: Good pineapples should be soft and sweet, never sour and crunchy. Cut the top knot off the fruit and slice off all the outer rind. Then slice the inside yellow fruit into slices and eat around the hard center core or remove the hard core, which is usually round and about one-inch or so in diameter. Special cutting tools can be purchased to remove the outer rind and core of the fruit. Eat the fresh fruit all by itself or in a fruit salad or use it in cooking and desserts. Great on pizzas or shish kebabs.

Pomegranates

Special Information: Grown along the middle and southern coastline of the USA in Georgia, and especially Florida and California. This fruit is used to make grenadine.

Selection: The reddish-white fruit is similar in size and shape to a round apple, except that the skin is hard and bumpy and the stem top is different. Ripe fruit has a very thin, bright scarlet skin. Available around September to December.

Storage: These will ripen on a countertop. Refrigerate when ripe or opened. May be refrigerated up to one or two weeks.

Serving: The pomegranate is made up of red juicy fruit surrounding each of its many seeds. Discard the coarse outer skin of the fruit. Either chew the fruit off around each seed and discard the seeds or eat the seeds too. The fruit also may be juiced and the juice mixed with other fruit juices or used by itself. One can roll the fruit on a hard surface to break up the pulp and then insert a straw and drink out the juice if desired. These can also be frozen. May also be used in jelled desserts and sauces.

Pumpkins

Special Information: These are in the gourd family, like melons, and since they are eaten like a fruit, they are included here. Although these are similar to squash, pumpkins have softer rinds and harder stems. They are very high in vitamin A and contain a variety of other vitamins and minerals including C, and B's, and iron.

Selection: Choose pumpkins with firm outer rinds that sound a bit hollow when knocked upon gently.

Storage: Whole pumpkins will keep up to one or two months at room temperature. Cut pumpkins should be wrapped and refrigerated or cooked and frozen. Refrigerated pumpkin will keep about six to ten days.

Serving: Very small pumpkins are best for cooking and eating purposes. Choose a pumpkin that will fit whole into your largest cooking pot. Then boil the whole pumpkin until its very soft and a knife runs through it easily. Cut pumpkins can be boiled, baked, or steamed, but more vitamins are lost when they are cut. Keep a lid on while the pumpkin cooks. Use the cooked pumpkin in any favorite recipe calling for fresh or canned pumpkin. It is especially delicious in pies, cakes, breads, and puddings. Pumpkin seeds can be toasted in the oven at medium temperature along with sea salt, tamari soy sauce, and herbs until nicely toasted. Serve the seeds warm. They are very hard to digest, unhulled and should only be eaten by those with strong stomachs or those using digestive aids. The hulled pumpkin seeds (pepitas) are easier to digest. (See Pepitas and Pumpkin seeds)

Rhubarb

Special Information: Here is a vegetable that is eaten like a fruit, so it is included in this section. Rhubarb is rich in vitamin A and calcium. It also contains some C and B vitamins and a variety of minerals.

Selection: When picking rhubarb from a garden or supermarket, choose only the long, thick stalks. If harvesting them from a garden, pull the stalks off the plant by twisting them near the base of the plant. Never cut them. Mature stalks are large and red and green in color.

Storage: Discard the leaves and store the stalks, wrapped, in the refrigerator. They will keep up to seven to ten days. Or, chop them in one-inch long pieces, double-wrap them in plastic bags, and freeze them raw for later use.

Serving: Never eat rhubarb leaves, because they are highly poisonous. The stalks themselves are edible but tart. Some people like to munch on them raw with a little salt, but most people prefer cooked rhubarb. They can be chopped and stewed with an inch or so of water in a saucepan. Honey or other sweetening should be added for flavoring and possibly a dash or two of cinnamon. When the rhubarb cooks down completely into sauce, it is similar to applesauce and can be used instead of applesauce in most recipes. Cooked rhubarb is also commonly used in breads, cakes, puddings, and jams. (See recipe.)

Star Fruit

Special Information: Also called carambola. A yellow-green, oblong, star-shaped tree melon which originated in Malaysia and is now grown throughout Asia. In North America it grows in the West Indies, Hawaii, and Florida. This tall evergreen tree produces about three crops per year. Contain good amounts of vitamins A, C, and potassium.

Selection: These little four or five inch melons have deeper ridges than an acorn squash. Choose a firm (but not hard), unblemished, mainly yellow fruit with only bits of green around the outer ridges. Too much green may denote a sour or unripe fruit. Make sure fruits are fairly ripe when purchased as they spoil easily if you try to ripen them at home.

Storage: Store on an open counter up to one or two days only if not fully ripe but check fruit often and refrigerate immediately as it softens. Keeps refrigerated for two to four days cut, longer if whole.

Serving: Cut crosswise, this fruit resembles a lovely pointed star. This succulent, delectable melon can be eaten alone, in a fruit salad, in jams, puddings, blender drinks, or it can be used in baking. Peel before using. Especially tasty in fruit flans. Dried star fruit is sometimes available in specialty and health food stores. There are actually sweet and sour varieties, but only the sweet ones are made widely available.

Ugli

This fruit is a cross between a grapefruit and a tangerine. It can be peeled by hand and eaten like a tangerine.

Wildberries

Special Information: Wildberries include sweet berries such as raspberries, strawberries, blackberries, blueberries, and Saskatoons, and tart berries such as currants, gooseberries, and huckleberries. Most berries are high in vitamin C and a variety of vitamins and minerals.

Selection: Wildberries are usually smaller than cultivated berries. Pick bright colored, ripe, soft berries that fall or pull easily from their plants. When buying, choose firm, bright-colored fruit.

Storage: Wildberries are most delicious and nutritious when eaten very soon after picking. Do not wash them unless absolutely necessary to preserve as many vitamins as possible. They may be kept refrigerated from one to three days or a bit longer.

Serving: All berries may be eaten fresh by themselves, but whether eaten fresh or made into jams, pies, or other desserts, tart berries often taste better with honey or another natural sweetener.

Recommended Reading

1. Natural Food Primers

The Guide to Natural and Healthy Eating, Renee Frappier
Les Editions Asclepiades Inc., ISBN 2-9801115-3-8

Shopper's Guide to Natural Foods, East West Journal Editors
Avery Publishing Group, ISBN 0-89529-233-5

Goldbeck's Guide to Good Food, Nikki and David Goldbeck
Ceres Press, ISBN 0-452-26171-6

The Wellness Encyclopedia of Food and Nutrition, Sheldon Margen, MD
Rebus, ISBN 0-929661-03-6

2. Nutrition and Vitamin Guides and Reference Books

Prescription for Nutritional Healing, James F. Balch and Phyllis A. Balch
Avery Publishing Group Inc., ISBN 0-89529-429-X

Healthy Healing, Linda Rector-Page
Healthy Healing Publications, ISBN 0-912331-21-6

Nutrition Almanac, Lavon J. Dunne
McGraw Hill, ISBN 0-07-034912-6

Return to the Joy of Health, Dr. Zoltan P. Rona with Jeanne Marie Martin
Alive Books, ISBN 0-920470-62-9

Diet and Nutrition, A Holistic Approach, Rudolph Ballantine
Himalayan International Institute, ISBN 0-89389-048-0

Your Body Knows Best, Ann Louise Gittleman
Pocket Book, ISBN 0-671875922

Vitamin Bible, Earl Mindell
Warner Books, ISBN 0-446-30626-6

3. Foods and Additives

Empty Harvest, Bernard Jensen and Mark Anderson
Avery Publishing Group, ISBN 0-89529-416-8

Food as Medicine, Dr. Earl Mindell
Distican, ISBN 0-671-98582-5

Diet for A Poisoned Planet, David Steinman
Ballantine Books, ISBN 0-345-37465-7

A Consumer's Dictionary of Food Additives, Ruth Winter
Crown Publishers Inc., ISBN 0-517-531615

The Poisons Around Us, Henry A. Schroeder
Keats Publishing, ISBN

The Safe Shopper's Bible, David Steinman and Samuel S. Epstein
Macmillan US, ISBN 0-02-082085-2

Safe Food, Michael F. Jacobson, Lisa Y. Lefferts and Anne Witte Garland
Living Planet Press, ISBN 1-879326-01-9

4. Allergies

The All Natural Allergy Cookbook, Jeanne Marie Martin
Harbour Publishing, ISBN 1-55017-044-9

Allergies Disease in Disguise, Carolee Bateson-Koch
Alive Books, ISBN 0-920470-42-4

Freedom from Allergy, Dr. Ron Greenburg and Angela Nori
Blue Poppy Press, ISBN 0-88925-905-4

Taste and See: Allergy Relief Cooking, P. King
Family Health Publications, ISBN 0-89529-397-8

The Self-Help Cookbook, Marjorie Hurt Jones
Rodale Press, ISBN 0-87857-505-7

The Allergy Cookbook: Diets Unlimited for Limited Diets
Allergy Information Association of Canada, ISBN 0-458-80690-0

5. Sugar and Related Health Disorders

Complete Candida Yeast Guidebook, Jeanne Marie Martin and Zoltan P. Rona
Prima, ISBN 0-7615-0167-3

The Yeast Connection Cookbook, William Crook, MD and Marjorie Hurt Jones, RN
Professional Books, ISBN 0-93347816-X

Who Killed Candida?, Vicki Glassburn
Teach Services, ISBN 0-945383-12-6

Diabetes and Hypoglycemia, Michael T. Murray
Prima, ISBN 1-55958-426-2

Hypoglycemia: A Better Approach, Paavo Airola
Health Plus, ISBN 0-932090-01-X

Sugar Blues, William Duffy
Warner Books, ISBN 0-446-89288-2

Breaking the Vicious Cycle (Food and the Gut Reaction), Elaine Gottshall
Kirkton Press, ISBN 0-969-2768-1

Chronic Fatigue and the Yeast Connection, William Crook, MD
Professional Books, ISBN 0-933478-20-8

Chronic Fatigue Syndrome, Gregg Charles Fisher
Warner Books, ISBN 0-446-39004-6

6. Children's Health and Cookbooks

Pretend Soup and Other Real Recipes, Mollie Katzen and Ann Henderson
Ten Speed Press, ISBN 1-883672-06-6

Vegetarian Baby and Child, Petra Jackson
Macmillan Canada, ISBN 0-7715-7316-2

Vegetarian Baby, Sharon Yntema
ISBN 0-935526-01-3

Vegetarian Children, Sharon Yntema
McBooks Press, ISBN 0-935526-22-6

Pregnancy, Children and the Vegan Diet, Michael Klaper
ISBN 0-9614248-2-6

Healthier Children, Barbara Kahan
Keats, ISBN 0-87983-475-7

Tracking Down Hidden Food Allergies, William G. Crook
Professional Books, ISBN 0-933478-05-4

7. Recipe Books

Including Meats:

Jeanne Marie Martin's Light Cuisine, Jeanne Marie Martin
Harbour Publishing, ISBN 1-55017123-2

Recipes for Romance, Jeanne Marie Martin
Forthcoming title

The New York Times New Natural Foods Cookbook, Jean Hewitt
Avon Books, ISBN 0-380-62687-X

Recipes from an Ecological Kitchen, Lorna J. Sass
William Morrow & Co., Hardcover ISBN 0-688-10051-1

About Vegetarianism:

Becoming Vegetarian, Vesanto Melina, Brenda Davis and Victoria Harrison
Macmillan Canada, ISBN 0-7715-9045-8

The Gradual Vegetarian, Lisa Tracy
Dell Publishing, ISBN 0-440-53124-1

Food for Thought, Ananda Mitra
Nucleus Publications, ISBN 0-945934-07-6

Why Vegetarian?, Lynda Dickinson
Gordon Soules, ISBN 0-91957489-0

Vegetarian Cookbooks:

The Moosewood Cookbook, Mollie Katzen
Ten Speed Press, ISBN 0-89815-490-1

Moosewood Cookbook Cooks at Home, Moosewood Collective
Fireside Books, ISBN 0-671-67992-9

Vegetarian Times Cookbook, The Editors of Vegetarian Times
Macmillan, ISBN 0-02-010370-0

Horn of the Moon Cookbook, Ginny Callan
Harper Collins, ISBN 0-06-096038-8

Cabbagetown Cafe, Julie Jordan
The Crossing Press, SBN 0-89594-192-9

The Vegetarian Feast, Martha Rose Schulman
Harper Collins, ISBN 0-06-095001-3

On the Road to Vegetarian Cooking, Anne Lukin
Second Story Press, ISBN 0-929005-28-7

The New McDougall Cookbook, John A, McDougall and Mary McDougall
Duton Books, ISBN 0-525-93610-6

Vegetarian Soup Cookbooks:

Hearty Vegetarian Soups and Stews, Jeanne Marie Martin
Harbour Publishing, ISBN 1-55017-050-3

Soups for All Seasons, Nava Atlas
Amberwood Press, ISBN 0-9630243-1-0

Old Classic Vegetarian Cookbooks:

The Vegetarian Epicure, Anna Thomas
Vintage Books, ISBN 0-394-71784-8

Ten Talents Cookbook, Rosalie Hurd and Frank Hurd
Ten Talents, ISBN 0-9603532-0-8

Diet for a Small Planet, Frances Moore Lappe
Random, ISBN 0-345-32120-0

Recipes for a Small Planet, Frances Moore Lappe
Random, ISBN 0-345-32492-7

Survival into the 21st Century, Viktoras Kulvinskas
21st Century Publications, ISBN 0-933278-04-7

Veganism:

Diet for a New America, John Robbins
Stillpoint Publishing, ISBN 0-913299-54-5

May All Be Fed: Diet For A New World, John Robbins
Avon Books, ISBN 0-688-11625-6

Vegan Nutrition: Pure And Simple, Michael Klaper
Gentle World Inc., ISBN 0-9614248-2-6

Vegan Cookbooks:

Vegan Delights, Jeanne Marie Martin
Harbour Publishing, ISBN 1-55017-079-1

Country Kitchen Collection, Silver Hills Guest House
ISBN 0-88925-933-X365

Simply Vegan, Debra Wasserman
Lazarus Publication, ISBN 093-141-105X

The American Vegetarian Cookbook, Marilyn Diamond
Warner Books, ISBN 0-446-51561-2

A Celebration of Wellness, Natalie Cederquist and James Levin
Avery Publishing Group, ISBN 0-9628698-1-3

A Diet for All Reasons, Paulette Eisen
Alive Books, ISBN 0-920470-68-8

Macrobiotics and Macrobiotic Cooking:

Zen Macrobiotic Cooking, Michel Abehsera
Avon Books, ISBN 0-380-09151-5

Aveline Kushi's Guide to Macrobiotic Cooking, Aveline Kushi
Warner Books, ISBN 0-446-38634-0

The Macrobiotic Way, Aveline Kushi
Avery Publishing Group, ISBN 0-89529-222-X

The Vegetarian's Ecstasy, Natalie Cederquist and James Levin
Avery Publishing Group, ISBN 0-9628698-0-5

Macrobiotic Community Cookbook, A. Lerman
Avery Publishing Group, ISBN 0-89529-396-X

Raw Foods:

Raw Energy Recipes, Susannah and Leslie Kenton
Ebury Press, ISBN 0-09-178470-0

Vibrant Living, Natalie Cederquist and James Levin
Avery Publishing Group, ISBN 0-96286982-1

Ethnic and Specialty Cooking:

The World in Your Kitchen/Vegetarian Recipes, Troth Wells
Second Story Press, Hardcover ISBN 0-929005-45-7

From the Global Kitchen/A Collection of Vegetarian Recipes
Plenty International, ISBN 1-577067-006-4

The Spice of Vegetarian Cooking/Ethnic Cooking, Martha Rose Shulman
Inner Traditions, ISBN 0-89281-399-7

A Taste of the Mediterranean/Vegetarian Style, Mary Salloum
Centax Books, ISBN 1-895292-17-4

Vegetarian Cuisine/Caribbean Style, Dr. Betty "K"
Gutax Books, ISBN 1-895292-18-2

Hot, Spicy and Meatless, Dave Dewitt, Mary Jane Wilan and Melissa T. Stock
Prima, ISBN 1-55958-361-4

Indian Vegetarian Cooking, Jack Santa Maria
Samuel Weiser Inc., ISBN 0-87728-220-X

Greek Vegetarian Cooking, Alkmini Chaitow
Harper Collins, ISBN 0-7225-0725-9

Italian Vegetarian Cooking, Jo Marcangelo
Inner Traditions, ISBN 0-89281-343-1

Chinese Vegetarian Cooking, Jack Santa Maria
Harper Collins, ISBN 0-916360-36-9

Jewish Vegetarian Cooking, Rose Friedman
Harper Collins, ISBN 0-7225-2471-4

Mexican Vegetarian Cooking, Edith Metcalfe de Plata
Harper Collins, ISBN 0-7225-0789-5

Cooking with Tofu:

Tofu, Quick and Easy, Louise Hagler
Book Publishing Co., ISBN 0-913990-50-1

Tofu Cookery, Louise Hagler
Book Publishing Co., ISBN 0-913990-38-8

The Tofu Book, John Paino and Lisa Messinger
Avery Publishing Group, ISBN 0-89529-409-5

The Book of Tofu, William Shurtleff and Akiko Aoyagi
Ballantine Books, ISBN 0-345-27809-7

About Soybeans:

Earl Mindell's Soy Miracle, Dr. Earl Mindell
Distican, ISBN 0-671-89820-5

The Simple Soybean and Your Health, Mark and Virginia Messina and Ken Setchell
Avery Publishing Group, ISBN 0-89529-611-X

Legume Cookbooks:

Romancing the Bean, Joanne Saltzman
H.J. Kramer Inc., ISBN 0-915811-48-0

Bean Cuisine, Janet Horsley
Avery Publishing Group, ISBN 0-89529-446-X

Fabulous Beans, Barb Bloomfield
Book Publishing Co., ISBN 0-91399017-5

Lean Bean Cuisine, Jay Solomon
Prima, ISBN 1-55958-438-6

Whole Grain Cookbooks:

Amazing Grains, Joanne Saltzman
H.J.Kramer Inc., ISBN 0-915811-21-9

Grains for Better Health, Maureen Keane and Daniella Chace
Prima, ISBN 1-55958-486-6

Quinoa The Supergrain, Rebecca Wood
Japan Publications, ISBN 0-87040-780-5

From Grits to Gourmet, T. Chikalo
Pheylonian Publishing Kohr, ISBN none

Bread and Baking Books:

The Tassajara Bread Book (Revised & Updated Version), Edward Espe Brown
Shambhala Books, ISBN 0-87773-343-0

Uprisings, The Cooperative Whole Grain Educational Association
Book Publishing Co., ISBN 0-913990-70-1

Breadtime Stories: A Cookbook for Bakers, Susan Jane Cheney
Ten Speed Press, ISBN 0-89815-315-8

The Village Baker/Classic Regional Breads From Europe And America
Ten Speed Press, ISBN 0-89815-489-8

Bread Machine Baking for Better Health, Maureen B. Keane and Daniella Chace
Prima, ISBN 1-55958-419-X

Grains for Better Health, Maureen B. Keane and Daniella Chace
Prima, ISBN 1-55958-486-6

Sugar-Free Desserts:

Fruit-Sweet and Sugar-Free, Jamie Feuer
Healing Arts Press, ISBN 0-89281-449-7

Naturally Sweet/Desserts Sweetened With Fruit, Fran Raboff and Lynn Bassler
The Crossing Press, ISBN 0-89594-619-X

Naturally Sweet Desserts, Marcea Weber
Avery Publishing Group, ISBN 0-89529-443-5

8. Healing Foods and Recipes

The Healing Power of Foods, Michael T. Murray
Prima, ISBN 1-55958-318-5

The Healing Cuisine/India's Art of Ayurvedic Cooking, Harish Johari
Inner Traditions, ISBN 0-89281-382-2

Food and Healing, Annemarie Colbin
Ballantine Books, ISBN 0-345-30385-7

Foods That Heal, Maureen Salaman
Statford Publishing, ISBN 0-913087-025

Foods That Heal, Bernard Jensen
Avery Publishing Group, ISBN 0-89529-563-3

9. About Fats And Oils

Fats That Heal, Fats That Kill, Udo Erasmus
Alive Books, ISBN 0-920470-38-6

The Facts About Fats, John Finnegan
Elysian Arts Book, ISBN 0-927425-12-2

10. About Herbs And Spices

Spices: Seeds and Barks, Jill Norman
Bantam Books, Hardcover ISBN 0-553-05738-3

The Herb Book, Arabella Boxer, Philippa Back
Octopus Books, Hardcover ISBN 1-85052-038-0

The Encyclopedia of Herbs, Spices and Flavorings, Elisabeth Lambert Ortiz
Reader's Digest Press, Hardcover ISBN 0-88850-304-0

11. About Chlorophyll and Green Foods

The Healing Power of Chlorophyll from Plant Life, Bernard Jensen
No ISBN

Cereal Grass/What's In It For You!, Edited by Ronald L. Seibold
Wilderness Community Education Foundation, ISBN 0-9628126-0-9

The Wheatgrass Book, Ann Wigmore
Avery Publishing Group, ISBN 0-89529-234-3

Green Barley Essence, Yoshihide Hagiwara
Keats, ISBN 0-87834-8-8

Chlorella, William Lee, Michael Rosenbaum
Keats, ISBN 0-87983464-1

Spirulina, Jack Joseph Challem
Keats, ISBN 0-87983-262-2

12. About Herbal Remedies

Back to Eden, Jethro Kloss
Back to Eden Books, ISBN 0-940676-00-1

The Herb Book, John Lust
Bantam, ISBN 0-553-23827-2

The New Age Herbalist, Richard Mabey
Penguin Books, ISBN 0-14-012682-1

Indian Herbalogy of North America, Alma Hutchens
ISBN 0-87773-639-1

Healing Plants, M.Pahlow
Barron Books, ISBN 0-8120-1498-7

13. About Juicing

Healing with Herbal Juices, Siegfried Gursche
Alive Books, ISBN 0-920470-34-3

Getting the Best Out of Your Juicer, William H. Lee
Keats, ISBN 0-87983-586-9

Juicing for Life, Cherie Calbon and Maureen Keane
Avery Publishing Group, ISBN 0-895295-12-1

The Juicing Book, Stephen Bauer
Avery Publishing Group, ISBN 0-8952925-3-X

The Complete Raw Juice Therapy, Thorsons Editorial Board
Harper Collins, ISBN 0-7225-1877-3

Fresh Vegetable and Fruit Juices, Norman Walker
Norwalk Press, ISBN 0-89019-067-0

14. Fasting, Cleansing and Parasites

Juice Fasting and Detoxification, Steve Meyerowitz
Sprout House, ISBN 1-878736-64-7

Miracle of Fasting, Paul C. Bragg
Health Sciences, ISBN 0-87790-002-7

Colon Health: The Key to Vibrant Life, Norman Walker
Norwalk Press, ISBN 0-89019-069-0

Tissue Cleansing Through Bowel Management, Bernard Jensen and Sylvia Bell
Bernard Jensen International, ISBN 0-960836-07-1

Inner Cleansing, Carlson Wade
Parker Publishing Co., ISBN 0-13-465575-3

Achieve Maximum Health/Colon Flora, David Webster
Hygeia Publishing, ISBN 0-9647537-1-5

The Body-Smart System, Helene Silver
Healthy Healing Publications, ISBN 1-88433460-1

Guess What Came to Dinner/Parasites and Your Health, Ann Louise Gittleman
Avery Publishing Group, ISBN 0-89529-570

Parasites: The Enemy Within, Hanna Kroeger, MS.D and Jerald Foote
Kroeger Products (1122 Pearl Street Boulder CO 80302), ISBN

15. Vegetarian Restaurant Guidebooks

Vegetarian Journal's Guide to Natural Foods Restaurants in the U.S. and Canada,
Vegetarian Resource Group, Avery Publishing Group, ISBN 0-89529-571-7

The Canadian Vegetarian Dining Guide, Lynne Tomlinson
ISBN 0-9697539-0-X

16. Journals and Magazines

alive, Canadian Journal of Health and Nutrition
Box 80055
Burnaby BC V5H 3X1
604-435-1919 Fax: 604-435-4888

Health Naturally
Box 580
Parry Sound ON P2A 2X5
705-746-7839 Fax: 705-746-7893

Healthy and Natural Journal
100 - 100 Wallace Avenue
Sarasota FL 34237
941-366-1153 Fax: 941-366-5743

Natural Health
PO Box 7440
Red Oak IA 51591-0440
800-526-8440 (US only)

Veggie Life
Box 412
Mt. Morris IL 61054-8163
800-345-2785 Fax: 510-671-0692

Vegetarian Times
PO Box 570
Oak Park IL 60303
708-848-8100 Fax: 708-848-2031

Recipe Index

Breads

Desserts

Beverages

Index

Wildberries, 408, 416

Yams, 32, 38, 46, 143, 145, 235, 267, 280, 403, 407

Yeast, 20, 47, 52, 57-60, 69-70, 89, 97, 115, 118, 120, 127, 195, 198, 202, 248-249, 284, 286-288, 291-292, 296, 339-340, 354, 358, 367, 369, 372-374, 379, 381, 384, 387-388, 418-419

Yellow split peas, 183-184, 221

Yoga, 6, 42, 69

Yucca, 389

Zinc, 60, 192, 377, 380, 390, 399

Zucchini, 32, 39, 101, 114, 143, 145, 152, 154-156, 158, 193-194, 197, 199, 202, 219-220, 224, 228, 235, 237, 244, 277, 298, 405-407, 430

Zwieback, 115, 294

Notes:

Notes:

Recipe Reminders:

Recipe Reminders:

Family Favorites:

Family Favorites:

About the Author

JEANNE MARIE MARTIN lectures internationally on topics concerning natural foods and wholistic lifestyles. Her more than 25 years of experience has led her to write seven health cookbooks and over 250 magazine articles. Jeanne Marie has also contributed chapters on healing treatments and diets to two books by doctors, most recently *Return to the Joy of Health* working with Dr. Zoltan Rona. Her recipes also appear in Cathi Graham's *201 Fat Burning Recipes* and *Sunrise Tofu Cookbook*.

As a nutrition consultant, Jeanne Marie has worked with more than thirty wholistic medical doctors, naturopaths, and chiropractors whose clients have special health problems. She specializes in creating customized diets for people with allergies, Candida albicans, chronic fatigue syndrome, high or low blood sugar, cancer, heart problems, and weight control problems.

In addition to her nutrition consultations, Jeanne Marie teaches cooking classes in Western Canada and in the Seattle/Tacoma area and lectures on nutrition at universities, schools, hospitals, clinics, and on TV and radio shows.

Jeanne Marie is also a professional floral designer, published poet, singer, arts and crafts enthusiast, and qualified yoga instructor.

For an information packet and full details on consultations, please send $5.00 (refundable with consultation) to:

Jeanne Marie Martin
c/o PO Box 4391
Vancouver BC V6B 3Z8
Canada

Or, for lecture information please call 1-604-878-8787.

(All calls will be returned collect.)

Other Titles by Alive Books

Return to the Joy of Health
Natural medicine and alternative treatments for all your health complaints.
Dr. Zoltan Rona, 408 pp softcover

Fats That Heal Fats That Kill
The complete guide to fats, oils, cholesterol and human health.
Udo Erasmus, 480 pp softcover

Allergies: Disease in Disguise
How to heal your allergic condition permanently and naturally.
*Carolee Bateson-Koch DC ND,
224 pp softcover*

Diet for All Reasons
Nutrition guide and recipe collection.
Paulette Eisen, 176 pp softcover

Kombucha Rediscovered!
A guide to the medicinal benefits of an ancient healing tea.
Klaus Kaufmann, 96 pp softcover

The Breuss Cancer Cure
Advice for prevention and natural treatment of cancer, leukemia and other seemingly incurable diseases.
*Rudolf Breuss (translated from German),
112pp softcover*

Healing with Herbal Juices
A practical guide to herbal juice therapy: nature's preventative medicine.
Siegfried Gursche, 256 pp softcover

**The All-in-One Guide to Herbs, Vitamins &
Minerals**
The quick and easy reference for everything you need to know.
Victoria Hogan, 64pp softcover

**Devil's Claw Root and Other Natural
Remedies for Arthritis**
A herbal remedy that has helped free thousands of arthritis sufferers from crippling pain.
*Rachel Carston (Revised by Klaus Kaufmann),
128 pp softcover*

Silica - The Forgotten Nutrient
Healthy Skin, Shiny Hair, Strong Bones, Beautiful Nails - A guide to the vital role of organic vegetal silica in nutrition, health, longevity and medicine.
*Klaus Kaufmann, 1990, 1993,
128 pp softcover*

Silica - The Amazing Gel
An essential mineral for radiant health, recovery and rejuvenation.
*Klaus Kaufmann, 1993, 1995,
159 pp softcover*

**Available at your local health food store, pharmacy, bookstore or from
Alive Books, PO Box 80055, Burnaby BC V5H 3X1**